THE IRISH BORDER AS A CULTURAL DIVIDE

DR. M. W. HESLINGA

THE IRISH BORDER
AS A CULTURAL DIVIDE

A CONTRIBUTION TO THE STUDY OF REGIONALISM
IN THE BRITISH ISLES

With a Foreword by
DR. E. ESTYN EVANS,
Emeritus professor

of geography and Irish studies
in The Queen's University Belfast

Third, unrevised edition

VAN GORCUM ASSEN, THE NETHERLANDS 1979

The publication of this book was made possible through a grant from the Netherlands Organization for the Advancement of Pure Research (Z.W.O.)

ISBN 90 232 0864 1

Printed in The Netherlands by Van Gorcum, Assen

FOREWORD

Of the histories of Irish Partition there is no end, but this study of the historical geography behind Partition is the first to come from a professional geographer. Dr. MARCUS WILLEM HESLINGA, who is lecturer in human geography at the Free University of Amsterdam, is, however, not the first Dutchman to concern himself with Irish affairs: leaving aside a famous political figure, one thinks, in the field of natural history, of GERARD BOATE (1604-49) and of LLOYD PRAEGER, author of that classic work, *The Way that I went*, whose father came from The Hague.

Dr. HESLINGA takes British and Irish geographers to task for neglecting the subject he has chosen for his doctoral thesis at the University of Utrecht. Some of us could claim that we have honestly sought, by field study and research, to contribute to a better understanding of the Irish environment and of man's responses to it; and whether we are concerned with historical or present-day geography we are bound to recognize that regional differences are an essential aspect of the island's personality. It is our duty to study the roots of regionalism, and it is our profound hope that the differences between North and South may find expression in ways that will facilitate, rather than frustrate, the full development of the material, cultural and spiritual wealth of the island. But 'the border' is such a lively political issue that our motives would be suspect, on one side or the other and probably on both, if we were to concentrate our attention on it. Any student who approaches the subject must pick his way delicately through hard spikes of political prejudice.

I am personally grateful to Dr. HESLINGA for taking on this task, and I believe that he has pursued it with a high degree of objectivity. He first came to Ireland in 1959 as a fellow of the Netherlands Organisation for the Advancement of Pure Research at The Hague. Both in 1959 and on other visits in 1960 and 1961 he travelled throughout the island and made contacts with people in all walks of life, north and south. He has obviously read extensively around his subject and he is to be warmly congratulated on his mastery of the intricacies and niceties of English style. A glance at the Table of Contents will show how widely and thoroughly he has pursued his enquiries.

Approaching the problems of Irish Partition externally, Dr. HESLINGA sees clearly the mythical and even mystical nature of several popular beliefs. There is the myth of the 'natural geographical unit', the God-given inviolate island, which reason quickly dispels. Geographers are the first to recognize that regionalism is a cultural force, to be understood by reference to human responses and not to theoretical 'natural' areas. On the other side there is the myth, exploded scientifically by the findings of physical anthropology but more effectively by the extravagances of Nazi racial theory, of a superior or at least a distinctive 'race' of planters who settled in the North from Scotland. Then there is the superficial view, apparently still held in some quarters, that the Ulster problem was created by English politicians and militarists.

Much more tenacious is the belief in 'the historic Irish nation' – and to a lesser degree in a politically independent Ulster – although Irish scholars have long ceased to defend it.

Most historians agree that throughout the pre-Reformation centuries, Ireland was never effectively united in a political sense, whether by Gaelic kings or English lords. Nationalism as a creed is largely a product of the last two hundred years, in particular of the Romantic period, and its adoption by Irish leader-heroes gave it great emotional appeal. Concepts of political consciousness and the struggle for national independence have been projected backwards into centuries when they had little or no meaning. As Dr. HESLINGA points out, it was the decentralized nature of Gaelic society that enabled it to survive.

"An outsider might expect that Irish Nationalists would be proud of having sprung from a civilization which so maintained itself, but modern Irish Nationalist theory owes it origin not to the Gaelic Irish but to the Anglo-Irish".

The modern Irish Republic goes back to the mediaeval English colony, and it is a fact that Irish nationalism has expressed itself mainly and most effectively in the English language. Here we come across another myth: Gaelic is officially the national language but it would be an understatement to say that English is freely spoken. Indeed it is so freely spoken in the Republic and so persuasively written that the outside world is made familiar with the cause of Irish unity, whereas the taciturn North gets a poor press.

Dr. HESLINGA sees both sections of the Irish Border, land and sea, as in the last resort religious frontiers. Separation and Partition alike are manifestations of the importance of religious factors in shaping the major socio-cultural regional contrasts in the British Isles. Yet it must be admitted that accounts of the attitude of the Catholic Church in the nineteenth century towards the Irish language and towards militant action, whether by peasants or intellectuals, must make strange reading to Irish nationalists. The Church stood for established law and authority and it was, by definition, 'the antithesis of a nationalistic faith'.

As a human geographer Dr. HESLINGA sees that any study of Irish regionalism must take account of regionalism in the British Isles as a whole. Regionalism has inspired the English genius for compromise, and in this respect the Southern Irish are more English than the English. The proudly independent Republic, technically a foreign state, allows itself to have the most intimate social and economic links with the mother country of the Commonwealth. In the end the author finds justification for the view tenaciously held in Northern Ireland, that it was not Ireland but the British Isles that suffered partition in 1921:

"The main problem is not why the majority of the people of the 'Six Counties' refused to cut through their constitutional links with Great Britain and throw in their lot with the people of the 'Twenty-Six Counties', but rather why the majority of the people of the 'Thirty-Two Counties' desired to withdraw from the United Kingdom of Great Britain and Ireland".

The North, so bitterly opposed to Home Rule, had to accept a large measure of it as a result.

I warmly commend this book for its honest endeavour to discover the realities behind politics and thus contribute to better understanding. I do so as one who has many friends north and south and who admires their great and varied gifts. I hope the book will be widely read in Britain as well as in Ireland.

E. ESTYN EVANS

PREFACE TO THE FIRST EDITION

It is a pleasant duty, on completing the text, to look back and call to mind all the kindness and assistance afforded me in its preparation. To mention all the scholars, officials, ecclesiastics and politicians who of their kindness assisted me in various ways would, I am afraid, be impossible. Yet I cannot but at least make acknowledgement of my debt to His Excellency, B. Gallagher, Irish Ambassador at The Hague, and Mr. F. O'Riordan, Secretary of the Irish Embassy; His Excellency, Dr. P. A. Kasteel, Netherlands Ambassador at Dublin, and Mr. M. van Oordt, Secretary of the Netherlands Embassy; Dr. A. Farrington, the then Secretary of the Royal Irish Academy at Dublin; Dr. E. Estyn Evans, Professor of Geography at the Queen's University of Belfast; Dr. M. D. McCarthy, Director of the Central Statistics Office at Dublin; and Mr. L. C. Mulligan, Registrar-General for Northern Ireland at Belfast. I am more grateful than I can say to two friends, one in the South and one in the North of Ireland, each of whom gave mucht criticism and advice.

I need hardly emphasize that the views expressed in this book are entirely my own and that nobody mentioned above may in any way be considered to have given approval of them. Nor can I expect that my views wil be received as did the lecturer on a similar theme who felt selfconfident enough to write: "Judging by the comments of Belfast and Dublin people present I succeeded in putting the Irish case without antagonizing anyone, and the English also seemed to understand".

Amsterdam, June 1962

PREFACE TO THE THIRD EDITION

The present book which was completed in manuscript in July 1961, was first published as a dissertation for the doctorate of Letters at the University of Utrecht in March 1962. As such, it was not expected to draw much attention outside a small circle of academic colleagues, family and friends. When, however, it became apparent that there was a demand from other quarters, it was decided to publish the book anew. The text and the title were left unchanged but the original author's foreword in Dutch was replaced by a foreword by Professor Estyn Evans. This book was published in June 1962 in the series *Sociaal-Geografische Studies*. It was reprinted in 1971.

When asked to consent to a new official edition, I have considered the need for a revision. There was a temptation to shorten the text and enhance its readability by removing the many references and footnotes which go with a dissertation. The re-issuing also provided the opportunity of drawing on a whole range of new publications on British and Irish affairs. But when I realised that this would not bring about major changes in my argument, it did not seem reason enough to attempt to write what could well become a new book.

Neither did I feel inclined to up-date the text by referring to the tragic events in Northern

Ireland since the publication of the first edition. My study was not so much intended to comment on the current political situation but rather to place the Northern Ireland problem within a much longer historical and a much wider geographical context. This emphasis has not changed. However, it is my sincere hope that the people of that pleasant land will soon see the constraints of their historical geography loosened so that, to paraphrase one of my sources, all of them can live, and love, and worship, and die in peace.

Amsterdam, July 1979

CONTENTS

LIST OF TABLES

LIST OF FIGURES

"Geography is not the mistress of the life of nations. The only final cause in history is the human mind, the thoughts it creates, the ideals which, under Divine inspiration, it attains. Geography neither predestined Ireland to be independent, nor foredoomed it to be dependent. It is men, and the wills of men, which make it the one or the other. .. Seas may divide, but they may also unite, according as men will to use them".

ERNEST BARKER

"Partition does not depend upon a physical boundary which can be removed by political action; it depends upon very important differences in outlook between two groups of people; and though these differences may be accentuated by political division they will not necessarily disappear as a result of enforced political union. The real partition of Ireland is not on the map but in the minds of men."

J. C. BECKETT

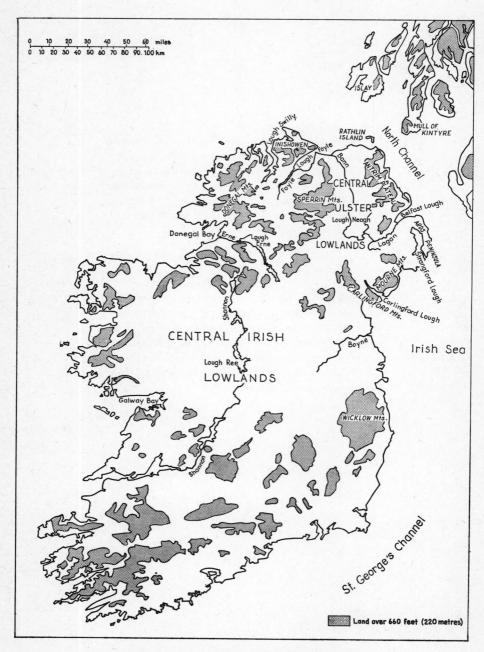

FIG. 1. The location of physical features mentioned in the text

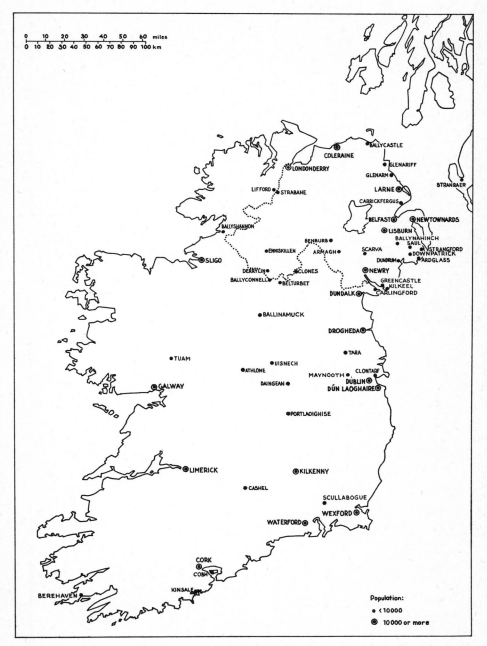

FIG. 2. The location of towns mentioned in the text

FIG. 3. The administrative counties and provinces of Ireland

Fig. 4. The Roman Catholic dioceses and ecclesiastical provinces of Ireland (after Jean Blanchard)

PART ONE

THE STUDY OF THE IRISH BORDER

Chapter 1

THE SUBJECT OF THIS STUDY

INTRODUCTION

When man took possession of the earth's surface, he found many obstacles which hampered his movements and hindered his contacts. Through the centuries he has endeavoured to conquer or to neutralize these natural barriers, by clearing forests and draining swamps, by building bridges and constructing ships. Thus, travel, commerce, and exchange of ideas have been facilitated to an unimaginable extent. On the other hand, man has often found reason to preserve or even to accentuate natural barriers, for only behind them did he feel safe from attack. And indeed, where there were no obstacles he has even created new barriers to traffic and trade or to the free course of thought.

Only in a very few instances are these new barriers visibly demarcated in the landscape. Sometimes they are merely a matter of posts and stones, set at intervals, or of spikes erected across roads. These boundaries, however, may be just as perceptible as natural barriers – if not more so – in political or economic or social life. Many of these man-made barriers have disappeared. Occasionally their only reminder is an abandoned earthwork or a solitary boundary post. But many of these have only been shifted – shortened or extended – whereas others still have a meaning in social life.

Because of their appearance and course, because of the territories they give size and shape to, because of their impact on daily life, and above all because of the influences they exert upon the feelings of the people they unite or divide, boundaries form a fascinating theme. In the last resort they are symbols: they can stand for possession and loss, for hopes and disillusions, for patriotism and for oppression, for rights and wrongs. People may hate them and want them abolished and people may revere them, even long for them.

Geographers generally take a keen interest in boundaries or frontiers [a], since they are much concerned with the determination and characterization of regions. It might even be possible to outline a history of geography by showing the nature of the borders past generations of geographers have studied, and how they have studied them. Most

---

[a] In this study the two words are alternatively employed. As their etymology suggests, a frontier and a boundary were in origin two different things. Historically the 'frontier' was not a line but an area, the foreland of a civilization or state, the borderland of an 'ecumene', or a 'march'. The term 'boundary' has always indicated well-established limits or bounds within which a political unit is bound or confined. It must be understood that gradually the borderlands, the old 'marchlands', were defined more and more precisely until they became, in principle, exact border lines. (For other differences between frontiers and boundaries, see: KRISTOF, *passim*).

important in human geography are the international frontiers, separating sovereign states, for they delimit all kinds of human interests and activities.

"The location of a boundary may.. determine for millions of people the language and the ideas which children shall be taught at school, the books and newspapers which people will be able to buy and read, the kind of money they shall use, the markets in which they must buy and sell, and perhaps even the kinds of food they may be permitted to eat".[1]

The frontier this book is concerned with is that which separates the Republic of Ireland, the former Irish Free State, sometimes called Éire (population: 2.8 million), from the United Kingdom of Great Britain and Northern Ireland (population: 52.7 million). On the analogy of the Scottish and the Welsh Border it will be called the 'Irish Border' – or simply the 'Border'. The Irish Border consists of two parts, one northern and the other southern. The northern section is the land boundary which crosses the island of Ireland, separating Northern Ireland, sometimes called Ulster[a], a self-governing province of the United Kingdom (population: 1.4 million), from the Irish Republic. The other section is formed by the southern and central part of the Irish Sea between Ireland and Great Britain.[b]

The Border dates back to the early nineteen 'twenties. It was derived from the so-called *Anglo-Irish Treaty*, officially styled: *Articles of Agreement for a Treaty between Great Britain and Ireland*, negotiated between the revolutionary (Southern) Irish government and the British government in 1921. The land boundary was first defined by a British act, the *Government of Ireland Act, 1920*, which provided for two subordinate governments in Ireland within the framework of the United Kingdom: one in Dublin for Southern Ireland and the other in Belfast for Northern Ireland (this act was effective only in regard to Northern Ireland; in the rest of the island it became a dead letter). The land boundary was confirmed by a treaty between the Free State government, the British government, and the Northern Ireland government in 1925.

THE PARTITION CONTROVERSY

Hitherto geographers have paid little attention to the Irish Border. My search for geographical literature on this frontier has produced only one thesis, written by a German geographer in the early nineteen 'thirties, and two articles by British geographers, which appeared last year. (The library of the Geography Department of the Queen's University of Belfast contains two theses which have not been published.) Geographical treatises

[a] A peculiar difficulty which presents itself when writing about Ireland is how to designate the two parts of the island which the land boundary establishes. Several phrases are used for both areas, each with a distinctly emotional appeal. It appears that some names are used only in certain circles while in others a more or less familiar alternative is deliberately preferred. These terms have indeed become shibboleths. They are constituent elements in opposed national mythologies: they have come to function in different systems of historical beliefs. A business man may be worried by these alternative terms when he is not sure what name a customer may prefer. A geographer must be no less concerned with the political implications of the terms which of necessity he must employ in any research on Ireland. He may well try to offend as few people as possible but he must avoid straining his 'geographical conscience'! In Chapter 3 I will set out the different meanings and values attached to 'Ulster', 'Éire', and other geographical names.

[b] In this study by 'Irish Sea' is understood the whole sea dividing Ireland from Great Britain, including the North Channel in the north and St George's Channel in the south. People speak generally of the 'Irish Sea' though they refer to the trade across the Irish Sea as 'cross-Channel' trade. The term 'cross-Channel' probably derives from St George's Channel.

of a more general nature only refer casually to the Irish Border. The scope of this literature is limited. Moreover, it deals only with the land boundary. [a] A new study which also takes regard of the connected sea boundary is long overdue.

At first sight it is rather surprising that, so far, geographers have dealt with only one part of the Irish Border. Perhaps the main reason is that the land boundary is disputed whereas the sea boundary is generally accepted by all parties concerned. Indeed, the land boundary has recently been the scene of hundreds of acts of violence. It is the only state frontier within Western Europe which has witnessed – for five or six years in succession – a whole series of 'border incidents'.

These incidents are caused by small armed bands of the I.R.A., the (illegal) *Irish Republican Army* which does not acquiesce in the political division of Ireland and wants to see Northern Ireland included in an all-Ireland republic. (The majority of the people of Northern Ireland, however, want to stay in the United Kingdom.) Border incidents include raids on customs huts, police stations, electricity transformers, telephone exchanges, bridges and other 'strategic objects' on the northern side of the land boundary, and attempts to ambush members of the R.U.C., the *Royal Ulster Constabulary, i.e.* the Northern Ireland police force.

In fact, the great majority of the people in the Irish Republic, and a minority of the population of Northern Ireland as well, dislike 'Partition', as the political division of the island is called in common parlance. This does not mean that they all support the I.R.A. As a matter of fact, most people in Ireland disapprove of the Border raids. They are even very unpopular among the minority in Northern Ireland, however anxious they may be to join the Republic. Prominent members of the minority have repeatedly repudiated the I.R.A. The I.R.A. has been outlawed in the Republic as well as in the United Kingdom. The *Gárda Síochána* (civic guard), the police force of the Republic, co-operates, to some extent, with the R.U.C. in its suppression. [b] The I.R.A. in its turn does not recognize either of the two governments set up in Ireland.

One wonders why a campaign of violence against Northern Ireland was launched in December 1956, thirty-five years after the land boundary had come into being. A primary reason may have been that the I.R.A. realized that the land boundary was becoming generally accepted in Ireland. It is well to remember that more than half of Ireland's population have grown up with it and increasing numbers of people on both sides have become materially concerned with its continuation. Another aim of the recent I.R.A. campaign may have been to arouse interest in the Irish land boundary dispute in Great Britain and abroad. Indeed, few people outside Ireland are aware of this border problem – even, oddly enough, in Great Britain. [c]

[a] In the next Chapter I will examine briefly what various geographers have said about the Irish Border, or more particularly about the land boundary.

[b] Recently it was estimated that "the hard core of those actively engaged in raiding, drilling and supplying arms" is about one hundred and fifty (*The Sunday Times*, Nov. 26, 1961).

[c] According to Mr Liam Kelly (an exponent of extremist Nationalist opinion), "the Republicans had no hope of military success in the North". Their hope was "that if sufficient damage could be done it would be brought home to the British that there would never be peace in that area" and "that they would be the instrument of re-opening talks on the Irish question between the Governments concerned" (*The Mid-Ulster Observer*, June 5, 1958). One theory has that the I.R.A. campaign was triggered off by the Hungarian uprising two months before (*The Observer*, June 21, 1959).

Nowadays it is seldom realized that hardly half a century ago the idea that Ireland should be separated from Great Britain evoked as much emotion as the idea that Ireland should be partitioned does today. At the time the conception of a sea boundary was as much resisted as the land boundary is today. Therefore, if one wonders why a political frontier runs across Ireland, one could ask with almost equal right why a political frontier runs through the Irish Sea. Moreover, as this study will show, the two problems are closely related: if the idea of a sea boundary had not arisen, there would not have been a land boundary.

IRELAND AS A REGIONAL UNIT

There is a second reason why geographers who have dealt with the Irish land boundary have given no substantial thought to the sea boundary. The idea which underlies almost all studies and statements made by geographers with regard to the Irish Border is that the land boundary is 'incongruous' while it is too obvious that there is a sea boundary. This idea derives from two traditional theories: one of the geography of the British Isles, and the other of the merits of so-called natural boundaries.

The well-established picture of the geography of the British Isles is of two main natural entities, clearly separated by the Irish Sea, which are, culturally, sharply distinguished from each other. This simplified version of geography has been reinforced again and again by the way geographers have dealt with these islands.

There was a time when many geographers assumed that a natural region tends also to become a 'cultural region' [a] owing to "the paramount influence exerted by Nature upon Man". Nowadays geographers no longer attach very much importance to this idea. Most of them will agree with ROBERT DICKINSON's observation that "a natural region with clearly defined frontiers cannot, and does not, give rise to a corresponding unity in the human relations within it, be they cultural, social, political or economic". [2] The old idea only lingers on as far as islands are concerned. The British Isles provide a striking example: there are still geographers who simply take for granted that Great Britain and Ireland are cultural regions because they are islands.

In this study I will examine in how far Ireland is a cultural region. This is a far-reaching problem which I examine only in so far as the Irish Border bears upon it. [b]

[a] By a 'cultural region' will be understood: "an area which is homogeneous in respect of certain interrelated characteristics of the make-up of its society, whether those characteristics be economic, cultural or political, or whether they apply to the past or the present" (DICKINSON, 19). Here the word 'cultural' is used in both a broad and a narrow sense. It will be clear from the context which meaning applies.

[b] A geographer who deals with the land boundary may be justified, to some extent, in delimiting his study to Ireland. He may examine, for instance, the impact of the land boundary on Ireland. But he must always be aware of the fact that Northern Ireland, although it has its own government and parliament, is not a sovereign state like the Irish Republic. It follows that the impact of the land boundary cannot be understood without full regard to Northern Ireland's integration in the United Kingdom. For instance, as Northern Ireland's autonomy in the field of economics is minimal, the significance of the land boundary as an economic barrier can only be studied properly in the context of the British Isles as a whole. A geographer who chooses to deal with both the land and sea boundary may still concentrate upon Ireland but he can never leave Great Britain out of consideration – for the simple reason that the frontier which he studies is the frontier between the Irish Republic and the United Kingdom of *Great Britain* and Northern Ireland.

My main purpose is to show how far the Irish land and sea boundary conform to major regional divisions of the British Isles.[a]

The picture which this study presents differs from the traditional picture of Ireland in two main respects. On the one hand it shows great contrasts within Ireland, more specifically between the two parts of Ireland which the land boundary has come to define. On the other hand it shows great similarities between Ireland and Great Britain, or more specifically between the two parts of Ireland and Great Britain. As for the Border: the land boundary represents in some respects a much greater division than is often thought whereas the sea boundary is in some respects a less marked division than is commonly supposed.

The popular view that Ireland and Great Britain are two separate cultural regions is also sustained by the practice among human geographers who, while not assuming that natural unity inevitably means cultural unity and even acknowledging all kinds of regional diversities within these islands, nevertheless deal with these diversities within the framework of natural rather than cultural entities. All the geographies of the British Isles which pay attention to cultural features treat these features in the context of natural entities, *i.e.* the islands of Great Britain and Ireland respectively.

If the human geographer is to deal properly with the spread and interrelations of cultural features he must not end his study abruptly at an apparent natural barrier when there is abundant evidence that spread has taken place beyond it at different periods in time. It is rather odd that no geographer who deals with the spread of cultural features in Ireland or in Great Britain is dissuaded by mountain ranges or lake belts but the same geographer rarely looks beyond the Irish Sea.

Human geographers might well learn from physical geographers for their approach to Ireland is not limited by the Irish Sea. They are very much aware of connexions between Ireland and Great Britain. Physical geographers always stress that Ireland is a natural unity only from the point of view of topography. Their maps show that the main natural features of Ireland are continuations of the natural features of Great Britain. Structurally, therefore, Ireland does not stand on its own.

[a] It should be pointed out that, "if in legal terms an international boundary is a line, geographically and politically it is a zone" (GOTTMANN). The common conception of state boundaries, which is expressed in such terms as 'frontier line' and 'border line', results from the normal human tendency to think of things in sharply defined compartments rather than from careful observation of the facts. (Fundamentally it supposes the establishment of firm, effective, sovereignty over a contiguous territory: the existence of a central government which exerts more than nominal control over the whole of its territory). A state frontier is, no less than any other regional divide, essentially "a zone in which the influences from the two sides mingle so as to lessen the abruption of the transition between the two strongly contrasted regions which it separates" (FAWCETT, 17-8, 24; GOTTMANN, *Politique*, 122-3, 135-7; DE VISSCHER, 258-67).

Apart from the fact that a state boundary is often drawn within a pre-existing 'transitional belt', there will in time develop on both sides of this line "the unmistakable features of a political frontier zone: custom-houses, quarantine stations, and their counterpart, a smuggler's economy". Often also there are "towns south of the border" performing services outlawed by the state north of the line, and *vice versa* (*Frontiers*, 7). The concept of the political frontier zone is also accepted in international law. I might point to the *zone contigue*, the strip between the 'territorial' and the 'high' seas (cf. GIDEL, *passim*), and to the agreements between neighbouring states concerning well-defined areas on both sides of their common frontiers for which special regulations are in force. I might instance provisions facilitating short-distance traffic across the border and reciprocal obligations to communicate information about the occurrence of contagious diseases of persons and animals.

This study will show that in the same way Ireland is not a self-contained cultural unit: the major cultural regional diversities within Ireland can only be understood fully within the framework of cultural regional entities which extend across the Irish Sea into parts of Great Britain. While not denying that these islands have distinctive features, I will point out that, in some respects, the northern parts of both islands have more in common with one another than they have with the southern. The reverse seems also true: the southern parts have some features in common which are shared only to a small extent by the northern parts. The usual view of the British Isles is of a large eastern island and a smaller western island. It is also possible, in my opinion, to divide the British Isles into a large southern part and a smaller northern part.

The fact that to many geographers it is only too obvious that there is a state frontier in the Irish Sea can also be connected with the traditional view that, if at all possible, a state should be defined by prominent natural features.

At one time this idea was wide-spread. Most geographers, however, have recognized that so-called 'artificial frontiers', *i.e.* frontiers which have no relation to conspicuous natural barriers, are not necessarily unworkable and unsatisfactory frontiers. A great number of international boundaries have been stable for a long time although they most strikingly disregard natural divisions – being either straight lines drawn by compromise, or adjusted to capricious cultural conditions. On the other hand, a boundary chosen so as to correspond with natural features may be the cause of friction because all too frequently it disregards human activities and interests.

Many a geographer, however, while no longer prejudiced against 'artificial' land boundaries, still has a weakness for sea boundaries. But a sea not only keeps peoples apart: it also binds them together. This study will show that this maxim can be perfectly well applied to the Irish Sea. In many respects contacts across the Irish Sea are more numerous and more intensive than those across the land boundary. While the popular view of the British Isles holds that they are clearly distinctive entities and that therefore the land boundary is incongruous, my view tends to find the sea boundary hardly less incongruous.

GEOGRAPHICAL ARGUMENTS IN THE PARTITION ISSUE

In Part Two I will examine how far the Irish land and sea boundary conform to some actual regional divisions of the British Isles, and in Parts Three and Four how far they conform to major historical regional divisions. For obvious reasons this study cannot cover all aspects of the regional differentiation of the British Isles. Some geographers, perhaps, will be surprised at my lengthy treatment of 'spiritual' divisions whereas I pay relatively little attention to economic divisions. My approach was first suggested by the survey of a considerable amount of anti- and pro-Partition literature. [a]

This literature confirms the conclusion of RICHARD HARTSHORNE in his essay on the boundary disputes in pre-War Europe:

"Even granted that claims to areas are still being based on 'historic rights' or on the 'law of the conquest', the arguments which are keeping border disputes alive, and therefore dangerous, are now based primarily on real or supposed geographical associations. .. It is asserted that these associations – whether 'natural', ethnographic, economic, or historical – cause an area to belong justly to a certain state".[3]

[a] In the next Chapter I will mention some specimens of this literature.

A great deal of anti- and pro-Partition writing is concerned with the "real or supposed geographical associations" of Northern Ireland – with the rest of Ireland on the one hand, and with Great Britain on the other. An analysis of a fair sample of this literature shows that the basic theories and prevailing arguments, nursed and cherished on either side during the last forty or fifty years, have on the whole changed very little if at all.

The most common argument put forward for the abolition of the land boundary is that the frontier is repugnant to the unity of Ireland, both natural and cultural. The arguments advanced in favour of maintaining the land boundary stem from a similar way of thinking. They emphasize Northern Ireland's close natural and cultural ties to Great Britain while stressing certain differences between 'Ulster' and 'Éire'. These contrasting views of Northern Ireland's geographical associations may also be found in some of the writings of geographers who have dealt with Partition. There are geographers who, while appreciating the tragic side of Partition, consider Northern Ireland's case for retention of the union with Great Britain a strong one. Others, however, are in favour of the theory that Ireland, as a natural entity, ought to be a political entity, and therefore Northern Ireland should be united with the rest of Ireland.

HARTSHORNE, after pointing out that any physiographical association of a disputed territory with a neighbouring state does not in itself unite it to that state, is no doubt right when he says:

"In an area of physiographic unity the human characteristics and activities of its various parts may or may not be associated together. If they are, then those human associations are the factors to be considered in any border dispute. This condition cannot *a priori* be assumed, however".[4]

The human associations which, according to HARTSHORNE, clearly do tie regions together are of three types:

(1) *cultural associations:* "When neighbouring territories belong to the same cultural area, particularly in so far as nationality is concerned [a], they have a strong bond even if they have never been part of the same political area and even if there are natural barriers between them which make communication difficult";

(2) *socio-economic associations:* "communications, both of people and of goods" (transport and trade); and

(3) *historical associations* (memories and concepts derived from a common past): "When neighbouring areas have had a common experience over a long period of time in the same political unit, they inherit common memories and common political and social ideals. The historical associations, however, cannot be measured simply by length of time, for they have less to do with historical records than with the people's thoughts and memories about their past".[5]

In Part Two I will consider not only certain geographical associations of Northern Ireland with the Irish Republic and with Great Britain, but also some associations of the Republic with Great Britain. The selection of these associations has been prompted primarily by the great significance which both sides in the Partition controversy attach to them. In Chapter 4 I will discuss the natural associations of both parts of Ireland. Chapter 5 has regard to what HARTSHORNE calls the historical associations. Chapters 6 and

[a] By 'nationality' HARTSHORNE understands: "a feeling of loyalty to a particular country, both land and people", which is generally based on a common culture. A common culture results, usually, from a common language, but in some cases religion or particular social and political concepts may be the most important factors in determining nationality (*Aspects,* 168).

7 deal with some cultural associations – 'cultural' in the narrow sense in which HARTSHORNE uses the word.

The other category of human associations which HARTSHORNE distinguishes, the socio-economic associations, play a far less important role in the Partition issue. At first sight this may appear strange. It is therefore not amiss to have a look at the socio-economic associations of the two parts of Ireland.

THE BORDER AS A SOCIO-ECONOMIC DIVIDE

We have been experiencing after the Second World War the gradual whittling away of many travel restrictions between the Western European countries. But here is a state frontier where such travel restrictions never existed, though the frontier was created after a period of guerilla warfare and has witnessed many 'border incidents'. An outsider is surprised to find that one can cross and re-cross the Irish Border freely – by land as well as by sea – without passport, travel documents, or any other identity document [a]: the United Kingdom and the Irish Republic form a single control area for immigration purposes.

In fact, in spite of Separation and Partition, the British Isles in many vitally important respects still form a social unit. Citizens of the Republic who are resident in the United Kingdom enjoy many privileges not enjoyed by citizens of any other foreign country. As a matter of fact – in the words of the *Ireland Act, 1949* – "notwithstanding that the Republic of Ireland is not part of His Majesty's dominions, the Republic of Ireland is not a foreign country for the purposes of any law in force in any part of the United Kingdom".[b] When, in 1948, the South of Ireland ceased to be formally part of the Commonwealth of Nations and became the Republic of Ireland, J. M. JONES writes in his *British Nationality Law*,

"it was felt that considerations of geographical propinquity, the long historical associations of Ireland with the rest of the British Isles, and similar factors, made it inappropriate that citizens of Éire, even though not British subjects or Commonwealth citizens, should be aliens. .. It is not necessary, or even possible, for citizens of Éire to become naturalized as citizens of the United Kingdom and Colonies; they are entitled, however, to become such citizens by registration if eligible under the *British Nationality Act*".[c]

Under the *British Nationality Act, 1948*, citizens of the Republic have for almost all purposes of the internal law of the United Kingdom the same privileges and duties [c]

---

[a] Cars and some other goods are however liable to customs duty as on practically all international frontiers. Motorists need driving licenses and may cross the land boundary only by a dozen so-called 'approved roads'. These are the only travel restrictions, apart from occasional shortage of accommodation on the cross-Channel boat and air services. Only since the I.R.A. campaign began have the border roads been blocked, more or less provisionally, in order to prevent motorized raids. (Except on the roads, there is not the slightest sign in the landscape of a state frontier in Ireland.)

[b] The ambiguous position of the Irish Republic is recognized by the fact that her representative in the United Kingdom is an ambassador, not a high commissioner (for the Republic is not within the Commonwealth), but he conducts his relations with the London government through the Commonwealth Relations Office, not the Foreign Office (for the Republic is not a foreign country according to the United Kingdom law) (WHEARE, 138).

[c] Citizens of the Republic were even liable to conscription after two years' residence in Great Britain. (There was never conscription in Northern Ireland or in the Republic).

as citizens of the United Kingdom.[7] On the other hand, the *Irish Nationality and Citizenship Act*, passed by the Dublin parliament in 1956, contains the provision that:

"Where the Government are satisfied that under the law of any country .. Irish citizens enjoy in that country some or all of the rights and privileges of a citizen of that country, the Government may .. declare that citizens of that country shall enjoy in the State similar citizenship rights and privileges to those enjoyed by Irish citizens in that country, but subject to such conditions (if any) as the Government may think fit to impose".

In a few respects Northern Ireland stands more on its own than the Irish Republic does. For example, there are no employment restrictions in Great Britain for citizens of the Republic nor in the Republic for British citizens, whereas in Northern Ireland there are some restrictions which apply to people from both Great Britain and the Republic. Another example is that citizens of the Republic have the franchise in the British general elections on the same residence conditions as British citizens. By the Republic constitution only citizens may vote, but it appears that British residents in the Republic may vote in local elections. (Republic citizens who are resident in Great Britain are not only entitled to vote in general elections but in local elections as well.) On the other hand, Northern Ireland has a separate code for its local government elections and for its own parliamentary elections.

If the Irish Border can hardly be considered a social divide in view of all the social associations between the United Kingdom and the Republic, it is not an important economic barrier either. On both sides of the border the same monetary system is in use. True, there are two coinages (since the late 'twenties), but the coins and notes have the same value. [a] The currency notes, although of different colour and language, both carry the promise that they are payable to the bearer on demand in London.[b] The United Kingdom currency circulates freely in the Republic; that of the Republic circulates in Northern Ireland but not in Great Britain.

Economic life in the Republic is in myriad ways tied to the United Kingdom economy. It is dependent upon the United Kingdom as the dominant outlet for its chief export – live cattle – and for a large portion of its own supplies of materials, goods and services.[8] The Republic grants the United Kingdom a special preferential tariff. This tariff is lower than that given to other Commonwealth countries (excluding Canada) and that given to other countries. On the other hand, exports from the Republic enter the United Kingdom free of all duty and restrictions with but a few, rather insignificant, exceptions. In fact, the free access to the United Kingdom market is one of the principal inducements offered by the Dublin government to foreign industries wishing to settle in the Republic. The Dublin authorities are even anxious to advertise this advantage! (As this provision exists as a result of bilateral agreement, they must feel quite confident that it is one which is going to continue.)

[a] The only difference is that the farthing has recently been withdrawn from the United Kingdom coinage. The farthings of the Republic are however perpetually in short supply. With one exception, the coins of both sides fit the telephone boxes of the other.

[b] The Irish pound is tied by law to the pound sterling and the security for the Republic note issue is almost entirely British money and securities (cf. *Appraisal*, 20). The Dublin central bank, constituted in 1942, performs only some of the functions of a central bank – the others are still discharged by the Bank of England.

Indeed, a report, prepared for the Dublin government in 1952 by American economists, states that "the extraordinary degree" of the Republic's economic linkage to the United Kingdom is "inconsistent with its passionate commitment to political independence".[9] However, these economic ties – so far from being repugnant to the great majority of the people of the Republic – are welcomed by them: they are regarded as a source of strength. Even the I.R.A. takes care that its actions do not interfere with economic interests. When a British customs hut on the land boundary is blown up, the connected installations for the transit of live cattle are spared. (Most of the I.R.A. members are farmers' sons.)

In 1960 the Dublin government suggested an even closer economic integration with the United Kingdom, under which arrangement British goods would receive even greater preference and in due course have completely free access to the Republic market, and British agricultural subsidies would be more fully granted to Republic agricultural producers.[10] If the British government had accepted these astute proposals, the British Isles would have become once more a free trade area – as they were prior to 1922. [a]

THE BORDER AS A SPIRITUAL DIVIDE

In his essay on *Geography and International Relations* JEAN GOTTMANN observes: "The most stubborn facts are those of the spirit, not those of the physical world". While history shows how stubborn are the facts of the spirit, "geography demonstrates that the main partitions observed in the space accessible to men are not those in the topography or in the vegetation, but those that are in the minds of men".[11] Any geographer who goes into the problem of the political division of the British Isles, or into that of Ireland in particular, cannot, I think, fail to agree with this conclusion. Nor can he fail to recognize that the most stubborn facts of the spirit are such factors as religious and nationalist feeling.

The great attention this study pays to those feelings rests on the assumption that the political division of the British Isles hinges on spiritual oppositions rather than on economic theories and realities. As I see it, the Irish Border in a sense represents an attempt to translate into 'geographical terms' those decisive regional spiritual cleavages.[12] In his *A Geography of Europe* GOTTMANN notes:

"To be distinct from its surroundings, a region needs much more than a mountain or a valley, a given language or certain skills; it needs essentially a strong belief based on some religious creed, some social viewpoint, or some pattern of political memories, and often a combination of all three. Thus regionalism has an *iconography* as its foundation: each community has found for itself or was given an icon, a symbol slightly different from those cherished by its neighbors".[13]

Although the subject of this book is a political frontier, it should not therefore be regarded as a 'political geography' of, say, Ireland. For on the political side it is less comprehensive than might properly be expected of a political geography, whereas it

---

[a] I propose to deal at greater length with the socio-economic associations of the two parts of Ireland, with one another and with Great Britain, in a study (now under preparation) which examines the impact of the Irish Border on social and economic life in Ireland since 1922.

includes many items which would probably have been out of place in such a treatise. [a]
As the Irish Border will be studied with regard to the regional differentiation of Ireland
and, by extension, of the British Isles as a whole, this book could perhaps be conceived
of as a 'regional geography'. It is not, however, a regional geography in the encyclopaedic
sense this term often bears. Rather is it intended as a contribution to the study of 'regionalism' in the British Isles.

The concept of 'regionalism' has been defined in various ways. [b] Fundamental is the
'regional spirit' which is always made of many components:

"a historical background, and its interpretation, common to the members of the community, but
alien to those beyond the border. The common link is preserved and often reinforced by the education that
family and school give the younger generations. The local environment always plays a part among the
foundations of such national or regional spirit, but the important thing is what the people are *taught to
see* in the physical and social conditions they live in".[14]

By 'regionalism' I understand a feeling of solidarity which unites the people living
within a certain area, or at least the majority of those people. This feeling is institutionalized
in social organizations but it is not necessarily recognized by legislation and administration.
It implies people's awareness of distinctness, whether intuitive or artificially aroused,
and an attachment to their 'own' region. This 'regional consciousness' corresponds to
the 'region' as a 'psychological complex', as defined by a Hindu sociologist:

"a common and co-ordinate set of stimuli, eliciting a similarity of responses, habits and feelings which
are reinforced by gregariousness and which are moulded and stabilized into a characteristic mental type
and pattern of living".[15]

The concept of regionalism grades into that of 'nationalism'. Stubborn regionalisms
indeed have often evolved towards nationalisms in modern times.[16] This holds good for
Ireland also. Nationalism is, generally speaking, activated, intensified and magnified
regionalism. It can be distinguished from regionalism in so far as it implies a theoretical
justification and a development of political demands. It follows that a discussion of the
roots and evolution of the nationalist movements in Ireland is not inappropriate in this
study.

IRELAND AS A HISTORICAL UNIT

After having shown in how far the Irish land and sea boundary conform to some actual
regional divisions of the British Isles (Part Two), I will examine at rather great length

---

[a] It is true that, although it is one of the oldest branches of geography, there is as yet no consensus of
opinion as to the approach and content of political geography. The same applies indeed to other branches
of human geography, such as economic and social (or sociological) geography. Moreover, there is still
much controversy about human geography as a whole.

[b] For an account of the development and use of the concept of regionalism from the eighteenth century
to the present day, both as a tool for research and as an approach to problems of practical administration, see: *Regionalism in America*, edited by MERRILL JENSEN and published in celebration of the hund-
redth anniversary of the founding of the University of Wisconsin in 1952.

in how far they conform to historical regional divisions of these islands (Parts Three and Four). As DICKINSON says:

"The extent to which a natural entity has in fact functioned in the past as a cultural entity can only be based on a full appraisal of the human relations – cultural, political and economic – in their geographical aspects. These relations must be both assessed for the past and evaluated in the light of the present".[17]

The firmly established picture of the geography of the British Isles, which is that of two main cultural regions clearly distinguished from each other, applies not only to the present but to the past as well. It corresponds to an equally firmly established picture of the history of these islands which is that of an everlasting war, of British aggression and Irish resistance. This simplified version of history is supported by the emergence of the Irish Republic which claims succession from "the generations of Irishmen who resisted British imperialism and colonialism", and which, of course, claims that its jurisdiction should extend over the whole island.

EOIN MACNEILL (who was professor of ancient Irish history in University College, Dublin) notes in his introduction to GERARD HAYES-McCOY's study of the *Scots Mercenary Forces in Ireland*:

"One of the difficulties in the way of a better understanding of Irish history is the habit of importing notions of our own time and of extraneous origin, especially political, juristic, and economic notions, which have not a valid application and must lead, as they have led, to the misunderstanding and misrepresentation of the facts".

A distortion of Irish history which results largely from the habit of thinking about history in relation to modern political conceptions is, according to MACNEILL, "the view that the people of Ireland, throughout most of their history, were a people of 'warriors'".[18] Another instance is the view – which was, essentially, MACNEILL's too – that the people of Ireland, throughout most of their history, constituted a 'nation'. As MICHAEL TIERNEY (the president of University College, Dublin) observes:

"A very popular way of looking at our history is to conceive of it as having been guided in all its phases by one true doctrine, the doctrine of Nationality, all other explanations being dismissed as aberrant. This one true doctrine is often believed to be of immortal native origin and is invoked with equal rigour to explain the course of events in the twelfth, the seventeenth, or the nineteenth century. Thus construed and invoked, it makes nonsense of a great part of our history; for in this rigid form it is a product of the late eighteenth century and was first popularly preached only a little more than a hundred years ago".[19]

It is well to remember that, throughout the nineteenth century and even in the beginning of the present century, the study of history in Ireland was, to a very large extent, bound up with nationalism. In 1905 it could still be said that, "with a few exceptions, Irish history has been written by novelists, fanatics, and politicians".[20] Gradually, however, historical research has disentangled itself from nineteenth-century political prejudice. Meanwhile the Partition issue has generated new prejudice.

The polemic note in contemporary studies, introduced by the Partition controversy, may be as apparent by omission as by commission. It would seem that there is among scholars in the Republic some reluctance – unconscious rather than conscious – to lay stress on the north-south contrasts which are as inherent in early Irish history, secular and ecclesiastical, as they are in modern history. The underlying motive may be not to provide material for a modern 'North-South rivalry' to Ulster Unionist partisans, comparable with the controversies which raged among scholars of a past generation – even if the ancient north-south divisions arise from different causes than the modern political conflict.

As a corollary of the view that of old the Irish – both of the north and the south – have formed a 'nation', it is generally believed in Ireland (and in Great Britain) that 'the Irish' have always kept very much apart from 'the English' or 'the British'. It is seldom realized that there has been a continuous movement of population across the Irish Sea. Not only Irish geography but also Irish history is influenced in its approach by late-eighteenth- and nineteenth-century ideas of the sea as a natural frontier and therefore falls short in providing a proper understanding of the diversity of life within these islands.

In her essay on Irish-Welsh relations CECILE O'RAHILLY observes: "Nothing could be more fatal to the scientific investigations of .. early problems than to bring to such researches the ideas and conceptions of the nineteenth and twentieth centuries". It is difficult for modern students of sedentary habits, *Stubenmenschen* as HEINRICH ZIMMER calls them, to realize that "in far-off barbaric days seas often connected, and lands separated, distant countries".[21] This is perhaps most evident in the north of the British Isles where the two main islands come very close.

A typical instance of 'geographical prejudice' is the way in which many Irish historians have dealt with the Scots who settled in Ulster in the seventeenth century. These Scots looked upon the narrow North Channel rather in the same way as other Scots looked upon the Firth of Forth. They never felt any particular attachment to a natural unit called Ireland but rather regarded themselves as a cross-Channel extension of Scotland. Viewed in that light it is hardly surprising that their descendants – who are still conscious of their Scottish extraction – really care for the union of Northern Ireland with Great Britain.

One who thinks in (nineteenth-century) terms of Ireland as a self-contained unit clearly separated from Great Britain by the Irish Sea can never understand the position of the seventeenth-century 'immigrants' – nor that of their twentieth-century descendants. Modern Scottish historians also fail to grasp it. They rarely pay any attention to the population movements from Scotland into Ulster in the seventeenth and previous centuries since, in the nineteenth century, they became, in retrospect, the Scottish counter-part of the Cromwellian Settlement and other acts of English 'colonialism' and 'imperialism'.

On the other hand, Irish, or rather Southern Irish, authors pay very little attention, if any, to the role of Scotland in Irish affairs prior to the eighteenth century. They are sometimes as 'anglo-centric' in their views as are many English authors, in the sense that they concentrate upon England as the undoubtedly most important part of Great Britain and have regard to the other parts only in so far as these territories are important from the English point of view. It is seldom realized in Ireland – and in England – that till 350 years ago Great Britain was divided into two states [a] which were often at war with

---

[a] For practical purposes we can ignore Wales. It had largely been conquered and at no time has it existed as anything like a 'state', not even in a twelfth-century context.

one another and were allied to different warring states on the continent. [a] Till 250 years ago these two states, though united under one crown, retained separate sovereign parliaments.

An English king invaded Ireland in 1169 but a Scottish king, or rather his brother, did so in 1315. An English king began the conquest of Ireland but a Scottish king completed it. [b] The omission of the role of Scotland in Irish affairs leads to many historical errors but also to a totally wrong conception of the historical geography of the British Isles. (It is well to remember that Scotland covers about one-fourth of the land area of the British Isles, *i.e.* 30,000 square miles – which is almost the size of Ireland.)

In fact, just as there is no study which deals systematically with the present-day contacts and contrasts between the main parts of the British Isles, equally there is no study – a 'historical geography' or a 'geographical history' – which deals systematically with such contacts and contrasts in the past. This book does not pretend to meet the need for such a study. It only deals with the development of contrasts and contacts between the north and the south of Ireland on the one hand and of their relations with the northern and southern parts of Great Britain on the other. [c] Special attention will be given to the growth – and decline – of various concepts of Ulster.

The historical or historical-geographical part of this study has been divided into two Parts which deal with the pre- and the post-Reformation period respectively. This division rests on the assumption that the Reformation and its political implications

[a] England's attempt to conquer Scotland, begun by the first Norman king, ended in failure. Scotland was indeed conquered and her kingship and parliament extinguished. But she revived and drove out the English and remained a menace to England's security in succeeding centuries. The bloody pitched battles of Flodden (1513) and Pinkie (1547) were large engagements by continental standards. The Scottish royal family had marriage alliances with continental dynasties. Mary, Queen of Scots, was married to the *dauphin* of France (1558), and for a brief period (1559-60) Scotland and France were united under one crown. Had Mary's husband, Francis II, lived, their children married and had children, Scotland and England might yet be separate states. (Even as it is they have retained separate legal and educational systems.)

[b] It will be objected that Edward Bruce landed in Ireland on the request of Irish princes to eject the English. But Henry II also invaded Ireland on the request of an Irish prince and with the avowed intention of reforming Irish manners and religion. Moreover, Henry's action had the approval of the pope, Edward's had not. Henry's invasion succeeded, Edward's failed. But had Edward succeeded he would have established a new state with a Gaelic-Norman-Scottish aristocratic basis (he was half-Norman by descent). Had he died childless would Ireland and Scotland have been united? And as for the completion of the English conquest in the beginning of the seventeenth century: James I who presided over the destruction of the Gaelic order in Ulster had been king of Scotland for forty years and king of England for only four years when he initiated the Plantation of Ulster (1607).

[c] I have availed myself of the opportunity to pay full regard to some of the theories which modern scholars like THOMAS O'RAHILLY, KENNETH JACKSON, D. A. BINCHY and JAMES CARNEY have advanced. These theories on early Irish history are still little known outside Ireland, except to Celtologists. They have upset a great many conceptions which have hitherto been looked on as established facts and some of which are key-stones in the Nationalist mythology. (Nationalists often find it difficult to appreciate this disrespect of the traditional views by modern scholars; cf. MACNEILL, *Phases*, 105).

In spite of the rather overwhelming abundance of material that has come to light during the last few decades, the pictures of Ireland in each of the early periods have still many nebulous spots. However, of all evidence stored in ancient texts (especially laws) and scattered over and enclosed in the soil, only a part has hitherto been touched, let alone thoroughly examined. Therefore, the conclusions drawn from the present material may be subject to revision.

have exerted a decisive influence on the regionalisms in the British Isles, or in Ireland at any rate. Indeed, it is one of my principal contentions that the present Irish Border is rooted in the Reformation. It is true, the present state frontier shows conformity to regional divisions of the British Isles which are much older. This does not mean, however, that it must have any relation to those older divisions. The latter are 'locational' rather than 'functional' forerunners of the modern frontier. [a]

Finally it is not amiss to stress the tentative nature of the historical-geographical part – and of the rest of this study. It is but a first attempt to deal with regionalisms in the British Isles in this way.

Chapter 2

LITERATURE ON PARTITION

GEOGRAPHERS ON PARTITION[b]

The first geographer to carry out research on the Irish land boundary was a German, FRIEDRICH MÜLLER-ROSS, who delivered a thesis on *Die irische Grenzfrage* (*Ulster, Irland und Grossbritannien*) in 1931. (Only part of his study has been published.) Some points of his study will be outlined below. What MÜLLER-ROSS calls the Irish boundary problem surpasses, in his opinion, by far all other boundary problems of his time because of its many-sidedness.[22] The main facets of this problem are, according to MÜLLER-ROSS:

(1)   The land boundary is not a 'natural' boundary. The only 'natural' frontier between the United Kingdom and the Irish Free State is the Irish Sea. The constitutional linkage with Great Britain of what MÜLLER-ROSS styles 'North-East Ulster' is, therefore, just as absurd as a possible claim of 'Ireland' (the Free State) to the western part of Scotland would be.[23]

(2)   The land boundary has been imposed against the wishes of the majority of the population of Ireland.

[a]   A state frontier is very rarely an entirely new dividing line, a fresh creation in no way derived from an earlier division. In most cases it will be found that the boundary has succeeded to an older border, whether a line or zone. I should emphasize that any striking resemblance between a modern state frontier and an ancient boundary is often very deceptive because the latter may have served quite different purposes. The only true forerunner of a modern frontier is that boundary which has performed, essentially, the same 'functions', no matter what its location. (Of course, strictly speaking, a frontier does not perform functions but it limits the exercise of functions by governments and other bodies.)

Therefore, we should clearly distinguish between two types of predecessor boundaries:

(1)   the 'locational' or 'formal' predecessor boundary, which is any older boundary having exactly or approximately the same 'location' as the present frontier, irrespective of the functions of the older division and the extent and kind of the regions it defined; and

(2)   the 'functional' or 'material' predecessor boundary, which is any older boundary performing exactly or approximately the same 'functions' as the present frontier, irrespective of the location of the older division. (It is possible that a locational forerunner of a modern boundary is a functional forerunner too.)

It is clear, then, that the question of how far a state boundary does go back can be answered in two ways.

[b]   The purpose of this Section and the next one is to give some idea of the kind of things geographers have said about Partition. While one would feel inclined to comment on these statements it would be premature to do so at this stage as I shall need to elaborate later on many of the point sraised and their implications.

It is a counterpart of the international frontiers which the 'Central Powers' (Germany, Austria and Hungary) were forced to accept after the First World War. Northern Ireland is "an important British bridgehead", a 'glacis' for their military control of the Free State. The creation of this 'buffer state' finds many analogies in the *divide et impera* policy which England uses with regard to other Dominions, such as Australia and New Zealand (1923), Canada and Newfoundland (1927), and India and Burma (1931).[24]

(3)   The land boundary is the only frontier in the world the justification of which is based on a difference in religion: Northern Ireland is predominantly Protestant whereas the Free State is almost wholly Roman Catholic. However, the actual course of the boundary does not provide a practicable dividing line between both denominations. It is, in fact, not easily possible to draw such a line, as Roman Catholic and Protestant Ireland are not clearly spatially separated. The land boundary has been delimited in such a way that the Ulster Unionists, who are the government party in Northern Ireland, can maintain an absolute majority of Protestants in the Belfast parliament. The Irish boundary problem is, therefore, not a 'geographical-denominational' but a minority problem.[25]

(4)   The land boundary cuts off most of Ireland's industries from the Free State. Ireland is, economically, a 'harmony', in the sense that the industries of Northern Ireland are the necessary complement of the predominantly agricultural Free State. The land boundary is a 'sociographical' boundary since it marks out "the area in which Ulster-Protestant capital-ownership constitutes the principal factor in economic and political life".[26]

(5)   Only the 'Ulster basin' in the north-east may be considered essentially distinct from the rest of the island. This is a virtually Protestant area, colonized by English and Scottish Protestants in the seventeenth century. It must be attributed to the geographical compactness of the 'Ulster colonization' that these settlers have not been absorbed by Roman Catholicism as happened to their predecessors in other parts of Ireland.[27]

There is a strong contrast between the scope and approach of MÜLLER-ROSS's study and the dissertations of A. E. LINTON and W. D. SCARLETT (1957). The latter studies, encouraged by Professor Evans of the Queen's University of Belfast, are straightforward accounts of conscientious detailed fieldwork on certain economic and social effects of the land boundary on some minor service centres. Miss LINTON's thesis deals with Ballyconnell and Belturbet in Co. (county) Cavan and Derrylin in Co. Fermanagh, and SCARLETT's mainly with Clones in Co. Monaghan. I regret that these studies have not been published.

EMRYS JONES (a Welsh 'social geographer' who was at the time lecturer in the Department of Geography of Queen's University), in his essay on *Problems of Partition and Segregation in Northern Ireland* (1960), points out that the land boundary was arbitrary in two senses:

(1)   It was the result of dealing with a bloc of counties which had an overall majority of Protestants, though the local variations in the ratio of Roman Catholics and Protestants within this area were very great indeed.

(2)   As a consequence of this the land boundary – as it was finally accepted in 1925 by the Free State in return for substantial financial concessions from the United Kingdom – was no more than a series of county boundaries which bore no relevance to the issue and brought with them serious difficulties in detail.[28]

JONES has dealt especially with the disruption and tension which arose in Northern Ireland as a result of Partition. Tension arose not only along the land boundary itself but wherever minority groups (*i.e.* Roman Catholics) were exclusive and fairly numerous: in the more western and southern districts, in the larger towns, and particularly in the new capital Belfast.

J. H. ANDREWS (an English geographer who is a lecturer in Trinity College, Dublin) treats of the forecast published by an English newspaper in 1925 on the findings of the *Boundary Commission* (cf. Fig. 5). The task of this commission, which was envisaged by the *Anglo-Irish Treaty, 1921*, was to suggest adjustments of the course of the land boundary.[a] Its report was not published, and according to the British prime minister it was not to be published until such time as the Irish Border aroused no more excitement than Offa's Dyke (on the Welsh Border) or Hadrian's Wall (a forerunner of the Scottish Border). ANDREWS has carefully reviewed all indirect and second-hand evidence available and his conclusion is that the *Morning Post* forecast cannot have been far from the truth.[29]

BRITISH GEOGRAPHIES ON PARTITION

In this Section I will examine what geographical treatises of a more general nature say about the Irish land boundary. First I want to refer to two recent articles on Ireland, one by A. J. ROSE (a New Zealand geographer who stayed in Ireland in 1956), and one by N. C. MITCHEL (a Northern Ireland geographer who is at present a lecturer in Queen's University, Belfast).

ROSE concludes that, during the time the land boundary has persisted, "the strength of its presence has increased rather than diminished". The two parts of Ireland have drawn apart economically and in many other ways. The policies of the Dublin and Belfast governments, for instance with regard to education and social security, "have accentuated rather than diminished the differences between the two parts of the country". Unlike MÜLLER-ROSS, ROSE does not consider the political link between Northern Ireland and Great Britain incongruous. On the contrary, it "supplements the economic ties with Clydeside and Lancashire that make Ulster a cross-Channel projection of northern Britain".[30]

MITCHEL observes that "Partition was a compromise between two seemingly irreconcilable Irish outlooks and demands". To speak of Ireland, in his opinion, is to speak of two nations. MITCHEL, too, holds the view that the political division of Ireland has been strengthened rather than weakened, since nothing has been done to lessen the effects of the economic and religious factors responsible for its conception. As he points out, the maintenance of the land border is "the core of Ulster's political life, signifying its close ties with Britain and the Commonwealth, in contrast with the Republic's secession".[31]

T. W. FREEMAN (an English geographer who was a lecturer in Trinity College, Dublin) in the second (revised) edition of his standard work, *Ireland: A General and Regional Geography* (1960), makes various comments on the land boundary. His opinions may be summarized as follows:

(1) While the land boundary is in no sense a geomorphological divide over most of its course, the regional geographer cannot neglect this separation if he wants to divide Ireland into a number of regional units.[32]

---

[a] The Treaty laid down that, if the powers of the parliament and government of the Free State should come to extend no longer to Northern Ireland (as happened), a commission should be appointed by the Dublin, Belfast and London governments to "determine in accordance with the wishes of the inhabitants, so far as may be compatible with economic and geographical conditions, the boundaries between Northern Ireland and the rest of Ireland".

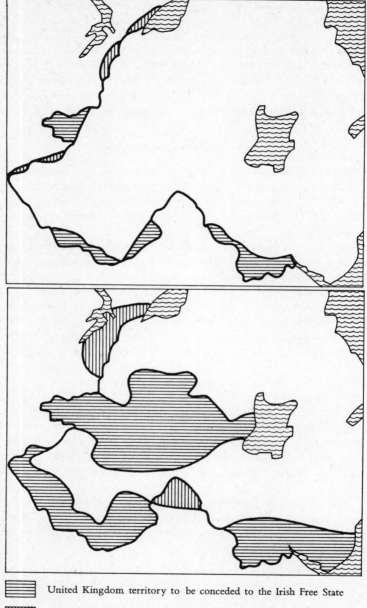

United Kingdom territory to be conceded to the Irish Free State

Free State territory to be conceded to the United Kingdom

FIG. 5. Adjustments of the Irish land boundary, recommended by the Irish Boundary Commission, according to *The Morning Post*, Nov. 7, 1925

FIG. 6. Probable changes of the Irish land boundary on the basis of a plebiscite by parishes, according to *Foreign Affairs*, 1923, 328-9

(2) The dominantly Roman Catholic communities in Northern Ireland are spread through an area so discontinuous that no new frontier could be drawn without leaving Roman Catholic majorities in a truncated Northern Ireland, or local Protestant majorities in an enlarged Republic.[33] (cf. Fig. 6).

(3) Partition, whatever its merits, is already deeply rooted in the life of the land. The two parts of Ireland "differ so radically in policy and outlook on many social and economic questions that it is hard to see how they may eventually be united". The appeals for a united Ireland are normally made on "non-economic grounds such as historical and geographical unity, and national pride". If Ireland ever becomes one governmental unit, "hard thinking will be necessary to provide satisfactory economic arrangements among people whose interests have become so diverse".[34]

(4) "It is difficult to resist the impression that the two units draw farther apart in their economic life year by year", and not least by the divergent policies of the two governments. The Republic's policy is "protectionist within its boundaries, in order that its small industries may be preserved". Northern Ireland's policy is "imperial, as there is both a desire and a need for co-operation with the eastern neighbour".[35]

(5) Trading interests in both areas lie with Great Britain which is both the source of coal, many raw materials and manufactured goods, and also the main consumer of Ireland's agricultural produce. Ireland's closest human relations, too, are with Great Britain.[36]

(6) "There is much to be deplored in the present situation and it would be unjust to fail to recognize the strong feelings of the Nationalist party in Northern Ireland. But the Northern Ireland case for retention of the union with Britain is strong".[37]

It is of interest to compare the few references to Partition which occur in geographical works on the British Isles as a whole:

(1) STAMP and BEAVER observe that the contrasts between the two parts of Ireland are deeply rooted. They draw a parallel between "the close connection in geological structure and relief between Northern Ireland and Scotland" and "human associations between the two countries through the ages". They also note that the Northern Ireland border towns Londonderry and Newry (Co. Down) are hampered in their trade by the frontier.[38]

(2) HANS DÖRRIES (1934) states that the political division of Ireland seems strange to non-Britons but "whoever travels in the country sees very soon the basic differences which the last settlement of the Irish question could not overlook". He also notes that political development since 1921 repeatedly confirms that "the wall of hate between Ulster and the Free State is by no means abolished; it is as it were even higher than the sharp customs boundary between the two countries".[39]

(3) ALBERT DEMANGEON's only reference is that the boundary is disputed at certain points, as the Free State claims the Roman Catholic areas of Northern Ireland [a], at least those adjacent to its territory.[40]

(4) JOHANN SÖLCH (1952) makes the complaint that the land boundary handicaps the undertaking of any regional division of Ireland, apparently because it is not a natural frontier. He recognizes also that it is not a *Volksgrenze*. A clear separation between what he calls 'Irish' and 'Britons' could be achieved by comprehensive transferences of people but he doubts whether the Irish would be satisfied by such a far-reaching measure. He further believes that Partition has caused various economic difficulties on both sides.[41]

General political geographies throw hardly any new light on the matter.

<h2>OTHER LITERATURE ON PARTITION</h2>

HARTSHORNE in his paper on the various boundary disputes in pre-War Europe has given a 'tentative evaluation' of these problems which includes the Irish Partition issue. It is

---

[a] This is, however, as I have already shown, not true: the Republic claims not parts but the whole of Northern Ireland, and the land boundary is disputed as a whole.

Table 1. Ratings for the human geographical associations of certain disputed territories with their claimant-states, for the year 1938 (after RICHARD HARTSHORNE).

Disputed Territories	Population in Thousands		Geographical Associations with Claimant-State (Ratings)		
	Total Number	Speaking Language of Claimant-State	Cultural	Socio-Economic	Historical
Northern Ireland	1,287	0	D	B-C ?	D
Alsace	1,219	1,153	D ?	B	B-D
Saar	713	1	E	C	E
Lorraine	655	481	D ?	B-C	B-D
Corsica	291	290	D-E ?	D	D
South Tyrol	250	215	A	B	A
North Schleswig	160	40	D	C	D
Åland Islands	27	19	B	D	D

of interest to examine how he has evaluated the human-geographical associations of Northern Ireland with the Irish Republic. In Table 1 his evaluations are shown in abbreviated form; for comparison there are added some other territories which were disputed in the year 1938. [a]

Associations are graded in five levels, from A to E. The letter A represents percentage ratings from 80 to 100 per cent, B from 60 to 80 per cent, etc. HARTSHORNE suggests that, when the ratings for all three associations are high, *i.e.* A or B, the 'total geographical association' of the disputed territory is predominantly with the claimant-state and not with the state holding the area. Where the three ratings differ considerably, there is obviously no possible basis for computing a resultant.

It is apparent from Table 1 that HARTSHORNE has considered Northern Ireland's associations with the Republic rather weak, with the exception of the socio-economic associations. He has graded the latter B-C but has added a question mark. Northern Ireland gets a zero in the language column and HARTSHORNE remarks that "the most important factor here is religion; Roman Catholics form a minority in Northern Ireland".[42] (Apart from that, I may point out that the language of the Republic is, *de facto*, English, as is the language of Northern Ireland – so the figure O has virtually no significance at all.)

If there is no comprehensive geographical study on Irish Partition, neither is there a history of the origins of the land boundary, at least no scholarly one. There is DENIS GWYNN's *The History of Partition, 1912-1925*, but it covers only a short period and it is rather one-sided. The author (who is research professor of modern history in University

[a] Alsace and Lorraine were French but were claimed by Germany, the Saar was German but was claimed by France, Corsica was French but was claimed by Italy, South Tyrol was in Italy but was claimed by Austria, North Schleswig was in Denmark but was claimed by Germany, while the Åland Islands were Finnish but were claimed by Sweden.

College, Cork) describes his purpose as "an attempt to establish the true history of how and why the partition of Ireland was imposed in 1920, against the wishes and convictions of all parties concerned".

GWYNN treats the creation of the land boundary as "an arbitrary improvisation", an "artificial arrangement", "the outcome of many extemporized compromises which were always devised in haste and imposed against the considered judgment of all parties".[43] The weakness of his book is that it shows, as another Southern Irish writer says, no awareness of the profound and decisive nature of

"Northern opposition, first, to Home Rule for all-Ireland, and later, when the North might have been prepared to consider Home Rule of a moderately nationalist or Redmond [a] brand, to a politically isolated Ireland inspired by an extreme or separatist nationalism. Partition was then, in fact, the consequence of the North's refusal to be party to the South's regional isolationalism and the expression of an essential demand to preserve her intimate connection with British, Dominion and international life".[44]

DENIS GWYNN's book is valuable in providing a record of negotiations between Irish Nationalist leaders, the British government, and the Ulster Unionist leaders, and it deals in considerable detail with the various boundary proposals made at these negotiations.

Whereas there are few geographical and historical studies on Partition, other literature is abundant. A full bibliography of books, essays, articles and pamphlets might easily amount to hundreds of titles. It is well to remember that Partition is a subject which embraces most of the political history of both parts of Ireland since the first proposal was made that the island should be (temporarily) divided. For four or five decades the most contentious issues in Ireland's political life have been those connected with the land boundary – in the beginning over its creation, and later over its arbitration or maintenance.

In view of this, one is not surprised to find that most Partition literature deals with its political aspects. Many of these writings are in the nature of political propaganda: they are either vehemently against or strongly in favour of Partition. They supply the student of political science or social psychology with very expressive though rather unwieldy source-material.

A geographer is rather inclined to disregard this shower of rhetoric and emotion with which he is deluged as he travels through Ireland. However, if he wants to engage in any comprehensive research of the land frontier, he should not entirely neglect it. It shows him what this border means to various groups of people living north and south of it. And it demonstrates more clearly than anything else, in the severe division of opinion over a wide range of aspects, that the frontier really has become – and indeed originated in – a mental gulf. It also reveals that the anti- and pro-Partitionists think in quite different geographical terms.

It struck me that both sides in the dispute sometimes use the same words to denote their opponents. In doctrinaire Republican circles the term 'Separatist' stands for those people who wanted the separation of Northern Ireland from the rest of Ireland, and among their adversaries it means those people who wanted the separation of Ireland

[a] John Redmond (1856-1918), the last leader of the Irish Nationalist Party. DENIS GWYNN wrote the 'official' biography of Redmond for which the latter's papers were entrusted to him. *The History of Partition*, too, is to a large extent based on previously unpublished papers of Redmond.

from the United Kingdom of Great Britain and Ireland. The word 'Partitionist' is also used in two senses. It is often employed as a nickname for those people in Ireland who approve of the partition of the island, whereas the other side argues that

"The true Partitionists are those who would (in a political sense) remove Ulster from what anyone who glances at a map of Europe will recognize as a national, geographical, social and economic unit, namely the British Isles".[45]

Although both sides use the same words, they think in different terms.[a] One side thinks in terms of Ireland alone, the other in terms of the British Isles. One view is that the land boundary is an 'unnatural' dividing line between two areas which together form the island of Ireland. The other view is that the land boundary *and* the connected sea boundary are a no less 'unnatural' dividing line between two areas which together constitute the British Isles.

In the following Section I will survey some examples of anti- and pro-Partition literature.

ANTI- AND PRO-PARTITION LITERATURE

The most balanced statement of the anti-Partition viewpoint, and the only full-scale representation of their case by the Dublin government, is still the *Handbook of the Ulster Question*. It was issued in 1923 with an eye to the forthcoming *Boundary Commission*. In my opinion the *Handbook* is still the most important book on the land boundary, providing material which cannot easily be obtained from other sources. It comprises four parts which deal respectively with:

(1)   the historical background from which the 'Ulster problem' emerged, and "the development and application of the policy of Partition in the light of history, reason, and the national idea";

(2)   the wishes of the population with regard to Partition, that is to say for or against an all-Ireland parliament in Dublin, as shown for the smallest as well as the largest administrative units;

(3)   the geography of the former (English) administrative province of Ulster (which covered nine counties, six of which are now in Northern Ireland), and the effects of Partition on the economic and financial interests of "the partitioned area" (*i.e.* Northern Ireland), the Ulster province, and Ireland as a whole; and

(4)   a comparison of the 'Ulster problem' with similar questions elsewhere, "with a view to discovering whether a political solution founded on separation accords with international precedents".

As the introduction of the *Handbook* states, "the facts and figures contained in the volume are derived from authoritative sources which cannot be seriously challenged". Not everyone, however, will agree with the conclusions drawn from the material, which are "against any form of Partition, and particularly the form of Partition set up by the Act of 1920" (the *Government of Ireland Act, 1920*, passed by the British parliament, which in fact created the land boundary as it exists today).

A similar book, though on a more limited scale and more prejudiced, is W. A. McKNIGHT's *Ireland and the Ulster Legend*. The author claimed to be the first to treat the

---

[a]   In this study the term 'Partition' will be used exclusively for the political division of Ireland, whereas the political division of the British Isles will be referred to as the 'Separation'.

'Ulster subject' statistically. He proposed to ascertain whether the assertion of "Ulster's superiority in prosperity and civilisation", put forward by the Ulster Unionists as justifying a demand for special treatment, was true. Needless to say, he concluded that this assertion was entirely unfounded. [a] In the same category of writing belongs *The Case of Ulster: An Analysis of Four Partition Arguments*, by SEAN MILROY. [b]

The most recent and best written statement of the 'Partition problem' from the orthodox Dublin viewpoint is contained in FRANK GALLAGHER's *The Indivisible Island* (1957). As the author is an ex-director of the Dublin government information bureau and copies of his book are distributed through official channels, it may be regarded as having official approval. It must be pointed out, however, that not all Nationalists are happy with this book. DONAL BARRINGTON, for instance, in his valuable essay on *Uniting Ireland*, says that

"The very title reveals a weakness that has bedevilled all Nationalist thinking on the Partition problem for the past forty years: a complete refusal to face unpleasant facts. There is little use telling us that Ireland is an indivisible island when, in fact, it has been divided since before many of us were born and is further from unity today than at any point in modern history. Surely it is time we faced the fact that our country is divided and is in danger of remaining divided forever?"[46]

Another Nationalist opponent of GALLAGHER, EARNÁN DE BLAGHD (Ernest Blythe), writes in a comprehensive review of the book that its author

"makes no attempt to be objective or to revise old judgments in the light of subsequent developments, or to question old prejudices or to scrap stale doctrinaire assumptions. He gives us mainly an elaborate rehash of the widely accepted but misconceived and lopsided propaganda which has heretofore prevented us from facing up to the many difficulties that must be overcome if we are to end Partition".[47]

There is no counterpart to the *Handbook of the Ulster Question*, or to GALLAGHER's book, on the other side. There is, indeed, comparatively little pro-Partition literature. [c] The best book is *Ulster and the Irish Republic: A Brief Survey of Irish Republican Propaganda and an Exposure of its Fallacies*. It is written by WILLIAM A. CARSON (a former Registrar-General for Northern Ireland) and has an introduction by a former American ambassador

[a] McKNIGHT's "statistical tests of morale" include even the proportions of illegitimate births and habitual criminals in 'Ulster'. Most of his reasoning is rather ambivalent as it refers primarily to the former Ulster province in which area the Protestants and the industrial population formed minorities. In some places the book deals with two other concepts of Ulster, namely:
(1) 'East Ulster', which means here Cos (counties) Antrim, Down, Armagh, and Londonderry, with Belfast C.B. (county borough); and
(2) 'West Ulster', which consists of the 'Pro-Irish-Rule Counties' of Donegal, Tyrone, Fermanagh, Cavan, and Monaghan.
[b] The arguments which, in MILROY's opinion, covered "the whole position of the advocates of Partition" were that Northern Ireland was "a homogeneous non-Irish entity", and that in the case of a submission of this area to an all-Ireland government in Dublin its alleged superior prosperity, the civil and religious liberties of the Protestants, and the industry and commerce of Belfast would be jeopardized. MILROY attempted to show the absolute fallacy of these arguments and concluded that "Partition, instead of being an intelligent device to safeguard the material interests of the North-east of Ulster, is nothing more than a reactionary outcome of savage political bigotry".
[c] It is, perhaps, not surprising to a psychologist that anti-Partition literature outnumbers – and generally 'outsizes' – pro-Partition writing.

in Dublin, David Gray ("to whom Mr de Valera sent his famous protest against the landing of U.S. forces in Ulster" during the War). CARSON's book deals with some of "the stock arguments which are incessantly being put forward to persuade world opinion that Ulster should be incorporated in the Irish Republic":

(1)   That the decision of Northern Ireland to remain in the United Kingdom and the Commonwealth has involved the dismemberment of a very ancient and hitherto united nation: on 'racial', historical, and geographical grounds Northern Ireland should form part of an all-Ireland republic;

(2)   That Northern Ireland's present status as an integral part of the United Kingdom was not her own choice, but was forced on her by British politicians and is maintained by a British army of occupation; and

(3)   That Northern Ireland is at present a police state where freedom of speech and action does not exist, and where minorities are subjected to political and religious oppression by a totalitarian regime.

Chapter 3

'IRELAND' AND OTHER GEOGRAPHICAL NAMES

'IRELAND' AND 'IRISH FREE STATE'

The name 'Ireland' for the whole island comes from Old English 'Ir(a)land', literally: land of the Irish.[48] This word has been the accepted name of the island not only in the Germanic but also in the Romance languages. The Irish name for Ireland is 'Éire', which comes from Old Irish 'Ériu'. The Welsh name for Ireland, 'Iwerddon', is a cognate word. The hypothesis has been advanced that the Irish name was originally given by Celtic-speaking immigrants to one of the earlier population elements, the 'Érainn', who lived in the south of the island. According to M. A. O'BRIEN it is absolutely uncertain what 'Ériu' meant originally: it may not be Celtic or even Indo-European at all.[49] Other familiar names for Ireland are 'Erin'[a] and 'Hibernia'.[b]

'Ireland' has been recognized as a 'political' concept since before the Viking invasions. There were pre-Viking Gaelic kings claiming the title *high-king of Ireland*. Neither in practice nor in theory, however, was the claim admitted. But, however little actual control was vested in the high-kingship, the concept of 'Ireland' existed. It was also recognized by the Anglo-Normans who established themselves in the island in the latter part of the twelfth century. Indeed, Ireland was not fused with England but remained a separate lordship with a semi-independent legislature till 1541. But, like the previous Gaelic high-kings, none of the English *lords of Ireland* exercised undisputed sway over the

---

[a]   'Erin' is a poetic name which was common especially in late eighteenth- and nineteenth-century romantic literature in English. No nineteenth-century meeting of Irish Nationalists, or a St Patrick's Day parade among the Irish (especially Roman Catholic emigrants and their offspring) in America, was complete without a banner *Erin go bragh*, meaning: Ireland for ever. (That the grammar of this slogan was incor‑ rect, as I am given to understand, points to a then already prevailing lack of knowledge of the Irish language.)

[b]   The Latin name 'Hibernia' goes back at least to Caesar. It has been appropriated particularly by the Roman Catholic population of the island; cf. *Hibernia*, a leading Irish weekly, and the *Ancient Order of Hibernians*, the counterpart of the Orange Institution (cf. STRAUSS, 212-3, 235).

whole island. It was the Tudors who finally succeeded in effecting the political unity of Ireland.

In 1541 Henry VIII abandoned the title *lord of Ireland* and took the title *king of Ireland*. The kingdom of Ireland with its semi-independent parliament continued till 1801 – with a brief interim under Cromwell's Protectorate (1653-60) when the British Isles were formally a single political unit. Ireland as a political concept was not even extinguished by the *Act of Union, 1801*. The Union of England and Scotland had been verbally symbolized in the introduction of the term 'United Kingdom of Great Britain'. But when Ireland was included formally, there was no attempt to find a new name like 'United Kingdom of the British Isles': the new kingdom was simply styled 'United Kingdom of Great Britain and Ireland'. (In spite of the Union Ireland continued to have a separate administrative existence – as, though in rather a different way, Scotland also continued to have.)

'Ireland' and cognate terms, then, are well-established names which for two thousand years or more have always been used in the same sense, *i.e.* for the whole island. Nowadays, however, 'Ireland' and its Irish equivalent 'Éire' are often used in a more restricted sense, *i.e.* for a part of the island albeit the greatest part. This sometimes gives rise to serious misunderstanding; it has even led to diplomatic complications. Confusion really dates from 1937 when a new constitution was adopted in the Irish Free State and the name which had been in use since 1922 to denote that territory was officially discarded.

The original name for the Free State area was 'Southern Ireland', the counterpart of 'Northern Ireland', a term still in official usage. Both names had been legally adopted in 1920 under the *Government of Ireland Act*. After the truce of the 11th July 1921 had ended the so-called Anglo-Irish War, and negotiations between the revolutionary (Southern) Irish government and the British government had commenced, a title had to be found to take the place of the obviously non-viable term 'Southern Ireland'.[a] The name 'Saorstát Éireann', in English: 'Irish Free State', was adopted.

When, in the early nineteen hundreds, Irish Nationalists attempted to define their political aims in the Irish language, which they sought to revive, they coined two new words. One was 'poblacht' (republic), from 'pobal', an early Irish derivation of Latin 'populus'. The other term was 'saorstát', derived from 'saor' (free) and 'stát' (state). At the 1921 negotiations the latter term was preferred by Lloyd George, the British prime minister, because it had less obvious political implications than 'poblacht': a 'free state' was not necessarily a republic in the modern sense of the word (cf. the Orange Free State in South Africa).

The new name, however, did not receive general acceptance in the Irish Free State itself. The more doctrinaire Nationalists (first among them Mr de Valera) could not approve of it for two reasons. They objected because, in the first place, the term 'Free State' came to stand for a state which was, in fact, a member of the British Commonwealth and not a completely sovereign republic. And, secondly, the term was already coloured because it covered only the territory south of the land boundary: it implied, as it were,

---

[a] Strictly speaking a name had to be found for the whole island as the Irish Nationalist leaders negotiated for Ireland at large (or at least claimed to do so). As it was clear that, in accordance with the Treaty provisions, Northern Ireland would vote itself out of the new state, the new name would apply only to 'Southern Ireland'.

a *de jure* recognition of Partition. It is not surprising then that, once Mr de Valera had risen to power (1932), the days of the term 'Irish Free State' and its Irish equivalent were numbered.

'ÉIRE' AND 'REPUBLIC OF IRELAND'

The names 'Irish Free State' and 'Saorstát Éireann' were officially abolished with the enactment of the 1937 constitution. The Free State constitution had been specifically designed for the area of that state; the 1937 constitution was meant to be a constitution for the whole island, including Northern Ireland. It declared (Art. 4) that the name of the state was "Éire, or in the English language, Ireland". The 'national territory' was described (Art. 2) as "the whole island of Ireland, its islands and the territorial seas". However, it was also stated that (Art. 3):

"Pending the re-integration of the national territory, and without prejudice to the right of the Parliament and Government established by this Constitution to exercise jurisdiction over the whole of that territory, the laws enacted by that Parliament shall have the like area and extent of application as the laws of Saorstát Éireann and the like extra-territorial effect".

But, as the terms 'Saorstát Éireann' and 'Irish Free State' were now dropped, no official name remained which could be used, legitimately, to describe the *de facto* area of the state. In semi-official publications (*e.g.* in statistics) and in Dublin newspapers the gap was filled by the term 'Twenty-Six Counties'. This unwieldy phrase refers to the division of the island into 'counties' (English administrative units). There are thirty-two in all, six of which are now in Northern Ireland. The term 'Twenty-Six Counties' was used already in doctrinaire Nationalist circles, who refused to recognize the Free State, as a mere factual description of the territory of that state. The term remained in semi-official use till 1953. [a]

Outside Ireland the term 'Twenty-Six Counties' did not find wide acceptance. Instead, the term 'Éire' was adopted in the English press and in British official usage to denote the Free State territory.[50] Strictly speaking this was a terminological inexactitude for 'Éire' is only the Irish for 'Ireland'. Its adoption into English had the charms and advantages of every new loanword. 'Éire' was quite unknown outside Ireland and, with the exception of Irish speakers, its spelling did not immediately associate it with the familiar 'Erin'.

In Dublin the use of 'Éire' as an equivalent for 'Irish Free State' was not appreciated. It was regarded in some quarters as "another wrong to Ireland", another "malicious act of the British". It was frequently pointed out that the constitution stated that the name of the state in the English language was 'Ireland', and that 'Éire' could only correctly be used in the Irish language; that it was as improper as the use in English of 'Deutschland' for 'Germany'. [b]

[a] In that year it was officially announced in Dublin that, when it was necessary to refer to the area of the Twenty-Six Counties, either the expression "Ireland (exclusive of the Six Counties)" or the word 'Ireland' with an asterisk and a footnote reading "Exclusive of the Six Counties" should be used (cf. *Reports Commission on Emigration*, xii).

[b] However, the preamble of the 1937 constitution says: "We, the people of Éire .. do hereby adopt .. this Constitution". Here 'Éire' is deliberately used in the English language. As the preamble is printed

Since 1948 the situation has been eased, more or less accidentally, by the passing of the *Republic of Ireland Act* by the Dublin parliament. By that act the last formal political tie with the British Commonwealth was removed and the state was formally declared a republic. The act did not change the official name of the state, 'Éire' or, in English, 'Ireland' – since this is embedded in the constitution (which can only be altered by referendum). The act stated however: "The description of the State is the Republic of Ireland". Though this title was not a new name for the state, but only a legal description of it, in practice it came to be used as such. It implies the equivalent of the old Irish Free State and therefore does not mean the whole island of Ireland. [a]

In official phraseology the usage of the term 'Republic of Ireland' is very precisely confined. It is generally avoided in Dublin, at least since 1950.[b] Its use by foreign governments is as a rule refused by the Dublin government. Practical considerations seem to prompt one very important exception, that made by the United Kingdom. The *Ireland Act, 1949*, which recognized that "the part of Ireland heretofore known as Eire" ceased to be part of 'His Majesty's dominions', laid down that this area henceforth may be referred to by "the name attributed by the law thereof, that is to say, as the Republic of Ireland". [c]

Thus there are no less than four terms in use for the Free State territory: 'Ireland', 'Éire', 'Twenty-Six Counties', and 'Republic of Ireland'.[d] 'Twenty-Six Counties' conveys nothing to a foreigner. 'Ireland' is even less practicable because it is very confusing. Some British and continental geographers speak of 'Eire' (they always omit the accent) – a custom, however, which disregards both the literal meaning of the word and the emotional values it has for sincere Irish Nationalists. Therefore, I will speak of the 'Republic of Ireland' (or 'Irish Republic'). Legally this term may not be strictly accurate but it is a convenient geographical description and gives least offence.

before the constitution, an unwary foreigner might be pardoned for believing that it was correct and even desirable to use 'Éire' as the name of the state in English. (The whole situation is not without an element of that 'Irish humour' so beloved of English writers on Ireland but which, in this case at any rate, is not appreciated in Dublin.)

[a] The situation is paralleled in Korea and Germany, countries which were also partitioned. In the case of Korea there are two states which claim to be the successor-state of the previously unpartitioned Korea: the 'Republic of Korea' (commonly known as South Korea) and the 'Democratic Republic of Korea' (North Korea). In the case of Germany there are a 'German Federal Republic' (West Germany) and a 'German Democratic Republic' (East Germany).

[b] During the years 1949-50 'Republic of Ireland' was used as the name of the state. This may appear from the *Trade Agreement between the Government of the Republic of Ireland and the Government of the Netherlands*, Dublin, Nov. 25, 1949 (cf. *Irish Treaty Series*, No. 11/1950, etc.). Occasionally the phrase has also been used in a geographical sense, meaning the *de facto* territory of the state (cf. *Irish Treaty Series*, No. 8/1951, Art. II).

[c] By mutual agreement the British ambassador is accredited to the *President of the Republic of Ireland*. All other heads of missions in Dublin are accredited to the *President of Ireland* (whose competence is *de facto* confined to the territory of the former Free State). When, a few years ago, Australia wanted to follow the British practice, the credentials of the ambassador designate were refused and since then there has been only a *chargé d'affaires* at Dublin.

[d] In Northern Ireland the Republic is still colloquially known as the Irish Free State. Older people in the Republic, too, still speak of the Free State.

'NORTHERN IRELAND'

The designation of the northern part of Ireland produces difficulties similar to those encountered in describing the area of the Republic. Its constitutional name is likewise vehemently denounced, both on political and geographical grounds.

Irish Nationalists usually refer to Northern Ireland as the 'Six Counties', the counterpart of 'Twenty-Six Counties'. For more than twenty years successive Dublin governments also have employed this term. (They could not, of course, refrain from using the correct name 'Northern Ireland' for legal purposes.) In 1948 'Northern Ireland' was even removed from the Dublin statistical publications and replaced by 'Six Counties'.

There are, however, certain recent indications of a change in the Dublin attitude. The prime minister, Mr Lemass, who took office in 1959 when Mr de Valera was elected president, has on several occasions attracted attention by referring to 'Northern Ireland', and even to the 'Northern Ireland government'. This avoidance of the revolutionary terminology has been regarded in Dublin as well as in Belfast as "a gesture towards a *rapprochement* and co-operation between the two countries", and "a first step towards an acknowledgement of the constitutional position of Northern Ireland".

Apart from the Dublin government's tactical move, there is, to my mind, no reason why a geographer who is not involved in Irish political disputes should employ the term 'Six Counties' – the more so as he is not likely to use the term 'Twenty-Six Counties.' It is true that 'Northern Ireland' does not cover the whole north of Ireland and indeed does not include the most northern part of the island, *viz.* the peninsula of Inishowen (Co. Donegal). It would, in fact, be more correct to designate it 'North-Eastern Ireland', and especially so as

"It is in the north-east that one may most clearly discern those physical and cultural links with Great Britain that have played a large part in differentiating Northern Ireland from the other major regions of the island".[51]

The term 'North-Eastern Ireland', however, has a deprecatory sound in the ears of most Northerners. It has found some acceptance only in Nationalist circles, and among their continental sympathizers. Though 'Northern Ireland' is not topographically correct, it does not lead to the slightest misunderstanding. It is only one of the many geographical names which are objectively not precise but nevertheless are very convenient in daily usage, such as 'Southern England' and the 'Southern States' of the U.S. So, throughout the present volume, 'Northern Ireland' will be used.

As an alternative, for brevity, I shall speak of 'the North', and, accordingly, of 'the South' for the Republic – which merely means north and south of the land boundary (though, of course, Co. Donegal is actually 'west' of it). In doing this I am simply copying the example of many Irishmen (including Nationalists in Co. Donegal!) who refer to the two parts of Ireland in this way.

Similarly, I shall speak of 'Northerners' and 'Southerners' for the people of Northern Ireland and the Republic respectively. I realize that some people in the South do not like being called 'Southerners', at least by Northerners, probably because they sense in it something of the alleged 'racial' superiority complex of the Unionist Northerners (cf. the derogatory overtones of 'Southerners' in Yankee mouth). I will use the term simply for its obvious convenience.

There is another alternative for 'Northern Ireland', namely 'Ulster'. The term is derived from 'Ulaid', the Old Irish name of a people who were once dominant in the north. The suffix -ster is often regarded as Norse, and therefore it cannot be older than the ninth century.[52] It may come from Old Norse 'staor', meaning: stead. [a] The term 'Ulster', too, involves us in complications.

For centuries 'Ulster' was the name of one of the four provinces of Ireland which, in their present form, are creations of the English administration. Thus the province of Ulster was first defined in edicts of 1603 and 1610. In one way or another, however, these 'English' provinces originated from Irish (Gaelic) kingdoms or 'provinces'. 'Ulster' indeed goes back to a kingdom which, according to traditional evidence, extended over the greater part of the north of the island towards the end of the first century A.D. Eventually 'Ulster' was confined to the north-eastern part of Ireland, the territory east of the Bann river and Lough Neagh (the great inland lake). This area approximates to the modern counties of Antrim and Down, the 'core' of modern Ulster.

The four English provinces have never had much practical importance except, since the nineteenth century, for statistical purposes and as a framework for a whole range of modern social activities, especially sport. Apart from that, the provinces of Leinster and Munster have no significance whatsoever in daily life. No one will say, for example, "I am going to Leinster", or "I was in Munster". Connacht, the name of the province in the west, has retained some meaning: people may speak of going to Connacht – though without any exact notion of the area involved.

With 'Ulster' the case is obviously different. The term retained a certain topographical significance in the seventeenth and eighteenth centuries but it regained a political meaning in the nineteenth and twentieth centuries. It has therefore become once more a geographical reality. It infers, however, deviating sentimental values and, occasionally, divergent geographical meanings.

To the Nationalists the word 'Ulster' carries the proud implication that the 'kingdoms of Ulster' were the last part of Ireland to be conquered by the English in the late sixteenth century. In Dublin the phrase is officially used to designate the English province of that name, which contained nine counties – the six counties of Northern Ireland together with Cos Donegal, Cavan and Monaghan which are now in the Republic. In Southern statistics the phrase "Ulster (part of)" is used for the latter three counties. [b]

To the Ulster Unionists the term 'Ulster' has opposing historical and political associations. These emerged in the second half of the nineteenth century, and particularly when the first Home Rule bills were introduced in the British parliament. As *The Times* wrote in 1912:

---

[a] The names of the provinces of Leinster (in the south-east) and Munster (in the south) are similarly formed: they are derived from 'Laighen' and 'Mumhan' respectively, names of certain peoples.

[b] The other six components of the former administrative province are in extremist Nationalist circles ostentiously referred to as "the lost counties of Ulster", or simply as "Occupied Ireland". There are writers in the North who, obviously to offset their opponents, refer to the three Ulster counties which are in the Republic as "the lost counties of Ulster".

"The term Ulster has come to connote, for reasons of general convenience and by mutual consent, the driving force of Protestant opposition to Nationalist aims; and to say that one is an Ulsterman is just to say that one will not have Home Rule at any price".[53]

It is probable that in 1922 the Northerners, if they had felt as free as the Southerners did to choose a new official name for their state for consideration by the London government, they would have chosen 'Ulster'. They were, however, more bound by the provisions of the *Government of Ireland Act, 1920*, which introduced the names Northern and Southern Ireland. The Belfast government was, in fact, set up on the basis of that act, whereas the Dublin government was a continuation of the more or less underground revolutionary government, founded in 1919 on the ruins of the 'Republic of Ireland' proclaimed by the 1916 insurgents.

In one of the first acts passed by the Belfast parliament the Northern Ireland police force was named, with the British Home Office's consent, the *Royal Ulster Constabulary*.[a] The official emblem of the Belfast government is the *Red Hand of Ulster*, derived from the device of the most famous of northern Irish princely families, the O'Neills – who styled themselves *kings of Ulster*. The official statistical publication of Belfast is the *Ulster Year Book*. It seems that, when in 1925 London, Dublin and Belfast had agreed to leave the land boundary as it was, an attempt was made by the Northern Ireland government to have the region's name changed to 'Ulster'. In 1945 the *Ulster Unionist Party* made the same proposal.

The popularity of 'Ulster' among the Protestant population of Northern Ireland is manifest in the number of companies, firms, associations, societies, committees and clubs in the North, whose names begin with 'Ulster'.[b] As Mr Faulkner (the Northern Ireland Minister of Home Affairs) recently said:

"Around the word Ulster a new separate image has grown in people's minds of a modern, progressive industrial community. We want to make the image clearer still so that the world will picture us as we are: an entity entirely separate and distinct from the South but as much a part of the United Kingdom as is Scotland".[54]

This usage of the word Ulster is most strongly objected to in Dublin. It is somewhat surprising to an outsider to note that Southern opinion contends that the phrase must be reserved for the territory of the former English administrative province – and that the boundary of that province, which was entirely an English creation, has become almost sacrosanct in the eyes of Nationalists. Moreover, the other provincial boundaries have very little significance or sentimental value.

[a] The name recalled the pre-Partition *Royal Irish Constabulary*. They were greatly admired in the North because they had borne the brunt of the guerilla warfare of the I.R.A. (the so-called Anglo-Irish War).

[b] Only a few of these names date from before Partition. According to the Northern Ireland telephone directory there are no less than 163 such names, whereas about fifty names begin with 'Northern Ireland'. The figure of 163 excludes all local branches which carry the same names, such as the ninety stations and depots of the *Ulster Transport Authority* which are scattered all over the North. There are only two 'Ulster' names in the Southern telephone directory, both dating from pre-Partition times: the *Ulster Bank Ltd* (with some fifty branches), and the *Ulster Arms Hotel* in Cavan. (The Northern directory contains some sixty names with 'Irish' in them, including branches and agencies of Dublin organizations and newspapers; about forty-five names with 'British'; and about twenty names with 'Scottish' or 'Scotch'.)

Apart from that, in the course of one-and-a-half millennia 'Ulster' has stood for many different territories which, however, were always located in the northern or north-eastern portion of the island. During almost a third of that period the name was connected with an earldom of English creation, dating from 1205. In the fifteenth century the earldom merged in the English crown and since then it has only been held by members of the royal family. (In 1928 the earldom of Ulster was bestowed upon the duke of Gloucester.[55])

Historically, therefore, there is as much or as little justification for the modern Northern definition of 'Ulster', comprising six counties, as for the pre-Partition definition covering nine counties. In using the term, it should be clear from the context what is understood by it: an Irish kingdom, an Anglo-Irish earldom, an English province, Northern Ireland, or the three Ulster counties which are in the Republic.

THE 'BRITISH ISLES'

Finally something must be said of the name 'British Isles', and of some cognate terms whose various meanings easily bewilder a foreigner. These phrases are all derived from the earliest inhabitants of the British Isles to whom a name can be assigned, the 'Pretani' or 'Priteni'. Presumably they were the ruling people of these islands, when they first became known to the Greeks, some time after the founding of the Greek colony at Massalia, about 500 B.C.[56]

It appears that the term 'British Isles' has a longer history than any of the names by which its parts have since become known. The term goes back some 2,500 years to the 'Pretanic' or 'Bretanic Islands' of the Greek geographers. It is, in fact, as well established in scientific and popular usage as, say, 'Scandinavia'.

In the Irish Republic, however, the phrase has become less popular. There are not a few doctrinaire Nationalists who "refuse to be connected even geographically with England".[57] There is a tendency in the Republic, even in scientific circles, to refer to the British Isles as 'these islands'. This is a rather poetical variation which it is impractical for geographers to follow – at least for those who do not confine their interest to those islands. A few German geographers in the 'twenties and 'thirties tried to introduce the term 'Britisch-Irische Inseln', but, so far as I am aware, this has not become fashionable.

I cannot see any reason to drop the term 'British Isles' as it is one of our oldest geographical names and it is still unequivocal. In essence it has no political implications, no more, for instance, than the term 'Iberian peninsula'. The dislike of the term among fanatical Irishmen may perhaps be explained because they rank it with other uses of the word 'British', which indeed have a certain political significance. However, as I will show, these meanings of 'British' are not applicable to Ireland, or to the Irish Republic in particular.

'BRITAIN' AND 'GREAT BRITAIN'

The name of the Pretani is also kept alive in names which have always been reserved for the largest of the British Isles or even for parts of the island. When the Pretani were pushed towards the north by new invaders of Great Britain, their name underwent a natural restriction of meaning. This may be inferred from Welsh 'Prydyn' and Irish (Gaelic)

'Cruthin' or 'Cruithni', meaning: the people or the land of the Picts, *i.e.* the north of Great Britain.[58]

However, there can be no doubt that – notwithstanding the encroachments of later invaders – the island as a whole continued to be regarded as the 'land of the Pretani'. So much is clear from Welsh 'Ynys Prydain', a name of great antiquity which may have served as a model for Mid. Irish 'Inis Bretan', literally: the island of the Britons. In ancient Latin the names in regular use are 'Britannia' for the island, and 'Britanni' for the people (variants are by no means unknown: -tt- for -t-, and -n- for -nn-). There is also 'Brittones', originally used by poets in the first century A.D. [a], apparently as synonymous with 'Britanni'.[59]

Today the English term 'Britain' is sometimes used to denote the island of Great Britain, and sometimes as a convenient synonym for the whole United Kingdom of Great Britain and Northern Ireland. Accordingly 'British' may mean an inhabitant of, or anything belonging to or made in, Great Britain, *or* the whole United Kingdom.

There are authors who, in writing of the peoples of the British Isles, classify the Irish as 'British', together with the English, the Welsh, and the Scots. Apart altogether from the fact that "'the British' in many an Irish mouth has implications only equalled by those of *les boches* in France"[60], it is historically and politically incorrect. In the past 'British' was often used to describe the colonists from Great Britain in Ireland, the native population being described as "the mere (pure) Irish".

In contrast to the Irish Nationalists, the Ulster Unionists are proud to be called 'British', instead of – or as well as – 'Irish'. A slogan in the heart of Belfast proclaims that *Ulster is British*. The inhabitants of Northern Ireland, Unionists as well as Nationalists, are indeed 'British citizens', and goods manufactured in the North are entitled to the description *British Made*.[b]

In contrast to 'Britain', the term 'Great Britain' has an explicit meaning, *i.e.* England, Wales, and Scotland. Prior to the second half of the sixteenth century the phrase was used only as a historical name for the island and for poetical and rhetorical purposes. Since then it has become a definite political conception, occasionally deliberately used in juxtaposition with 'Ireland'. This conception was especially fostered by Scots. In 1603 King James, anxious to give expression to his being sovereign of England (and Wales) *and* Scotland, assumed the title *King of Great Britain, France and Ireland*.

[a] In the course of the Roman occupation of the greater part of Great Britain, the names 'Britanni' and 'Brittones' ceased to be applied to all the inhabitants of the island. They then came to be confined to the population of Roman Britain, in the main descendants of the post-Pretanic immigrants. Hence 'Briton' in English, 'Brython' in Welsh, and 'Bretain' in Irish. Eventually, in the Latin writings of Welsh and Irish authors of post-Roman times, 'Brittones' again underwent a restriction of meaning. It was retained exclusively for the surviving remnants of the population of Roman Britain as distinct from the later invaders of the island, the Anglo-Saxons in the south-east, and the Irish (Scots) in the west. When, as a result of the loss of their independence, the 'Britons' of Cornwall in the south-west and of Strathclyde in the north-west were assimilated, the only 'Britons' left in Great Britain were the Welsh. Accordingly in Irish 'Breatain' has been narrowed down to mean Wales, and 'Breat(h)nach' to mean Welshman (cf. THOMAS O'RAHILLY, *History*, 446-7).

[b] However, certain commodities produced in Northern Ireland are marketed abroad as *Made in Ireland*, such as Irish linen table cloths. Moreover, occasionally they carry nineteenth-century romantic Irish 'national symbols', such as harps, shamrocks, and round towers. The chief reason may be commercial, because of the large numbers of Irish in Great Britain and overseas.

In 1707, when the union of England and Scotland was achieved, the phrase 'United Kingdom of Great Britain' was adopted as a formal designation. In 1801, when Ireland was united with Great Britain, the term 'United Kingdom of Great Britain and Ireland' was employed. This name lasted until 1922 when it was changed into 'United Kingdom of Great Britain and Northern Ireland'. In 1927 the royal style became *King of Great Britain, Ireland, etc.* (the Irish Free State still being a dominion). In 1948, after the Irish Republic had severed the link with the British crown, the title was changed to *King of the United Kingdom of Great Britain and Northern Ireland.* [a]

'West Britain' is also a term demanding explanation. It seems to date back to the eighteenth century when the phrases 'South Britain' and 'North Britain' were frequently used in acts of parliament for England (including, of course, Wales) and Scotland respectively. So Ireland was called, "humorously or polemically", 'West Britain'.[61] Among Irish Nationalists the term 'West British' came to be employed as a term of violent abuse, directed to those who believed in co-operation with Great Britain.[62] On the other hand, as the name 'North Britain' (or 'N.B.') is still in occasional, chiefly postal, use – which the Scots dislike – the employment of the term 'West Britain' was not unknown as a postal address for irritating Irish susceptibilities.

[a] A similar change was affected by legislative measures in the dominions, with the exception – due to constitutional hindrances – of Canada. This incidentally leads to the anomaly that the Canadian ambassador, who is accredited to the *President of Ireland*, is sent out by the *Queen of Great Britain, Ireland, etc.*

REFERENCES PART ONE

1 BOGGS, 5
2 DICKINSON, 19-20
3 *Aspects*, 165-6
4 Ibid., 167
5 Ibid., 167-9
6 J. M. JONES, 174-5
7 Cf. ibid., 3, 126; VAN PANHUYS, 32
8 Cf. *Appraisal*, 82
9 Ibid., 20, 27, 92
10 Cf. *The Spectator*, Apr. 29, 1960
11 GOTTMANN, *Relations*, 164
12 Cf. *Ulster since 1800*, vol. ii, 233
13 GOTTMANN, *Europe*, 70
14 GOTTMANN, *Relations*, 162-3
14 *Regionalism*, 123
16 GOTTMANN, *Relations*, 163
17 DICKINSON, 126-7
18 HAYES-McCOY, vii
19 O'CONNELL, 151. Cf. MACALISTER, *Archaeology*, x-xii

20 BONN, vol. i, v
21 CECILE O'RAHILLY, 9-10
22 MÜLLER-ROSS, v-vi
23 Ibid., 62, 70
24 Ibid., 1, 62-5
25 Ibid., vi, 41-2
26 Ibid., 63-4, 68
27 Ibid., vi, 57
28 EMRYS JONES, *Problems*, 97
29 ANDREWS, 103-4
30 ROSE, 182
31 N. C. MITCHEL, 1, 6
32 FREEMAN, *Ireland*, 258, 465
33 Ibid., 152-6
34 Ibid., 6, 111, 228, 503
35 Ibid., 172, 228
36 Ibid., 6, 228
37 Ibid., 146, 172-3
38 STAMP & BEAVER, 708-9, 729, 738
39 DÖRRIES, 320-1

[40] DEMANGEON, 115
[41] SÖLCH, vol. ii, 1110-1
[42] *Aspects*, 170-3
[43] DENIS GWYNN, 7, 235
[44] SHEEHY, 38-9
[45] CARSON, 55. Cf. SHEEHY, 10
[46] BARRINGTON, 379
[47] *The Leader*, Aug. 3, 1957
[48] PARTRIDGE, 314
[49] *View of Ireland*, 188. Cf. KENNEY, 133; THOMAS O'RAHILLY, *History*, 297
[50] WILLIAMSON, *History*, vol. ii, 355
[51] *Belfast*, 15

[52] *View of Ireland*, 189
[53] Cf. CARTY, *Ireland 1851-1921*, 131
[54] *Belfast Telegraph*, Apr. 8, 1960
[55] *Encyclopaedia Britannica*, vol. xxii, 674
[56] THOMAS O'RAHILLY, *History*, 84, 342
[57] HARVEY, 50
[58] CHADWICK, 66; THOMAS O'RAHILLY, *History*, 444, 450
[59] CHADWICK, 66-8; KENNEY, 133-4; THOMAS O'RAHILLY, *History*, 449-51
[60] HARVEY, 51
[61] *Oxford English Dictionary*, vol. i, 1113
[62] HARVEY, 50-1

PART TWO

THE IRISH BORDER AS A REGIONAL DIVIDE

Chapter 4

IRELAND AS A NATURAL UNIT

THE ORDER OF NATURE

The essence of the orthodox Irish Nationalist case against Partition and for Separation is summed up in the following quotation from the *Handbook of the Ulster Question*:

"Ireland is by natural design a complete geographical entity. This natural design enforced on the political life of Ireland at a very early date the ideal of national unity, and it is doing violence, not only to nature, but to the whole trend of the political life of the island to divorce politically at this late date in her national existence a considerable section of the northern part of the country from the motherland".[1]

The two basic elements in this reasoning are 'natural' and 'national' unity. In this Chapter I am primarily concerned with the issue of Ireland's natural unity. The argument that present-day Ireland represents also a national unit will be discussed in Chapter 5.

The idea which dominates a great part of anti-Partition writing and oratory (and also MÜLLER-ROSS's Partition study) is that the land boundary is "contrary to nature". Not only is Ireland considered a 'natural unit', the frontier itself is condemned because it is not a 'natural frontier'. (Sometimes it is even asserted that the Republic has a 'natural right' to the six counties of Northern Ireland.)

The absolute claim which the Republic makes to Northern Ireland ultimately rests on the assumption that "Ireland was always regarded as one nation, clearly defined and bounded by the hand of God".[2] To many Irishmen it is almost a dogma that the Creator has predestined Ireland to be a national and political unit, because it is "a perfect geographical entity", in the sense of a natural (physical) entity. This belief, a typical instance of confusion between natural features and Divine will, has many parallels.[a]

The idea, JEAN GOTTMANN observes in his *La politique des états et leur géographie*, that "the order of nature, as physical geography has shown it on maps", is "the model of a normal and desirable political order", is a common illusion.[3] The belief that 'natural' (physical) frontiers were the preordained confines of political entities gained prominence in the last quarter of the eighteenth century. Since then the concept has haunted the minds of many statesmen.[4]

We must realize, however, that all international frontiers are, in the final analysis,

---

[a] The French revolutionary leaders justified the annexation of the Low Countries and the German provinces on the left bank of the Rhine by explaining that this rounded out the natural frontiers of the nation: from the Alps to the Ocean, and from the Pyrenees to the Rhine. One may also think of the alleged coincidence of 'Deutschland', as a politico-cultural entity, with a distinct physical framework which afforded a basis for the Nazi policy of territorial expansion (cf. DICKINSON, 125; *Frontiers*, 10; KEDOURIE, 122).

political phenomena, that is that they are drawn by man to delimit the sphere of state authority.[5] That sometimes it was possible and convenient to adopt a line which was already marked by nature does not alter the fact. It is man who determines whether natural features will be used and, if so, which. This explains the remarkable fact, noticed by JAN BROEK, that nations usually envisage their natural frontiers as lying beyond their actual borders.[6] There is some truth in the statement that "a natural frontier is simply that particular natural feature beyond a state's present boundary to which its leaders would like to expand".[7]

That orthodox Irish nationalism still clings to "the idea that geographical and political unity are necessarily identical"[8], can, perhaps, be largely explained by the fact that Ireland is so obvious a natural entity, surrounded as it is on all sides by the sea.

This Chapter deals mainly with four questions:

(1)   How far can Ireland be considered as a 'natural unit', both with regard to its morphology and its structural relations with Great Britain and the continent?
(2)   To what extent has geomorphology conditioned or checked the growth of regional and 'national' unity?
(3)   In what way has the appreciation of Ireland's geographical position changed in the course of history?
(4)   Is the land boundary related to natural features?

THE NATURAL REGIONAL DIVERSITY OF IRELAND

The most concise exposition of the significance of Ireland's natural environment is Y. M. GOBLET's:

"Being an island whose morphology favours penetration by invaders and hinders political unification, Ireland is weighed down by two heavy burdens of geographical position: isolation at the extreme end of the western frontier of Europe, and proximity to the great island of the British archipelago".[9]

In the following pages I will examine first the main features of Ireland's morphology and the parts which they have played in the moulding of Irish life. Next follows a very brief inspection of Ireland's structural links with the outside world and an analysis of the major changes in the appreciation of Ireland's 'geographical position'.

At first sight Ireland has a very compact shape – something that is often regarded as an asset to a country, because it may facilitate internal communications and would be a strategic aid in defence. For the more compact a territory is, the shorter its outline in relation to the area and, hence, the smaller its vulnerability to attacks from outside. But on closer examination it appears that Ireland has a rather long coastline, due to the number of deep sea inlets and bays. In ancient times these sea 'loughs' enabled any invader to gain a foothold relatively deep in the interior without losing his contacts by sea. [a]

[a]   The bays partly account for the fact that no part of the island lies more than 55 miles from the sea. The actual length of the coastline amounts to no less than 2,610 miles. This is equivalent to the length of the coasts of the Iberian peninsula (Spain and Portugal), to that of the continental part of Italy, and to that of the mainland of Greece. (The areas of these three peninsulas are respectively seven, three, and $1\frac{1}{4}$ times the size of Ireland.)

Many travellers to Ireland are struck by its mountainous appearance. But most of the mountains are to be found near the coast. Indeed, it is not surprising to find that the surface of the island is often described as 'saucer-shaped'. It consists, essentially, of a broad central lowland, rimmed by uplands. The mountains, however, do not form a continuous barrier: in many places they are interrupted by the sea loughs.

The broadest gap is on the east coast, between the Wicklow mountains south of Dublin and the Carlingford mountains north of Dundalk (Co. Louth). A Dutchman, however, would still describe this gap, no less than fifty miles wide, as a 'hilly coastal strip'. This is what R. A. S. MACALISTER called "Ireland's frontdoor opening" which has always invited invasion from Great Britain and by way of which, especially in later years, most of the influences of general European culture have filtered through.[10]

The most outstanding feature of Ireland's morphology is the Central Lowlands. They extend over almost the whole breadth of the island, dividing the northern from the southern upland areas. Much of their surface is covered by 'bog' (peat deposits) and strewn with lakes; streams and rivers meander sluggishly towards the sea. The topography is further diversified by many winding 'eskers' [a], and by a number of isolated uplands.[11]

The general physiographical plan, a central basin surrounded by groups of mountains and hills, is repeated on a smaller scale in the north-east of the island.[12] Here the Central Irish Lowlands have their counterpart in the Central Ulster Lowlands which are surrounded by:

(1)   the Antrim plateau in the extreme north-east;
(2)   the Down and Armagh hill country with the Mourne mountains in the south-east and south; and
(3)   the Sperrin mountains in Cos Londonderry and Tyrone in the west.

The centre of the basin is constituted by Lough Neagh, by far the largest lake in the British Isles: a shallow quadrilateral sheet of water, nearly as large as the Lake of Geneva. Three corridors connect the Central Ulster Lowlands with the sea:

(1)   the valley of the Lower Bann, between the Sperrins and the Antrim plateau, with the Atlantic in the north;
(2)   the Lagan valley, between the Antrim plateau and the Down hill country, with Belfast Lough in the east; and
(3)   the 'Newry gap' (a glacial overflow-channel) with the Irish Sea via Carlingford Lough in the south-east.

To the south there is a continuation of the narrow Newry gap leading through the Carlingford mountains (between Cos Armagh and Louth), the 'Gap of the North'. This pass has been since Norman times "the main gateway between Ulster and the south".[13]

In the north-west of the island there is another, much smaller basin, similarly enclosed by uplands. This is the Foyle valley, surrounded by the Sperrins in the east, the Donegal highlands in the west, and the hills of the Inishowen peninsula in the north. Its main outlet is at Londonderry C.B. via Lough Foyle.

Perhaps the most easily recognizable of the minor morphological features of Ireland are the drumlins. There are many thousands of these smooth oval hills, often separated

[a] Sand and gravel ridges which were laid down in glacial times. Their Irish name has been adopted for denoting similar features in other parts of the world.

by bogs and lakelets. They are concentrated in the so-called 'drumlin-belt' which extends from Co. Sligo in the west to Co. Down in the east. It not only covers the northern parts of the Central Irish Lowlands but spreads also northward into the Central Ulster Lowlands. Only the northern uplands are void of drumlins.[a]

AN EVALUATION OF IRELAND'S MAJOR MORPHOLOGICAL FEATURES

In the *Handbook of the Ulster Question* we read:

"Ireland is by natural design a complete geographical entity, and there is no better instance in either hemisphere of a country all of whose parts are bound closely together, and which has no area throughout its whole extent separated by natural barriers from the main body of the country".[14]

This statement is not altogether borne out by our brief survey of Ireland's major morphological features. The "main body of the country" is essentially the Central Irish Lowlands with their upland rim. The Central Ulster Lowlands clearly stand apart. So does the Foyle valley.

It would seem obvious to think of the Central Irish Lowlands as an ideal 'historical kernel area'.[b] It appears, however, that any unifying effects of the large plain are of relatively recent date. They had to await the removal of great tracts of forests, bogs and marshes, and the construction of modern lines of communication – canals in the eighteenth and railways in the nineteenth century.[15] This does not mean that the Lowlands were not inhabited, but population was for long confined to small and detached communities.[16] Indeed, with the exception of their eastern coastal portion, the region between the Wicklow and the Carlingford mountains, the Central Irish Lowlands have for thousands of years served as a 'natural dividing zone'[c] between the north and the south of the island rather than as a unifying force.

The drumlins on their northern flank accentuated this dividing function. As E. ESTYN EVANS has shown, the drumlin belt must have been very difficult country for early man.

---

[a] The drumlins are abundant memorials to the glaciation of the lowlands. They consist mostly of glaci-fluvial sands and gravels, and boulder clay. Their long axes are parallel to the direction of the ice motion. The name 'drumlin' which, like the word 'esker', has become a familiar term to physical geographers all over the world, means little ridge. 'Drum' is one of the anglicized forms of Irish 'druim', literally: back, metaphorically: long hill or ridge. It is one of the most common root words in Irish place-names. About 2,400 names of townlands, etc., begin with 'drum', 'drom', or 'drim', besides the countless names which contain this prolific root in other combinations (JOHN GRAHAM, 1-4).

[b] *I.e.* an area in which a political unit has originated or about which it has crystallized. Roughly speaking there are three types of such kernel areas: (1) fertile lowlands, strengthened by a nexus of water and land routes; (2) easily defensible highlands; and (3) coastal footholds, more or less depending on reinforcements from overseas. It should be stressed that not all historical kernel areas have expanded into a modern state. In the course of time many of them have come to be dominated or superseded by another core which, because of its situation or resources, was apparently in a more advantageous position – or in which a stronger central authority appeared (such as a bridgehead backed by an energetic maritime state). In most countries a number of overshadowed or neutralized historical kernel areas can be discerned.

[c] A 'natural dividing zone' is an area (land or water) which imposes difficulties on communication and political or cultural expansion. Its opposite is the 'natural unifying zone' which facilitates communication and expansion. It must be remembered that whether a certain area hampers or fosters contacts is "a relative matter, depending upon the human ends and means" (*Frontiers*, 14). A dividing zone may be turned into a unifying zone, and the reverse has occurred as well.

He suggests that it was not until the Iron Age, which brought in superior tools and new techniques (about 250 B.C.), that the heavily wooded drumlins began to be utilized.[17]

It is not by chance that the boundaries of the modern administrative provinces (which are believed to correspond roughly to ancient kingdoms) meet in the heart of the lowlands, along the line of the middle Shannon north and south of Lough Ree. The lough is the geometrical centre both of the lowlands and of the whole island.

"Near-by Athlone, therefore, serves as the centre of Eire's broadcasting system, but in no terrestrial sense is this bog-strewn central lowland a dominant cultural region. Its function has been largely negative, for it has served as a refuge area remote from the contacts of the coastal fringe and the urban forces which radiate from it."[18]

The same things can be said of the physiographical counterpart of the Central Irish Lowlands, the Central Ulster Lowlands in the north-east. They also served as a natural dividing zone; their geometrical centre, Lough Neagh, still does. Their dividing influence is, perhaps, most clearly illustrated by the fact that the boundaries of no less than five counties (five of Northern Ireland's six counties) meet in the lough, namely Antrim, Down, Armagh, Tyrone, and Londonderry.

In conclusion it may be said that the often-repeated Nationalist argument that the natural unity of Ireland should have imposed a national unity from an early date, is one very hard to sustain in the light of historical geography. If it was relatively simple to gain a foothold on Irish soil, it was very difficult to establish an effective supremacy over the whole island. J. C. BECKETT rightly observes:

"Though the interior can be reached easily from the coast, Ireland has no natural focal point, no great crossing-place of routes, no centre from which influence spreads naturally to the circumference. This was one of the factors which helped to prevent the establishment of political unity from within".[19]

The importance of the fact that physiographical conditions favoured separate communities, rather than any form of central authority, cannot be overexaggerated. On the other hand, Ireland's weakness has long been Ireland's strength. Although the absence of central authority made a co-ordinated resistance impossible, resistance could not be easily paralyzed by the central government falling into the hands of the invader.[20] EVANS's observation with regard to the 'north-eastern bridgehead' is also true of the other corners of the island: "Again and again the invader has come into the loughs and penetrated the valleys, but always there were hills where the older folk could find refuge".[21]

The scattered grouping of the uplands made it impossible for any invader to confine the indigenous population within one 'reservation'. All upland areas served as 'natural fortresses' and inaccessible places of refuge for the older population groups.[22] The same applies to the bogs and lakes which are strewn over the island. Therefore, Ireland's morphology has, until modern times, ruled out the possibility of gaining "a comparatively short frontier against the native population". Moreover, the latter soon became masters in the art of making use of the difficulties of the terrain, in some cases simply by obstructing the trails through the dense forests.[23]

IRELAND'S NATURAL STRUCTURAL RELATIONS

If Ireland can hardly be regarded as "a perfect natural entity" in view of its morphology, it is certainly not a natural entity considering its structural relations with Great Britain.

FREEMAN says: "The physical geography of Ireland is so closely related to that of Great Britain that to the imaginative eye the intervening seas exist only as a geological creation of yesterday".[24] Or, as EVANS puts it: "In geology as in history, it is as difficult to consider Ireland apart from Britain as the islets of Ireland apart from Ireland."[25] Structurally Ireland is a mere extension of Great Britain: its insular character is simply an accident of sea level.

Similarly, it could be argued that Great Britain is an extension of the European mainland. It can be regarded as a cut-off peninsula like Jutland except that the latter has retained its connection with the continent.[26] Great Britain and Ireland are indeed not 'oceanic' islands in the sense of being surrounded on all sides by very deep seas, as are the Azores. They are true 'continental' islands, embedded in the European continental shelf. Ireland is really, as GRENVILLE COLE said, "the last outpost of Eurasia against the oceanic depths of the Atlantic".[27]

Ireland's structural relations with the continent are most apparent in its mountain ranges. They represent two of the major European mountain building epochs. The trends of both systems converge through Great Britain to meet in the west of Ireland. Therefore one may say that, in terms of physical geography, there is as little reason for considering Ireland on its own as there is for the British Isles to be considered apart from the continent. On the other hand, there may well be a case for thinking of the British Isles as a major natural region standing on its own, if we consider the proximity of the two main islands. From Snae Fell, the peak which rises from the Irish Sea to form the highest summit of the Isle of Man, the mountains on all four sides of the sea are visible.[28]

THE APPRECIATION OF IRELAND'S GEOGRAPHICAL POSITION

What makes Ireland's geographical position unique, according to ERHARD RUMPF, is that – though an island – she has in fact only one neighbour: Great Britain. Most small continental countries throughout history have had to withstand pressure from at least two and frequently three neighbours. But these pressures often cancelled each other out, which helped in the maintenance of national identity and independence. The most striking example, according to RUMPF, is Poland:

> "Despite all partitions and foreign rule, Poland has remained more Polish than Ireland Irish, and has preserved her language, which Ireland has as good as lost. Ireland had, however, only one neighbour and only one adversary, and throughout the long centuries all attempts to withdraw from its influence came to grief, and even today have succeeded only in a limited fashion".[29]

Nature has placed Ireland and Great Britain in such close juxtaposition that it seems inevitable that their destinies should be interwoven in various ways.[30] It has often been observed that Ireland was near enough to Great Britain to enforce connection, yet far enough to discourage intimacy, or in the famous saying of Grattan (the late-eighteenth-century 'Anglo-Irish' statesman): "The ocean protests against separation, and the sea against union".[31] However, 'the sea', in casu the Irish Sea, has always acted as a unifying rather than a dividing factor. Parts Three and Four will show that of old there has been a continuous interplay of cultures between both islands – not only westward but eastward as well.

The popular view of the British Isles is of *deux sœurs jumelles et ennemies*.[32] It is generally taken for granted that of those sister islands the larger should be dominant. But Great Britain has not always exerted a preponderant influence. In fact, the preponderance of Great Britain, or rather England, was not definitely established before the sixteenth century. It was not until England built her power on commerce and on the rule of the seas that, as GOBLET says, she ceased to look on Ireland as an island of secondary importance. Only then did she undertake effective annexation in order to bring the whole of the British Isles under English rule.[33]

One could say that since the sixteenth century, since the Tudor conquest of Ireland, the Irish Sea is an 'English Sea'.[a] In view of the maintenance of links between Scotland and Ulster, we should allow for the North Channel remaining a 'Scottish Sea'. It is, therefore, perhaps more appropriate to call the Irish Sea, since the sixteenth century, a 'British Sea'.[34]

The major motive for Ireland's subjection was strategic. It was in the sixteenth century that Ireland's strategic significance became evident. A Jesuit is reputed to have said to King Philip II of Spain: "He that will England win, let him in Ireland begin" (as a contemporary phrased it in English). Since the second half of the sixteenth century, when Spain supported Irish resistance against English rule, "Ireland has repeatedly caught the eye of hostile strategists as a stepping-stone to England". The strategic problem of Ireland in relation to England reappeared, as CYRIL FALLS says,

"at the end of the seventeenth century, when French arms supported in Ireland a king who had been driven from the English throne. It reappeared at the end of the eighteenth century, in the wars of the French Revolution, when the last battle against the land forces of a foreign invader was fought at Ballinamuck. It reappeared in the First World War in the early twentieth century, and once more, as a very important issue, in the Second World War".

FALLS also states that Ireland's strategic position influences the attitude of British governments to Partition and reinforces the plea of Northern Ireland to remain a part of the United Kingdom:

"The dependence of Great Britain upon supplies carried across the Atlantic has increased the strategic significance of Ireland. And behind this lies the inescapable truth that Ireland alone, however friendly an Ireland she may be, cannot successfully defend herself against invasion by a major power".[35]

Ireland's close spatial relations with Great Britain tend to divert attention from her position *vis-à-vis* to the continent and from her 'Atlantic connexion'. Miss O'RAHILLY writes:

"The obvious route for a modern continental traveller to Ireland lies through England. Matters have been so, more or less, since the days of Agricola. But .. this route was not the older route. Previous to the Roman conquest of Britain, Ireland received her share of continental culture exclusively by means of direct intercourse with West-Gaulish harbours".[36]

[a] Certain areas off the English and Welsh coasts, enclosed by base-lines between the most western points of Cornwall and Wales, and between Holyhead and the Isle of Man, are still known as 'the King's (or Queen's) Chambers'. Throughout the seventeenth century the crown claimed a right to keep the peace and exclusive fishing rights within these areas. Officially these rights have never been abandoned: as recently as 1920 the British Attorney General declared that the British claim to the King's Chambers stood "perfectly good" (*The Irish Times*, Jan. 1, 1960).

There is a great deal of evidence for contacts between southern Ireland and the south-western parts of the European mainland in prehistorical times, especially in the Bronze Age. But these contacts lasted for a long time after the Roman conquest of Great Britain. An obvious example is found in the commercial links between Irish ports – including Limerick and Galway on the west coast – and the continent, down to the sixteenth century. [a] Miss O'RAHILLY herself gives several instances of this direct trade.[37] It is only with the rise of England to mercantile and naval power that Ireland became more and more detached from the continent. Since then it can truly be said that the obvious route from the mainland to Ireland is via Great Britain. An anti-British Frenchman in this connexion refers to Great Britain as "that high prison wall" and as "the obstacle which halts the intellectual and economic exchange with Erin, and the isolator which intercepts the flow of civilization".[38]

What GOBLET calls Ireland's 'insularization' by Tudor England[39] was not counterbalanced by her participation in the rapidly growing long-distance navigation.[40] In fact, the Irish share in trans-Atlantic shipping was gradually reduced to nothing. As DEMANGEON observes:

"From the beginning there was no room for both British and Irish shipping, and at the end of the eighteenth century Irish ships were forbidden to carry colonial produce from one colony to another. In 1728 England had monopolized two-thirds of the Irish shipping trade; in 1778 the proportion had risen to seven-eighths, and by the middle of the nineteenth century she had taken the whole. Thenceforth Irish produce was shipped and exports received only in English vessels. Today Ireland still communicates with the world almost entirely by means of British ships and, moreover, usually through British ports".[41]

Although this 'subordination' has been somewhat loosened, since 1921, by the efforts of the Dublin government [b], it is still largely true that "the world's commerce passes close to Ireland, but scarcely touches her shores".[42] It is true that, in the nineteenth century, many hundreds of thousands of Irishmen emigrated to America – but most of them went through British ports, especially Liverpool, and on British ships.

Twice, in the nineteenth and twentieth centuries, has the appreciation of Ireland's space relations been temporarily changed, when advantage was taken of Ireland's westward position. As H. C. BROOKFIELD has said, "successively at sea and in the air, technological changes have at first operated to give Ireland's location maximum significance, but ultimately have undermined the basis of her connection with the transatlantic routeway". [c]

[a] Evidence of early Irish-Gaulish connections is the history of the Irish word 'gall'. From its original meaning of a 'Gaul' it has come to denote a 'foreigner'. As CECILE O'RAHILLY says (24), Gaulish merchants were for a long period the commonest foreigners in Ireland. Their name, becoming the general term for foreigner in the Gaelic language, was from the ninth till the eleventh century commonly applied to the Vikings, and from the twelfth century on to the Anglo-Normans and the English.

[b] Nowadays at least 60% of incoming and outgoing cargoes in the foreign trade of the Republic are carried by British vessels (Appraisal, 20). British transport concerns still enjoy a practical monopoly of sea traffic between the Republic and the United Kingdom.

[c] In the early days of the Atlantic ferry, steamers by-passed Ireland entirely. It was speed in the carriage of mails that caused a number of liners to call in Ireland – by the middle eighteen 'fifties even in Galway on the western seaboard. But when the speed of the ocean liners increased, the advantage of the Irish call was reduced. By contrast to the sea route, Ireland was closely involved in the development of cross-Atlantic aviation from the outset. After the Second World War Shannon Airport near Limerick became the principal forward staging point in the greatly expanded Atlantic air traffic. In the jet-age, however,

Finally I will discuss the situation of the land boundary. I agree with JOHN MOGEY that "geography fostered some degree of isolation in the north, although it is important not to exaggerate this factor or to imply that it affords a major explanation of Partition".[43] The land boundary itself does not conform to any major natural divide except in the extreme east, in the Carlingford mountains. Anyone travelling from Dundalk (Co. Louth) northward via the Gap of the North to Newry (Co. Down) really gets the impression of crossing a grim natural barrier. The boundary is based, over most of its length, like all county boundaries, on such natural features as rivers and brooklets [a] (cf. Fig. 7). But hardly any of these pre-existing natural lines tends to constitue a barrier to communication.[44]

The boundary cuts off half of the Foyle valley in the north-west and even a small section of the Central Irish Lowlands. The latter is in Co. Fermanagh, the only Northern Ireland county which has no part in the Central Ulster Lowlands. Co. Fermanagh itself is divided into two parts, a north-eastern and a south-western, by the lakes of the middle course of the river Erne. Both the upper reaches and the short outfall of the river from the lower lake to the Atlantic are in the Republic. The Erne lake belt of old acted as an obstacle to communication. It formed, for instance, a frontier in peasant architecture.[45] Until the twentieth century the only practicable route crossing the middle portion of the lake basin was at Enniskillen, the Irish Interlaken – a passage which has been contested many times.[46]

As a corollary of the argument that the land boundary is to be condemned because it is not a natural frontier, in the sense that it is not based on natural barriers, it has frequently been pointed out in anti-Partition literature that the delimitation of the frontier is highly impracticable.[47] This criticism, however, has essentially nothing to do with the land boundary not being a natural frontier. There are many natural frontiers following impracticable courses whereas many 'artificial' frontiers have proved to be very suitable indeed.

The argument that the land boundary as a whole is not based on any major natural divide has only academic significance. The criticism that its actual course is inconvenient, is more relevant. And, as is easily shown, the validity of the argument cannot be questioned. According to the *Handbook of the Ulster Question*, "no barrier has ever pursued a more tortuous or irregular path". (It also tells us that, when the boundary was set up, it cut across twenty or more rail tracks and ran through no less than fourteen hundred agricultural holdings). For very few miles at a time does the boundary follow "a reasonably straight course".[48]

The irregularity of the frontier is expressed in its length which amounts to no less than 256 miles. Some idea of this length can be obtained from the fact that the land boundary is more than three times as long as the direct distance from Newry (Co. Down)

the advantages of Shannon's westward position has largely been destroyed (BROOKFIELD, 69–70, 73–6). (The development of Shannon as a special industrial centre by the Dublin government is designed to offset this.)

[a] According to EVANS, the Irish county boundaries follow broadly the lines of older political units and reflect in the use of rivers as boundaries "an early stage of settlement around hill-masses" (*Belfast*, 20; cf. *View of Ireland*, 189).

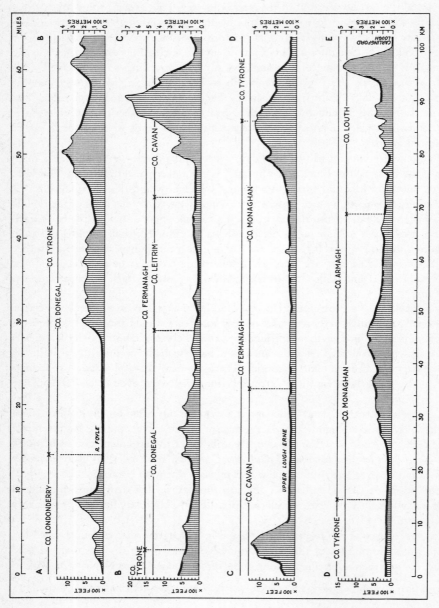

Fig. 7. Profile of the Irish land boundary showing that the boundary over most of its course follows rivers, brooklets or other waters (indicated by heavy lines)

to Londonderry, the cities situated near its two extremities; and that the longest distance in Ireland, calculated along a straight line from the north-east to the south-west of the island, amounts to c. 300 miles.[49]

The impracticability of the delimitation of the land boundary was never more apparent than during the Second World War when the boundary was *de jure* the frontier between a belligerent and a neutral – the Republic staying outside the War. Throughout the War the boundary remained practically an 'open' frontier, in the sense that no effort was made to check cross-Border movement. The United Kingdom government always held that no form of control could be wholly effective. As it was not practicable to enforce travel restrictions along the land frontier, travel between Northern Ireland and Great Britain had to be regulated upon the same basis as travel between the Republic and Great Britain.[50]

The fact that no practicable method of closing the long, staggering, frontier could be found was among the reasons why Northern Ireland was totally excluded from the *Military Training Act, 1939*: compulsory national service was not extended to the North. It was pretty certain that many of those who objected to conscription, either on political or moral grounds, would seek to cross into the Republic. Mr Winant cabled to Mr Roosevelt that policing the land boundary could have absorbed as many men as conscription in Northern Ireland would have added to the armed forces.[51]

The situation of the frontier is taken full advantage of by illegal organizations. Small armed bands of the I.R.A. usually operate from some remote, thinly populated, corner in the Southern Border Counties. When recently the British ambassador in Dublin expressed to the Dublin government his government's deep concern at the continued raids on the Border and the murder of a Northern policeman, the prime minister of the Republic pointed out that it was virtually impossible to watch every mile of the long boundary and, therefore, it was very difficult to stop Border raid plans.[52]

THE 'COMPARTMENTIZATION' OF IRELAND

A 'geographical' argument against Partition that may be dealt with here, is that Ireland is far too small an island to contain two separate political units. [a] This is, however, merely a matter of opinion. There is no objective standard for such a judgment. The inhabitants of small old countries on the continent will certainly not easily be persuaded by reflections of this kind. For the area of Ireland amounts to 32,400 square miles which is roughly twice the area of Denmark or that of Switzerland. The land boundary divides the island into a northern part of 5,400 square miles and a southern of 27,000 square miles. The area of Northern Ireland is still about half that of Belgium, while the area of the Republic just exceeds that of the Benelux as a whole.

That this argument carries some weight is simply because the Irish are accustomed to but one yardstick, used whenever a comparison is sought, that is Great Britain. If one realizes that the whole of Ireland corresponds to only one-third of the area of Great Britain, then the Irish Nationalists's complaint can more easily be understood.

---

[a] Ulster Unionists will, of course, hold that Ireland is not divided into two separate political units as Northern Ireland is an 'integral part' of the United Kingdom.

Table 2. Indices of fragmentation by international frontiers, of each continent (after S. WHITTEMORE BOGGS) and of certain smaller territories, for the year 1937.

	Index of Compartmentization	Index of Interruption
Europe	4.0	480
Europe except the USSR[1]	7.3	1,400
Asia	1.6	120
Asia except the USSR[2]	1.7	190
North and Central America	1.3	27
South America	2.7	33
Africa	2.5	32
Ireland	7.0	930
Hispaniola	5.8	893
Scandinavian peninsula[3]	3.4	105
Iberian peninsula[4]	3.3	477

[1] Omitting the boundaries of the USSR and her five pre-War European neighbours, and the area of European USSR.
[2] Omitting the pre-War boundaries of the USSR in Asia, and the area of Asiatic USSR.
[3] *I.e.* Sweden and Norway; omitting the boundaries with Finland and the USSR.
[4] *I.e.* Spain and Portugal; omitting the boundary of Spain with France.

Perhaps there is a more useful way of assessing the argument. The American geographer S. WHITTEMORE BOGGS, has devised what he calls a *compartmentization index* which enabled him to compare the extent to which each of the continents has become dissected by international boundaries. This index gives the approximate number of miles of international frontiers per thousand square miles of area in each continent. Sea frontiers are omitted from this calculation as they are conceived as 'national', not as 'international', boundaries.[53] (Hence the areas of those islands for which there are no international land frontiers, such as Greenland and the Philipines, are not taken into account.)

I suggest that the index could be applied adequately on a much smaller scale, that is to say to islands and peninsulas which are divided into 'national compartments'. The value of this index for each of the continents in the year 1937, as computed by BOGGS, is shown in the first column of Table 2. For comparison I have added the corresponding figures for the islands of Ireland and Hispaniola [a], and the Scandinavian and Iberian peninsulas; these figures also relate to 1937. The figures confirm the impression that in proportion to its size Europe is more minutely partitioned than any other continent.

It is apparent that the relative compartmentization of Ireland surpasses that of the Caribbean island and contrasts strongly with the dissection of both European peninsulas. On the other hand, the extent to which Ireland has been broken up by the land boundary is almost equal to the fragmentization of the whole of Europe (exclusive of the U.S.S.R. and Iceland). This shows that the 'degree of compartmentization' of Ireland is not as

[a] Hispaniola is also known as Santo Domingo, or as Haiti. Both the latter names are somewhat confusing because of their resemblance to the names of the two states on the island: the largely white, Spanish-speaking, Dominican Republic, and the chiefly negro, Creole-speaking, Republic of Haiti.

exceptional as the anti-Partitionists's argument under consideration implies; it conforms to the pattern established upon the European mainland.

This impression is confirmed by the index numbers in the second column in Table 2, which relate to another measurement proposed by BOGGS, *i.e.* the *interruption index*. This index is obtained by multiplying the number of miles of boundary per thousand square miles of area by the number of the population per square mile. It is based on the assumption that – other things being equal – the greater the population density, the greater will be both the pressure upon the boundaries and the complexity of the problems that arise from their presence.

Chapter 5

IRELAND AS A NATIONAL UNIT

PRINCIPLES OF IRISH NATIONALISM

Nationalism is described in a recent study by ELIE KEDOURIE as a doctrine, invented in Europe at the beginning of the nineteenth century, which

"pretends to supply a criterion for the determination of the unit of population proper to enjoy a government exclusively of its own, for the legitimate exercise of power in the state, and for the right organization of a society of states. Briefly, the doctrine holds that humanity is naturally divided into nations, that nations are known by certain characteristics which can be ascertained, and that the only legitimate type of government is self-government".[54]

This is a definition which includes all the various definitions of Irish nationalism put forward by Irish Nationalists. The basic concept of Irish nationalism can, perhaps, be defined as follows: the people of the island of Ireland have a right, established by history, to constitute a sovereign state; invasion from the neighbouring island, and the consequences of that invasion, cannot alter that right. There are, however, other additional definitions of the Nationalist doctrine, not necessarily held by all Nationalists. The principal one is that enunciated by Padraic Pearse (1879-1916), president of the Provisional Government established in the 1916 Rising: "Ireland, not free only but Gaelic as well, not Gaelic only but free as well".

The two primary objects of the Dublin government's policy, as has frequently been stated by the heads of government, no matter what political party they may belong to, are: (1) the revival of the Gaelic language, and (2) the abolition of Partition. According to Mr de Valera the language issue is even more important than the Border issue. In 1939 he stated in the Dublin senate:

"If I were told to-morrow: 'You can have a united Ireland if you give up your idea of restoring the national language to be the spoken language of the majority of the people', I would, for myself, say no. .. I would say it for this reason: that I believe that as long as the language remains, you have a distinguishing characteristic of nationality which will enable the nation to persist. If you lose the language the danger is that there would be absorption".[55]

There are many Nationalists, however, who do not believe in the necessity of the language revival. [a] (I omit the very many who do not agree with the methods used but who are in favour of the revival itself.) An Irish Nationalist, therefore, has come to mean first and foremost: an Irishman believing in the necessity of the abolition of Partition, or – to put it more positively – believing in the concept of the island of Ireland as a sovereign state.

The fundamental principle of Irish nationalism is that "the whole of Ireland must be regarded as the national unit".[56] In the words of the Dublin prime minister, Mr Lemass:

"It is, indeed, the simple truth that Ireland is one nation, in its history, in its geography and in its people, entitled to have its essential unity expressed in its political institutions. .. Ireland is, by every test, one nation. It is on that essential unity that we found our case for political reintegration".[57]

There are, in fact, various conceptions of the Irish nation. The 'official' conception, as represented by Mr Lemass, embraces, in principle, the total population of the 'national territory' – which coincides, according to the 1937 constitution, with the whole island. In practical terms, however, the Irish nation embraces only those people, north and south of the land boundary, who feel themselves part of the nation – or who are supposed to do so because of their political or religious allegiance. One could say that the two ideas are related to each other as theory and practice.

The important thing, however, is that both conceptions are expressed in terms of the whole island. As GEORGE O'BRIEN states in his *The Four Green Fields* (i.e. the four Irish provinces): "The island has always been the unit to which nationalist sentiment has been attached". Irish nationalism, in O'BRIEN's opinion, is "a love of the country rather than a love of the people in the country, a local rather than a racial patriotism".[58] Generally speaking this may be true. But, if the "love of the country" is attached to the whole island, the "love of the people" is certainly not attached to the whole population. For practical purposes "the Irish people" excludes "the outlanders of Ulster". In 1922 (!) EOIN MACNEILL, who was heart and soul opposed to this exclusivism, rebuked those people "who look upon the 'Black North' as a diseased limb which should be cut off from the Irish social body".[59] Other Nationalist leaders, too, have criticized this exclusivism.

There are, however, two sides to the question. Many Northerners reject, even detest, the idea of being considered part of the Irish nation. They argue that essentially they are profoundly different from the 'Southerners', and that they constitute a different people. According to the Northern Ireland prime minister, Lord Brookeborough: "The border between Northern Ireland and Eire exists because of the ideological gulf which divides the two peoples".[60] People who "feel Ulster", or who are supposed to do so because of their political or religious allegiance, often like to call themselves 'Ulstermen', and occasionally they are called so by friend and foe. [b]

[a] In Chapter 7 I will dwell at rather great length on the Gaelic language revival.
[b] Formerly the phrase 'Ulsterman' was used in a wider sense, including all sections of the population of the Ulster province, whether 'natives' or 'colonists'. It still happens that Northerners who reckon themselves 'Irish', call themselves Ulstermen. Professor EOIN MACNEILL (1876-1944), one of the outstanding Nationalist leaders in the first quarter of the century, used to call himself an Ulsterman – which did not, as he said, make him any the less an Irishman. In order to avoid misunderstanding I will employ the term in its modern colloquial meaning only.

"Feeling Ulster" – as opposed to "feeling Irish" – points at a certain 'regional consciousness', if not to a 'national consciousness'. Hardly any Irishman will question the existence of an 'Ulster consciousness'. Many Irishmen, however, would take offence at the idea that there is such a thing as 'Ulster nationalism'. At most they would speak of 'Ulster regionalism'. A non-committed observer, when discussing typical Ulster sentiments and their expressions, spoke to me of 'Ulsterism'. I will adopt this phrase because it leaves the question open.

In the following Sections I will inquire into the basic elements of Ulsterism as a contribution to the question whether one is justified in speaking of Ireland as of two nations. The existence of a nation can be judged by various criteria. [a] Criteria which seem most obvious in the case of Ireland are: (1) separate political affinities; (2) separate religious affinities; and (3) separate traditions and symbols. The latter distinction is, of course, to a very large extent inherent in the combined contrasts in political and religious allegiance.

THE TWO BRITISH COLONIES

Before turning to the question whether the Ulstermen form a separate nation, I should make it clear that not all references in literature to the existence of two nations in Ireland explicitly mean that one is the 'Ulster nation'. Before the Border was drawn, a distinction frequently made was between the 'Irish nation' and the 'Ascendancy'. The latter, sometimes denoted as the 'Anglo-Irish nation', were a narrow caste, almost entirely composed of English (Episcopalian) stock, who since the end of the seventeenth century had dominated public life in Ireland. Originally they had owned the greater part of the land in Ireland, but in the nineteenth century the British government had dispossessed them in a sweeping piece of social reform which made Ireland a land of peasant proprietors. In GALLAGHER's *The Indivisible Island* this exclusive hereditary class has been pictured as follows:

"It was a small group of overlords opposed politically to the national ideals of the majority, rejecting Ireland's distinctive culture, despising the symbols of her separate nationality and usually differing in religious persuasion from the mass of the people. The group stood for British supremacy and against the nation though from it there had come individuals to participate in and to lead the great movements for freedom... The group as a whole gave themselves the name of the 'British garrison' and put first the British interests. All major official appointments were given to them: the franchise was for long restricted to them and when it had to be widened was designed still to preserve their domination". [61]

---

[a] "While certain primary elements – a common homeland, a common stock and, less invariably, a common language – are to be found in the composition of most nations, the word defies a precise all-inclusive academic definition. But it is generally agreed that in its essence nationhood is always a matter of the spirit" (COUPLAND, xix). Here by 'nation' is understood: a distinct cultural entity, a community aware of real or imagined differences between themselves and other people, adhering to their own way of life, and aspiring to become or to remain a separate political entity.

Things which make a nation are, in the words of RENAN in his famous essay on *Qu'est ce qu'une nation?*: "the common possession of a rich heritage of memories", also "the actual agreement and desire to live together", and "the will to preserve worthily the joint inheritance... To share the glories of the past and a common will in the present: to have done great deeds together and to desire to do more of them – these are the essential conditions of a people's being" (306).

It has frequently been suggested by Nationalist authors that the focus of this "ancient and evil system" has been shifted from Dublin to Belfast after 1921: "In Northern Ireland at the present day, the old system of ascendancy still holds sway; the outward forms are somewhat altered, but the essential underlying conditions are those of the eighteenth century".[62] As GALLAGHER sees it: "There the national minority has been able to continue the system by which a group ruled, excluding from all true participation in government the members of the national majority".[63]

It is true that Northern Ireland preserves some Ascendancy features [a] – but so does the rest of the United Kingdom. It is absurd, however, to consider the rank and file of Ulstermen as representatives of the pre-revolution Ascendancy as defined above. There were, in fact, two 'British colonies' in Ireland. On the one hand there was the Ascendancy, exclusively English and Episcopalian, who were distributed over the whole island. On the other hand there was – and still is – the 'colony' with its predominating Scottish and Presbyterian element in the (administrative) Ulster province.

It was their Presbyterianism which brought the 'Ulster planters' into conflict not merely with the Roman Catholic Irish but also with the Anglican Ascendancy represented by the Established Church (of Ireland).

"This Presbyterian element in the Northern colony was, like the Catholic Irish if to a lesser degree, persecuted by the Established Church and by the British and Irish Parliaments. It was this protracted two-sided struggle, with the Catholic Irish on the one hand and the Protestant Anglo-Irish on the other, which bred in the Northern planters that inflexible determination which has marked their history.

The resistance of the Presbyterian colony to the Irish and Anglo-Irish was aided by their concentration in a restricted area in the north-east of the island. The Northern plantation had depth through its own middle-class and peasantry, unlike the Protestant (Anglican) Ascendancy who were spread horizontally, as a landlord–class, over the body of the Irish Catholic peasantry. Thus when in the second decade of the present century the Catholic Irish rose in rebellion against English rule, the Ulster planters were in a position to resist the demand for an Irish government and the Protestant Ascendancy were not".[64]

If Northern Ireland has preserved some Ascendancy features which have been swept away in the South, this can be attributed to the determined resistance of the Ulster colony to Irish demands for Home Rule and Separation. The prospect of Home Rule, and even more so of Separation, was among the chief factors which led to a *rapprochement* between the Ascendancy and the Ulstermen. The two parties, however, had essentially different loyalties and objects: the Ulster farmers and artisans were opposed to the incorporation of Ulster in an all-Ireland state, while the Ascendancy – feeling no particular loyalty to Ulster – wished to preserve the Union in entirety and to prevent any Irish state being set up. The fact that after the Separation and subsequent Partition the Ulster gentry continued to be of importance in Northern Ireland may lend some support to the 'vestigial colony' theory. But their position has come to rely entirely on the Ulsterism of farmers and artisans.

[a] A certain social exclusivism can be noted in the succession of members of the old landed aristocracy to parliamentary seats, as far as the Protestant population is concerned – even if the majority of the electorate might have preferred less exalted candidates to represent them. That, as GALLAGHER suggests, "the members of the national majority", *viz*. the Roman Catholics, are excluded from "all true participation in government" is, in my opinion, a gross oversimplification.

At the outset I should note that, however much the Ulstermen may stress their distinctness from other Irishmen, they rarely speak of themselves as a separate nation. They eschew the term 'nation', probably because the concept implies a desire for political independence. The Ulstermen want, of course, to be independent from the Republic, but at the same time they want to be in the United Kingdom. Therefore, if an Ulsterman speaks of the nation he belongs to, he always refers to the British. For him one of the main differences between Ulstermen and other Irishmen is simply that the Ulstermen feel proud to belong to the 'British nation'.

WILLIAM CARSON makes this quite implicit when he says that, tried by Renan's tests, "Ulster is British". He adds: "Despite Separatist arguments, the fact that one is British does not involve ceasing to be Irish any more than it involves ceasing to be Welsh or Scottish".[65] Indeed, the majority of the Northerners, as EVANS observes, "while proud to call themselves Irish on St Patrick's Day or at Twickenham on the rugby football field, think of themselves first and foremost as British".[66] Needless to say, to the Nationalists, north and south of the land boundary, the epithets 'Irish' and 'British' are mutually exclusive.

To an Ulsterman, to "feel British" means in the first place to be loyal to the British crown. In the field of politics this loyalty finds expression in voting 'Unionist', that is for candidates of the *Ulster Unionist Party*. Although the Ulster Unionist representatives at Westminster vote with the Conservatives who represent English, Welsh and Scottish constituencies, the Ulster Unionist Party is no mere branch or extension of the British Conservative party.

The Ulster Unionist Party can hardly be called a political party in the usual sense of the word. It is "composed of all levels of society to a degree not often encountered in parliamentary democracies", and "a blend of people of many political sympathies".[67] If it cannot be compared with the Conservative and Labour parties in Great Britain, neither is it comparable with one of the denominational political parties in the Netherlands. It is, essentially, a manifestation of a separate 'nationhood' eager to preserve their identity.

But, however often the Ulstermen may profess their 'Britishness', their ultimate loyalty is to 'Ulster'. They are not Ulstermen because they are British but they are British because they are Ulstermen. Apart altogether from their social and spiritual links with Great Britain, the Ulstermen are Unionist because, as they see it, the constitutional (and economic) links with Great Britain are the sole guarantee for the preservation of their identity.[a] D. W. BROGAN is perhaps right when he says: "The Ulstermen are far too sensible to be real loyalists." They refuse to sacrifice any of their real or alleged interests to English needs. "Their first duty is to Ulster".[68]

---

[a] Even the small Northern Ireland Labour Party (which holds four of the fifty-two seats in the Belfast parliament) believes that "there is nothing to be gained in any direction by the abolition of the Border" (*i.e.* the land boundary), and that "Ulster must find its own solution to its own problems" (*The Times*, June 29, 1961).

The Irish Nationalist ideology – as it was first formulated at the end of the eighteenth century and as it is embodied in the constitution of the Irish Republic (1937) – is essentially 'non-sectarian'. This means that it envisages a sovereign state which embraces the whole population of the island of Ireland, irrespective of religion and descent (cf. p. 54). The doctrine which dates from the end of the nineteenth century and which holds that Ireland should not only be free but Gaelic-speaking as well – however exclusive it may be – is, too, essentially 'non-sectarian'.

In practice, however, Irish nationalism has become very much associated with Roman Catholicism. This is hardly surprising as three-quarters of the population of Ireland are Roman Catholics, and as Irish resistance against the Union with Great Britain was bound up with Roman Catholicism. [a] It is, I think, hardly too much to say that, to many Nationalists, one of the attributes which define a 'true Irishman', and exclude a spurious one, is the 'Catholic faith'.[b] This exclusivism finds daily expression in such phrases like "I am Irish, so, of course, I am a Catholic". The 'most true Irishman' would be the Gaelic-speaking Roman Catholic. (Not all Nationalists are happy about this – growing – tendency towards "religious racialism"; they realize that it makes the attainment of "national reunion" all the more difficult.[69])

If it is true that every nationalist movement has one major stimulus – whether 'race', language, or some other inherited cultural attribute which would distinguish one nation from another[70] – then the main impetus of Irish nationalism is religion, in casu Roman Catholicism. Irish nationalism is not the only nationalist movement which has drawn much from "the powerful and tenacious loyalties which a faith held in common for centuries creates".[71] The moving force of Ulsterism, too, is religion, in casu Protestantism. If for an Irish Roman Catholic his nationality is hardly separable from his religion, the same is broadly true of the Ulster Protestant.

ARLAND USSHER assumes that but for their religion Irishmen would probably have forgotten Separatism.[72] It may also be assumed that but for their religion Ulstermen would have forgotten 'Partitionism'. To "feel Ulster", therefore, not only means: being a Unionist, but also: professing the 'Protestant faith'. One may even say that being an Ulster Unionist presupposes one's being a Protestant. [c]

Today the most pronounced expression of Ulsterism as a politico-religious movement is found in the Loyal Orange Order, known as the Orange Institution. This organization

---

a In his address at the closing of the recent Dublin Patrician Congress, the Republic prime minister, Mr Lemass, said that "in the story of our island, nationality and religion had been interwoven in an unusually intimate degree. Throughout the centuries the free exercise of our religion had always been linked with our aspirations for national independence and our people rallied again and again to the cry of 'Faith and Fatherland' " (The Irish Press, June 26, 1961).

b Even members of the Dublin government are inclined to equate 'Irish' and 'Catholic'. The prime minister recently observed in a public address that "the Irish remain steadfast in their devotion to the Faith of St Patrick and in their loyalty to the Apostolic See" (The Irish Press, June 26, 1961).

c When it was suggested by some young Unionists that the party in the future might admit Roman Catholics as members, it was stated by a Unionist senator: "It is difficult to see how a Roman Catholic, with the vast differences in our religious outlook, could be either acceptable within the Unionist Party as a member, or, for that matter, bring himself unconditionally to support its ideals" (The Irish Times, Oct. 10, 1959).

which was founded in Co. Armagh at the end of the eighteenth century is "a voluntary association of English-speaking Protestants, organized throughout the world in defence of Civil and Religious Liberty". The principles which the so-called Orangemen uphold are symbolized by the 'Open Bible' and the British crown.[73] The Ulster Orangeman, states an official publication of the (Northern) Irish branch of the order, is

"deeply loyal to the British crown and a faithful Protestant, and is bound to support our constitutional system which maintains the Protestant religion and preserves the Union between Great Britain and Northern Ireland. The Border [land boundary] is as secure a bulwark to his religious faith and his political freedom, under the ample folds of the Union Jack, as were the grey old Walls of Derry beneath her Crimson Banner three centuries ago".[74]

The (Northern) Irish branch of the Orange Institution is 'interlocked' with the Unionist Party. Most members of the Belfast government, if not all, belong to it. The order publishes no membership figures. It is probable that over 100,000 adult male Protestants in Northern Ireland belong to it; the number of active members in Belfast alone may be assessed at 20,000.

Finally I should point out that, however much Ulsterism may be linked up with Protestantism, not all Irish Protestants – not even all Protestants who still "think British" – sympathize with Ulsterism, to say nothing of Orangeism. Sympathy among the Protestants in the Republic is practically confined to those Protestants whose families have always lived in the Southern Border Counties (the three "lost counties" of Donegal, Cavan and Monaghan), or who originally came from 'Ulster', i.e. the nine counties of the former administrative province.

The other Protestants in the Republic rarely feel attached to their co-religionists in 'Ulster' – not even those who feel that they do not quite 'belong' in the South. [a] Quite a number of them even share with their Roman Catholic fellow-countrymen the traditional allergy to – if not dislike of – the Ulstermen. Although disapproving of acts of violence and disliking the tragic nature of recent events, occasional Protestants in Dublin expressed to me a certain enjoyment at seeing "those stolid Ulstermen" being harried by the I.R.A.! Here it is well to remember that the majority of the Southern Protestants are Episcopalians (Anglicans) of English descent, whereas Ulsterism originated with Presbyterians of Scottish descent.

The Southern Protestants who sympathize with Ulsterism – we might call them 'Southern Ulstermen' – number only a few thousands. In proportion to their numerical strength there are a considerable number of Orangemen among them. It is likely that not a few of them will settle across the land boundary as soon as Northern Ireland can offer them prospects of earning a reasonable living. In this way many have already settled in the North. Needless to say the other Southern Protestants would not contemplate emigration to Northern Ireland: rather do they gravitate towards England.

[a] A rather fair observer (of Southern Protestant descent) concludes that the 'non-Catholic' in the Republic often feels himself far more cut off than does a Roman Catholic in present-day England. "The life of his countrymen is an intricate pattern of fasts and festivals, pilgrimages and retreats, in which he has no part. ... In these circumstances it would be surprising if the non-Catholic did not feel himself something of a stranger and a 'foreign body' in Eire. If he is sensitive, he will sometimes feel even the toleration he enjoys as more exasperating than persecution would be" (USSHER, 75).

W. B. STANFORD (a Southern Protestant who is a member of the Dublin senate) says that "Unionism has no poets, no orators or writers, no culture or mythology, to rival those of Irish Nationalism".[75] This is undoubtedly true from the point of view of the arts. EVANS (a Welshman) notes that "Ulster regionalism has failed to inspire great music or an impassioned literature such as have so often heralded political self-determination."[76] Nor can Ulsterism rival Irish nationalism with regard to the antiquity, real or supposed, of its mythology. However, a nationalist mythology which does not look farther back than three or four centuries, like that of Ulsterism, can be emotionally as satisfying to its adherents as a mythology, like that of Irish nationalism, which looks back over the whole Christian era and even farther (!).

As EVANS observes: "The heroes of the Williamite campaign – William of Orange, whose title the Loyal Orange Order bears, and his general Schomberg – stand as heroes of an earlier period do for the Roman Catholics".[77] The Ulstermen still revere the prince of Orange, of "glorious, pious and immortal memory", as "William the Deliverer" who saved the cause of Protestantism in Europe and incidentally secured the survival of the Ulster colony. In STANFORD's opinion the Battle of the Boyne, the decisive victory of William III over James II in 1690 near Drogheda (Co. Louth), is no substitute for a major saga.[78] Apart altogether from the international issues at stake in this battle, this opinion is quite unfounded. Each year William's victory is celebrated by hundreds of thousands of Ulstermen with great ceremony and pageantry. [a]

The anniversary, known as "The Twelfth" (of July), is a real 'national feast-day'. It is celebrated by long processions of Orangemen, sometimes led by delegations of the "Brethren of the South" (Southern Ulstermen) who are loudly cheered on by the crowds.[b] The processions head for 'field services'. [c] At these rallies, which are a mixture of religious services and political meetings, the Orangemen and their supporters hear speeches delivered by Protestant ministers and Unionist statesmen. Afterwards they profess their faith, pledge loyalty to the Queen, and renew their determination "to watch over Ulster's

---

[a] The anniversary is heralded by the erection of arches, the painting of pictures of "Dutch William" on corner-houses, and the chalking on walls and streets of such slogans as *Remember 1690* (the year of the Boyne battle), *No Popery*, and *Not an Inch*. The latter watchword means that the Ulstermen are determined not to cede an inch of the territory of Northern Ireland. On the eve of the holiday numerous bonfires are burned in the streets and on the hills.

[b] There is an interesting parallel in the fact that at the famous St Patrick's Day Irish Parade in New York, which is composed of associations representing the thirty-two counties of Ireland, the "Six-County associations" are put at the head of the procession – a symbol perhaps borrowed from the Ulster precedent.

[c] In 1960 Twelfth processions were held in twenty places, including a small town just across the land boundary in Co. Donegal (!). In these marches 75 to 80,000 Orangemen took part. As is usual, Belfast had the largest parade with about 18,000 participants (representing about three hundred lodges), twice marching a distance of over five miles. This procession took almost three hours to pass through the town centre. All parades are enlivened by pipe, flute, accordeon and silver bands – each lodge patronizes or hires a band. They are adorned with large silk banners which carry pictures of Biblical scenes (such as *The Star of Bethlehem*, and *Abraham offering up Isaac*), and of historical themes, either taken from Ulster's past (such as *The Drowning of the Protestants in the River Bann*, and *King William leaving Belfast Castle*) or derived from the history of the United Kingdom as a whole (such as *The Battle of the Somme*, and *The Secret of England's Greatness*).

integrity". [a] According to MOGEY, "this emotional mechanism, making use of many separate devices, has been an important factor in maintaining the unbroken record of the Unionist Party at the polls since 1920".[79]

The Twelfth is not the only annual public manifestation of Ulster Orangeism and Unionism in which huge crowds take part. Another instance is "The Battle of Scarva", a reconstruction of the Boyne battle performed on "The Thirteenth" (of July) in Scarva (Co. Down), a little village situated on the Black Pig's Dyke. [b] *The Battle of the Boyne* is not the only epic tale of Ulsterism. Other stories which still stir the imagination of thousands of Ulstermen are the cycle of *The Siege of Derry*. [c] The city of Londonderry holds a special place in the hearts of Ulstermen as "Ulster's Maiden City" – so called because she was "wooed but never won" by the Jacobite army during the Williamite campaign.[80]

An Ulsterman wrote, somewhat rhetorically:

"The symbols, heroes and traditions of Irish nationalism which deeply move the emotional and rhetorical temperament of the people of Eire, only bore and repel the practical and executive temperament of the people of Northern Ireland".[81]

Overlooking his remarks on the temperament of the Southerners and the Northerners, it could be said, with equal justification, that the symbols, heroes and traditions of Ulsterism are boring and repellent to the Irish Nationalists. The latter identify themselves with the Jacobite party in the Williamite campaign; they have learnt to interpret the Siege of Derry and the Battle of the Boyne as stages in the defeat of the 'Irish nation'. [d]

---

[a] Some of the themes developed at the 1960 demonstrations were: the rejection of the proposal made by the Republic prime minister for the setting up of an all-Ireland free trade area; the upholding of Christian principles by the royal family in their daily lives; and the trend towards laxity in observing the Sabbath in Northern Ireland (it was deplored that Orangemen cross the boundary in their cars on a Sunday to frequent public houses in the Republic). The various addresses may well be summed up in the Northern Ireland prime minister's words at a meeting in Co. Fermanagh: "There will go out from these great demonstrations the message that in spite of threats and cajolery, talk and terrorism, the heart and soul of Ulster remains staunch and true" (*Belfast Telegraph*, July 12, 1960).

[b] In 1960 the Battle of Scarva and the connected religious field service were attended by 30 to 40,000 people. The sham fight is preceded by a "Black Parade", a procession of *Royal Black Preceptories*. Preceptories are lodges of the *Black Institution*, a more exclusive and purely religious offshoot of the Orange Institution. Its membership is open only to persons who have received the degrees of an Orangeman.

[c] Each August there is a "Relief Parade" in Derry, a procession of *Apprentice Boys*. Apprentice Boys are an offshoot of the Black Institution. Membership can only be conferred within the sacrosanct "Grey Walls of Derry". The Relief Parade in 1960 included about 10,000 Apprentice Boys, assembled from all parts of the United Kingdom and from Canada. The parade (enlivened by 130 bands) was proceded by a thanksgiving service in "historic St Columb's Cathedral where the Siege defenders prayed for deliverance", and a ceremony in which about 500 new members (including the Northern Ireland premier and several Canadians and Scots) were initiated into the order. The Apprentice Boys take their name from one of the episodes of the Derry cycle, *The Closing of the Gates*. It tells how the governor of Derry (a Protestant) was ready to surrender the city, in which thousands of Protestants had sought refuge, when thirteen apprentice boys took the law into their hands and shut the gates in the face of the oncoming foe. Each December the exploits of "The Brave Thirteen" are also commemorated "with a deep religious and patriotic fervour" (DEWAR, *Portraits*, 27-8).

[d] It falls outside the scope of this study to examine how these contrasting traditions are fostered by the ways in which history is taught in school. Protestant schools in the North are rarely taught any 'Irish' history. Of history-teaching in the Republic it has been said that "the Gaelic Republican ideal" has

They are most profoundly offended, however, by those symbols of Ulsterism which are purely British in origin. Nationalists cannot understand that the playing of the British national anthem, *God Save The Queen*, means as much to Ulstermen as does *The Soldier's Song* to themselves. The same applies to the display of the Union Jack and the Tricolour.

THE TWO NATIONS

In conclusion I feel justified in saying that, on the basis of the three criteria chosen, Ulstermen do form a separate nation. That they rarely call themselves a separate nation does not alter the fact. Ulsterism, then, is essentially a form of nationalism. It has too many political implications to be considered mere regionalism. On the other hand, its political implications do not reach as far as those of Irish nationalism. The fulfilment of the Ulster nation is not sought by the attainment of political independence but by the maintenance of the constitutional link with the British crown.

If therefore Ulsterism is not the true counterpart of Irish nationalism, it has, perhaps, more similarity to Scottish and Welsh nationalism. At least one could say that, if the Scots and the Welshmen constitute separate nations, the Ulstermen, too, constitute a separate nation. At any rate, the Ulstermen cannot be considered to belong to the Irish nation. I agree with ARLAND USSHER (a Southerner of Ascendancy upbringing) who observes:

"Since the people of North-East Ulster have seen fit to exclude themselves from the new Ireland, and so far have shown not the slightest disposition to revise their attitude, it seems both unreasonable and impertinent to consider them as part of the nation".[82]

And it is well to remember that, as *The Times* said in an article on *Both Sides of the Green Curtain*, in the meantime

"a new generation has grown up in the Six Counties which never knew a united Ireland and which does not regard itself as Irish in the wider sense. Ulster men and women under forty have no experience of an undivided island. They have looked, from their childhood, to Scotland and England. .. Southern neutrality in the War and the setting up of the Republic widened the ideological gap. This contemporary attitude of the North is different from the old Orange fanaticism. But it has added a no less powerful barrier. To move to and fro between the two camps is to be impressed by how little each knows of what the other is doing and thinking".

dictated the selection of events to be stressed (cf. *The Irish Times*, Febr. 27, 1960). According to a Unionist author, they are calculated to stir up feelings of hatred against "the brutal Saxon oppressors" of "an eminently Christian country"; the results of this teaching are to be seen in the I.R.A. (CARSON, 52-4).

One may certainly say that the average Irishman is remarkably ill-informed about the past – his historical knowledge often being acquired as part of his political, rather than of his historical education (GEORGE O'BRIEN, *Fields*, 5). MANSERGH notes that Irish Nationalists fail to see history in perspective: "Irish history has remained for many Irishmen no more than a series of incidents, unco-ordinated by a logical sequence of cause and effect, unsubstantiated by evidence of economic or social conditions, entirely dissociated from the events of the outside world" (*Age*, 254). The Editor of the *History of the Church of Ireland* refers to the extreme insularity of the outlook of most Irishmen, "which leads them to think that the abuses and oppressions of the past were the result of conditions peculiar to this country" (vi). It has been said that Irish history is a subject for Englishmen to remember and for Irishmen to forget. According to GEORGE O'BRIEN (*Fields*, 5) a more correct aphorism might be that "Irish history is a subject for Englishmen to learn and for Irishmen to learn properly". These observations apply *mutatis mutandis* to the Ulstermen.

The same article states that how remote the Northerners (*i.e.* the Ulstermen) feel themselves to be from what they regard as a "Celtic banana republic" is not realized in the South.[83] An argument repeatedly put forward by Ulstermen in defence of Partition is that "the people of Ulster" (read: the Ulstermen) and "the people of Eire" (read: the Nationalists) hold such different opinions on the rights of the individual [a] and the relation between Church and state.[b]

According to some Ulstermen the 'ideological gulf' between the two nations emerges most clearly from the compulsory use in the Republic of what is to Ulstermen "a dead language", instead of "a tongue which is almost universal".[84] When the Free State was set up, its government was faced with "a crucial paradox", as R. A. BREATNACH (professor of Old Irish in University College, Cork) says. Adherence to the Gaelic ideal, accepted by many doctrinaire Nationalists, could only make the attainment of a united Ireland all the more difficult. The decision that "that part of the historic Irish nation which had become independent would become Irish-speaking as well" could, of course, result only in "adding a cultural or linguistic dimension to the complex of historical, religious, economic and political differences and prejudices on which the Northern Unionists had rejected the Irish Nationalist ethos". If the Ulstermen had refused to come to terms with the Nationalists on the basis of a free Ireland,

"how could they be expected at a later time to agree to become part of a free Gaelic Ireland in which, whatever safeguards they might be offered, they would seem to be faced in the last analysis with cultural domination or assimilation".[85]

STANFORD is probably right when he says that in some quarters of the North there is an "astonishing antipathy" towards the Gaelic language. He suggests that it results from "an instinctive dread of racial exclusivism". In his opinion "Gaelic exclusivism" would indeed resemble "the pernicious continental forms of racialism, anti-Semitism, anti-Slavism and the rest".[86]

A DUAL COMMUNITY

Finally something must be said about the relations between the two nations. The res-

[a] According to a Northern Ireland cabinet minister, "the fundamental conception of the Ulsterman" is the right to think for oneself, to speak for oneself, the right to differ from one's neighbours, "the right – to use Bunyan's famous words – 'to be a pilgrim'" (*Border*, 9-11). Ulstermen dread that they would have to give up this conception if they were merged in the South. As Mr S. T. O'KELLY, the ex-president, once declared, the Free State government was "inspired in its every action by Catholic principles and Catholic doctrine" (*The Irish Press*, Oct. 10, 1933). According to Father JOSEPH COLLINS O.P., "with the exception of one article, which was the subject of dispute, it would be difficult to find a clearer and more comprehensive statement of Catholic teaching on fundamental social problems than was to be found in the [1937] Irish Constitution" (*The Irish Times*, Nov. 21, 1959).

[b] It is obvious that the Roman Catholic Church has a great influence in political affairs in the Republic (cf. BLANCHARD, 50; O'FAOLAIN, *De Valera*, 167-9). As Father JOHN A. O'BRIEN puts it: "Ireland is a Catholic nation; the activities of the Church and her priests are intertwined with the daily life of the Irish people" (in: *Vanishing Irish*, 11). A few years ago one of the bishops declared that "the clergy should never be apologetic in their efforts to impose the teaching of the Church in legislation" (*The Irish Times*, Oct. 25, 1956). A recent example, which has figured largely in the Ulsterman's thinking, is that of the mother-and-child health service. The Minister for Health who proposed such a scheme – which was very much in line with United Kingdom legislation – was forced to resign when the hierarchy objected to his proposals (cf. *The Irish Times*, April 12, 1951; BLANSHARD, 73-80).

pective positions in the South and the North are quite different. It is, in my opinion, fair
to say that no Ulsterman left south of the land boundary disputes the right of his fellow-
countrymen to have a government of their own choosing. He will not feel such a need
to profess loudly his loyalty to the new regime as his co-religionists in the South who have
become politically converted and who express obedience to the laws of the land even
when Roman Catholics may express indifference or contempt. The few thousands of
'Southern Ulstermen' do not, however, in one way or another constitute a threat to
their government.

The situation of the politico-religious minority in the North is different. Their
attitude towards their government may well be summed up in the following statement
made by an ecclesiastic at the 1955 *Catholic Truth Society* congress in Londonderry:

"Catholics, almost without exception, not because they are Catholics but because they are Irish, are
fixed in their opposition to this state of Northern Ireland, an unnatural organism conceived in deceit and
maintained by force, and they hunger after the day when they will be united with the nation".[87]

As the leader of the Nationalist Party in Northern Ireland [a] told a rally of the *Ancient
Order of Hibernians* (the counterpart of the Orange Institution) on St Patrick's Day, 1960:

"We who are Irish claim every inch of our country for our own people and if those in this north-
eastern territory who glory in their connection with the British imagine that we are going to abdicate
one iota of our political faith to placate them, then all I can say is they do not know us. We can see no
point in trying to come to terms with people utterly alien in their outlook and so remote from the traditions
of this nation".[88]

If the number of Southern Ulstermen is negligible, and even tends to shrink further,
the number of Northern Nationalists is considerable and tends to increase. Some of my
Northern Nationalist informants expressed confidence that sooner or later they would
achieve numerical majority, which automatically would bring about the political unification of Ireland. Roman Catholics number about one-third of the Northern Ireland
population (cf. Table 3) but Roman Catholic pupils number over 45 per cent of all
pupils on rolls of primary schools in the North. [b] According to a Dublin newspaper the
Belfast government finds itself in a dilemma:

"The more it does to create full employment and improve living standards, the more it harms its
own political position. For a prosperous economy will reduce emigration which mainly affects Catholics
and the more Catholics remaining at home the greater the threat to the Unionist's long dominance".[89]

The "precariousness of the balance of power"[90] has influenced the electoral policy
in the North. The Northern Nationalists complain of a restriction of the franchise and
of the 'gerrymandering' [c] of the boundaries of certain local government electoral areas,

---

[a] Curiously enough the Northern Ireland Nationalist Party has no central organization or functioning
local branches as has the Ulster Unionist Party or the political parties in the Republic. As DESMOND
FENNELL (15) puts it, "there are some M.P.'s who call themselves Nationalists".

[b] They are now in an absolute majority in the primary schools of four of the six counties. In 1924 the
percentage of Roman Catholic pupils in all Northern primary schools was 34.8, in 1934 36.5, in 1945
39.4, in 1951 41.5, in 1954 42.8, and in 1957 45.5% (cf. *Ulster Year Books*).

[c] The term 'gerrymandering' comes from governor Gerry of Massachusetts who – in 1812 – carved out a
freak legislative district of the state in order to ensure automatic electoral advantage to his own party
(*The Irish Times*, Dec. 5, 1960). GALLAGHER (234) calls Partition itself "a giant gerrymander": "By that
major boundary manipulation a minority in the whole of Ireland was given a veto on the majority's

Table 3. Percentage of Roman Catholics in the population of Northern Ireland by county and county borough, at each census since 1911.

	1911	1926	1937	1951	1961
Co. Antrim	20.5	20.2	20.2	22.1	24.4
Belfast C.B.	24.1	23.0	23.8	25.9	27.5
Co. Down	31.6	30.4	30.6	30.2	28.7
East Ulster	*25.1*	*24.3*	*24.7*	*26.1*	*27.0*
Co. Londonderry	41.5	41.6	42.1	43.0	42.6
Londonderry C.B.	56.2	60.0	61.3	63.1	67.1
Co. Tyrone	55.4	55.5	55.3	55.4	54.8
Co. Fermanagh	56.2	56.0	55.3	55.5	52.9
Co. Armagh	45.3	45.4	45.5	46.4	47.3
Northern Border Cos	*50.0*	*50.5*	*50.6*	*51.1*	*51.2*
Total Northern Ireland	34.4	33.5	33.5	34.4	34.9

notably in Co. Tyrone and in Londonderry C.B.[a] DENIS GWYNN in *The History of Partition* speaks of an "intolerable deprivation of fair representation for the Nationalist and Catholic majority" in the North[91] ('majority', of course, refers to the whole island). According to some of my Ulster Unionist informants this policy is expedient so long as the Northern Nationalists are not prepared to accept the constitutional position of Northern Ireland.[b]

Though there are some who maintain that "the Catholics of Northern Ireland are gradually moving towards an acceptance of the political *status quo*", and that there are Roman Catholics who vote Unionist[92], this must be a matter of speculation. The fact remains that a Roman Catholic who admits to being a Unionist, or a Protestant who is a Nationalist, still "is reckoned by his co-religionists in their kinder moods as a phenome-

---

right to decide policy for the nation, just as today by boundary manipulations minorities in the Nationalist areas inside the partitioned territory are allowed to veto the local majority".

[a] The seven rural councils of Co. Tyrone, which originally included 82 Nationalists and 63 Unionists, now consist of 62 Nationalists and 99 Unionists (GALLAGHER, 232-3). The most bitter conflict is the struggle for municipal supremacy in the Border town Londonderry C.B. This struggle goes back to the last quarter of the nineteenth century when the Roman Catholics reached the majority (cf. CURRAN, *passim*). Although nearly two-thirds of the population are Roman Catholics, only two-fifths of the seats on the corporation are held by Nationalists (GALLAGHER, 227-8). Gerrymandering, such as it is, does not, however, seriously affect Nationalist representation in the Belfast parliament and at Westminster. (It may be noted that the term 'gerrymandering' is also applied by opposition parties in the Republic to occasional changes in electoral districts accomplished by the government party. Such a complaint is likely enough to arise in any country which adheres to the principle of territorial representation.)

[b] They also pointed out that there is no government in the world which does not discriminate, in one way or another, against a political grouping which reserves its loyalties for a foreign government. The Northern Nationalists cannot be regarded as a constitutional opposition party, and they do not want to be regarded as such. A few days before the 1959 general election Nationalist members of the Belfast parliament went to Dublin and "in the name of hundreds of thousands of Nationalists pledged their loyalty to the president of Ireland" (*Sunday Independent*, Oct. 11, 1959).

non, and on more ordinary occasions as one who has betrayed his faith".[93] Essentially, "the Ulster community" still is, as STANFORD says[94], "a dual community". [a]

However peaceably neighbours of different politics and religion may live side by side [b], below the surface there still goes on a "silent struggle between the two races", the one possessed by hate, the other by fear.[95] There is some truth in the picture which LYNN DOYLE (the novelist, who may, perhaps, be called a Protestant Nationalist of moderate views) gives of their opinion of each other[96]: To the Northern Catholic the Protestant is "a foreigner and an interloper, with no right to the land he holds", and "a sycophant of a foreign power, to whom he pretends loyalty merely because it pays him"; to the Ulster Protestant the Roman Catholic is "a traitor to the lawfully established government by the majority, which he is for ever scheming to upset", and "a bigot and a potential persecutor". [c]

Nowhere in Northern Ireland is social tension more acute than in Londonderry – the only town in the United Kingdom where the British national anthem is not played in cinemas at the conclusion of performances. History may say that the Siege of Derry lasted 105 days. As DOYLE remarks: "It began on April 26, 1689, and has been going on ever since: the Irish are still besieging .. and though the tide is setting the Irish way the spirit of 'No Surrender' is as strong as ever".[97] And a Roman Catholic ecclesiastic, speaking of the Ulstermen's attempt to retain the City inside the Walls as "a sort of Orange Mecca where the unbeliever may not enter", stated: "Three hundred years of history should have shown them the futility of attempting to build a Protestant island in a Catholic sea".[98]

[a] It must be noted that the main division follows politico-religious rather than socio-economic lines. It is not possible to identify one side with 'workers' and the other with 'capitalists' (*Ulster under H.R.*, 12-3), as both sides comprise all classes of society. This does not preclude the fact that certain trades are dominated by Protestants and other by Roman Catholics. Most publicans, bookmakers and cattle-dealers are Roman Catholics; hardware, drapery and clothing shops are mostly owned by Protestants; grocer's and butcher's shops and footwear stores would be fairly evenly divided (FENNELL, 2; MOGEY, *Community*, 87; *Ulster under H.R.*, 11). In those towns where the two sections are rather evenly matched in numbers there is a duplication in retail shops (especially grocery), which are exclusively supported by the respective communities.

[b] In many towns even a kind of territorial *apartheid* is observed as, for instance, in Kilkeel (Co. Down) (BLOOMFIELD, 108-10). Perhaps the most striking example is provided by certain parts of Belfast, especially working-class areas, which are either exclusively Protestant or Catholic (cf. EMRYS JONES, *Geography*, 172-204).

[c] ROSEMARY HARRIS (lecturer in the Geography Department at Queen's in Belfast) found that Nationalists in Co. Tyrone still regard themselves as the dispossessed and that Protestants still think – despite all avowals to the contrary – that, in the turmoil that would preceed the unification of Ireland, they would be turned out. The latter recall that, during "the Troubles" which preceded Partition, in several parts of Co. Tyrone the Nationalists raffled tickets for the farms of Protestants (3-4). "Out in the west a farm can still burn down in the night because it passes from Protestant to Catholic ownership – or vice versa" (*The Observer*, June 21, 1959). DOYLE tells how a man in Downpatrick (Co. Down) "let house-property lie idle for years that he might in the end fill it with voters of his own politics" (109).

Chapter 6

'NORTHERNERS' AND 'SOUTHERNERS'

THE CAUSES OF PARTITION

Explanations of Partition can roughly be divided into two categories. The one theory which is almost generally accepted by Irish Nationalists is that, to quote a speech of Mr de Valera, "the erection of the Six-County area into a petty state" was

"a purely arbitrary act, inspired solely by considerations of British Imperial policy, and contrary to every interest of the Irish people. Imposed by force and maintained by subsidies, Partition is the worst of all the many crimes committed by British statesmen against the Irish people during the last 750 years".[99]

According to one of the *Mansion House Committee* pamphlets [a], "the fact that Ireland was a national unit was never questioned until a British government for its own purposes decided to cut the country into two parts". The "British ruling class and its extension, the colonial Ascendancy in Ireland", inspired by the old English political doctrine of *Divide and Rule*, first attempted to frustrate the Home Rule movement by playing on sectarian fears and prejudices among "the religious minority in the north-east". When finally national independence had to be conceded, sectarian fears had been so successfully aroused that six counties, which taken together had a pro-Partition majority, had to be excluded from the control of the new Dublin parliament.

The *Handbook of the Ulster Question* takes much the same line:

"The problem of North-east Ulster is unique in only one respect – it is the only religious minority in the world which has, through the assistance of powerful outside influences, been able to frustrate the organic development of the nation for more than a century, and then to insist on cutting off from the nation not only its own adherents but a large minority whose traditional allegiance was to the nation as a whole" [100]

As we have seen in Chapter 2, the German geographer, MÜLLER-ROSS, looks at the Partition problem in exactly the same way. Recently there have appeared a few essays by young Nationalist authors which display a quite different attitude to the Partition problem – and, as it seems to me, a more realistic one. They argue that the division of Ireland is "the result of a fundamental internal spiritual opposition". Of the geographers whom I have quoted in Chapter 2, N. C. MITCHEL and HANS DÖRRIES have expressed similar views.

DONAL BARRINGTON in his essay on *Uniting Ireland* stresses that it is quite misleading to say that Partition was forced on Ireland by the British government against the wishes of North and South. According to BARRINGTON it is more correct to say that Partition was forced on the British government by "the conflicting demands of the two parties of Irishmen".[101] JOHN HORGAN in his introduction to MICHAEL SHEEHY's *Divided We Stand* writes:

[a] Issued by the *All-Party Anti-Partition Conference* in Dublin in 1950 and distributed via official channels all over the world.

"To say that Partition was created, and is maintained, by England for ulterior motives, is .. untrue. On the contrary all the English parties without exception have sought at one time or another to find a solution, even to the extent of betraying their Northern adherents. It was only through the determined clash of rival Irish wills that Partition became inevitable".

And SHEEHY himself calls it "the most childish of evasions" and "the most ignoble of pretences" to place the responsibility for Partition on England, and to ignore "the many and fundamental differences which more than adequately explain the political division of Ireland".[102]

In the previous Chapter I have already examined "the determined clash of rival Irish wills" – having left it open to question whether this clash of wills was evoked or accentuated by English politicians. In this Chapter I propose to deal with some other of "the many and fundamental differences" between the people of Ireland, *i.e.* with certain differences in outlook and way of life. These 'mental' differences, however inexhaustible a theme of conversation and however important a factor in politics, have not yet evoked any systematic research. [a]

REGIONAL DIFFERENCES IN WAY OF LIFE

According to many observers, Irish and non-Irish, there are two 'regional' or 'national characters' in Ireland. Some others, however, maintain that there is one 'basic Irish' character with regional variations. As for myself, I do not think that there is any alleged 'typical Irish' characteristic which is not found among people outside Ireland, in Great Britain or on the continent. While leaving it open to question whether there exist regional or national characters[b], I do not deny that there are certain regional differences in habits, attitudes, norms, etc. – in other words, of personal outlook and way of life – in Ireland.

Before going into these subtle regional differences it is not amiss to make some reservations. Apart from the fact that these differences are rather intangible, it should be realized that the appreciation of these differences depends very much on the observer's attitude of mind and frame of reference, which are influenced by his personal background and other imponderables. And, of course, there is always room for a divergence of opinions as unity and difference always go hand in hand. Here an observation of LEWIS MUMFORD may be recalled:

"When one searches for unity, the human race is obviously one. When one looks for differences one discovers not only national types and regional types, one discovers likewise important differences between .. a Glasgow man and an Edinburgh man, even differences in language, accent, gesture, feeling, between villages that are but a day's walk apart. Finally, one reaches the primordial unit of individuality and realizes that no two identical finger prints of different persons have yet been discovered. Unity does not annul difference; and difference does not undermine a dynamic unity".[103]

[a] The literature, apart from occasional references in historical and geographical studies, biographies, books of travel, and other works, is hardly more than some essays. I have relied much on the opinion of a few ecclesiastics and some other people whose personal experience of the people north and south of the land boundary extends over most of a lifetime.

[b] For a discussion of various definitions of the term 'national character' and a review of the most important tendencies in contemporary research on this controversial subject, see DUIJKER and FRIJDA, *National Character and National Stereotypes*. Their book also contains a bibliography of nearly a thousand titles of studies on national character and national stereotypes.

In this Chapter I will concentrate upon those differences which are associated, in one way or another, with the north and the south of Ireland. Many people in Ireland connect differences in way of life with political contrasts. It has often struck me that 'Ulsterman' and 'Nationalist' are more than political concepts: both terms stand also for different 'mental types and attitudes'. The Ulsterman and the Nationalist in the political sense are in sharp contrast. The socio-psychological concepts of the Ulsterman and the Nationalist, however, cannot as easily be distinguished from each other. Mental characteristics are less tangible than candidly expressed political opinions. At any rate, this much is clear that the 'characters' of the Ulsterman and the Nationalist grade into each other.

There are people who prefer to speak of the 'Ulster' and the 'Irish' character. In their opinion the main 'Ulster' peculiarities are shared not only by the Ulster Unionists but, to a greater or less extent, by all inhabitants of Ulster, i.e. the English administrative province of nine counties. Other authors and informants speak of 'northern' and 'southern' characteristics, and accordingly of the 'northerner' and the 'southerner' as of two, more or less distinctive, 'personalities' or 'spiritual concepts'. This division is practically identical with that between the 'Ulster' and 'Irish' peculiarities as the traditional regional concepts of the 'north' and the 'south' approximate to the Ulster province and the rest of Ireland.

Some authors compare the people of Northern Ireland with those of the Republic. Since the land boundary was drawn it has, for the sake of convenience, become customary to project all sorts of traditional contrasts between the 'north' and the 'south' on the two political units (which I denote as the 'North' and the 'South', with capital letters). The identification of the traditional 'north' and 'south' concepts with the modern political units is justified only to some extent. In the present instance one could at best say that the North is dominated by 'northerners' and the South by 'southerners'.

In this Chapter I will deal with 'northerners' and 'southerners' (i.e. people living in the 'north' and the 'south' of Ireland), rather than with 'Northerners' and 'Southerners' (i.e. the people of Northern Ireland and the Republic respectively), or with 'Ulstermen' and 'Nationalists'.

THE 'NORTHERNER' AND THE 'SOUTHERNER'

Stereotypes which the southerners and the northerners hold about each other [a] and which various outsiders consider to be rather valid assertions are: "the northerner is dour", and "the southerner is easy-going". Many observers are inclined to call the northerners more obstinate and stubborn, more steadfast and 'dogged', and more austere and strict, than the southerners. Some say that the northerners are, on the average, more punctual, more law-abiding, and less unpredictable than the southerners. The former are also said to be less versatile and engaging than the latter, less courteous, and less given to flattery.[104]

It is often noted that it is in "the vigorous field of administration" that the northerner makes his mark rather than in the fine arts. As JOHN HARRISON says, Ulstermen are not

---

[a] Here by a 'stereotype' is understood: an apodictical and evaluative schematic judgment about a certain category of people, more or less generally held either by the same or by another population group (cf. DUIJKER and FRIJDA). These traditional opinions, however undifferentiated they may be, are useful because they form first approximations from which we can build more accurate judgments (cf. BRINTON, 67).

much given to the arts of poetry and oratory.[105] Expressive of their character, as EVANS sees it, is their habit of negative understatement. "It is immortalized in the political watchword of the North [*i.e.* the Ulstermen], *Not an Inch*, which the visitor will see chalked up in strange places; it will be accompanied by another slogan, similar in its emphatic brevity, *No Surrender*".[106] ST. JOHN ERVINE calls the Ulstermen "rocklike in their rigid attachments and extra-ordinarily unmoved by swift emotions, though quick in response to moods according with their principles".[107]

Sometimes the northerners are accused of being greedy. However, as LYNN DOYLE puts it, the northerners are no more greedy than the southerners, but the latter will spend more recklessly whereas the former will in general save, or spend more frugally. Occasionally it is said that on the whole the northerners are more provident whereas the southerners lean more on Providence.[108] An old saying in Ireland is that the southerner works to live whereas the northerner lives to work. Or, in the words of an ecclesiastic (who comes from Dublin but who lived for considerable time in the North), the southerner is more concerned with living and the northerner with making a living. [a] NICHOLAS MANSERGH (who also comes from the South) observes that the people of the Ulster province "lack neither a capacity for genuine hard work nor a determination to bring a difficult task to a successful conclusion".[109] The southerners are sometimes 'accused' of sheltering under the motto: "Sure it'll do".

It is suggested that the north-south difference is reflected in the retail trade. According to DOYLE it may be laid down as a rough rule that, while in the south the shopkeeper aims at a moderate turnover with a high profit, his northern colleague rather cuts profits and competes bitterly for turnover.[110] J. LOGAN suggests that the southerner will perhaps secure more orders as a commercial traveller by "his charming manner and gift of words", but his opposite number from the north will outdistance him "in persistence, punctuality in delivery and in keeping his promise".[111]

I give this selection of opinions for what they are worth. It is probable that some of these judgments will be challenged by future psychological research. Various authors, in order to illustrate the contrasts between the northerners and the southerners, have compared both population groups with continental people. A German notes that – although they speak the same language – the northerners and the southerners are as distinct from one another, in character and attitude towards life, as are 'Mecklenburgers' (people in northern Germany) and southern Italians.[112] This is rather far-fetched. It is not at all necessary to traverse the whole continent in search of contrasts which are more or less similar to the differences between the people of the north and the south of Ireland.

PADRAIC COLUM observes, with regard to the north-south contrasts in Ireland: "Every country, large or small, polarizes itself", in the sense that it makes itself a 'north' and a 'south'. There are indeed a series of countries which present such a polarization. It is of interest to see how some authors have framed this contrast. According to COLUM

---

[a] American economists (*Appraisal*, 80) recently referred to the fact that the actively voiced ambitions for economic expansion and betterment in the Republic are frequently qualified by "expressions of a conflicting, anti-materialist philosophy, of an asceticism that opposes material aspirations to spiritual goals, and hence writes down the former as unworthy". (In their opinion the first need in the Republic's economic programming is "for a clarification of aims, and for a confident and wholehearted commitment to their fulfilment".)

the north prides itself on "its progressiveness, its purposefulness, its practicality", and the south on "its traditionalism, its old-world grace, its loyalty to unprofitable causes".[113] According to JAMES WOODBURN the people in the north are marked by "energy, grit, and industry", and those in the south by "grace and courtesy". He compares the northern Irish with the Prussians in Germany, the Lombards in Italy, and the Yankees in the United States.[114]

It is not my task to attempt explanations of why there should be a more or less marked contrast between northerners and southerners in other countries than Ireland. Nor will I engage in an appreciation of the comparisons made between those countries and Ireland. It is sufficient to say that there is, generally speaking of course, a somewhat different approach to work in the north and in the south of Ireland; that the northerners on the whole radiate more energy than the southerners; and that the northerners pride themselves on their progressiveness, purposefulness, and practicality – like northerners in a number of other countries. In the following pages I shall look at some explanations of this difference often put forward in Ireland.

THE SCOTTISH PRESBYTERIAN TRADITION

How does one account for the dissimilarities between the northerners and the southerners in Ireland? One of the most popular explanations is that the northerners, at least many of them, are of a different 'race' from the 'Gaelic' or 'Irish' southerners. Here the term 'race' merely means 'people'. 'Gael' or 'Irish', like 'Scot' and 'Englishman', are cultural rather than 'racial' notions: none of the constituent peoples of the British Isles is 'racially pure'. [a] The 'racial' contrast between the north and the south would derive from the Plantation of Ulster by Scottish and English colonists in the seventeenth century, and from the preceding and contemporaneous – more spontaneous – influx of Scottish settlers into Cos Antrim and Down.

The late-sixteenth- and early-seventeenth-century immigrants have left their mark on the population no less heavily than on the landscape. [b] Undoubtedly, the Scottish is the stronger of the two traditions. "To this day, the traveller in Ulster will note influences that he can identify as Scotch". One of these influences is "a certain uncompromising

[a] As WALTER FITZGERALD (Europe, 16) observes: "The racial composition of the British and Irish peoples illustrates the falsity of any theory that nationality is derived from community of race". He also notes that the often expressed view, which differentiates the Irish nationality from the English on grounds of racial divergence, "results from a complete lack of appreciation of the very similar racial histories of the two peoples".

[b] Some of the northern towns still show in their morphology clear evidence of the intermingling of the Scottish and English colonists with the pre-Plantation population. Carrickfergus (Co. Antrim) and Downpatrick (Co. Down), for instance, have 'Irish' and 'Scottish' quarters and a 'Church district' which originally was inhabited by (Episcopalian) English.

The three cultural strands are also recognizable in the countryside. The many little differences which usually exist between one rural district and another are often emphasized by differences due to the cultural heritage of the three population groups. EVANS (Portrait, 64) points to the apple orchards and rose gardens of Co. Armagh and the Lagan valley where 'West Country English' settled; to "the virtual absence of gardens from the Irish districts, compensated along the coasts by a profusion of flowering fuchsia hedges"; and to "the better kept hedges and neat stone-dykes of the Scottish areas, clean and 'Protestant-looking', as the phrase goes" (cf. HUME, Elements, 117-8).

dourness of character, allied with a dry humour".[115] The northerner's alleged shrewdness is but one of his traits which are generally explained as a Scottish heritage. One also thinks of his lack of feeling for the fine arts.[116] It is even pointed out that, if the northerner excels as a fighting-man, it is because he has the dash of an Irishman in taking a position and the determination of the Scot in holding it. The official War history of Northern Ireland states that to "the fierce recklessness of the Irishman" he not rarely adds "the grim determination of the Scot".[117]

It is clear that the north-south contrast cannot be explained without taking full account of the large-scale immigration of Scots into the Ulster province during the seventeenth century. A fact which is often overlooked is that prior to the seventeenth century the north had already received considerable numbers of Scottish immigrants. This influx, perhaps, affords some explanation of the fact that the so-called Scottish traits in the northern character are not exclusive to the descendants of the seventeenth-century immigrants. (There has also been some immigration by English – Anglo-Normans – in the Middle Ages, mainly into south-east Co. Down.)

On the other hand, there was also notable immigration from Great Britain into the south, at least since the Anglo-Norman invasion at the end of the twelfth century. I need only point to the Pale, the great English colony on the east coast, and to the many mediaeval English towns in the south. The majority of those immigrants came from England; the others came mainly from Wales. [a] There is no evidence of any substantial immigration by Scots into the south.

The reason for the difference in mental type and pattern of living between the northerners and the southerners is also sought frequently in the predominance of Protestantism in the north, and more especially in the strong influence of Presbyterianism – just as the difference between the people in the northern part and those in the southern part of the Netherlands is frequently ascribed to (or at least considered to be connected with) the fact that the former are mostly Protestant (Presbyterian) and the latter predominantly Roman Catholic.[118] One of the authors who thinks this way is SEAN O'FAOLAIN (a Southern Nationalist).[119] When noting that the north and the south have "very different ideas as to what is worth while in this life", he points to religion – "meaning a different focus of the mind". [b]

Many observers, Irishmen as well as foreigners, associate the most marked characteristics of the northerner – such as his self-assertion, his robustness and his sturdiness –

---

[a] In 1612 it was stated that "there have been so many English colonies in Ireland, as that, if the people were numbered at this day by the poll, such as are descended of English race would be found more in number than the ancient natives." In 1640 it was stated that the Irish people were "now for the most part descended of British ancestors" (WOODBURN, 23). In Parts III and IV I will dwell at length on the various population movements into the south and the north.

[b] According to O'FAOLAIN (*Journey*, 242), nowhere can one see that contrast better than in Strabane (Co. Tyrone) and Lifford (Co. Donegal): "Two communities more different spiritually, while so close to each other geographically, would be hard to imagine". Of Enniskillen (Co. Fermanagh) he says: "Like all Northern towns it has the sturdy, clean, smart, efficient air of an English market-town. It has the same reticence, too, and the same heaviness. The contrast between it and, say, Sligo is the contrast between two foreign countries" (239). And of Coleraine (Co. Londonderry): "one of the cleanest market-towns in these islands, solid and bright and comfortable. .. I felt myself at a great distance from home in Coleraine" (253).

with those of the Protestant, more especially the Calvinist (Presbyterian), rather than with the Roman Catholic.[120] As almost all Protestants are of seventeenth-century Scottish and English descent, the two most common explanations of the northerner's distinctive character – 'race' and 'religion' – come to virtually the same thing.

The conclusion that the Scottish tradition in Ulster is more pronounced than the English corresponds with the conclusion that Presbyterianism has exercised the dominant influence on mental type and pattern of living – as it has done in Scotland. As WALLACE NOTESTEIN says: "That hard Presbyterianism did more than any factor to create the disciplined Scot of today, the Scot of stern moral convictions and sober conduct". It was, for instance, their Church government which gave them experience in making their own choices as to who would govern them.[121] These observations apply just as much to the Scottish Presbyterians who settled in Ulster. T. W. MOODY says:

"The stronghold of Ulster Protestants has always been the Presbyterian Church, rooted in the Scottish Reformation and maintaining close and continuous contact with Scotland. Probably the most important social institution of Protestant Ulster, it is the only large Church in Ulster whose members are concentrated in the province and whose structure and government are provincial".[122]

What MORAY MCLAREN says with regard to present-day Scotland holds almost equally good for present-day Ulster, or rather Northern Ireland:

"Modern Scotland may be far from being entirely Presbyterian, Protestant, or even entirely Christian, but it is a Scotland which was fashioned and is still shaped by the Protestant Reformation and the Presbyterian Kirk".[123]

PROTESTANT AND CATHOLIC NORTHERNERS

The observant traveller in the north can often distinguish those districts which are predominantly Roman Catholic or Protestant. Broadly speaking the Catholic farms, whether great or small, are less well kept, the houses less tidy. Protestants in general seem to be, as the phrase goes, more 'houseproud': they are keen on cleanliness. The others would seem to care less for those things. The difference in appearance does not hold good in all cases. As DESMOND FENNELL notes in his essay on *The Northern Catholic*[124]: "There are slovenly Protestants in Co. Fermanagh and in some areas the Catholics have learned the virtues of thrift and orderliness from their Presbyterian neighbours". [a]

[a] The upland areas are usually occupied by Roman Catholics. These areas were never systematically settled by the seventeenth-century Protestant immigrants, and they therefore became 'reservations' for the 'native' population. The immigrants as a rule preferred the lowland areas: they drained and cultivated great tracts of land which were at that time thinly populated. In many lowland districts, however, Catholic families are mingled with Protestant ones. Sometimes it is alleged that these areas at the time of the Plantation were bogs which, like the mountains, "had least to offer to the cupidity of conquerors", and therefore were occupied by Roman Catholic refugees (HUME, *Elements*, 116). This is a simplification. Apart from later changes in the distribution of Protestants and Catholics – some areas have lost a very considerable part of the Protestant population – various lowland districts always remained, as Nationalists usually say, "in Irish hands". I would rather say that they remained "in Catholic hands" for not all inhabitants were 'Irish'; many were descendants of mediaeval immigrants from Great Britain.

One of the flat regions where Roman Catholics predominate, and which are "well-to-do and progressive" (FENNELL), is the barony of Lecale, a fertile peninsula in south-east Co. Down. This region was colonized at the end of the twelfth century by Anglo-Normans (cf. Chapter 11). Although these

Northerners – irrespective of their creed – sometimes lay great stress on the mental differences between the two denominational groups. The reason is obvious: a northern Protestant is almost inevitably an Ulsterman (in the modern political sense of the word), and a northern Catholic an Irish Nationalist. But the "different qualities of character" of the two groups shade into each other. The extremes are typified by the stereotypes which the two groups hold about each other. According to W. R. Rodgers:

> "The Catholic is a charming and courteous person, open in manner and eloquent in speech. His faults are those of volatility; 'easy come, easy go'. 'A glib person', says the Protestant. .. The Ulster Protestant is a cautious, logical and far-seeing person in speech and action, and he distrusts eloquence. His virtue is that of stability. 'A stiff person', says the Catholic".[125]

If people in the north are inclined rather to emphasize the contrasts between the two denominations, people in the south often have a keener eye for what the northerners have in common. The opinions of many of my informants from the south correspond more or less to Eoin MacNeill's view that the northern Catholic is "hardly less grave, sedate, unresponsive, taciturn, laconic, keen at a bargain, tenacious of his own, critical towards others, than the typical Ulster Presbyterian".[126] Many a southern Catholic regards his northern co-religionist as being 'sharper' and more businesslike than himself. The northern Catholics may be as hospitable and charitable as their southern co-religionists but they have a 'hard core' which is not found in the south.[127] These opinions are, to some degree, paralleled by the views expressed by Protestants from the south. As they see it, their northern co-religionists are on the whole more dogmatic and pugnacious. [a]

In their turn northern Catholics find their southern co-religionists "sometimes feckless, sometimes charming but unreliable".[128] The 'northerness' of the northern Catholics is reflected, perhaps, in the vigour of Northern nationalism. The "rigid and uncompromising attitude" of the Northern Nationalists and the "grim determination" of the Ulstermen are well matched. It is clear that, if both sections of the population of Northern Ireland have anything in common, it is their concern with politics and religion. One may perhaps say that in those areas where Northerners, or northerners generally, most vehemently disagree, *viz.* politics and religion, they are bound together by their common deep concern with those matters. [b]

---

settlers remained Roman Catholics (like nearly all the mediaeval settlers), they were left undisturbed during the Plantation. As Buchanan has shown, the barony still preserves many features of 'Anglo-Norman culture' (*Isle Lecale*, 22). He suggests that a particular technique of thatching, found in Lecale, locally referred to as 'English thatch' (as distinct from the 'Irish thatch'), is part of the mediaeval heritage, introduced by English craftsmen of Anglo-Norman times (*Thatch*, 27). In many respects this district indeed resembles the Pale north of Dublin.

[a] Most Protestants in the south are Episcopalians of English descent, many of whom rather dislike "the puritanical expression of Protestantism" which prevails in the north. According to some observers Episcopalianism in the north has more Calvinistic (Presbyterian) traits than in the south. It is, I think, fair to say that the more Catholic-thinking Episcopalians feel more at home in the south with its "Roman atmosphere", whereas 'Low Church' Episcopalians would find the more Calvinistic atmosphere of the north more congenial. (In Dublin the Holy Week and the Saint's Days are observed by the whole community; in Belfast there is less emphasis on the Church's Calendar.)

[b] Catholics and Protestants alike often take great pains to find out the religion of a stranger or, as they say, "with which foot he digs". This oblique way of referring to someone's religious conviction goes back to the seventeenth century. As Evans has explained, the old Irish spade is operated with the right foot,

In this respect one can at any rate endorse MOODY's conclusion that "Protestant Ulster is not just an outlying part of British society nor is Catholic Ulster indistinguishable from the rest of Catholic Ireland". MOODY also observes that "some of the attributes of a common society have long existed in Ulster speech (though it is English) [a], in Ulster humour, in a certain stern and realistic attitude to life".[129]

I incline to J. WHITE's view that, in the absence of political tension, both northern Protestants and Catholics would feel "a sense of regional fellowship, a sense of difference from southerners, that mixture of contempt and defensiveness that is typical of the strongly-marked provincial character" of Ulster.[130] There is little of a sense of regional fellowship, or of what may be called a 'positive regional consciousness', which embraces both denominations. Both population groups, however, harbour a sense of difference from southerners.

It is beyond doubt that this 'negative regional consciousness' is far more vivid among Protestants than among Catholics. At any rate, a Protestant will more frankly admit such feelings whereas a Catholic will rather repress them. But, of course, the northern Protestants (especially the Presbyterians) have very few sentimental ties with the south whereas the northern Catholics have many. One could even say, perhaps, that Ulsterism has drawn much from this 'negative regional consciousness' whereas Irish nationalism to some extent has suffered from it. It has been suggested that the fact that the Northern Nationalists have so long refrained from allying themselves with either *Fine Gael* or *Fianna Fáil*, the two main political parties in the Republic, can be attributed to their essential difference in character from the southerners.[131]

THE CORE OF THE NORTH

The preceding Sections have shown that, so far as 'race' is concerned', the northern traits are seen most clearly in the people of Scottish descent. So far as 'religion' is concerned, we may say that the northern characteristics are seen most clearly in the Protestants, more particularly in the Presbyterians – in fact, those northerners who claim ancestry from the seventeenth-century Scottish immigrants. This analysis poses the question of how to delimit 'the north' as a socio-cultural region.

It is true that, as WHITE says, "the northern heritage" is not by any means exclusive to the six counties of Northern Ireland. "It is shared, to a greater or less extent, by all the

---

whereas the 'Ulster spade', derived from styles introduced by Protestant immigrants in Plantation times, is normally used with the left loof (*Portrait*, 27).

There are many other phrases which *both* sections use for distinguishing their friends from their foes in order to maintain segregation, such as: "What school was he at?", and "Is he the right colour?", *i.e.* orange or green? (cf. *The Irish Times*, Nov. 28, 1959).

[a] The speech of Ulster is generally recognized as being distinct from that of each of the other regions of the British Isles. It resembles the English spoken in Canada. Like that and other overseas varieties of English it is, as G. B. ADAMS has shown, the result of a mixture of divergent types of English and has arisen only in recent times. Ulster English is, as ADAMS puts it (61-2), "a reblending of two divergent streams of one original language" (the same applies to Ulster Gaelic which is of mixed Irish and Scottish origin). Ulster English represents a combination of "a northward thrust from the Pale" and "a more gradual and widespread southwestward expansion from the southern half of Scotland".

nine counties of Ulster".[132] All those counties have witnessed a considerable influx of Scots, either prior or during the seventeenth century.[a] (In comparison with this movement the number of Scottish immigrants into the rest of Ireland is negligible.) But there is no doubt that the most Scottish part is east Ulster (Cos Antrim and Down with Belfast) and neighbouring districts of Cos Londonderry and Tyrone – in fact, those parts of Ulster which are nearest Scotland.

Ancestry, however, is very difficult to establish and therefore it is of little help for a more precise definition of the north. Religion is a more useful criterion in that the denominations of the people are known from the census reports – though, so far as Northern Ireland is concerned, by county and county borough only. Tables 3 (p. 65) and 4 confirm the opinion that the 'core' of the north is east Ulster. The rest of Northern Ireland (Cos Londonderry, Tyrone, Fermanagh, and Armagh), together with the three Southern Border Counties (Cos. Donegal, Cavan, and Monaghan), may be considered as a broad transition zone in which the north gradually loses its identity.

R. P. McDermott and D. A. Webb in their demographic study of Irish Protestantism also divide Northern Ireland into two sections: (1) the 'Belfast area', which is roughly the districts within a thirty-mile radius of the city (i.e. east Ulster, excluding north Co. Antrim and south Co. Down, but including north Co. Armagh); and (2) the rest. In their opinion, conditions in the remainder of Northern Ireland are closer in nearly every way to those found in the Republic. "When people talk of Ulster and its characteristics it is generally the Belfast area which they have in mind. Densely populated, highly industrialized, and Presbyterian in its atmosphere, it is the predominant partner of the two".[133]

According to many observers, Irish and non-Irish, contrasts between the northerners and the southerners express themselves most clearly in the people of the two capital cities, Belfast and Dublin. It is indeed natural enough to regard the Belfastmen as "the most typical northerners". As Demangeon says: "Belfast, lying opposite Scotland, is itself a Scottish town both by the origin of its inhabitants and the character of its industries".[134]

For the moment I will leave the question open as to whether we have as much right to consider the Dubliners as the most typical southerners. [b] (For the definition of the core of the south the religious criterion is of no use as practically all southerners are Roman Catholics.) Dublin's atmosphere is English rather than Gaelic. Demangeon rightly noted: "Dublin, which faces England is an Anglo-Saxon capital city and the

---

[a] It is perhaps significant that the modern Donegal Irish word for Protestant is 'Albanach', literally: Scotsman. (On the other hand, the *Protestant Lane* in Dublin was renamed on the streetsign: *Raedh Na Sacsan*, literally: Englishman's lane.)

[b] It is well to remember that the two cities have strongly contrasting histories. Dublin is a mediaeval English city, whereas Belfast at the beginning of the seventeenth century was a tiny village and at the beginning of the eighteenth century still "a remote provincial town" (*Social Life*, 21). Dublin in the eighteenth century was the second city in the British Isles, and "the seventh in Christendom", and – according to a visitor – "there never was so splendid a metropolis in so poor a country" (Carty, *Ireland 1783-1850*, xxii). Dublin still has a 'residential atmosphere'. This is to be attributed in no small part to the aristocratic architecture of the eighteenth-century Ascendancy class: "Georgian Dublin still provides a framework of frozen dignity for the central nucleus which remains the focus of the city's life" (*View of Ireland* 237). Belfast, on the other hand, is essentially "a successful nineteenth-century city" (*Social Life*, 26-7).

Table 4. The population of Ireland by religious denominations (percentage distribution), by county, county borough or province, at the census of 1911.

	Population 000	Roman Catholic	Episcopalian	Presbyterian	Methodist	Other
Co. Antrim	193.9	20.5	21.7	50.1	2.0	5.7
Belfast C.B.	386.9	24.1	30.5	33.7	6.2	5.5
Co. Down	204.3	31.6	23.0	38.0	2.2	5.2
East Ulster	*785.1*	*25.1*	*26.4*	*38.9*	*4.1*	*5.5*
Co. Londonderry	99.8	41.5	20.1	34.3	0.8	3.3
Londonderry C.B.	40.8	56.2	17.6	21.3	2.9	2.0
Co. Tyrone	142.7	55.4	22.7	18.6	2.0	1.3
Co. Fermanagh	61.8	56.2	34.2	2.0	6.5	1.1
Co. Armagh	120.3	45.3	32.5	15.8	4.2	2.2
Northern Border Counties	*465.4*	*50.0*	*25.7*	*19.3*	*3.0*	*2.0*
Co. Donegal	168.5	78.9	10.7	8.9	1.0	0.5
Co. Cavan	91.2	81.5	14.2	3.1	0.9	0.3
Co. Monaghan	71.5	74.7	12.2	11.9	0.6	0.6
Southern Border Counties	*331.2*	*78.7*	*12.0*	*7.9*	*0.9*	*0.5*
Dublin Co. and C.B.	477.2	78.8	16.5	1.8	1.0	1.9
Rest of Leinster	684.8	89.7	9.0	0.6	0.4	0.3
Munster	1,035.5	94.0	4.9	0.4	0.4	0.3
Connacht	611.0	96.2	3.1	0.4	0.2	0.1
Rest of Ireland	*2,808.5*	*90.9*	*7.5*	*0.7*	*0.4*	*0.5*
Total Ireland	4,390.2	73.9	13.1	10.0	1.4	1.6

headquarters of English culture".[135] As O'FAOLAIN put it: you feel no jar in arriving in Dublin from London, as you may, without a jar, cross back from "clanging Belfast" to "clanging Glasgow".[136]

On the stage the Belfastman is usually portrayed as a bourgeois, a man who lacks 'culture' (or at least refinement), a man whose religion consists in "objecting to the religion of other people", and a man who is "wholly occupied in making money". HUGH SHEARMAN admits that "a love of the practical and tangible" is very strong in Belfast.[137] The Dubliners do not seem to bother so much about material things. If "Belfast people are reserved and stolid for the most part, Dublin folk are lively, sociable and friendly", LOGAN observes. If people "rush and hustle" in Belfast, in Dublin they merely stroll.[138] And from my own experience I may say that time does not mean in Dublin so much as it does in Belfast.

According to a publication of the Dublin government, the atmosphere of Belfast is one of "hard work and self-denial" which the visitor will find "grim or tonic according to his temperament".[139] While, as O'FAOLAIN says, there is "an atmosphere of profitable commerce" about the shipyards and factories of Belfast, "a tradition of metropolitan dignity and opulence still glows from the slightly decrepit Georgian face of Dublin".[140] An old saying in Ireland is: "Dublin *is* the capital but Belfast *has* the capital", that is in the sense of owning the money. [a] The contrast between the two cities is aptly summed up by LOGAN who calls Dublin "Grecian and artistic" and Belfast "Romanesque and utilitarian".[141]

THE LAND BOUNDARY AS A CULTURAL DIVIDE

In conclusion we may say that the Irish land boundary represents, however arbitrarily, an important spiritual divide. This regional divide is, essentially, a broad transition zone which, for the sake of convenience, may be considered to coincide with the area of seven Border counties, four in Northern Ireland and three in the Republic. The north-south contrast is most marked in the field of religion (cf. Fig. 8) and as such it has become ever more marked as a result of heavy emigration of Protestants from the South since the setting-up of the Free State in 1921, or rather since the beginning of the Anglo-Irish guerilla warfare and the boycot-actions in 1919. The land boundary itself, too, has become more pronounced as a dividing line as a result of the movement of quite a number of Southern Ulstermen from the Southern Border Counties into Northern Ireland.

According to the census returns the number of Protestants in the South has fallen by just over one-half between 1911 and 1946 (cf. Tables 5 and 6). As may be inferred from Tables 7 and 8, this decline still continues. The great reduction in their membership in the Republic – which has been set off by an increase in Northern Ireland – presents the Protestant Churches with many problems.

The Presbyterian Church recently decided to group together all presbyteries south of the land boundary in one synod. This radical measure did not, as was stated, result from a desire to partition the Church. It was designed to help to dispel "the present atmosphere of apathy and hopelessness among Presbyterians in Eire" as it was to provide "some effective means of letting Presbyterians in the Republic work out together the general problems and vocations with which they are faced through living in different political conditions, from the great bulk of the Church".[142]

According to McDERMOTT and WEBB, the Presbyterian Church has in many ways suffered less from the changes in the distribution of its members than has the (Episcopalian) Church of Ireland:

"The environment of the latter has hitherto been the whole island, and its administrative centre has necessarily been Dublin. The environment, the native territory of Presbyterianism has always been the North-eastern corner of Ireland. It could to-day lose its whole membership outside the Six Counties without any profound alteration of its essential structure, without suffering any organic modification. It would be weakened by such a loss, but not transformed. But the changes in the distribution of the members of the Church of Ireland might, if they were to continue, entail very important modifications of its whole character and ethos. .. The Church of Ulster would not be the same as the Church of Ireland".[143]

[a] In Scotland the phrase goes that Edinburgh may be the capital but Glasgow has the capital. There are indeed some parallels between Edinburgh and Dublin, as there are many between Glasgow and Belfast.

Table 5. The population of the Irish Republic by religious denomination (in thousands and percentage distribution), at each census since 1911.

	1911 000	1926 000	1936 000	1946 000	1946 1911=100
Roman Catholic	2,812.5	2,751.3	2,773.9	2,786.0	99
Episcopalian	249.6	164.2	145.0	124.8	50
Presbyterian	45.5	32.4	28.1	23.9	53
Methodist	16.4	10.7	9.6	8.4	51
Other	15.7	13.4	11.8	12.0	76
Total Irish Republic	3,139.7	2,972.0	2,968.4	2,955.1	94
	%	%	%	%	
Roman Catholic	89.6	92.6	93.4	94.3	
Episcopalian	8.0	5.5	4.9	4.2	
Presbyterian	1.4	1.1	1.0	0.8	
Methodist	0.5	0.4	0.3	0.3	
Other	0.5	0.4	0.4	0.4	
Total Irish Republic	100	100	100	100	

Table 6. Percentage of non-Roman Catholics in the population of the Irish Republic by county or province, at each census since 1911.

	1911	1926	1936	1946
Co. Donegal	21.1	18.1	16.5	14.7
Co. Cavan	18.5	15.9	14.5	13.1
Co. Monaghan	25.3	21.5	18.9	16.8
Southern Border Cos	*21.3*	*18.2*	*16.5*	*14.7*
Dublin Co. and C.B.	21.3	14.2	11.5	9.7
Rest of Leinster	10.3	6.9	6.2	5.3
Munster	6.0	3.6	3.1	2.7
Connacht	3.8	2.6	2.3	2.0
Rest of Republic	*9.1*	*6.2*	*5.5*	*4.8*
Total Irish Republic	10.4	7.4	6.6	5.7

The two authors dread that if their Church continues to shrink into what they call "a Six-County body", "the awareness of all Ireland as its environment and the consciousness of the Anglo-Irish cultural tradition might weaken almost to the point of extinction".[144] According to another Episcopalian author, "there is no essential northernism or southernism in this national church".[145] As it appears to me, a considerable part of the members of the Episcopalian Church in the North have already become very much 'regionalized' in their outlook, in the sense that today they feel more congenial to the

Table 7. The number of families in the Presbyterian Church in Ireland by county aggregate (percentage distribution), at each decade since 1919.

	1919 %	1929 %	1939 %	1949 %	1959 %	1959 1919= 100
Belfast C.B.	29.4	32.7	34.1	35.3	38.6	183
Rest East Ulster	39.2	39.3	39.3	39.7	38.6	137
Northern Border Counties	20.7	19.9	19.4	19.0	17.6	118
Northern Ireland	*89.3*	*91.9*	*92.8*	*94.0*	*94.8*	*148*
Southern Border Counties	6.8	5.0	4.3	3.5	3.0	62
Dublin C.B. and Co.	1.8	1.6	1.6	1.5	1.3	101
Rest of Republic	2.1	1.5	1.3	1.0	0.9	50
Irish Republic	*10.7*	*8.1*	*7.2*	*6.0*	*5.2*	*66*
Total Ireland	100	100	100	100	100	139
Numbers	89,979	93,950	98,056	107,323	125,033	

Table 8. The number of members (including junior members) of the Society of the Methodist Church in Ireland by county aggregate (percentage distribution), at each decade since 1919.

	1919 %	1929 %	1939 %	1949 %	1959 %	1959 1919= 100
East Ulster	37.5	49.7	54.9	58.6	62.1	228
Northern Border Counties	28.0	26.1	24.4	23.8	23.8	117
Northern Ireland	*65.5*	*75.8*	*79.3*	*82.4*	*85.9*	*181*
Southern Border Counties	9.5	6.1	4.8	4.3	3.1	44
Dublin C.B. and Co.	8.9	7.3	7.1	6.3	5.6	86
Rest of Republic	16.1	10.8	8.8	7.0	5.4	46
Irish Republic	*34.5*	*24.2*	*20.7*	*17.6*	*14.1*	*56*
Total Ireland	100	100	100	100	100	137
Numbers	35,625	41,813	44,132	46,212	48,924	

'Ulster tradition' than to the 'Anglo-Irish tradition'.[a] (Some Northern Episcopalians criticize what they call "the top-heavy influence of the clergy in the Dublin area to the detriment of the populous Ulster parishes"[146], alleging that in this case the tail is wagging

[a] This certainly does not apply to the Episcopalian clergy and dignitaries. Most of the clergymen come from the South (a few years ago more than three-quarters). Explanations are: (1) the Southern Episcopalians are on the whole more educated and well-to-do than the Northern; (2) the lack of opportunities in other professions in the South leads to more students for the ministry; (3) the influence of the Roman Catholic environment with its emphasis on "the privilege of a son in the priesthood"; and (4) the clergy are trained in Dublin.

the dog. [a] Indeed, the land boundary is becoming as much of a reality in ecclesiastical life as it is in politics. [b]

However palpable the land boundary (zone) may be as a spiritual divide, it is not in every respect a cultural divide. The North and the South, or rather the Ulstermen and the Nationalists, may not share the same religion and political loyalties but they have various things in common. For instance, both sides share an interest in history – mythology perhaps rather than history – but labourer and professional man are equally interested. Whether as heroes or villains, the same historical figures are well-known to all Irishmen. A Twelfth of July procession and meeting is much the same as a Southern equivalent: there is the same addiction to bands, rhetoric and drinking – though the sentiments are different. [c] And there is what I might call the notion of morality common to both sides. [d]

But the people of Ireland have also many things in common with people in Great Britain. I have often wondered whether there is anything typically Irish, or Northern and Southern Irish, which is not found in Great Britain. At any rate, there are many basic similarities between the two islands. These similarities are often overlooked by authors on Ireland because most Irishmen – and certainly most Englishmen – take them for granted. An outsider, however, cannot but observe them.

CRANE BRINTON (an American), for instance, notes that no one can travel in Ireland without realizing that "the Irish really have absorbed a good deal from their long life in common with the English". (He adds: "Or perhaps they never were very wild" – which refers to the image generations of English had of the Irish.) The absorption is most apparent from the fact that the language remains English – "with a brogue, perhaps, but still English: you can travel a long way in Eire without hearing a word of Gaelic". [147] FENNELL (who comes from the South) even says that:

"Though the life of the people in Ireland – and in particular in the Republic of Ireland – has characteristics of its own, these characteristics do not make Irish life [e] more than a regional variant of life within

[a] There are some Episcopalians who maintain that there should be a second entry into the clergy in the North. Apart from the fact that the Church is too small for two clerical training colleges, some Church authorities think that it would do Northern students some good to spend a few years in Dublin. Other Episcopalians take offence at the fact that Belfast has never been considered worthy of a bishopric – although at least one of its many parishes is more populous than some Southern dioceses (cf. *Belfast Telegraph*, Aug. 6, 1960).

[b] The land boundary also affects the Methodist Church. For instance, there is a tendency to bring ministers with children or who suffer from bad health into the North and unmarried ministers or childless couples into the South taking account of the differences between educational and health service facilities in the North and the South.

[c] Some popular 'patriotic' songs of the Ulstermen are sung to traditional Irish tunes whereas at least one Nationalist song is sung to a (Lowland) Scottish tune, *viz.* the best known of all Nationalist songs, *The Wearing of the Green*.

[d] One only needs to compare any Belfast or Dublin paper with English equivalents. The Irish notion seems to me more akin to the Scottish than the English. A native *Daily Mirror* or *News of the World* does not seem possible in Belfast any more than in Dublin. The attitude to divorce, pornography, etc., is the same north and south of the land boundary, though the legal position differs. The Speaker of the Northern Ireland parliament recently complimented a Nationalist member on raising the issue of some imported 'obscene' books.

[e] FENNELL uses the word 'Irish' to refer to what he calls "the oldest and truest Irish, the present carrier-group of Irish destiny – the Irish Catholic peasantry, whether living in the cities, towns or countryside".

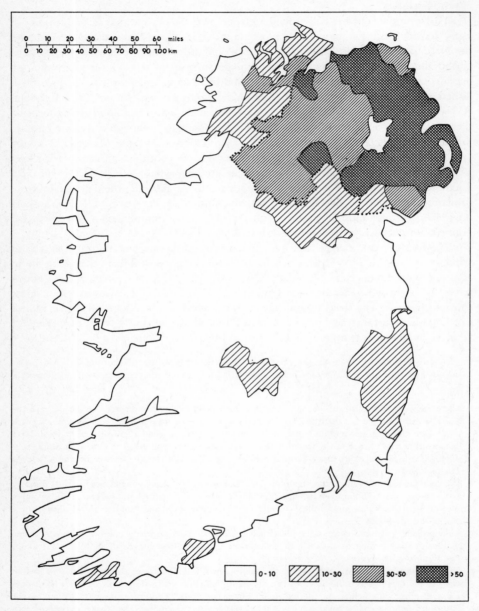

FIG. 8. Percentage of Protestants in the population of Ireland by rural district, for the year 1946 (after FREEMAN, *Ireland*, 157)

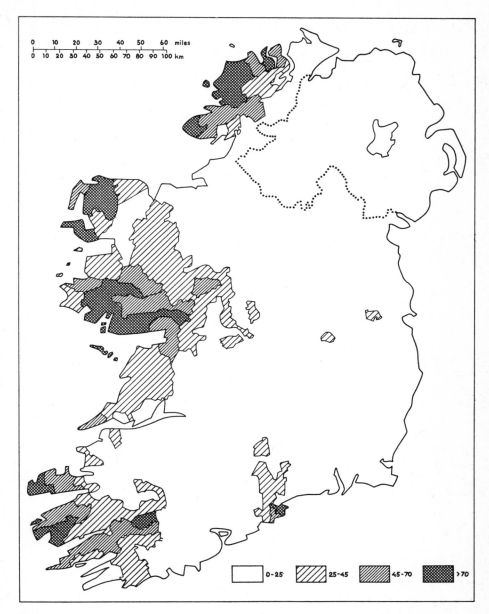

FIG. 9. Percentage of Irish speakers in the population of the Irish Republic by dispensary district, for the year 1946 (after *Census of Population of Ireland*, General Report, 203)

the British Isles. The flavour of Yorkshire life is very different from that of the Scottish Highlands or the English South-East: the 'local flavour' of Irish life is not any greater in degree".[148]

This is a rather brutal avowal, at least for a (Southern) Irishman. After all, the Republic is politically independent; neither Yorkshire nor the Highlands are – whatever the reason.

In the next Chapter I propose to examine the degree to which Ireland and Great Britain form a cultural unity. (Great Britain will be taken into account only in so far as it is relevant for the discussion of Irish cultural features.) First I will discuss how FREEMAN in his general and regional geography of Ireland has valued the human associations of the two islands. Special attention must be given to the Republic for it is a separate state – a fact which is often taken as to imply that in many respects the South is totally different in its human characteristics. In fact, the Republic in many ways fosters this impression. Here one thinks first and foremost of the language policy.

Chapter 7

THE UNITY OF THE BRITISH ISLES

SOME DIFFERENCES BETWEEN IRELAND AND GREAT BRITAIN

The foreign traveller who, coming from England, sets foot on Irish soil in or near Dublin, finds himself in an apparently familiar world. He will readily agree with MORITZ BONN that "Everything around him bears the features which he became familiar with in England; everything is like England, although it seems to be a somewhat disordered England". BONN, however, takes the view that this similarity is only superficial. It does not take a long time, he says, to recognize that "this English shell conceals a kernel of an entirely different nature".[149] His conclusion is shared, to some extent, by another German author who suggests that England and Ireland are connected materially rather than spiritually.[150]

FREEMAN expresses a similar view of the human associations of the two islands. In the introduction to his textbook he states that from writing this work he has "learned beyond doubt that Ireland is a fundamentally different country from either England, Wales or Scotland".[151] Later FREEMAN remarks that "Ireland is itself a natural unity, differing in its social geography from even its nearest neighbours, in spite of its long-continued contacts with them through invasions, trade and population movements".[152] Historically, he says, Ireland has "a clear individuality that reflects its distinctive space relations, for it is not now and probably never could have been made merely a detached fragment of an entity known as the British Isles". FREEMAN recognizes that there are similarities in the physical environment, but, he continues:

"As soon as the human landscape comes to the mind's eye contrasts emerge, for the farms are smaller, the towns farther apart, and industry everywhere of less significance than in Britain, if one excludes the city of Belfast and its hinterland. And there are deeper contrasts still, not least in religious allegiance, in social customs and in outlook which, though varied from one person or group to another, inevitably reflect a difference both of historical development from Britain and hardly less of the impact of current world problems and struggles on the country".[153]

FREEMAN admits that Ireland has qualities in common with the western or Atlantic side of Great Britain, but, he concludes, it is nevertheless "sharply distinct" from it. "Even the north-east, though part of the United Kingdom, has a social complexion quite different from that of Scotland, and a rural landscape of small farms that is peculiarly its own".[154] Ireland's "clearest claim to uniqueness" – still according to the same author – is its population history: "in a century of vast world population increase, the number of its people at home has fallen almost to half". This population decline makes Ireland "a land unique in Europe – perhaps in the world".[155]

FREEMAN is obviously right when he stresses various differences between Ireland and Great Britain. But are the two islands as fundamentally different as he suggests? As far as the 'cultural landscape' is concerned: in Great Britain there are also areas where farms are small, the towns far apart, and where industry is of little importance. England is undoubtedly better cultivated, better drained and better wooded than Ireland but the same applies to great parts of Wales and Scotland. The American, CRANE BRINTON's observation seems to me to be more appropriate:

"The 'look of the land' in Ireland is not wholly different from that in Great Britain, and indeed suggests regional and local variations in the British [Isles] scene rather than a different order of human geography".[156]

Nor is Ireland's demographic history unique, certainly to nothing like the degree which FREEMAN would have. Apart from the fact that Ireland is not the only European island which has witnessed a declining population (cf. Corsica), there are large parts of Great Britain which have lost a considerable proportion of their population since the eighteen 'fifties – and are still experiencing a net outward movement.[157] On the other hand, not all parts of Ireland have lost population over the last hundred years. In fact, some parts, east Ulster and the Dublin area, have gained population in this period.

Population decline in rural Ireland can be largely explained by the migration to urban and industrial districts, often using small country towns as stepping stones. This is a phenomenon which can be observed all over Europe. In Ireland's case the two main cities, Dublin and Belfast, are not able to absorb all the 'rural drift'. The surplus moves on to the urban districts across the Channel. From the very beginning of the Industrial Revolution there has been a continuous flow of people from the Irish countryside – as from rural districts in Scotland and England – into (and via) Merseyside and Clydeside (the Liverpool and Glasgow areas) and other urban districts in Great Britain.[158] The fact that practically the whole population surplus of Ireland goes to Great Britain epitomizes, more clearly perhaps than anything else, the socio-economic integration of the two islands.

Today Ireland sends about 60 to 65,000 persons per year to Great Britain. Approximately 50,000 come from the Republic – because of the lack of frontier control no exact figures are available. [a] The number of people from the Republic who have migrated to Great Britain since 1921 probably amounts to one million. Statistically these migrants are 'emigrants' as the Republic is a sovereign state. But in no other formal sense are they emigrants. They do not settle 'abroad': they are not 'aliens' in Great Britain. They have

[a] In 1960 emigration from the Republic to the United Kingdom was estimated to have increased to 72,000 (*The Sunday Times*, Nov. 5, 1961).

the same rights, privileges and duties as the citizens of the United Kingdom. In fact, they have easier access to Great Britain than British subjects coming from outside the United Kingdom as they enter through ports where there is no immigration control. [a]

'DEEPER CONTRASTS' BETWEEN IRELAND AND GREAT BRITAIN

There remain for consideration what FREEMAN calls the 'deeper contrasts' between the two islands, such as in religious allegiance, in social customs, and in outlook: contrasts which reflect differences both of historical development and of the impact of outside influences. Such contrasts as FREEMAN has in mind do occur within Ireland itself, as Chapters 5 and 6 have shown, but they occur in Great Britain as well. It is true that the great contrasts, even conflicts, that exist in Ireland between Catholics and Protestants (more specifically, Ulster Protestants) are not found in Great Britain. But, if I am not mistaken, the difference is a matter of degree rather than of kind. In some districts which have absorbed many immigrants from Ireland, North and South, inter-denominational relations resemble very much relations in Northern Ireland.

In Merseyside, the principal port of entry into England for Irish migrants, it has been noted that the 'Irish' and the 'Ulster' elements did not mingle but tended to congregate in different areas[159] – like they do in Belfast. [b] The 'Ulster problem' is most clearly reflected in the quarrels between Protestants and Catholics in Clydeside just opposite east Ulster. According to McLAREN these quarrels originated with the Ulster immigrants who brought their own 'religious warfare' with them, which they continued to wage in the poorer streets of Glasgow with whom he calls "their Catholic compatriots".[c] McLAREN also thinks that the Glasgow gang warfare for which the city is still, perhaps exaggeratedly, notorious has its origin in "this now century-old segregation of the Irish into rival groups".[160]

But 'anti-Catholic prejudice' in Clydeside is by no means confined to the Ulster Protestant immigrants. The (Protestant) Scots are not blameless either. As McLAREN also

---

[a] The recent announcement that legislation will be introduced in the United Kingdom to control the immigration of British subjects from other parts of the Commonwealth, has caused widespread apprehension in the Republic. As citizens of the Republic, although not technically British subjects, are not aliens in British law, it is hardly possible to exclude them from the working of the new bill. The British government finds itself in a difficult position. According to *The Irish Times* (Oct. 12, 1961), "there is a strong desire in Whitehall to be as broadminded and accommodating as possible as far as Ireland is concerned". But confidential talks between the London and Dublin governments about 'special provisions' for Irish labour are not well received by, particularly, the Pakistani and West Indian High Commissions, who are opposing the bill in principle and seeking in practice an assurance that it will not be a legalized colour bar (*The Irish Times*, Nov. 1, 1961; *The Sunday Times*, Nov. 5, 1961).

[b] The 'zoning' of the immigrants – some people refer to it as 'segregation' – in Merseyside has an occupational aspect too, for the 'Irish' were mainly unskilled labourers.

[c] HANDLEY notes that the large Roman Catholic population of Clydeside is to a considerable extent "more Irish in name than in sentiment". Many people of Irish descent in Scotland today have "only the slightest of connections through grandparents or great-grandparents with the motherland. In other countries such people would have become absorbed into the native stock. In Scotland, however, 'Catholic' and 'Irish' are synonymous terms. The writer has even heard natives of the Catholic Highlands referred to as 'the Hieland Irish'. While this attitude persists, the O'Reillys and Dochertys and O'Donnells will always be Irish to the native", though their connection with Ireland may be a tenuous one going back as far as the end of the eighteenth century (in: *Féilscríblinn*, 31-2).

observes, the Catholic Irish immigrants became unpopular with Glasgow Scots and in particular with Lowlanders [a] – apart from their being Roman Catholics – on account of their readiness to accept low wages for almost any work.[161] On the other hand, much of the anti-Catholic prejudice in nineteenth-century Belfast seems to have sprung from Glasgow. As DAVID KENNEDY writes, "imported into the new Belfast shipyards by artisans from the Clyde, it helped to inflame further Protestant-Catholic relations here".[162] Sectarian strife, then, provides another instance of cross-Channel interaction in the north of the British Isles.

In the next Sections I will deal with other alleged 'deep contrasts' between Ireland and Great Britain and more specifically with the attempts to create deep contrasts between the two islands.

THE POLICY OF 'LINGUISTIC SEPARATISM'

The aim of Irish nationalism has often been defined, rather negatively, as "to undo the British conquest". To most Nationalists this means the ending of the 'physical domination' of the Irish nation. This aim was achieved, at least for the majority of the Irish nation, in 1921. To a minority of Nationalists, however, the conquest will not be undone as long as Ireland is dominated culturally by Great Britain, more specifically by England. They maintain that, "in order to restore Irish nationhood in its full sense", political independence is not enough: the Irish people must again become Irish-speaking.[163] It was this spirit which led to the inclusion in the Free State constitution of the declaration that (Art. 4):

"The National language of the Irish Free State is the Irish language, but the English language shall be equally recognized as an official language. Nothing in this Article shall prevent special provisions being made by the Parliament of the Irish Free State for districts or areas in which only one language is in general use". [b]

Since 1922 the view has been expressed by almost all Southern politicians that – in the words of EARNÁN DE BLAGHD – "the only thing that could preserve the nation from ultimately being simply absorbed into the British people, sharing their minds, their literature, their world outlook, and their way of life, was a separate and vigorous culture".[164] As Mr Kevin Boland (Minister of Defence of the Republic) stated a few years ago:

---

[a] The cleavage is periodically re-affirmed in the "Old Firm Game", the football match between *Celtic* (pron. in this instance: seltic) and *Rangers*. 'Celtic' is of course the Roman Catholic team which is predominantly 'Irish' – incidentally the team flies the Tricolour. The 'Rangers' are Protestants – Scots and Ulstermen (many of them are Orangemen). As FINLAY (21) rightly notes, the meeting of the 'Rangers' and 'Celtic' is more than a football match. "It is a collision, symbolically, between the native Scot and the immense Irish influx to the Clyde basin, a collision between all they stand for. Feeling runs high, and there is more than just sporting give-and-take between the rival hordes of spectators". The 'ceremony' used to degenerate into hand-to-hand fighting in which thousands participated: an outburst of pent-up feeling.

[b] This declaration was retained, slightly modified, in the 1937 constitution (Art. 8): "The Irish language as the national language is the first official language. The English language is recognized as a second official language. Provisions may, however, be made by law for the exclusive use of either of the said languages for any or more official purposes, either throughout the State or in any part thereof".

"The most fruitful way in which we can prove our claim to be a distinct nation is to use our own language in our normal conversation at any rate. It is the principal test by which our claim can be objectively assessed by impartial outsiders. It is the proof of whether our claim to being a separate people is either sound or merely an illusion".[165]

The chief methods of the policy of 'linguistic separatism', introduced by the first Free State government and pursued by all successive Dublin governments "in the interests of self-fulfillment", are:

(1)   the introduction of compulsory teaching of Irish in the schools, combined with a system of rewards to teachers teaching other subjects through the medium of Irish and to pupils answering in Irish at public examinations, in order to establish "infant Gaelic microcosms within an adult English macrocosm"[a];

(2)   the introduction of special educational and economic facilities for the population of the 'Gaeltacht' areas, the isolated pockets on the western seaboard where the Irish language still has a precarious hold as "the vehicle of a decaying culture", in order to preserve the language as the vernacular and to enable its spread as the vernacular or as an additional language to other parts of the country[166]; and

(3)   the making of a knowledge of Irish a prerequisite for civil service and other government appointment.[b]

The results of this 're-gaelicization' policy are, to some extent, reflected in the census returns for 1926 and 1946 (cf. Table 9 and Fig. 9). They reveal that the number of Irish speakers, aged three years and over, in the Republic has increased by 9 per cent. In 1926 it was 540,800, and in 1946 it amounted to nearly 590,000. These figures correspond respectively to 19.3 and 21.1 per cent of the total population of three years of age and over. During these two decades the number of non-Irish speakers, aged three years and over, decreased by 3.5 per cent.

The question arises how far these statistics can be relied upon. According to the Dublin Statistics Office the number of Irish speakers would appear to be far less susceptible of exact measurement than any of the other matters into which the census inquires.[167] DONAL O'SULLIVAN says that many persons, "from mistaken motives of patriotism", claim to know Irish when their acquaintance with it falls short of knowledge. Sometimes, perhaps, they cannot do much more than write their names in that language.[168] But even if the figures are reliable, they are not proof that any substantial progress has been made towards re-gaelicization. The only real test of the vigour of the language is its use as a vernacular.

It is natural to look first at the Gaeltacht. Census figures show that 'natural Irish' is still loosing ground. In fact, it is a rapidly dying speech. During the 1926-46 period the number of Irish speakers in the Gaeltacht fell by more than one-fifth (cf. Table 10). This

---

[a] There was an almost complete lack of teachers and *apparatus paedagogicus* in 1922. Few people at that time had mastered the vagaries of the phonology of Irish, the complexities of its vocabulary, writes BREATNACH (136). Compelling large numbers of teachers and others, in a matter of months, to acquire somehow a knowledge of the language and some competence to teach, use, adapt and develop it in accordance with the particular needs of a more advanced social milieu, has led to the development of a 'hybrid speech', "a travesty of Irish, pronounced as if it were English". This 'school-room speech' shows signs of spreading to the radio, to the stage – in fact, to wherever Irish is spoken by non native speakers (see also: *The Irish Times*, Oct. 13, 1961).

[b] It is obvious that the demands of administration make it impossible to provide 'native Irish speakers' in all capacities. There is a standing joke which ridicules the 're-gaelicization' of the Dublin administration. The *dramatis personae* are a Dublin civil servant of one kind or another (*e.g.* a school-inspector or a tax-collector) and a native of the Gaeltacht. When the former adresses the latter in 'official Irish' – 'book Irish' as the people of the Gaeltacht call it – he gets the reply: "I don't understand English, sir".

Table 9. The number of persons in the Irish Republic, aged three years and over, and able to speak the Irish language, by county or province, at the censuses of 1926 and 1946.

	Number of Irish Speakers		% of Total Population	
	1926	1946	1926	1946
Co. Donegal	51,684	45,935	35.8	36.1
Co. Cavan	8,840	10,227	11.3	15.4
Co. Monaghan	7,318	8,226	11.9	15.3
Southern Border Cos	*67,841*	*64,388*	*23.9*	*26.0*
Dublin C.B. & Co.	39,409	92,381	8.3	15.5
Rest of Leinster	61,693	88,374	10.2	14.7
Munster	197,625	189,395	21.6	22.0
Connacht	174,234	154,187	33.3	33.2
Rest of Republic	*472,961*	*524,337*	*18.8*	*20.8*
Total Irish Republic	540,802	588,725	19.3	21.2

Table 10. The number of persons in the Gaeltacht and in the rest of the Irish Republic, able to speak the Irish language, at the censuses of 1911, 1926 and 1946 (figures for the year 1946 refer to persons aged three years and over only).

	Number of Irish Speakers		Percentage Distribution	
	Gaeltacht	Elsewhere	Gaeltacht	Elsewhere
1911	313,508	240,209	56.6	43.4
1926	246,811	296,700	45.4	54.6
1946	192,963	395,762	32.8	67.2

decrease is often attributed to emigration. According to BRIAN Ó CUÍV, many of those left in the Gaeltacht have also given up speaking Irish because of economic conditions, which have "forced the people to turn their eyes to the outside world". Other influences, such as the radio, cinema and newspapers, also play a part.[169]

Statistically the decline of the number of Irish speakers in the Gaeltacht is outweighed by an increase in the rest of the country. In the period under consideration the number of Irish speakers outside the Gaeltacht increased by one-third; in the Dublin area the growth was even 135 per cent.[a] (These tendencies are reflected in the figures for the Southern Border Counties in Table 9: in Cos Cavan and Monaghan the number increased

[a] According to the 1946 census the percentage of Irish speakers is highest among teachers (nearly 90%). Other people who have "a vested interest in the language" (as the phrase goes) are civil servants and commissioned army officers: more than half of them have some command of Irish. The percentage is also very high for theological students (86) and monks (78). Groups with low percentages are: textile workers (16), metal workers (13), shopkeepers (12), and dock labourers (2). There are, relatively, far more Irish speakers among farmers with small holdings than among farmers with large holdings: in 1946 more than half of the 1-5 acres holders were returned as Irish speakers and only one-tenth of the farmers with holdings of 50 acres and over.

by 14 per cent, whereas in Co. Donegal, which county is partly recognized as Gaeltacht, it decreased by 11 per cent.)

The figures for the non-Gaeltacht areas, however, may not be taken to indicate an increase in the usage of the language as a vernacular. Generally speaking they mean little more than that, with wider educational opportunities, more people in Great Britain have become French speakers.[170] According to Ó Cuív the number of people who used Gaelic as their ordinary medium of speech in 1950 probably would not exceed 35,000. No more than 3,000 would be Irish-speaking monoglots.[171] Another expert gave me as his considered opinion that today the number of persons speaking Irish at home would lay somewhere between 15 and 25,000.

FAILURE AND SUCCESS OF THE RE-GAELICIZATION POLICY

An outsider notes to his amazement that there is in the Republic not a single newspaper in Irish, not even a weekly of general interest.[172] Even the monthly journal of the extreme Nationalist, by some people regarded as 'terrorist', organization is in the English language (*The United Irishman*). Not only is practically all reading matter still in English, the great bulk of it – with the exception of the daily papers – still comes from England. (A circulation in the Republic is one of the factors governing advertising rates for British papers and journals.) The bookshops as regards content might well be Birmingham bookshops, says JOHN SHERIDAN.[173] In this light it cannot be held that the policy of 'linguistic separatism' has yielded much result. How is one to account for this?

There are people who lay the blame on the government for its refusal to set an example and to take the consequences of its own policy. As a matter of fact, it was never decided to turn all government departments over to the use of Irish.[174] Apart from the army[a] exclusive usage of the 'national language' is virtually confined to futilities.[b] Only in a few instances have English place-names been completely replaced by native Irish names.[c] Bills are still introduced and passed in English. The members of parliament are

[a] Irish is being used, because of security reasons, for communications by the bataillon which serves as U.N. troops in the Congo.

[b] Irish has been prescribed, for instance, for the printed form used in acknowledging the receipt of letters addressed to government departments, and for the beginning and end of official letters (otherwise in English): *a chara* (dear sir) and *mise, le meas* (yours faithfully). Irish is also prescribed for the indication of the foreign origin of certain imported wooden goods; for stamps and postmarks; for notices like *Bainne ar díol* (milk for sale); and for various titles, such as *An Taoiseach* (the prime minister), *Dáil Éireann* (chamber of deputies), *Gárda Síochána* (civic guard), *Bord Fáilte Éireann* (Irish tourist board), and *Córas Iompair Éireann* (Irish transport authority).

[c] *I.e.* Kingstown (Co. Dublin) and Queenstown (Co. Cork), which are today invariably described as 'Dún Laoghaire' and 'Cobh' respectively. Both English names, which had become a standing source of offence and embarrassment to doctrinaire Nationalists, date only from the nineteenth century. (Cobh never had lost its old name completely in popular speech). On the other hand, neither 'Portlaoighise' nor 'Daingean' have quite replaced 'Maryborough' and 'Philipstown', the towns named in honour of Mary Tudor and her husband, Philip II of Spain, in the sixteenth century. The attempt to revive other native place-names has failed. The foreigner who, on his arrival in Dún Laoghaire, the terminal of the main cross-Channel ferry service, speaks of 'Kingstown' causes positive anger but if he, after having proceeded to near-by Dublin, speaks of 'Baile Atha Cliath' – supposing he can pronounce it correctly – he makes a fool of himself. The Irish name for Dublin is still obsolete except on postmarks and official notepaper.

still exempt from any qualification in the language – half of them are said not to understand it.[175] On various occasions it has come to light that members of the government are still unable to carry on a debate in Irish.[176]

The lack of success of the language policy is also ascribed to its methods, particularly in the field of education. A lot has been said about "the ill psychological effects" of teaching children in infant standards, whose home language is English, through the medium of a language that they do not understand. [a] There is also considerable opposition to the fact that each year hundreds of children fail the intermediate and leaving certificate examinations because of their failure in Irish. According to some, "the burden of compulsory Irish" is one of the reasons for the large-scale migration from the Republic.[b] Many people seem to favour the replacement of compulsory methods by voluntary ones.[c]

Some time ago it was proposed in parliament that a public referendum should be held to decide whether a majority of the people would prefer voluntary methods. The proposal was however flatly turned down by the prime-minister, Mr Lemass, who held that the language was "inextricably bound up with the life of the country", and thought it would be "an insult to ask the population if they wanted to abandon their national heritage".[177] One wonders what the outcome of a referendum on the revival policy would have been.[d]

It seems unlikely that a fundamental change of methods would produce more results. It is probable that, if there was any prospect of success, the government would jump at it. Its alleged 'half-heartedness' and 'inconsistency' are perhaps consequences rather than causes of the apathy which prevails in the Republic as far as the Irish language

[a] There are only two subjects which are invariably taught through English: English and Christian doctrine – the latter even, strange as it may seem, in the Gaeltacht itself to some extent (a modern example of 'compulsory English').

[b] For instance, a report presented to the General Assembly of the Presbyterian Church states that the teaching of Irish and of other subjects through the medium of Irish "meets with the disapproval of most people, both Protestant and Roman Catholic, as a serious waste of time, seeing that most children, unless seeking a government post, cease to use it on leaving school. So much time is taken up with this particular subject that other subjects suffer, and parents feel that their children are being handicapped and will not be able to take the place in life that they desire for them. One solution that offers itself is to leave the country, so that the children may have a better chance in life".

[c] Champions of 'voluntary Irish' often point to the love of the language which has developed in the North, that is to say among the Nationalist section of the population. In fact, the intensity with which youngsters study Irish in Northern Ireland, encouraged by their parents, compares very favourably with the situation in the South. But, as it appears to me, this enthusiasm seems rather to lie in the opportunity that it provides for expressing nationalism than in love of the language itself.

[d] Whenever the language issue is raised at a county council meeting, or in Dáil Éireann, there is always a vote for Irish. In fact, there is, MYLES DILLON says, "widespread disillusionment and irritation on account of the efforts of successive governments to force Irish upon the schools and on the professions; but few dare to say publicly what so many say in private, for the Language has become a sacred symbol" (in: *Modern Ireland*, 57). BREATNACH (143) held a similar view when he wrote, a few years ago: "Anyone in touch with the language movement over the last twenty-five years will have become aware of a growing tendency on the part of those in official positions and in public life generally to refrain from criticising the state's aims, activities and achievements. Whatever one may think or say in private, one must not appear in public to deny the gods of the state or doubt the efficacy of the practices that have been devised". (On the other hand, the considerable gain of the principal opposition party, *Fine Gael*, at the 1961 election, according to various observers, is primarily to be attributed to its stand against 'compulsory Irish' which it had recently adopted.)

is concerned. The language revival cannot be called a popular cause. But it never was –
as political nationalism was. When the Free State embarked on her language policy it had
already become clear that, as BREATNACH observes:

> "The language which the Government proclaimed to be the authentic voice of the new Irish inde-
> pendent state proved on close acquaintance not to be linked, or only to be vaguely linked, to the national
> cause of liberty as understood by modern Irishmen. Indeed, no better illustration of the truth of Davis's
> statement that a language is 'a surer barrier, and more important frontier, than fortress or river' could be
> found than the fact that in the Gaeltacht areas nationalism made but little impression".[178]

The attempts at the re-gaelicization of the Irish nation have not been confined to
matters of language. There is, too, considerable encouragement of 'Gaelic' games and
pastimes which would provide "an outlet for the sense of racial distinctiveness".[179] These
activities were initiated by the *Gaelic Athletic Association* (1884), "the first modern example
of a great democratic movement under completely Irish auspices".[180] This (non-Gaelic-
speaking) organization fosters 'Gaelic' forms of football, hockey (hurling), and handball. [a]

It is undeniable that the 'Gaelic' games have become very popular in the Republic
and, as far as Northern Ireland is concerned, among the Northern Nationalist population.
It is a matter of opinion whether this success may be interpreted as an indication of the
"progress on the road to national rehabilitation", as some fanatics allege. The 'Gaelic'
games and the pool on these games [b] provide for many thousands of Irishmen another
outlet for their mania for sport and gambling – a mania which the Irish share with the
English and the other inhabitants of the British Isles.

Critics of the G.A.A. hold that it fosters 'religious segregation' and "unnecessary
isolation from fellow-countrymen", especially in the North.[181] In fact, the G.A.A. has
never made any real effort to attract Protestants to its ranks. [c] The identification of
Gaelic games and Roman Catholicism is strongest in the North. "The playing or attending

---

[a] The 'Gaelic' ancestry of the games is mythical. Forms of hockey existed in Scotland and Ireland, as in
other countries, in early times. But the games as now played derive only from the nineteenth century.
'Gaelic' football has no Gaelic roots – it is merely a derivative of the English game. In the eyes of a part
of the people the Gaelic games have a nimbus which the 'foreign' (*i.e.* English) games have not. On the
other hand, there are also Southerners who look down upon the 'native' games, for no other reason
than that those games are not English, or are not played by the English.

[b] The pool is operated by *Gael-Linn*, a voluntary organization set up a few years ago by language enthusiasts
who realized "that, like agricultural and industrial rehabilitation, progress in the language movement
demanded a more comprehensive and inspired policy than that which was being followed, and that
there was no immediate likelihood of such a basic policy change from the State" (*The Irish Times*, Febr.
12, 1960). The pool provides capital for a whole range of activities, such as the production of a weekly
newsreel for cinemas and the sending of hundreds of children from the South and the North to schools
in the Gaeltacht. Gael-Linn contributes to the economic development of the Gaeltacht by providing
farmers, who are unable to get an adequate living out of the present pattern of farming, with an alternative
to emigration. It enables them to augment their income by part-time fishing on the seaboard with new
sturdy-engined boats, and by the growing of intensive crops such as vegetables for quick-freezing.

[c] One of the rules of the G.A.A. reads that "any member who plays, attends, or helps to promote Rugby,
Soccer [football], Hockey or Cricket, thereby incurs automatic suspension from membership". In other
words, sportsmen have to choose between 'native' and 'foreign' games. As a result, there are two groups
of players, even at university level: the 'Gaelic crowd' and the 'Rugby crowd'. The former is exclusively
Roman Catholic. Indeed, the formation of the G.A.A. was the reason that Protestants abandoned the
games in so far as they played them: at that time the only hurling club in Ireland was in Trinity College, Dublin, the university of the Ascendancy.

Gaelic games represents for the vast majority of Northern Nationalists their only intimate contact with Irish culture". At all the games – which are almost exclusively played on Sunday – the Tricolour is flown.[182] (The *Gaelic Football Club* in Co. Tyrone elected unanimously an I.R.A. man president who is serving a twelve-year sentence in Belfast prison for his part in the raid on Omagh barracks.[183])

THE REPUBLIC AS A 'BRITISH PROVINCE'

Language has been called "by far the strongest tie that binds men together into a nation or, by extension, different nations into a spiritual empire or community of thought".[184] The British Isles provide an outstanding example. As for the Republic, the English language is the spoken language of the whole people with the exception of perhaps some 20,000 Gaelic speakers in scattered rural communities in the west. (There are considerably more Gaelic speakers in Scotland!) On the face of present conditions it is quite improbable that English will ever be ousted by Irish. English is the language of the parliament, of the Churches, of the newspapers, of the administration, of business, and of everyday life. This does not necessarily imply a 'community of thought' with the motherland of the English language. But in the case of the Republic it does, to a very great extent. The great exception is politics – and pastimes.

Bookshops display a preponderance of English published books. Newspapers never review books in continental languages (nor are learned journals much better). The cinema is dominated by English films – English war-films are especially popular. English influence is no less apparent in other fields. In 1953 a team of American economic experts concluded that procedures in most economic fields "continue to be modelled upon British procedures even at a time when, demonstrably, they are working far from well in the country of origin".[185] According to the president of the N.A.I.D.A., the *National Agricultural and Industrial Development Association*, Irish industries "have little to offer that is not almost identical with the product of British industries".[186] (There are of course exceptions. [a])

Education, both primary and secondary, remains exactly as it was before 1922 except in so far as the Irish language has been made part of the curriculum. Nor has the legal system ever been fundamentally altered in spite of the adoption of a rigid constitution.[b] According to ROLAND SAVAGE, "with an imitativeness that may be fairly dubbed provincial" the Dublin government "has merely tried to keep in step with English legislation without seriously questioning whether the British method of going about matters was

---

[a] Apart from the peat industry, there is a new range of goods made by foreign firms, *e.g.* cranes (German), aluminium and cosmetics (American), transistor radios (Japanese), and plastic pipes, washing-machines, and pianos (Dutch). The equipment of the first hydro-electric scheme (the Shannon scheme, carried out by Germans), which dates from the late 'twenties, was then in advance of anything in the United Kingdom; the new Verolme shipyard in Cork is more modern than any British shipyard.

[b] The constitution makes provision for the continuance of laws inherited by the Free State and expressly continues such institutions as *habeas corpus*. On the other hand, it does provide directives binding on the courts which could lead to a break with certain British legal principles. This has, for instance, arisen in regard to the custody of children as the constitution provides for the equal rights of parents. The adoption of international conventions, not adopted by the United Kingdom, can also lead to differences. (The Republic has adopted the right of individual appeal in the European Convention for Human Rights while the United Kingdom has not.)

the wisest or most suitable for us".[187] The most curious thing, however, is that where deviations have occurred – such changes as have occurred, like those in the code of local government law – "the critics have assailed them as attacks on democracy".[188]

The slight extent to which the Republic has varied from the United Kingdom in its legal (and administrative) practice is as nothing compared with the great difference between the Anglo-Saxon and the continental system. Although the courts of the Republic are clearly not bound by any decisions of the House of Lords or of the English courts made after the setting up of the Free State, post-1922 English cases, and also Northern Ireland cases, are freely cited in the Dublin courts and have "persuasive authority".[189]

It must strike any continental who has some intimate knowledge of life in England and Ireland that people in the Republic find it very difficult to approach problems and tasks on other than English lines. There is rarely a Southerner who suggests that the Republic could learn from other small countries on the continent – or from the United States. [a] (All of the Dublin newspapers have London (and Belfast) editors but no regular correspondents in any other country – not even in Rome or New York.) Indeed, although English political power has receded, English influence remains predominant in many spheres of life.[190] Culturally the South of Ireland remains in many ways what SHERIDAN (referring to literature) calls 'a British province'.[191] According to many observers English influence has even increased since 1922. For instance, the president of the N.A.I.D.A. said recently: "in the past forty years we have done more ourselves to make a little England of our country than Britain succeeded in doing during seven centuries".[192]

The English influence is, of course, greatly helped by the ease with which people from the Republic can make careers in Great Britain – in politics, journalism, schools, universities, the theatre, etc. The majority of Irish university graduates – teachers, doctors, engineers, etc. – go to Great Britain on qualifying. There is a similar movement from Great Britain to the Republic, and a return of university lecturers, schoolmasters, radio artists, etc.

The English influence is to some extent assisted and to some extent countered by the American influence. Americanization is, to some degree, common to all (Western) European countries but it is all the more noticeable in an English-speaking country, especially through the influence of the new mass communication media. Then, of course, there are the many ties of kindred between the Republic and the United States – there are probably some twenty million people of Irish (Catholic) descent in the United States[b] – which causes America to be regarded in the Republic with particular sympathy. (This sympathy has been lately reinforced by the election of Mr Kennedy whose grandfather came from Co. Waterford.)

[a] Recently the government decided to set up a commission to examine the whole system of university education. In spite of the fact that the Minister for Education is, by virtue of his position and his own often expressed opinion, an enthusiastic language revivalist, he found it natural to appoint to the commission professors of British universities but no representative of any continental or American universities. Dublin newspapers criticized the make-up of the commission on other grounds but not a single voice of opinion found it strange that Great Britain should be the only country whose experience might be useful – which indicates the degree of insularity, i.e. British Isles insularity.

[b] Since the First World War there has been very little emigration to the United States. In the years 1946-59 c. 81,000 people emigrated to America – the annual immigration quota for the Republic is c. 17,800 (cf. Statistical Abstract of the United States 1960).

A special factor binding the Republic to the English-speaking world is the Church, both in the Commonwealth countries and in America, as can readily be observed from the names of the cardinals and bishops. Irish priests still go in large numbers to all these countries.[193] On the other hand, the religion of the Irish immigrants has served to divide them in the past from other immigrants from the British Isles. Even today it helps them to retain a certain 'consciousness of origin' in predominantly Protestant states. Thus the religious division of the British Isles has been continued in the other parts of the English-speaking world.

THE CORES OF THE SOUTH

In conclusion I cannot quite agree with BONN and DÖRRIES, the two German authors whom I quoted at the outset of this Chapter. Similarities between Irish and English life are not confined to externals. As it seems to me, there is a lot of truth in FENNELL's thesis that the 'local flavour' of life in the Republic is not any greater in degree than that in the various parts of Great Britain. This thesis needs however qualification in view of the regional diversity of the Republic itself.

I would prefer to put it this way, that the 'local flavour' of life in the various parts of the Republic – and of Northern Ireland – seems not any greater in degree than that in the various parts of Great Britain. This applies both to the English– and the Irish-speaking districts of Ireland. (The Gaelic-speaking areas are paralleled by the Gaelic-speaking parts of Scotland – and the Welsh-speaking area.)

The Republic can roughly be divided into three cultural sub-regions – ignoring the small areas of Scottish settlement in the Southern Border Counties:

(1)   the Gaeltacht, the rural areas on the west coast, where survive, in however altered a form and however much influenced by the encroaching English culture, some elements of the old Gaelic culture[a];
(2)   the urban and rural areas of English settlement, which are found chiefly in the east and south-east, and where the Anglo-Saxon culture first took root[b]; and
(3)   the remainder of the Irish countryside, which has adopted a great many elements of English culture, and where the old Gaelic culture is preserved only in a number of Gaelic words, expressions, and turns of speech.

[a]   Only one city in Ireland, Galway, has any sizeable number of Gaelic speakers, *i.e.* people using Gaelic as their home language.
[b]   The English settlers can be distinguished into those who came prior to the Reformation, and who remained almost invariably Roman Catholic, and those who came after the Reformation, and who were almost invariably Protestant. The former merged completely into the '(Southern) Irish people' – and accordingly into the Irish nation. But the areas of their settlement still preserve some traits of what is often called the 'Anglo-Norman' influence or culture.

   One of the counties where this influence still "hangs almost palpably in the air" (O'FAOLAIN), is Co. Kilkenny. "The very nature of the people is patently different to that of the contiguous county of Tipperary". This influence is most pronounced where the Anglo-Norman invaders established abbeys. Of a particular district O'FAOLAIN (*Irish*, 56 8) says that "the farmhouses have an air rather of Wessex than of Ireland .. with all the marks of a tradition of good husbandry. .. And there is all over the land the fragrance of a long memory of stable conditions, so different to the harsh south and west where the generations have lived for centuries from hand to mouth and have only in our own times cut free from the gnawing fear of poverty and famine".

The question presents itself which part of the Republic may be considered the spiritual kernel area of the South, or rather the south, the counterpart of the area of Scottish (Presbyterian) settlement in east Ulster. I would suggest two such areas which represent the two conflicting, though to some extent synthesized, cultural strands of Southern life: (1) the small and declining Gaeltacht districts, which bear witness to a past when Ireland (and part of Scotland) had a different culture; and (2) Dublin, the old centre of English administration in Ireland, with the Pale, the main area of settlement around Dublin. Dublin, although it has become the capital of the Republic, remains – however paradoxical it may seem at first sight – the chief centre of the triumphant English culture.[a]

ANGLO-IRISH AND ANGLO-ULSTER RELATIONS

Relations between the Republic and England have been described as a 'love-hate relationship: "Black or white, England is always at the centre of Irish vision".[194] An outsider, however, when travelling in the Republic, may notice far more symptoms of an attitude which amounts to anglomania than indications of anglophobia. He even may notice far more symptoms of anglomania in the South than in the North – something which at first sight seems incongruous in view of history and the actual political situation. (I leave the Northern Nationalists out of consideration, some of whom seem very resentful about anything British.) There is an old saying which goes: "In the South they dislike the flag but like the English, in Ulster they like the flag but dislike the English".

It is well to remember that the North always gravitated to Scotland rather than to England: there always existed close connexions across the North Channel. Many Northerners are of Scottish descent – and are very conscious of it. And, of course, a considerable part of them are moved by the same basic urges as are the majority of Scots – urges which clearly derive from their common Calvinist (Presbyterian) heritage. It is, I think, true to say that, generally speaking, the Ulstermen feel more akin to the Scots than to the English. Labourers and intellectuals alike, they often find Scots easier to get on with than Englishmen. They are easily irritated by an Englishman, especially by anything which could be interpreted as an expression of his presumed sense of superiority.

Another chief cause of annoyance to the Ulstermen is the average Englishman's ignorance of the 'Ulster position'. His ignorance is reflected in the letters he addresses to 'Belfast, Eire'. (It has even happened with correspondence from the Home Office to the Northern Ireland government.) And, in so far as the Englishman is aware that there is a Partition problem, he rarely takes any interest in it. The Englishman turned his back on the 'Irish problem' in 1922.

Then there is the widespread belief in the North – rightly or wrongly – that 'London' shows more concern about 'Dublin' than about 'Belfast', as "the English always seem to care less for their friends than for their former enemies". This view also lives in the South. Some Southerners derive pleasure from the idea – wishful thinking? – that the Ulstermen who are "more British than the British" are of little or no account in London. (People in the South often seem to think that the English think a lot about Ireland – which

---

[a] Recently a girl from the Gaeltacht was, after her arrival in Dublin, lost for over six hours because she could only ask directions in Gaelic. Finally she succeeded in holding a conversation in a telephone box with an operator who could understand her language (*The Irish Times*, Oct. 9, 1961).

they do not – and that sooner or later the British government will coerce the North into the Republic – which seems rather unlikely.[a]

Various observers hold that Englishmen prefer to deal with Southerners rather than with Ulstermen – and that Southerners know better than Ulstermen how to get on with English people.[b] Recently an English paper observed:

> "For all his political ties with the North, the Englishman is more easily at home in Southern Ireland, and indeed the Northern Ireland Protestant, while he has similarities to the Lowland Scot, is a creature wildly unlike an Englishman".[195]

According to LOGAN: if the Belfastman is not popular in the South – nor does he expect to be – neither is he exactly popular with English people. "He is too independent to play the part of suppliant, and .. for being loyal to England he naturally expects England to be loyal to him".[196] Some time ago *The Times* wrote that "Belfast has never been a city meekly to do what London and Westminster in their wisdom thought was right."[197]

It has been estimated that six times as many English people visit Dublin every year as visit Belfast.[198] Dublin, of course, is a charming capital-type of city. But, in addition, Dublin has an 'Irish touch' that no English city can provide[c], yet it is English enough to make an Englishman feel comfortable. "To an Englishman Dublin has the virtues of a foreign capital without the drawbacks".[199]

SOME OBSTACLES TO ANGLICIZATION

Cultural unity, such as has been brought about between Ireland and England, has been achieved by the same influence which has welded together the various parts of Great Britain, *viz.* by 'anglicization', that is the imposition – and adoption – of culture elements which originated in England. Anglicization is a complicated cultural development which

---

[a] The *Ireland Act, 1949*, declares "that in no event will Northern Ireland or any part thereof cease to be part of His Majesty's dominions and of the United Kingdom without the consent of the Parliament of Northern Ireland". For a critical review of the Dublin policy of solving Partition by bringing pressure to bear on the British government, see: BARRINGTON, 386–91.

[b] An ecclesiastic gave as his opinion that people in the South are inclined to say what they think the Englishman they are talking to would like them to say, whereas an Ulsterman says exactly what he thinks – no matter to whom he is talking – and expects the other to do the same thing (something the other – if a southerner! – rarely does).

[c] The corporation in a moment of extra-fervid nationalism decided to name new streets only in Irish (the Irish is often merely a version of an English name) but most of the principal streets retain their old names, given to them in honour of English viceroys or monarchy, *e.g.* Grafton St, Northumberland St, and Nassau St. Only a few streets are named in honour of Nationalist leaders, *i.e.* O'Connell St, Cathal Brugha St, Pearse St, and Wolfe Tone St (a small back-street). There is no street name to honour Hugh O'Neill, Patrick Sarsfield, Thomas Davis, John Mitchel, or Douglas Hyde. The suburban streets have names that might appear in the suburbs of any English town. (In the country there is somewhat more tendency to 'national' names or names associated with Roman Catholicism, *e.g.* saints' names.)

The most prominent landmark in Dublin is still Nelson's Pillar, an enormous statue to admiral Nelson, standing outside the General Post Office (the headquarters of the 1916 insurgents). Minor monuments have been removed – extremists still blow up an odd one – but hitherto the corporation has firmly refused to remove, or replace, Nelson. Wellington's gigantic obelisk, too, remains. (Perhaps they remain because the cost of removal is high.)

has never been systematically examined. I have only touched on certain results of this age-long process which is still going on. In Parts Three and Four I will distinguish various stages in this process which set in, as far as Ireland is concerned, in the course of the twelfth century with the first reform movement in the Irish Church.

Not all parts of Ireland have been affected in the same degree and in the same way – nor have all parts of Great Britain. The anglicization process presents at once a uniting and a dividing factor – which is, to some extent, reflected in the existence of a land boundary in Ireland. Ulster has been anglicized chiefly from Scotland, in particular by Scottish immigrants, whereas the rest of Ireland has been anglicized entirely and directly from England – by English immigrants and through many other cultural agents. This explains for instance why people in the South are reputed to speak 'better English' than in the North: 'Ulster English' has a very strong Scottish mark.

One could say, perhaps, that Ulster has, to a large extent, been 'scoticized', that is anglicized in the Scottish way.[a] It is clear, then, that anglicization does not necessarily lead to uniformity of culture. In fact, all the forces working in favour of uniformity have not yet been powerful enough to suppress regional distinctions in outlook and way of life. England itself has preserved a remarkable cultural regional diversity.

There are various cultural elements which offer resistance to uniformity. Here one thinks first of 'language'.

It has been asserted that, if the Welsh language had died out a thousand years ago and English had become the language of Wales, there would be today no more difference between a man from Cardigan and a man from Kent than now exists between a man from Durham and a man from Devon.[200] The survival of Welsh is "the greatest obstacle to the extension of English ways of life throughout the Principality".[201] It is their language which, according to WYN GRIFFITH, must be held largely responsible for "that sense of unity amongst Welshmen which has survived so many challenges and changes", and for their 'otherness' in habit of mind and in custom and in many other ways.[202]

The position of the Welsh language is weakening but its prospects are far more hopeful than those of Irish. As I have shown, all the efforts expended in checking the progress of the English language in the areas least affected – by preserving Gaelic as the vernacular in the Gaeltacht – and all the attempts to repel the English language from the areas where it had already taken root, have not scored a great success.

It has been observed that the popularization of the English language in Scotland did more perhaps than statesmen had ever been able to do for the unification of England and Scotland:

"Two neighbouring nations that spoke the same language could not in a time of the spread of the printed word escape interchange of ideas and community of thought. As the Scots came to talk and write like the English, political union with the nation south of the Border became more conceivable".[203]

That political union between England and Ireland, or rather the greater part of Ireland, did not become – or remain – more conceivable can, to some extent, be explained by the fact that the spread of the English language in Ireland began later than in Scotland and proceeded much more slowly. It is not always realized that the disap-

[a] The legal, administrative, and educational systems of Northern Ireland, however, are English rather than Scottish, as are those of the rest of Ireland.

pearance of Gaelic from much the greater portion of Ireland is a phenomenon of quite recent growth. In fact, it was not until the middle of the eighteenth century that Irish, "the language of a nation bordering on serfdom" (THOMAS O'RAHILLY), began seriously to decline.[204]

There are more cultural elements which stand in the way of uniformity. Two factors already brought up for discussion in the previous Chapters are 'race' and 'religion'. As far as anglicization is being promoted by personal contacts with English people, 'race' would seem to be a somewhat greater hindrance to assimilation in the case of the (Scottish) northerners than in the case of the southerners (who have absorbed many English). As far as 'religion' is concerned, it is rather obvious that the positions of the north and the south are reversed, in view of the contrast between Protestantism and Roman Catholicism.

Here it is well to remember the difference between (Scottish) Presbyterianism and (English) Episcopalianism (Anglicanism). That Scotland in spite of the Union has not merged, spiritually, in England may be attributed, to a greater or less extent, to the fact that the Reformation put between the two countries the "barrier of a different faith". At the time of the Reformation – and for a long time since – "the gulf between the Scottish Kirk and the Church of England was, in the eyes of her adherents, almost as great as that which divided her from Rome".[205] This 'barrier' or 'gulf' was extended through Ireland; it is preserved as it were in the land boundary. The Ulster Presbyterian still looks naturally to Scotland for his spiritual home whereas the Irish Episcopalian looks to England – as the Irish Catholic does when he does not look to Rome.

There are people in the Republic who contend that the only barrier which will ultimately remain between Southern Ireland and England, or, by extension, the United Kingdom, is the 'barrier of a different faith'. As MICHAEL TIERNEY remarked, the Catholic religion provided differences which made it impossible for England to assimilate Ireland and also provided impetus for independence.[206] A few years ago DAVID GREENE (professor of Irish in Dublin) said on the controversy between Protestants and Catholics in Ireland:

"I do not think we deceive the northern Protestants who see clearly that, behind the Gaelic facade, we are just as anglicised as they are. They do not forgive us for disrupting the United Kingdom in order to set up a Catholic state, that is how they would put it themselves, and I suggest that it is uncomfortably near the truth".[207]

Mr Kevin Boland, when speaking of "our fellow countrymen in the Six Counties" who "look to us to prove the case for co-operation", observed:

"They can hardly be very deeply impressed at our claims to distinctive nationality if they find us speaking, living and behaving generally almost entirely as a corresponding body of people in any part of England. It just does not make much sense to them".[208]

GREENE goes even so far as to say that there are nations and nations and that "as intensity of national feeling goes we rank pretty low". As he puts it:

"If we find, in the long run, that nothing divides us from the people of Northern Ireland but religion, our journey from the United Kingdom becomes unnecessary; Catholicism, as its very name implies, is the antithesis of a national religion, and the British Catholics do not seem to suffer any disabilities".[209]

CONCLUSION PART TWO

The development towards greater formal political independence of the South of Ireland since 1921 has been matched by a simultaneous development of close social and economic relations with the United Kingdom. The severance of the last formal ties with the Commonwealth and the formal declaration of the Irish Republic in 1948 – at a time when a propaganda war of considerable intensity was being waged against the British on the Partition issue – was followed immediately by the granting of rights, amounting to quasi-citizenship, to British subjects. This detail reflects the fact, so baffling to continental (and, to some extent, to American) students, that, in many respects, connexions between the South of Ireland and the rest of the British Isles have been preserved on a pre-1921 basis.[a]

The arrangement which fits a self-ruling state into a British Isles social and economic unit is a remarkable compromise. Whatever the compelling social and economic reasons for such an arrangement, it could not have been effected without the readiness and ability, both in London and in Dublin, to compromise. (The English are everywhere renowned as the masters of the art of compromise but the Irish – I mean the Southern Irish – are as much masters of this art as are the English.) Whether a vigorous "native Irish culture" can flourish in such an arrangement is another matter which only the future can tell.

Since 1921 the South of Ireland has been free to develop her own way of life and give her institutions "a more suitable basis". Officials like to point with pride to many achievements which they believe could not have taken place if Southern Ireland had still been ruled from London. The so-called "break-away from the colonial past" is popularly often referred to – rather cynically – as "painting pillar-boxes green". The Republic is dotted with pre-1922 pillar-boxes with the raised royal initials VR, ER, and GR. They have not been replaced but merely painted green – from their pristine red. This operation symbolizes many more complex changes of similar nature.

The Irish language is declared "the national language" but English is recognized as "a second official language" – with such consequences, for instance, as that the capital is still invariably described as 'Dublin' and not 'Baile Atha Cliath' (except on post marks). Similarly one finds that all kinds of institutions have retained their old 'imperial' titles, such as the *Royal Irish Academy*, the *Royal College of Surgeons*, the *Royal Bank of Ireland*, the *Royal St George Yacht Club*, and the many-sided *Royal Dublin Society* (which, *inter alia*, manages one of the most famous of Irish events, the *Dublin Horse Show*). The Roman Catholic clergy are educated in the *Royal College of St Patrick*, Maynooth (Co. Kildare).

There are regular outcries against this state of affairs by small extremist bodies but public opinion is quite unmoved. Indeed, as CRANE BRINTON notes, "the Irish, like the English, are not really good revolutionaries – not social revolutionaries".[210] The South-

---

[a] The continental student of the connexions between the Irish Republic and the United Kingdom comes across many ambiguities and paradoxes which he finds difficult to understand – especially so if he is used to think along straight lines and to seek clear-cut divisions. After some time he will realize that what to him are inconsistencies and anomalies are not felt as such by the Irish – nor by the English. A good deal of misunderstanding and, consequently, of misrepresentation with regard to 'Anglo-Irish relations' on the continent arises from the fact that, generally speaking, people on the continent approach political problems in a different way from the English and the (Southern) Irish, who seem to be, on the whole, less dogmatic and more empiric than most continentals.

erners are often more inclined to laugh at officialdom's tendency to make changes than to co-operate. To change the name of a hotel, which has always been known as *The Queen's* or *The Royal*, to *The Patrick Sarsfield* or *The Padraic Pearse* would simply arouse derision – strange though this may seem to outsiders. (According to the telephone directory there are no fewer than eighteen *Imperial Hotels* in the provinces.)

There are differences with the United Kingdom. The schools are organized on a denominational basis. Divorce has been abolished. Birth-control is prohibited. A rather rigid book censorship has been introduced. These and other changes reflect the religion of the people of Southern Ireland rather than the political aspirations of revolutionaries. In fact, the most outstanding, and perhaps the only fundamental, difference with the rest of the British Isles is that over 95 per cent of the population of the Republic are very devout Roman Catholics.

The Republic has unique social and economic ties with her neighbour, speaks the same language, and to a large extent shares the same civilization. That all these ties will grow even closer is likely. Religion alone will continue to make a division. Whether the religious contrast in itself necessitates self-government is a matter of opinion. In view of the religious contrast, however, and more particularly in view of the introduction of Roman Catholic moral ideas into the legal – and indeed constitutional – system of the Republic, it is hardly to be expected that a Dublin parliament would enact an Act of Union with the United Kingdom. On the other hand, the same religious contrast and legal principles make the ending of Partition, with the consent of the majority of the people of Northern Ireland – the declared object of Dublin political leaders – quite illusory.

In fact, the Republic's many ties with the United Kingdom are primarily with Great Britain, especially England: the South of Ireland is turned eastward rather than north-ward. The Irish land boundary is more of a social barrier than is the sea boundary in the sense that there is, absolutely and relatively, very little emigration across the land boundary. Practically all the 50,000 persons who annually leave the Republic settle in Great Britain. (So do the 15,000 persons who emigrate each year from Northern Ireland, whether Nationalists or Ulstermen.) It should be emphasized that this movement has hardly been influenced by the creation of the land boundary, if at all. If there had been no land boundary, the migration pattern would probably have differed very little from the actual pattern. The same applies to the sea boundary.[a]

The land boundary is also more of a 'spiritual' divide than is the sea boundary in the sense that the people of the Republic on the whole feel less attached to the people of the rest of Ireland – or rather to the majority of the Northerners – and their way of life, than to the people on the other side of the Irish Sea – or rather to the English – and their way of life. People in the Republic are as much aware of their differences with the majority of the Northerners as the latter are aware of their differences with the Southerners. The

---

[a] Similarly the land boundary is also more of an economic barrier in the sense that far less goods go from the Republic to Northern Ireland and *vice versa* than from the Republic to Great Britain and *vice versa*. This situation does not depend on any frontier regulations but merely on the fact that, economically, the South of Ireland is more closely linked with Great Britain than with the rest of Ireland – as is Northern Ireland. (An analysis of the trade across the land boundary shows that a considerable portion of the goods which pass the frontier go from the Republic via Northern Ireland ports to Great Britain or *vice versa*.)

land boundary, to some extent, may be interpreted as a cross-Channel extension of the Scottish Border as it marks off, in a rather arbitrary way, the 'scoticized' part of Ireland against the 'anglicized' part ('anglicized' taken in the narrow sense of the word).

Thus the two parts of the Irish Border, the land and the sea boundary, too, demonstrate that a so-called 'artificial' frontier (line) can be a greater cultural divide than a so-called 'natural' frontier (zone).

REFERENCES PART TWO

[1] *Handbook*, 91
[2] *Unification*, 62
[3] GOTTMANN, *Politique*, 20
[4] *Frontiers*, 9
[5] Ibid., 7. Cf. *Aspects*, 164; KEDOURIE, 125-7
[6] *Frontiers*, 11
[7] Cf. ibid., 11
[8] SHEEHY, 9
[9] GOBLET, vol. i, 1
[10] MACALISTER, *Archaeology*, 8. Cf. WALTER FITZGERALD, *Geography*, 3; MÜLLER-ROSS, 68
[11] Cf. *View of Ireland*, 2
[12] Cf. DÖRRIES, 338
[13] ARCHER, 6-7; CORR, 7-8; HOWARTH, 38
[14] *Handbook*, 90-1
[15] EVANS, *Folk Ways*, 17-8
[16] HOWARTH, 153
[17] EVANS, *Portrait*, 21
[18] EVANS, *Folk Ways*, 17
[19] BECKETT, 9
[20] SHEARMAN, *Relations*, 13. Cf. GOEDHEER, 110
[21] EVANS, *Portrait*, 18
[22] BONN, vol. i, 6-7; WOODBURN, 30
[23] BONN, vol. i, 6-7
[24] FREEMAN, *Ireland*, viii
[25] EVANS, *Heritage*, 16. cf. MACKINDER, 79
[26] DÖRRIES, 227. Cf. MACKINDER, 177
[27] COLE, 9
[28] MACKINDER, 20-1
[29] RUMPF, 17
[30] CURTIS, *History*, v
[31] BOWMAN, 31; *Constitution*, 251
[32] PAUL-DUBOIS, 4. Cf. CHATTERTON-HILL, 28-9, 55, 124
[33] GOBLET, vol. i, 1-2
[34] Cf. DEMANGEON, 147
[35] FALLS, 9-11; *Ulster under H.R.*, 80-1; Cf. *Speeches*, 88, 92; MACMANUS, 131-2
[36] CECILE O'RAHILLY, 10
[37] Ibid., 23-4, 27-8. Cf. KENNEY, 139

[38] PAUL-DUBOIS, 4
[39] GOBLET, vol. i, 1-2
[40] Ibid., 13. Cf. FELS, 481
[41] DEMANGEON, 147. Cf. PRIESTER, 78-82, 95-7
[42] DEMANGEON, 147
[43] *Ulster under H.R.*, 1-2
[44] Cf. *Handbook*, 90
[45] MOGEY, *Life*, 34
[46] IRWIN, 9-10; REILLY, 19-25
[47] Cf. *Handbook*, 98
[48] Ibid., 90, 98
[49] Cf. MÜLLER-ROSS, 62
[50] BLAKE, 84, 96-8, 172, 175-6
[51] Ibid., 194-8; WINANT, 186
[52] *The Irish Times*, Nov. 15, 1961
[53] BOGGS, 12-7
[54] KEDOURIE, 9, 73-4
[55] O'SULLIVAN, 17. Cf. MACMANUS, 370
[56] GEORGE O'BRIEN, *Fields*, 15
[57] LEMASS, 4, 14
[58] GEORGE O'BRIEN, *Fields*, 10-1. Cf. ALICE GREEN, 93
[59] CARTY, *Ireland 1851-1921*, 143
[60] *Border*, 6
[61] GALLAGHER, 199-200. Cf. ARMOUR, 11; USSHER, 7-13
[62] ARMOUR, 15, 22; GEORGE O'BRIEN, *Fields*, 23
[63] GALLAGHER, 200. Cf. PAUL-DUBOIS, 81-102
[64] SHEEHY, 27-8
[65] CARSON, 55-6. Cf. McLAREN, 7
[66] EVANS, *Portrait*, 7
[67] *Ulster under H.R.*, 55, 69
[68] BROGAN, 77n
[69] Cf. *The Irish Times*, Jan. 12, 13, 1960
[70] Cf. KEDOURIE, 62-76
[71] Cf. ibid., 76
[72] USSHER, 75
[73] DEWAR, *Orangeism*, 8, 15
[74] Ibid., 22
[75] STANFORD, 25

[76] EVANS, *Portrait*, 61
[77] Ibid., 57
[78] STANFORD, 25
[79] *Ulster under H.R.*, 10. Cf. DOYLE, 105-6
[80] MILLIGAN, *passim*
[81] SHEARMAN, *Developments*, 160-1
[82] USSHER, 74
[83] *The Times*, Sept. 17, 1957
[84] *Border*, 10. Cf. SHEARMAN, *Relations*, 241
[85] BREATNACH, 120-30. Cf. O'SULLIVAN, 20
[86] STANFORD, 26
[87] *The Irish Times*, June 30, 1955
[88] *Belfast Telegraph*, March 17, 1960
[89] *The Irish Press*, Dec. 21, 1959
[90] MOGEY, *Community*, 86
[91] DENIS GWYNN, 9, 234-5. Cf. CARSON, 26-8; FENNELL, 5-12; GALLAGHER, 208-21; MANSERGH, *Government*, 138-9; *Ulster under H.R.*, 207-8
[92] FENNELL, 21; *Ulster under H.R.*, 71
[93] MANSERGH, *Government*, 243
[94] STANFORD, 15. Cf. *Ulster under H.R.*, 11
[95] Cf. DOYLE, 88, 109-10; FENNELL, 1; SHEARMAN, *Relations*, 243
[96] DOYLE, 87
[97] Ibid., 92
[98] *The Irish Times*, June 30, 1955
[99] EAMON DE VALERA, 60
[100] *Handbook*, vi
[101] BARRINGTON, 381. Cf. SHEEHY, 19
[102] SHEEHY, 10, 102
[103] MUMFORD, 310-1
[104] Cf. ERVINE, 570; GRUBBE, 18; LOGAN, 35, 62; *Republic*, 3; WOODBURN, 396
[105] EVANS, *Portrait*, 60-1; HARRISON, 112, 114; RODGERS, 11
[106] EVANS, *Portrait*, 8
[107] ERVINE, 190
[108] DOYLE, 87, 103
[109] MANSERGH, *Government*, 319
[110] DOYLE, 94
[111] LOGAN, 41
[112] GRUBBE, 18
[113] COLUM, 111
[114] WOODBURN, 397-8. Cf. LOGAN, 62
[115] WHITE, 153
[116] Cf. NOTESTEIN, 161
[117] *The Belfast News-Letter*, June 27, 1960; BLAKE, 34. Cf. LOGAN, 16
[118] Cf. DUIJKER & FRIJDA, 8; COLUM, 111
[119] O'FAOLAIN, *Journey*, 242
[120] Cf. MCCARTHY, 314-7
[121] NOTESTEIN, xiii, 150. Cf. FINLAY, 17
[122] *Ulster since 1800*, vol. ii, 231
[123] MCLAREN, 17
[124] FENNELL, 1

[125] RODGERS, 18. Cf. DOYLE, 101-2
[126] CARTY, *Ireland 1851-1921*, 144. Cf. BLAGHD, 98
[127] Cf. FENNELL, 3
[128] Ibid., 12. Cf. ERVINE, 95
[129] *Ulster since 1800*, vol. ii, 232
[130] WHITE, 153. Cf. GOOD, 3-4
[131] *Ulster under H.R.*, 70
[132] WHITE, 153. Cf. *Belfast*, 15
[133] MUMFORD, 315, 319, 367
[134] DEMANGEON, 137
[135] Ibid., 137. Cf. HARVEY, 67
[136] O'FAOLAIN, *Story*, 12. Cf. FREEMAN, *Ireland*, 500
[137] SHEARMAN, *Ulster*, 159, 162. Cf. CLARKSON, 346-7; LOGAN, 60; USSHER, 130
[138] LOGAN, 59, 61
[139] *Ireland*, 18
[140] O'FAOLAIN, *Story*, 9
[141] LOGAN, 61
[142] *Belfast Telegraph*, June 10, 1960
[143] MCDERMOTT & WEBB, 2-3
[144] Ibid., 23
[145] STANFORD, 36
[146] E.g. *Belfast Telegraph*, May 16, 1960
[147] BRINTON, 20, 119
[148] *The Spectator*, Apr. 29, 1960
[149] BONN, vol. i, 1
[150] DÖRRIES, 334
[151] FREEMAN, *Ireland*, vii
[152] Ibid., 251
[153] Ibid., 3-4
[154] Ibid., 78
[155] Ibid., 251, 498
[156] BRINTON, 19
[157] Cf. e.g. SAVILLE, *passim*
[158] Cf. LYNCH & VAIZEY, 14
[159] *Survey*, 126-7
[160] MCLAREN, 92-3, 113. Cf. *Glasgow*, 12
[161] MCLAREN, 92
[162] *Ulster since 1800*, vol. ii, 178. Cf. EMRYS JONES, *Geography*, 190
[163] BREATNACH, 129. Cf. GILFILLAN, 466, 471
[164] *The Irish Times*, July 22, 1958
[165] *The Sunday Press*, July 7, 1957
[166] BREATNACH, 136-40; O'SULLIVAN, 19. Cf. O'FAOLAIN, *De Valera*, 166
[167] *Census Population Ireland 1946*, vol. viii, viii
[168] O'SULLIVAN, 18
[169] Ó CUÍV, 31
[170] Cf. *Republic*, 3
[171] Ó CUÍV, 32
[172] Cf. O'SULLIVAN, 18
[173] SHERIDAN, 81-2
[174] Cf. *Hibernia*, Oct. 23, 1959
[175] Cf. *The Irish Times*, Nov. 13, 1959

[176] Cf. O'SULLIVAN, 564-5

[177] *The Irish Times*, Febr. 25, March 3, Dec. 5, 1960, Sept. 28, 1961

[178] BREATNACH, 131

[179] *Hibernia*, Oct. 30, 1959

[180] *Modern Ireland*, 80

[181] BARRINGTON, 397; WHITE, 152. Cf. *The Irish Times*, Nov. 28, 1960

[182] *Hibernia*, Oct. 30, 1959. Cf. HARRIS, 20, 168

[183] *The United Irishman*, March 1959

[184] GOAD, 14

[185] *Appraisal*, 92

[186] *The Irish Times*, Nov. 25, 1959

[187] ROLAND SAVAGE, 3. Cf. McBRIDE, 7

[188] MEGHEN, 95

[189] NEWARK, 34

[190] BECKETT, 9-10

[191] SHERIDAN, 85

[192] *The Irish Times*, Oct. 8, 1959

[193] Cf. BLANSHARD, 27-8

[194] *The Economist*, July 30, 1960

[195] *The Observer*, Sept. 25, 1960

[196] LOGAN, 41

[197] *The Times*, Dec. 9, 1957

[198] *The Observer*, Sept. 25, 1960

[199] HARVEY, 15

[200] GRIFFITH, 64-5

[201] WALTER FITZGERALD, *Europe*, 19

[202] GRIFFITH, 15, 62, 64

[203] NOTESTEIN, 160, 342-4

[204] THOMAS O'RAHILLY, *Dialects*, 2

[205] McLAREN, 17-8

[206] *The Irish Times*, July 25, 1957

[207] *The Irish Times*, Dec. 14, 1957

[208] *The Sunday Press*, July 7, 1957

[209] *The Plough*, Febr. 1959; *The Irish Times*, Dec. 14, 1957

[210] BRINTON, 19

PART THREE

REGIONAL CONTRASTS AND CONTACTS
OF PRE-REFORMATION IRELAND

Chapter 8

DIVISIONS OF EARLY GAELIC IRELAND[a]

THE ANCIENT KINGDOMS

It is evident that for the early beginnings of political organization in Ireland we have to look not at the wilderness in the heart of the island but at the upland fringe. In fact, all attempts at establishing any effective form of central authority in pre-Reformation Ireland – and indeed in post-Reformation Ireland – have originated from centres which are more or less peripheral. It is most clearly demonstrated by the location of the capitals of the Republic and Northern Ireland, Dublin and Belfast.

It is only little less apparent in the ancient Irish 'provinces' (kingdoms), which seem to be of pre-Gaelic Celtic origin.[b] Each of these 'provinces' was based upon an upland massif – each a typical highland kernel region: 'Ulster' in the north, 'Leinster' in the south-east, 'Munster' in the south-west, and 'Connacht' in the west.[1] EVANS has no doubt that this "ground pattern of regional diversity" was already established in the megalithic era, by the first half of the second millennium B.C.:

"We may think of the four kingdoms as slowly crystallizing throughout pre-historic times around areas of primary settlement among the hills. The political organization of these areas had to await the coming of Celtic conquerors [c], but fundamental in their differentiation are the divergencies in megalithic practice".[2]

---

[a] There is no detailed history of early Ireland which has regard to the new theories advanced by modern scholars like THOMAS O'RAHILLY. The work of synthesizing the bewildering mass of new material is still at an early stage. A standard work is still EDMUND CURTIS's *History of Mediaeval Ireland* (1923). Valuable though it is, it is hardly more than a school text book; and CURTIS was not an Old Irish scholar. A real pioneer work is O'RAHILLY's *Early Irish History and Mythology* (1946). The materials available for ecclesiastical history have been detailed by LOUIS GOUGAUD's *Christianity in Celtic Lands* (1932). In a very general way, the essays issued by the *Cultural Relations Committee* (a body set up by the Dublin government) serve as an excellent guide to modern Irish studies. (Perhaps the least satisfactory of these booklets is that on the Patrick controversy: a reader may well give up in despair at the conflict of opinions!)

[b] Until recently it was assumed that the Gaels were the earliest 'Celts' (Celtic speakers) to arrive on these shores. THOMAS O'RAHILLY (*History*, 199-208) has supplied proof that the Gaels, far from being the first, were the last Celtic invaders. He also maintains that they did not come via Great Britain but direct from the continent. The difficulty in regard to their arrival from Great Britain is the utter absence of any trace of the Gaelic language in that island, except where it was introduced by later Gaelic immigration from Ireland (cf. CECILE O'RAHILLY, 5-34).

[c] It should be emphasized that 'Celtic' is primarily a linguistic term, applied to a group of closely related Indo-European dialects. It cannot be used to denote 'race'. All the so-called Celtic peoples must have been, from the physical-anthropological standpoint, very mixed. Moreover, Celtic speech was also imposed upon or adopted by comparatively large numbers of subjects whose cultures were by no means homogeneous (cf. DAVIES, *Archaeology*, 24-5; RAFTERY, 178).

According to tradition the ancient Irish kingdoms met at the hill of Uisnech (Co. Westmeath), north-east of Athlone, in the very centre of the island. We must, of course, beware of too simple a view, dividing Ireland into four political units whose boundaries actually met at the hill. It is rather likely that, as THOMAS O'RAHILLY has suggested, Uisnech did not belong to any one of the kingdoms.[3] The Central Lowlands for long must have been a march or no man's land. (A geographer cannot help but be struck by the coincidence of the conclusions reached by O'RAHILLY from textual criticism with those which might be expected from purely geographical premises.)

It is only relatively late, not before the Gaelic conquest of Ireland was well advanced, that some form of authority was established over and in the Lowlands. In the fifth century, probably[4], a fifth kingdom was added to the existing four.[a] This latest-born of the Irish 'provinces', which later was incorporated in the kingdom of Leinster, was called 'Meath'. The name is derived from Old Irish 'Mide', literally: the middle (place or region), originally the name of the district surrounding the hill of Uisnech. Eventually 'Mide' came to be used in a wider sense so as to cover "the whole territory from Athlone eastward to Dublin and Drogheda"[5], thus including the greater part of the Central Lowlands.

By contrast with the old 'provinces', the short-lived Midland kingdom is a rather shadowy affair. This is hardly surprising in view of the physical conditions of that time which did not permit the development of a kingdom in the very centre of the island.[b] It is obvious that the Midland kingdom gravitated towards the higher coastal portion of the Lowlands. The centre of the so-called Midland Gaels was the hill of Tara[c], north-west of Dublin, which may have remained their 'capital' down to the seventh century.[6]

In one of the *Annals* Tara is described as "a place from which there is a wide view". It is situated on the western ridge of the coastal hills and its view indeed "reaches almost everywhere to the hills and mountains that limit the extent of the central plain".[7] The location of Tara not far from the east coast, more precisely in the broad gap which occurs in the coastal mountains, suggests that the Midland kingdom originated in a coastal colony. This incidentally is the view of THOMAS O'RAHILLY from the literary evidence.[8]

It is significant that the main part of the Midland kingdom – that part of the Central Lowlands most favoured by nature[9] – became in turn the Viking kingdom of Dublin, the chief coastal foothold of the Vikings in Ireland. [d] The territory of the Viking kingdom in its turn was largely comprised within the 'Pale', the area around Dublin which was the main base of the English in mediaeval Ireland. It seems only natural, then, to see in

---

[a] Henceforth each of the Irish 'provinces' was known as a 'cóiced', literally: fifth part. The word is retained in Modern Irish as 'cúigeadh', meaning: (an Irish) province.

[b] None of the historians who has dealt with the Midland kingdom has ever paid much attention to 'geographical factors'. THOMAS O'RAHILLY (*History*, 167-9) has shown how gratuitous were the assumptions of MACNEILL (*Phases*, 118) that made Uisnech a royal residence. Any acquaintance with the historical geography of the midlands would immediately have ruled out MACNEILL's theory. We need not wonder that excavations of the alleged royal residence produced next to nothing.

[c] Recent excavations at Tara have shown that some of its sacred sites were 'passage graves' of the Early Bronze Age (c. 1500 B.C.) (information from E. E. EVANS).

[d] Its memory was preserved for a thousand years in the maritime jurisdiction of the later Dublin corporation over the whole central part of the east coast (ALICE GREEN, 351).

Tara the predecessor of Dublin. The parallel between the early Gaelic centre and the Viking and Anglo-Norman centre goes even farther.

Tara was not only a regional 'capital'. At one time or other we find the kings of Tara claiming to be kings of all Ireland and superior to the other provincial kings.[10] At the end of the twelfth century Dublin was proclaimed the capital of the English lordship of Ireland. Throughout the Middle Ages, however, Dublin was only the claimant capital of all Ireland (its authority extended over a small part of 'Ulster' only). Ultimately Dublin inherited the role of capital of the Irish Free State and of the Republic of Ireland – so becoming once more a claimant capital for the whole of Ireland (again its authority extends over part of 'Ulster' only).

THE NORTHERN AND THE SOUTHERN HALF

The dividing influence of the Central Irish Lowlands in ancient Ireland is most apparent in the division of the island into two 'halves', a Northern and a Southern. THOMAS O'RAHILLY says:

"All through Irish literature the Northern Half of Ireland is known as *Leth Cuinn*, 'Conn's half', the Southern as *Leth Moga Nuadat* (or, shortly, *Leth Moga*), 'Mug Nuadat's half'. We may take it that here, as often, the names of ancestors are used in a secondary sense to signify the peoples descended from them, so that *Leth Cuinn* properly means 'the half dominated by the descendants of Conn', and *Leth Moga Nuadat* 'the half dominated by the descendants of Mug Nuadat'. ... Our early historians usually prefer a picturesque explanation to a prosaic one; and so from the ninth century, if not earlier, we find them inferring from these names that Conn and Mug Nuadat had divided Ireland between them".[11]

These names occur in the earliest Irish literature and continued to be used commonly down to the eighteenth century, in later times especially in poetry. O'RAHILLY suggests that the names could hardly have come into existence until the Gaelic conquest was well advanced.[12]

The time and manner of the Gaelic invasion are still matters of doubt and controversy. But there is no doubt that from the time of the earliest records – or, more correctly, from the earliest picture to be derived from the existing (though later) records – that is from about the sixth century onward, there were two Gaelic dynasties, a southern and a northern.

The former were the 'Eóganacht', literally: race of Eógan. They were established in Cashel (Co. Tipperary), probably from the fifth century onward.[13] They dominated the two southern provinces (kingdoms), Munster and Leinster. The northern dynasty is usually known as the 'Uí Néill', literally: descendants of Niall (a fifth-century king of Tara). [a] While there is some controversy as to the manner in which the Uí Néill power grew[14], it is accepted that after the fifth century their power extended over the 'midlands' and the ancient provinces of Connacht and Ulster. It also accepted[15] that after the conquest

[a] Originally they may have been known as the 'Connacht', literally: race of Conn. This name is retained in the name of the Connacht province (THOMAS O'RAHILLY, *History*, 174-5).

of Ulster the Uí Néill had two branches: a 'southern' one which was based upon Tara, and a 'northern' one whose rule centred in Ulster. [a]

The political division of early Gaelic Ireland, thus, meant that there was in effect a Northern and a Southern Half.[16] While I use the words 'political division', they must not be strained too far in their modern sense. Gaelic society as it had spread over Ireland was, essentially, a collection of small kingdoms, the so-called 'tuatha'.[b] Each king exercised direct authority only over the people of his own tuath. In addition he might also be an 'over-king', which meant that the kings of some neighbouring 'tribes'[c] admitted his supremacy. And he in his turn would be subordinate to a 'provincial king'.[17]

The 'political history' of pre-Viking Ireland appears to be concerned to a large extent with the warfare between the two most powerful of the Gaelic royal dynasties, the Uí Néill and the Eóganacht, viz. roughly between the Northern and the Southern Half. Their rivalry culminated in the 'high-kingship' controversy. It was probably in the fifth century that the Uí Néill laid claim to be supreme kings not only of the Northern Half but of all Ireland.[18] In the beginning the title, such as it was, alternated irregularly between the two branches of the dynasty, i.e. the 'northern' and 'southern' Uí Néill. Eventually it became the prerogative of the 'northern' Uí Néill.

"But though .. the Uí Néill called themselves kings of Ireland for six centuries afterwards, this must have always remained a matter of fact not of right: sometimes they were powerful enough to compel recognition of their claim from the other provincial kings, sometimes they weren't. And we have evidence that even their theoretical supremacy was repudiated by writers of the Southern Half as late as the eighth century".[19]

Gaelic society, although it showed 'politically' very little cohesion, enjoyed a remarkable cultural unity. From the later fifth or early sixth century the Gaelic language was spoken throughout Ireland[20] – though pockets, however large or small, of pre-Gaelic language may have continued to exist. The Gaelic language produced a literature which was to become one of the great glories of the Irish, indeed of the European, cultural heritage. [d]

THE OLDEST CONCEPTS OF ULSTER

The oldest regional concept to which the name 'Ulster' can be attached is the 'cóiced nUlad', literally: the province (kingdom) of the Ulaid. This takes us back to the first four

[a] The territories of the 'northern' Uí Néill and of their dependencies were called collectively 'In Fochla', literally: the North. This term seems to have remained in general use until about 925 (MacNeill, Celtic 133-4). It is interesting to find the term 'the North' used at such an early date for Ulster or part of Ulster. (Hitherto no modern propagandist has seized on this fact for polemic purposes.)

[b] The territory of such a 'tribal state' roughly corresponds to the modern barony (baronies are the constituent elements of the counties).

[c] Here the word 'tribal' is used as a sociological concept without any of the emotional overtones which it acquired in nineteenth-century polemics.

[d] Two very significant developments were the establishment of a common code of law, and the building-up of a 'syncretic history'. This syncretic history, which absorbed all subject pre-Gaelic population elements, explained the population differences in Ireland by means of a series of invasions. It found its most complete expression in the Book of Invasions, a compilation which, in its earliest form, goes back to the eighth century (Thomas O'Rahilly, History, 193-4). The ancient sagas and legends were altered or recast in order to suit this synthesis; the unravelling of the more or less botched versions is a task which does not always result in agreement among Celtic scholars.

centuries A.D., if not earlier. The territory at the time dominated by the Ulaid seems to have covered all the uplands north of the Central Irish Lowlands, including the Central Ulster Lowlands. According to the traditional theory the Ulaid 'capital' (centre) was at Emain Macha near Armagh.[21]

The Ulaid were not the oldest inhabitants of the north. They may not even have been the first Celtic speakers who settled there. [a] THOMAS O'RAHILLY conjectures that the Ulaid belong to the second of four migrations of Celtic speakers to Ireland, and that they invaded Ireland from Great Britain.[22] Within the territory of the Ulaid, and probably subject to them, were scattered communities of Pretani (Irish: Cruthin), the first Celtic-speaking invaders of the British Isles.[b] Their most populous community appears to have been the 'Dál nAraidi', who occupied the greater part of Co. Antrim and the west of Co. Down, and survived into early-Christian times.[23] (Is it unlikely to see in this settlement a bridgehead colony of the Pretani in nearby Scotland?)

The Ulaid (or their predecessors) may have spoken Brythonic (British), the language which was also used in most parts of Great Britain and which has survived as Welsh. Eventually they were to adopt Gaelic, the language which later became known as Irish. According to THOMAS O'RAHILLY the Gaelic language was introduced into Ireland only with the latest wave of Celtic-speaking invaders. Though the Gaels must have been few in number in comparison with the indigenous population, they gradually won a dominant position because of "their skill in war and politics" and by "the prestige of a superior culture".[24]

It was in the fifth century, as O'RAHILLY and BINCHY have suggested, that a section of the Gaels who had established themselves in Tara, the Uí Néill, forced their way northward into the Ulaid kingdom. "Traditions embodied in several of the *Ulidian Tales* suggest very plainly that during an extended period an aggressive warfare was waged by the men of Tara, with the help of the vassals whom they employed as fightingmen, against the Ulaid".[25] Once the Ulaid were overthrown, and their 'capital' Emain razed, there was no longer any serious obstacle to completing the conquest of Ulster. As O'RAHILLY observes, the conquest of the entire province of Ulster must have enormously increased the power and prestige of the Tara dynasty. It is not unlikely that the claim of the king of Tara to be *king of Ireland* originated at this time.[26]

The end of the struggle is marked by the settlement of princes of the Uí Néill in the middle and western parts of Ulster. The Ulaid themselves were driven eastward into Co. Down where they were known as the 'Dál Fiatach'. Their kinsmen the 'Dál Ríada' were henceforth confined to a small territory in north Co. Antrim. The Ulaid retained a certain suzerainty over east Ulster, *i.e.* an area approximating to modern Cos Antrim

[a] We have no means of knowing what languages the pre-Celtic peoples in Ireland spoke. An intensive study of place-names might possibly reveal some pre-Celtic features but such a study has yet to be attempted (cf. *Society*, 37). While there has been considerable speculation – some of it rather bizarre – on possible non-Indo-European elements in the Gaelic language, there has been little agreement. EVANS suggests that the self-contained population groups of fishermen on Lough Neagh's banks (in the very heart of the Central Ulster Lowlands), who use strange unexplained words for their fishing gear, are descendants of pre-Celtic invaders (*Folk Ways*, 6; *Portrait*, 52).

[b] As we know, the Pretani remained much more prominent in Scotland where they preserved their independence down to the ninth century, from the third century onward being known to Latin writers as 'Picti' (THOMAS O'RAHILLY, *History*, 341-2).

and Down.[27] Hence, from about the middle of the fifth century onward the old title *rí Ulad* (king of the Ulaid) had a double significance: it meant king of the Ulaid (the Dál Fiatach), and suzerain of east Ulster. [a] This is the first time that east Ulster emerges as a separate, though a rather shadowy, regional concept.

THE BLACK PIG'S DYKE

It probably was at the time of the Gaelic conquest that a series of linear earthworks was constructed which runs discontinuously from the head of Carlingford Lough on the east coast to Donegal Bay in the west.[b] Known locally under different names, these earthworks have the picturesque collective title of the 'Black Pig's Dyke'.[28] An alternative, more suggestive, term is the 'Great Wall of Ulster'.

R. A. S. MACALISTER describes the Dyke as "a chain of earthen mounds, roughly about thirty feet thick at the base and twenty feet high, running between two trenches each about ten feet deep". He assumes that the gaps in the Dyke originally were filled by forests and bogs, like those in Offa's Dyke on the eastern border of Wales.[29] An unusual section is the 'Dorsey' (cf. 'doirse', doors), an enormous entrenchment in south Co. Armagh. It consists of an oblong mound which rises about fifty feet above the surrounding marsh and has a ditch on each side. Originally it was continued as a line of palisades across the bog (information from E. ESTYN EVANS).

Various archaeologists agree that the detached earthworks may be copies of the Roman frontier works in Great Britain, perhaps as seen from the outside, and that they mark the southern border of the original Ulster kingdom. Opinions differ as to the main function of the Dyke. MACALISTER and JOSEPH RAFTERY interpret the Dyke as a series of defence works, designed to check the aggression of the Tara kings between the third and the fifth century A.D. This was also the view of EOIN MACNEILL.[30] The Dorsey probably commanded the main approach road to the Ulaid capital, Emain Macha. [c]

SEÁN Ó RÍORDÁIN doubts whether the Black Pig's Dyke was planned as a singular defensive work: "Such a great earthwork could hardly have been effectively manned in a military sense".[31] O. DAVIES holds the same opinion:

"The social and political conditions of ancient Ireland would have precluded linear defence even along a few miles; even the Romans, with their elaborate military technique, could use Hadrian's Wall as little more than a protected sentry-walk. The purpose of the Irish dykes was to concentrate traffic at defined crossings. This is not very different from the first stage of the Roman frontier in Britain, apart from the fact that this was much longer and was supported by a standing garrison based on a road".[32]

Both Ó RÍORDÁIN and DAVIES suggest that the dykes have served as a deterrent to cattle-raiding. They also assume that the habit of constructing such earthworks may have prevailed for a long period. The Anglo-Normans in Ireland still built, or at least utilized, entrenchments across passages. The Pale, "a late earthwork of much less imposing

---

[a] It appears that at times the more extensive and populous state of the Pretani (the Dál nAraidi), east of Lough Neagh, won supremacy over the Dál Fiatach. Then their kings laid claim to the coveted title of *rí Ulad* in its wider sense (DOBBS, 73-8; THOMAS O'RAHILLY, *History*, 347).

[b] Unfortunately there is no precise map of these earthworks.

[c] Pottery finds would suggest a date about the third century for the Dorsey, according to EVANS who also reports that there are other, shorter, lines of defence between the Dorsey and Armagh.

character", built around the area of the same name, may have served a similar function.[33] DAVIES does not reject the view that the Black Pig's Dyke follows the border of the Ulaid kingdom:

> "On the assumption that the short entrenchments described straddled roads with the purpose of preventing cattle-raiding, it would be reasonable to connect them as a single frontier if there is evidence that the gaps were closed by bog or forest, through which it would be impossible to drive cattle".[34]

There is another series of linear earthworks running through south-west Co. Down, known as the 'Dane's Cast'. The view is held that the Dane's Cast is a later line than the Black Pig's Dyke, and that it was constructed when the Gaels of Tara had conquered the greater part of Ulster. It therefore probably demarcated the south-western border of the restricted Ulaid kingdom.[35] Its name, like those of many dykes in Great Britain and on the continent, is associated with the Vikings.[36] However, there is no evidence that the Dane's Cast was erected or employed by the Vikings, nor that it was used against them.

Some polemic writers in Northern Ireland have seized on the *Ulster Sagas* as an early precedent of Ulster Unionist mythology, and on the Black Pig's Dyke as a forerunner of the present land boundary. Their intrusion into the Partition issue has provoked uncharitable retorts from the side of Nationalists on the unlikelihood of the ancient Ulster heroes recognizing descendants in the bowler-hatted Belfast Orangemen. On the other hand, the apparent disinclination of some people in the Republic to see in the Black Pig's Dyke more than scattered local tribal defences may be based on the dislike of seeing any predecessor of the land boundary. In fact, the course of the Black Pig's Dyke very roughly coincides with that of the modern land boundary. The Dyke, then, is, to some degree, a locational predecessor of the present state frontier. It is clear that it cannot be considered a functional predecessor.

THE DICHOTOMY OF EARLY CHRISTIANITY

The first fixed date in Irish history, says THOMAS O'RAHILLY in his famous paper on *The Two Patricks*, is 431. In that year Pope Celestine ordained Palladius as first bishop *ad Scottos in Christum credentis*.[37] It is uncertain, however, what became of Palladius, and also what was at the time understood by 'Scottos' or 'Scotti'. The history of the introduction of Christianity into Ireland is a matter of vigorous, perhaps even embittered, controversy.[38]

The old theory, which is still widely accepted, is that the Roman mission of Palladius was unsuccessful and was followed by the successful mission of Patrick, a Briton, who founded Armagh as the ecclesiastical capital for the whole island. [a] Several points of the orthodox theory were already criticized in the nineteenth century[39]; the established views are also firmly criticized by a number of modern scholars. [b]

---

[a] Patrick would then indeed have had "a striking predilection for Ulster", or at least for the Dál Fiatach territory. He is supposed to have spent his period of slavery in Co. Antrim, he would have begun his missionary activity at Saul on Strangford Lough, and his grave, on this theory, is at Downpatrick in Co. Down.

[b] For instance, THOMAS O'RAHILLY believed that the Roman mission of Palladius was largely confined to the 'midlands' (Tara) and Connacht (the territories of the 'southern' Uí Néill), and that the later British mission of Patrick was concentrated in Ulster. He suggested that the Palladian and Patrician

Whatever the truth of the various theories concerning the Palladian and Patrician missions, there is no doubt that Armagh became an episcopal see as early as the fifth century. One may wonder why this see was established at Armagh. According to JAMES CARNEY Armagh was chosen because it was adjacent to Emain Macha, "the seat of northern power". The intention obviously was, he says, "that the bishop of the Scotti [a] should rule, as the Pope in Rome, from the capital city".[40] D. A. BINCHY holds a similar view. He observes that it was the practice of all the early missioners to set up their own headquarters as close as possible to the capital of the kingdom or tribe to which they were sent.[b] BINCHY suggests that Emain Macha was still the 'capital' of the Ulaid at the time when Patrick came to Ireland.[41]

The history of the early Irish Church, in so far as it may be considered as a national unit, reflects the age-long north-south dichotomy in Ireland. Various authors have suggested that the conversion of the Southern Half, or at least a large part of it, preceded that of the Northern Half. BINCHY, for instance, conjectures that as early as the fourth century there must have been a number of Christian communities in Munster and the south of Leinster.[42] (This would make it probable that the ecclesiastical centre of Munster, Cashel, is older than Armagh.)

missions have been synthesized by the later Armagh ecclesiastics who claimed primatial authority over the whole island (*Patricks*, 26, 37, 46, 50-1, 83; cf. KENNEY, 159-60, 309-12).

   JAMES CARNEY also thinks that Patrick was only posthumously enrolled among the early Armagh bishops in order to establish the claim of the see to jurisdiction over the entire island. But he maintains that Patrick was in no way connected with Armagh and that the see of Armagh was established not by a British but by a Roman missionary. In CARNEY's opinion all northern traditions concerning Patrick are a series of deliberate fictions and forgeries "which endeavoured to anchor Patrick to Armagh" (396-402). D. A. BINCHY, however, recently expressed as his opinion that Patrick was intimately associated with Armagh, and that he established his principal headquarters at Armagh. In this respect BINCHY agrees with "the most orthodox of the Patrician theorists". For the rest he also believes that the Patrician story is "a case of over-simplification which first came into being in the interest of Armagh, in order to support the claims of Armagh to the primacy": "in the Patrician story several missions have been telescoped" (15).

[a] CARNEY, who believes that the *primus episcopus Scottorum* was a Roman, lays much stress on the fact that Patrick, who described himself as a bishop in 'Hiberione', referred tenderly to the 'Hiberionaci' but was hostile to the Picts and Scotti (404, 407). "To Patrick the Scotti were a people of ill-repute whom he mentally associated with the Picts. This would suggest either that Patrick restricted the term Scotti to that portion of the Irish people whose chief city was Emain Macha, or else, but less likely, that he used it for that section of the Irish people who had established colonies in Britain and hence were neighbours of the detested Picts" (406).

   It is well to remember that the term 'Scotti' is applied by various writers from the second half of the fourth century onward to the invaders from Ireland who, like the Picts, undertook plundering expeditions in the northern districts of Roman Britain. The question raised by CARNEY is whether in those early times 'Scotti' was a generic term for all inhabitants of Ireland, or was confined to the people of the north. In fact, there are authors who believe that at the time the Scots were restricted within Ulster. For instance, LLOYD in his *History of Wales* (vol. i, 95-6) notes that the Scots were "dwellers in the North of Ireland, and thus their association with the Picts was natural, for the passage from Ulster to Galloway, which is known to have been a Pictish country, was easily accomplished" (cf. CECILE O'RAHILLY, 37-8). From the eighth till the eleventh century, however, the name is apparently used as the Latin word for the Irish without any qualification.

[b] There is a parallel with Canterbury which became the ecclesiastical capital of England because it was the capital of one of the most important English kingdoms, *i.e.* Kent. London did not become the national capital until very much later (BINCHY, 16).

The pre-Patrician conversion of the Southern Half is often attributed to British missionaries. It is likely that some knowledge of Christianity must have percolated through the Gaelic colonies in Wales.[43] According to THOMAS O'RAHILLY the repatriation of Irish colonists in the second half of the fifth century must have meant "an accession of British influence in religious matters".[44] And there remained close ecclesiastical relations between Wales and southern Ireland during the sixth century.[45]

The north-south duality is perhaps most evident from the rivalry between Armagh and Cashel. Their rivalry provides a striking counterpart of the rivalry between the two chief royal dynasties of early Gaelic Ireland, the 'northern' Uí Néill and the Eóganacht. As a matter of fact, the ecclesiastical controversies were closely related with the political controversies. As for Cashel: it is well to remember that this ecclesiastical centre was also the seat of the Eóganacht (it probably had become an ecclesiastical capital because it was the 'political capital' of Munster). From the end of the eighth century down to the first half of the tenth century secular and ecclesiastical power were even united in the persons of several king-bishops.

And as for Armagh: its claim to primatial authority over all Ireland – which met strong opposition in Cashel[a] – is paralleled by the claim of the Uí Néill to the political supremacy over the whole island – which claim, too, was most tenaciously opposed in Cashel. In fact, as BINCHY states, it was only after Armagh came under the dominance of the Uí Néill that we find the claim to the primacy advanced.[46]

It is certain, as LOUIS GOUGAUD has shown, that the supremacy claimed by the northern see until the twelfth century amounted to very little.[47] It could hardly have been otherwise in view of the peculiar organization of Early Christianity in Ireland (and Highland Britain). The episcopal organization established in the fifth century soon decayed, largely as a result from the temporary isolation of the Celtic lands from the Church on the continent. 'Celtic Christianity', from the sixth to the twelfth century, was 'monastic' in structure and 'abbatial' in administration rather than 'diocesan' and 'episcopal'.[48] This loose organization reflected – in fact, was adapted to – the loose political organization of Gaelic Ireland which, of course, was quite unlike the social organization obtaining in the former provinces of the Roman Empire which had experience of centralized administration.

Chapter 9

RELATIONS BETWEEN IRELAND AND HIGHLAND BRITAIN

THE CONTRASTS BETWEEN HIGHLAND AND LOWLAND BRITAIN

There is abundant evidence that throughout prehistorical times the Irish Sea tended to be "the centre of a vast cultural province frequently uniting its much fractionated and

---

[a] Some scholars even have conjectured that the traditions of a pre-Patrician introduction of the Faith in the south may have been "inventions of Munstermen in the eleventh and twelfth centuries, who sought a claim to more or less independence of Armagh at a time when the Irish Church was being reorganized on a territorial and episcopal basis and when Munster was making a bid for the political hegemony of the island" (KENNEY, 310-1).

indented coastlands under a single cultural stimulus" (BOWEN). The Irish Sea continued to perform this unifying function in the so-called Age of the Saints when 'Celtic Christian' missionaries were active in establishing churches and monasteries in Western Europe, *i.e.* between the sixth and eighth centuries.[49]

This ancient cultural region, bound together by the Irish Sea, did not extend over the whole of Great Britain. It included only what is often styled 'Highland Britain' in contrast with 'Lowland Britain'. This "simple yet fundamental distinction" (DUDLEY STAMP) was introduced by HALFORD MACKINDER in his now classic book *Britain and the British Seas* (1902). Highland Britain includes all the main hill masses and mountains, Lowland Britain the major stretches of plain and lowland. Highland Britain extends over Scotland, northern England, Wales and Cornwall, Lowland Britain over the rest of England. The two areas offer a striking contrast in elevation, relief of the ground, soils, and rainfall.[50]

Various scholars have adopted and developed MACKINDER's distinction. DUDLEY STAMP, for instance, has pointed out the great difference which exists between the patterns of human settlement in Highland and Lowland Britain. In Highland Britain human settlement is essentially discontinuous – the cultivated areas occupy valleys and plains separated by large expanses of uncultivated hill lands – whereas in Lowland Britain human settlement is essentially continuous and there the cultivated land of one parish merges into that of the next.[51] The first to show the significance of the major natural division of Great Britain in the pre- and early historical periods was CYRIL FOX. In his essay on *The Personality of Britain* he observes:

"In the Lowland of Britain new cultures of continental origin tend to be *imposed* on the earlier or aboriginal culture. In the Highland, on the other hand, these tend to be *absorbed* by the older culture. Viewed in another aspect, in the Lowland, you get *replacement*, in the Highland, *fusion*. The power of absorption, the tendency to fusion in the Highland, may at times result in a greater continuity of cultural character, or it may provide the west with a cultural character of its own".[52]

The contrast between the two areas was epitomized by the Roman occupation of Great Britain in the boundary between the civil and military areas. The military districts established in parts of Highland Britain differed from the civil zone in preserving much more of their pre-Roman, Celtic, character. They were much less thickly inhabited, almost entirely lacking the large towns and great rural 'villas' (estates) of Lowland Britain.[53] Evidence of the cultural continuity in Highland Britain is the survival of Celtic languages in Scotland, Wales, and (down till the end of the eighteenth century) Cornwall.[54]

It was the Highland Zone, and not the Irish Sea, which for long acted as an effective natural dividing zone between Lowland Britain, *i.e.* England, and Ireland. [a] The Welsh mountains and the Pennines have saved Ireland from various invasions and they have modified others. The most obvious instances of the barrier function of Highland Britain

[a] The effectiveness of the Highland Zone as a natural barrier preventing the advance of Lowland influence is strongly evidenced by 'Offa's Dyke', the boundary between the Celtic people of the Welsh mountains and the Anglo-Saxon kingdom of Mercia, erected at the end of the eighth century. Long recognized both by Welsh and English as their common boundary, it still has significance. The present administrative border of Wales, established in 1538, corresponds closely to the ancient frontier over two-fifths of its course (FOX, *Boundary*, 6, 11, 22).

are provided by the Roman and the Anglo-Saxon conquests. The Roman effort faded out on the shores of the Irish Sea [a], the Saxon conquest never even approached it.

RELATIONS BETWEEN SOUTHERN IRELAND AND WALES

Various geographers have pointed out that Ireland is essentially a detached portion of Highland Britain: "the natural if now insular continuation of Highland Britain".[55] This has applied, with varying historical emphasis, not only to Ireland's natural features but also to her cultural features. "Inevitably", JACQUETTA and CHRISTOPHER HAWKES say, "her fate was closely linked with that of the British Highlands that reached out towards her even while they walled her off from England and the continent".[56]

Such cultural influences and invasions that reached Ireland from Great Britain in early times were almost always those of the Highland Zone. And it would appear that, whenever an Irish culture expanded, it was carried no further than Highland Britain, and the northern outliers of the Lowland Zone: it did not effectively reach across the mountain barrier to southern England.[57]

In fact, contacts across the Irish Sea were so close that, if it is necessary to divide the ancient cultural region into sub-regions, the main division must be rather between a southern and a northern area than between an eastern and a western. There was a definite tendency for the southern parts of Highland Britain and Ireland to form one cultural sub-region as the northern parts formed another.[58] PIERRE FLATRÈS has suggested that human relationships between the "two pairs of countries" were greatly facilitated by the correspondence between the natural environments of the opposite shores of the Irish Sea.[59]

And, of course, in ancient times there was found "easier and swifter passage by sea than any mountain trail could allow" (HAWKES). We find the same idea in ZIMMER who suggested that, in earlier times, "intercourse between Britons in the south-west and Irish in south Ireland must have been easier and safer than intercourse with such of their own fellow-countrymen as lived inland at an equal distance".[60]

Commercial contacts between southern Ireland and south-west Britain are attested as early as the Bronze and Iron Ages.[61] From the third century A.D. on there is abundant evidence of invasions of Gaelic-speaking people from the Southern Half, especially Co. Waterford, into the south of Great Britain.[b] There was a dynasty of southern Irish kings established in south-west Wales, apparently from the end of the third century. They

---

[a] We know from Tacitus (*De Vita et Moribus Agricolae*, xxiv) that Agricola, after he had halted at the Forth–Clyde line, and with his subsequent conquest of Galloway on the south-west coast of Scotland in the early eighties A.D., contemplated the possibility of invading Ireland. He considered that "in soil and climate, and in the temperament and manner of its people", Ireland differed little from Great Britain. Tacitus also reveals that Agricola, "under a show of friendship", had received an Irish 'kinglet' whom he kept at hand to use if opportunity offered (cf. COLE, 34-5; COLLINGWOOD, 114, 117).

[b] Evidence for the existence of southern Irish colonies is provided by the widespread Gaelic inscriptions of a type well known in Ireland and dating from the fifth to seventh centuries. These inscriptions are in the cumbersome 'Ogam script', assumed to be based on the Latin alphabet as taught in the grammar schools of the later Roman Empire. There survive in Ireland to the present day a little over three hundred stone monuments with Ogam inscriptions, five-sixth of which are found in the three southern counties of Kerry, Cork, and Waterford. In addition there are forty in Wales, six in Cornwall, two in Devon, and two in Scotland, *viz.* in Argyll opposite north-eastern Ireland. Their rarity in Scotland parallels their rarity in northern Ireland (JACKSON, *Language*, 151-3; cf. BINCHY, 8-9).

continued to rule there until the tenth century. There is reason to think that they kept in touch with their homeland until at least the eighth century.[62] There were also Irish colonies in north Wales and in Cornwall but they are less well evidenced and may very likely have been less numerous.[a] Welsh-Irish relations were perhaps closest and most continuous in the sixth and seventh centuries.[63] Trade with southern Ireland was, without doubt, one of the earliest maritime contacts of Bristol; and it remained of great importance throughout the Middle Ages.[64]

A new situation was to arise once England had achieved internal unity and set out to conquer the rest of Great Britain, indeed the rest of the British Isles. It seems inevitable that contacts between Wales and southern Ireland should become overshadowed by Anglo-Irish relations. The first sign of this shift in cross-Channel connexions is perhaps to be seen in the linkage between the Viking kingdoms of Dublin and York.[65] For the time being, however, in a kind of transitional period, Welsh-Irish intercourse was replaced by a triangular connexion between Norman England, Wales, and southern Ireland.

From the eleventh to the middle of the twelfth century, while the Welsh struggled against the Anglo-Normans, they looked upon Ireland as "the natural refuge where they might hope for asylum and for aid against their enemies".[66] On the other hand, the so-called 'Anglo-Norman' invasion of Ireland had a very marked Welsh character. Not only did the invaders come from Wales but their leaders were half Welsh by intermarriage, and there were many pure Welshmen among the rank and file of the invading army.[67] Later on Welsh mercenaries swelled the 'Cambrian' element. Indeed, a century after the invasion had taken place, a charter claimed half the credit for the Welsh followers or kinsmen of the invaders.[68] And according to a common tradition there were substantial settlements of Welsh adventurers in the twelfth and following centuries. Many place-names are taken as proof of the existence of these colonies.[69]

Anyhow, we may assume that with the 'Anglo-Norman' invasion of Ireland the free and direct intercourse of the southern Irish and the Welsh came to an end. As CECILE O'RAHILLY says, "The later history of Wales, at least in as far as it concerns Ireland, is one with that of England".[70]

RELATIONS BETWEEN ULSTER AND SCOTLAND

However important the contacts between the southern parts of the British Isles, relations were most frequent, and had the most far-reaching effects, in the north. The distinctiveness of northern Ireland (Ulster) from southern Ireland may be implied, to some extent, in its isolation by the Central Irish Lowlands. It is also – if not mainly – conditioned by its proximity to Great Britain (Scotland). The North Channel is, at its narrowest point, between Antrim and the Mull of Kintyre, less than twelve miles wide.[71]

C. B. FAWCETT's conclusion that the relative effect of the different parts of the 'sea barrier' between Great Britain and Ireland has depended more on the character of the

---

[a] It seems that about 400 A.D. the Romans settled a British force from the north in north Wales as *foederati* to subdue the Irish there. JACKSON also conjectures that the Irish settlers in Cornwall "persisted as a separate entity, and kept up their language, in the sixth and perhaps as late as the seventh century" (*Language*, 156, 172).

shores than on the width of the waters, is generally speaking true. Fawcett has misjudged, however, the effects of Ulster's proximity to what he calls the 'British mainland':

"The North Channel lies between the highland districts of Antrim and Kintyre which, before the rise of the industrial regions of Ulster and the Clyde, were remote from the fertile and populous parts of the two countries and were comparatively poor and unimportant. Both Ireland and Scotland then faced east-ward and south-eastward, towards England and away from each other; and thus the importance of their close approach was only slight and occasional".[72]

This is a typical instance of the anglo-centric view of the historical geography of the British Isles. It is true that, prior to the Industrial Revolution, the highland districts on both sides of the North Channel were remote and comparatively insignificant. But it is not true that the importance of the close approach of the two islands was only "slight and occasional". I rather agree with Shearman that

"For thousands of years the inhabitants of north-east Ulster and of south-west Scotland have been aware of each other's existence and have looked across at each other's territory with a view to exploration, conquest, refuge or trade. There has been coming and going between the two since the earliest periods of human occupation".[73]

Ulster's proximity to Scotland made it a natural way of entry. According to Fox:

"Invaders and cultures of British origin show a tendency to concentrate in Ulster for the same reason that continental cultures show a tendency to concentrate in south-east Britain. This suggests that the aloofness of Ulster from the general life of Ireland has its basis in prehistoric times; indeed, the island at times presents as marked a duality as Britain does".[74]

The theory is generally accepted today that the earliest people to reach Ireland, Early Mesolithic folk who can be traced back to about 6000 B.C., entered the island in the north-east, i.e. via the North Channel.[75] As Raftery concluded, the distribution of certain Irish Bronze and Iron Age material can best be explained by stating that the north-east was but "a continuation, in the cultural sense, of Britain's Highland Zone".[76]

A distribution pattern which has attracted much attention is that provided by the 'horned' or 'court cairns'. They are a highly specialized and localized type of chambered megalithic grave: "a dramatic demonstration of prehistoric regionalism within the unmistakable unity of the West European megalithic culture" (Evans). The distinctive burial structures are found only in northern Ireland, with an extension in the north of Connacht, and in the north-west of Great Britain.[77] Evans and E. M. Jope[78] see in their distribution "an early example of the space-relations which have influenced the cultural geography of north-eastern Ireland through the ages".[a]

---

[a] Recently the theories about these monuments, first advanced by a group of Belfast archaeologists a quarter of a century ago, have been challenged by Professor De Valera of Dublin. While the former postulated the entry of the culture into the Irish Sea, Professor De Valera concluded that it was diffused across northern Ireland and Great Britain from the north of Connacht (Cos Mayo and Sligo). Evans, in his review of De Valera's paper, argues that "none of the known invasions or cultural innovations which can be traced in Irish history has had its starting point on the remote and wild west coast. One is tempted rather to think of the coastlands of Mayo and Sligo as areas where old fashioned ways persisted so long that they look like congested districts on the megalithic map. Why, if the voyagers came here from the south, did they not land on the south coast, or on the west coast south of Galway Bay? And why, having landed in Mayo, did they not move south-eastwards into Leinster instead of making north-eastwards into Ulster?" (Studia Hibernica, vol. i, 228-32).

One of the most important migrations across the North Channel has been that from east Ulster to west Scotland, which began in the second half of the fifth century A.D. We have seen already that, probably in the first half of the fifth century, the Ulaid kingdom was conquered by the Uí Néill who established themselves firmly in mid and west Ulster. The Ulaid retained only a certain suzerainty over a number of *tuatha* (petty kingdoms) east of Lough Neagh and the river Bann. THOMAS O'RAHILLY suggests that the impairment of their territory was one of the reasons for the subsequent migration from east Ulster into various islands and peninsulas of west Scotland.[79]

Most of the colonists seem to have come from north Co. Antrim, then known as the kingdom of Dál Ríada. That by this time the Ulaid had become gaelicized is apparent in the name of their first colony, 'Oir-Ghaeil', today: Argyll, traditionally translated as Eastern Gaels, alternatively explained as 'Erra-ghaidheal', literally: coastland of the Gael.[80]

This settlement was the counterpart of the migration of Gaelic-speaking people from southern Ireland to the southern parts of Highland Britain – a movement that had already begun before the end of Roman rule in Great Britain. The colonization by the Ulaid began later, perhaps because the Gaels did not encroach on their territory before the fifth century. There is another, more important, difference between the two movements: that in the north had much more lasting effects than that in the south.

One may ask why, of all the Gaelic invasions of Great Britain, only the last one, the one from Ulster, was successful in the sense that it was destined to be permanent.[a] In the south the Gaelic invaders lost their supremacy and gradually merged into their British surroundings, losing their identity and their speech.[81] The explanation is likely to be found in the proximity of northern Ireland and north Britain, which facilitated the maintenance of close connexions and the supply of new levies of colonists. Once the relationship between the two countries was established, subsequent migrations, in either direction, must have been made easier because of the similarity in social (and physical) environment.

It is frequently said that it was the Scots who made modern Ulster. There is as much reason for saying that it was 'Ulstermen' who made ancient Scotland. For the colonists from east Ulster gave Scotland her name, her first kings, her Gaelic language, and her faith. It is often suggested that modern Ulster is an extension or projection of Scotland, but the first concept of Scotland was really an extension or projection of 'Gaelic Ulster'.

Whatever the original meaning of 'Scotti' (see p. 112), there is no doubt that the emigrants from east Ulster carried the name to west Scotland. Nor is there any doubt that for centuries the name was shared by the mother country and the colony alike. It was only in the second half of the ninth century, following the absorption of the Picts by the immigrant Scotti, that the term 'Scotia' – or 'Scotia minor' as distinguished from

---

[a] There was a similar movement to the Isle of Man. Instead of being absorbed, as were the southern Gaelic colonies in Cornwall and Wales, this northern Gaelic colony absorbed the indigenous population. Thus Gaelic became the language of Man; evolving into 'Manx', it remained the language of the island till recent times. While now obsolete as a spoken language, it is still used a little in certain traditional and formal acts of the *House of Keys*, the Manx parliament, and there has been a revival of interest in it, somewhat like the 'Irish revival' in Ireland.

'Scotia (major)' which, till c. 1000, normally meant Ireland – began to be used as a convenient designation for the population of north Britain as a whole. [a] From the eleventh century the terms 'Scoti' and 'Scotia' (English and Norse: 'Scotland') came to be associated exclusively with the north of Great Britain. [82]

Until the Viking invasions the two territories, 'Irish' and 'Scottish' Dál Ríada, were ruled by the same kings. [83] The last king of 'greater Dál Ríada' died in 792. [b] It was under Kenneth (Cinead) MacAlpin, who died 858, that the Scots and the Picts were united under one crown to form the nucleus of the later kingdom of Scotland. The extension of Scotia led to the transference of the seat of government eastward. [c] The direct line of the Dalradian kings became extinct in 1285.

THE GAELICIZATION OF THE SCOTTISH HIGHLANDS

The cultural effects of the Gaelic conquest of west Scotland were no less far-reaching than the political ones. The early colonists in fact imposed their Gaelic culture on much of Scotland (and Man, which we may ignore). The Gaelic culture then came to embrace the whole of Ireland and a great part of modern Scotland. As KENNETH JACKSON observes:

"Until at least the end of the sixteenth century Ireland and the Highlands formed a single culture-province. The 'sea-divided Gael', as they were called, were closely linked not only by their language but also by their civilization, their customs and traditions, by intermarriages between their noble kindreds, and by their aristocratic social system". [84]

The Gaelic language of Ireland and Scotland did not begin to diverge at all until the tenth century. Irish Gaelic and Scots Gaelic cannot be regarded as reaching the stage of distinct dialects until the twelfth and thirteenth centuries. For four or five centuries afterwards, however, the literary language of both Ireland and Scotland remained identical – thanks to the hereditary bardic families who carefully preserved and cultivated the language as it was spoken, at least among the educated, in both countries in the twelfth and thirteenth centuries. [85] The development of this what JACKSON calls 'Classic Common Gaelic' language being the same all over the area, it is, up to the seventeenth century,

[a] At the same time it began to supersede the native geographical name of 'Alba'. This term had no static connotation either. It derives from the earlier Celtic name of Great Britain, 'Albiu', recorded as 'Albion' by Pliny (preserved in "perfide Albion"). There is reason to believe that, in one way or another, the term was connected with the Pretani, as eventually it was applied only to north Britain, the land of the Picts. In the period under review it appears to have been used sometimes with reference to Scotland as a whole and sometimes to the non-Dalradian part of Scotland. Anyhow, 'Alba' in Scots Gaelic and Modern Irish, and 'yr Alban' in Welsh, still mean Scotland as a whole (CHADWICK, 3, 68-9; MACDONALD, n. 46; THOMAS O'RAHILLY, History, 385, 448).
[b] The name of the kingdom is revived in the term 'Dalradian', applied to the great metamorphic series of pre-Cambrian rocks which builds up the Central Highlands of Scotland. It was thus named (in 1891) because its outcrop includes the area of the ancient kingdom. The Dalradian rocks continue in the north and west of Ireland (CHARLESWORTH, 11-5).
[c] Its symbol was the 'Stone of Destiny' which eventually became known as the 'Stone of Scone'. According to tradition the Stone, on which all Dalradian and later 'Scottish' kings had been crowned, was brought to Scotland by the first king of 'greater Dál Ríada'. It was carried away from Scone by Edward I of England as booty of war in 1296 and ever since it has formed the seat of the coronation throne in Westminster Abbey. In 1950 it was removed by Scottish Nationalist students but after some months it was restored to Westminster (COUPLAND, 70, 408; cf. RITCHIE, 129, 186n).

quite impossible to say from linguistic reasons whether a poem in Gaelic was written in Ireland or in Scotland.

It was not, says JACKSON, until the break-up of the Gaelic aristocratic order in the seventeenth century, and the removal of its powerful unifying influence, that the Gaelic civilizations of the two countries began to go each its own way, and new literature composed in the now divergent popular dialects of Ireland and the Scottish Highlands began to displace the old common literature.[86]

Another factor which was to bind the northern parts of both islands together was Christianity. About the middle of the sixth century Colmcille (Columba maior), who belonged to the Uí Néill, founded a monastery on the little island of Iona, off the Scottish west coast in the Dalradian kingdom. Iona abbey was the starting-point of an energetic missionary campaign which spread over the whole north of Great Britain, including Northumbria in the north of England. The extension of the Gaelic language over a great part of Scotland was, no doubt, greatly helped by the conversion of the Picts. On the other hand, as R. L. RITCHIE suggests, the Dalradians have owed much of their success over the Picts to their possession of Iona, "the religious centre of all Scotti".[87]

Iona became the centre of a confederation of monastic settlements, the *familia Columbae*, at the time "the most powerful religious body in the Irish world".[88] For a century, more or less, following Columba's death in 597, "his clergy dominated the religious life of Ireland – or at least northern Ireland – Scotland, and Northumbria", quite overshadowing Armagh.[89] Their power was shattered, however, by the Paschal controversy. In fact, the eclipse of the Columban order by their defeat on the so-called Easter question helped the growing prestige of Armagh. [a]

Chapter 10

THE VIKING AND ANGLO-NORMAN CONQUESTS

POLITICAL IMPACTS OF THE VIKING INVASIONS

The first assault on Gaelic society as it had expanded over Ireland and a great part of Scotland came from Scandinavia, in particular from Norway. [b] For a time the Irish Sea

[a] Although the dating of the Easter festival had been reformed in 457, the Church in the Celtic lands for a long time adhered to the term as fixed in the third century. After strong pressure from Rome, southern Ireland accepted the reform of the Paschal date in the second quarter of the seventh century. The northern ecclesiastics, however, stood by the old term. KENNEY (216, 424) notes that the 'Romans' formed a recognized party in the Irish Church for the remainder of the century; "their efforts to win over the northern Irish seem to have had a marked influence on the country's ecclesiastical history". Thus the Easter controversy, too, reveals the north-south polarization in Early Christian Ireland.

The northern Irish submitted only towards the end of the seventh century, save Iona and affiliated monasteries. At least part of Iona was won over in 716 (GOUGAUD, 193-4, 199; ZIMMER, 78-86). It was during the Easter controversy that the claims of Armagh to primatial supremacy were most vigorously pressed (and that the earliest extant lives of St Patrick appear). Here, it is worthy of note, is one definite instance of a 'unifying' effect of the Church, for the northern see was aided in its claims by what KENNEY calls 'the Roman party of the south" (221, 325).

[b] The traditional name in Ireland for the Vikings is 'Danes', but the greater part of them were Norwegians. Hence Irish historians usually refer to them as 'Norse'.

was a 'Scandinavian lake' in which the Isle of Man acted as the 'Malta' of the new maritime power.[90] In the beginning the Vikings were very destructive indeed: not one of the great monasteries – often temptingly situated (cf. Iona) – escaped their clutches.[91] In the course of the ninth century the Vikings established a great number of colonies on the Irish and Scottish coasts.

Traces of their settlements in the north are the names of Ulfriksfjord (now Larne), Strangford (Co. Down), and Carlingford (Co. Louth). The Vikings left their imprint more heavily on southern Ireland in the foundation of the first real cities in Ireland, some of which still bear their Viking names: Dublin (a 'vikingization' of a pre-existing Gaelic name), Wexford, Waterford, and Limerick.[a] In the eleventh and twelfth centuries these cities came to owe allegiance, even if at time nominal, to Irish provincial kings. Dublin, for instance, was controlled by the kings of Leinster. However, the cities retained much of their Viking character.[b]

By establishing strong settlements in the Hebrides and on the western peninsulas of Scotland the Vikings drove a wedge between the Scottish kingdom and its mother country in east Ulster. On the other hand, their invasions contributed a great deal to the development of the theory of the high-kingship, the theory of the overlordship of members of one royal family over all provincial kings. However, no high-king ever succeeded in uniting all forces against the invaders.[92]

The expansion of Gaelic culture over a great part of Scotland had raised the question – not necessarily in real terms, for we must not extend to the high-kingship modern ideas of statehood – whether the claim of the high-king to suzerainty over all Gaelic kings also stretched out across the North Channel. At any rate, it is clear that since the Viking invasions no high-king attempted to assert this right. In other words, the notion of a Gaelic high-kingship became definitely a conception of Irish high-kingship.[c]

The idea perhaps never came nearer to what we think of as central authority than in the rough-and-ready supremacy of Brian Boramha (926-1014), king of Cashel. Brian set aside the traditional claim to the high-kingship of the 'northern' Uí Néill in 1000 A.D. On the other hand, he confirmed the ecclesiastical claims of Armagh – which were as dubious almost as his own – by formally acknowledging its disputed primacy over Cashel. In 1004 he had his name written in the *Book of Armagh* (which survives) as Brian, *Imperator Scotorum*.[93] Indeed, Brian is the first figure who looks at all like an all-Ireland king. His

---

[a] Urban life in Ireland, since its introduction by the Vikings, has always been practically confined to coastal towns. All of the present seven county boroughs in the island are situated on the coast or at sea inlets. In 1951 the nine towns with a population of more than 20,000, and ten out of sixteen towns with a population between 10 and 20,000, were coastal. On the other hand, of the 24 Irish towns with a population between 5 and 10,000, no less than 17 were situated inland. According to the 1926 census of the Free State (vol. x, 10-1), 63.5% of the Free State population was 'littoral', *i.e.* resident within twenty miles of the sea coast.

[b] This is vividly summarized in the entry for the year 1170 in the contemporary *Annals of Innisfallen*, recording the first landing of the Anglo-Normans in Ireland: "A great slaughter of the foreigners of Waterford by the oversea fleet". The Waterford citizens were still 'foreigners', a word that from that time on was to be applied to the Anglo-Normans (cf. p. 48a).

[c] There was never a Gaelic kingdom of Ireland: there were always a number of kings in Ireland, a greater or smaller part of them recognizing the suzerainty of a particular high-king. The kingdom of Scotia, however, by its nature as an aggressive coastal colony pushing inland, from the start had a more centralized existence – though it, too, included a collection of small 'states, the 'clans' of later times.

title 'Boramha', literally: of the tributes, is symbol of his power. However, the Battle of Clontarf (1014) – claimed by many historians as "a national victory of the Irish over the Norse" – saw Brian opposed by the king of Leinster who was allied to the Norse king of Dublin, while "the North stood aloof".[94]

After Brian the high-kingship was fought for by members of three dynasties of provincial kings, one in the Southern Half: the O'Briens (successors of Brian in Cashel), and two in the Northern Half: the 'northern' Uí Néill, and the O'Connors of Connacht (who in the past had been tributary to the Uí Néill). The claim to the high-kingship was regulated in terms of the north-south division: if a king of Leth Cuinn could compel hostages from some parts of Leth Moga, or *vice versa*, this had sufficient force to make his claim felt generally.[95] Though some high-kings reached much greater power than any of the kings before Brian, all of them had to contend with rivals: the Irish annalists called them plainly "kings with opposition". The important fact, however, is that the title fought for was *king of Ireland*. Indeed, Gaelic Ireland had become recognized as a *potential* 'political unit'. [a]

THE REORGANIZATION OF THE IRISH CHURCH

If the Viking invasions had led to destruction and decay, after their conversion the Viking coastal colonies in southern Ireland developed a vigorous religious life.[b] Dublin, Wexford, Waterford and Limerick became – apart from the episcopal organization, such as it was, of the Patrician Church – the first ordinary episcopal dioceses in Ireland, *i.e.* sees which were occupied by a bishop who was not an abbot. An interesting detail concerning the new bishoprics is that their bishops were consecrated at Canterbury.[c]

[a] The popular view in Ireland is that "there was a national kingship and there was unbroken succession to it from among the descendants of Niall from A.D. 400 to 1022, with but two exceptions" (GALLAGHER, 12). This 'national kingship' is a product of nineteenth-century Nationalist theory, created at a time when the structure and history of Gaelic society had not yet been thoroughly examined. (That such pre-scientific concepts prevail in school textbooks shows the extent and influence of Nationalist mythology.) The era of the 'high-kings with opposition' is similarly misinterpreted:

"Just as Wessex, Northumbria and Mercia had come into armed conflict in England as to which should provide the ruling house; and as Normandy, Anjou, Aquitaine and Burgundy contested in France; so in Ireland, Ulster, Leinster, Connacht and Munster sought the leadership. For a century and a half after the death of Brian and his heirs there was continual strife in the effort to decide the issue. It was not a difference as to the oneness of Ireland that caused this struggle but a question of who should be the monarch of the unit" (GALLAGHER, 16).

It is not possible to evaluate post-Brian Ireland by comparison with centralizing feudal states in the neighbouring island and on the continent. Irish society was still essentially the Gaelic tuath-organization, conglomerative rather than centralized, where the concept of central monarchy remained rudimentary. But, if we may not turn Gaelic society into anything like a modern 'united kingdom', it is well to remember that it was a cultural unit, in the sense that it was bound together by a common law and language – and perhaps even a primitive kind of 'national consciousness'.

[b] The popular view in Ireland that the Battle of Clontarf (1014) was "a victory of Christianity over paganism" is a myth. The Norse king of Dublin, for instance, was converted about 943, and two of his successors died as monks in Iona abbey (BRØNDSTED, 101; GOEDHEER, 108; MACNEILL, *Phases* 212).

[c] The explanation commonly offered is that Scandinavian colonists preferred to form their ecclesiastical connexions with their kinsmen in England rather than with their Irish enemies. But, says KENNEY (758), "the facts that almost all these early bishops were Irish in blood (although trained abroad), that the towns were generally under the dominion of one or other of the Irish kings (who sometimes joined in the

At that time the archbishops of Canterbury claimed primatial authority over the whole of Ireland, "taking account", says GOUGAUD, "of the ill-defined and insecure nature of the supremacy of Armagh"[96] (cf. p. 113). They were the first 'English' leaders to adopt the conception of the essential unity of the British Isles – and the first to fail in its realization. It was largely at their instigation that a large-scale reorganization of the Irish Church was at last undertaken.

A synod in 1111 divided Ireland into twenty-four dioceses. The dioceses were grouped into two archbishoprics, Armagh and Cashel, which represented the Northern and the Southern Half respectively. Armagh was to retain a "supremacy of honour" over the rest of Ireland, with the exception, however, of the diocese of Dublin which remained attached to Canterbury.[97] The connexion of Dublin with Canterbury was ended at the synod of 1152 which established four instead of two archbishoprics: Armagh, Cashel, Tuam, and Dublin – approximating to the ancient provincial kingdoms of Ulster, Munster, Connacht, and Leinster respectively.[98] This organization still remains in the Roman Catholic Church (cf. Fig. 4) and in the (Anglican) Church of Ireland. [a]

In conclusion: if twelfth-century Gaelic Ireland had a common basis of law, it was without any national secular institution. It is true, there was some conception of national kingship but it had not proved sufficiently effective to produce a central monarchy with a fixed residential centre. The only institution organized on an all-Ireland basis was the Church, with its head, the primate, permanently residing in Armagh, and its synods acting as a kind of national parliament.

THE ANGLO-NORMAN INVASION (1169)

In the year 1166 when Rory O'Connor, king of Connacht, had seized the high-kingship[b], Dermot MacMurrough, king of Leinster, having supported the rival claimant, found his

recommendation of the episcopal candidate), and that there is no evidence of close association or sympathy between the Northmen [Vikings] of Ireland and the Gallicised Normans of England, render such a hypothesis dubious". More probably, according to KENNEY, the townsmen wished to regularize their position in the universal Church. "They made no objection to entering the Irish Church as soon as that had adopted a diocesan organisation in which their position was recognised".

[a] The age-old quarrel between the Northern and the Southern Half, or rather between the sees of Armagh and Cashel, survived the reorganization of the Church in the sense that Cashel's claims were assumed by Dublin. In the beginning of the thirteenth century the (English) archbishop of Dublin took the title *primate of Ireland* in defiance of the archbishop of Armagh who was entitled to this dignity. The dispute was settled in the fourteenth century when the archbishop of Armagh was endowed with the title *primate of all Ireland* (cf. BLANCHARD, 43-4). To this day both the Roman Catholic and Anglican archbishops of Armagh carry the title *primate of all Ireland* and those of Dublin the title *primate of Ireland*. (A similar compromise was effected in England: the archbishop of York is *primate of England* and the archbishop of Canterbury is *primate of all England*; this compromise survives only in the Church of England.)

The old division of Ireland into a Northern and a Southern Half is also preserved in certain practices in the Roman Catholic Church, for instance at marriages and funerals (BLANCHARD, 28, 92).

[b] A typical example of false history leading to false Nationalist theory is GALLAGHER's statement that the issue of the high-kingship was decided in 1166. "In that year Rory O'Connor was universally accepted as High King and Ireland, one for centuries in language, law and culture, was again under one supreme ruler" (17). This, of course, is apologetics, not history, but apologetics without a historical basis. The weakness of the argument may immediately be shown. Had the Anglo-Norman invasion occurred four

position threatened. He then crossed the Irish Sea in search of support.[a] This was the obvious course for him as his Viking seaports, including "the all-important city of Dublin", had a busy trade with those of south Britain, especially Bristol and Chester.[99]

The English king, Henry II (1154-89), issued a general license for any of his subjects to go to Dermot's aid. Dermot easily found allies among "the restless and frustrated Anglo-Norman and Flemish settlers of South Wales, perhaps the last stronghold of the pure Norman type of military adventurer so common in the previous century".[100] In fact, Dermot's alliance was not the first one established between a southern Irish king and Welsh-Normans – a detail which is almost generally overlooked.[b] It explains why Dermot was not in his own lifetime "universally execrated as the traitor that he appeared to be in the distant retrospect".[101]

The subsequent Anglo-Norman conquest of Ireland – the last stage in the 'Normanization' of the British Isles – is often misrepresented. First of all, Dermot's alliance was rather the occasion than the cause of the conquest. Secondly, as NEWARK says: "Those who suppose that an independent Ireland was brought under alien political domination as the result of a military campaign have not even begun to approximate to the truth". Ireland did not fall to Henry by conquest in the same way that England fell to William the Conqueror in 1066.[102] Nor can the Norman conquest of Ireland be compared with that of Scotland, which was not a conquest in the military sense but was primarily dynastic.[103]

It was – as to methods and results – more a replica of that inflicted on Wales, which was neither "a full-scale conquest by royal armies" but "a gradual, piecemeal, creeping conquest" by adventurous barons.[104] It was among these "greedy and pugnacious barons" that Dermot readily found allies: allies, however, who, once they had encroached on Irish soil, lived up to their tradition by establishing baronies for themselves – but who also paved the way for the English king.

Henry II, on his arrival in Dublin in 1171, had two objects in mind. The most urgent one may have been the assertion of his authority over the land-hungry barons and the land that had already been occupied by them – the first phase in the controversy between the central monarchy and the Norman magnates in Ireland, which was to endure right through the Middle Ages. Henry's second purpose reached farther: the imposition of his suzerainty upon the Gaelic kings of Ireland and the establishment of his

years before it did, the above paragraph could have been written by GALLAGHER as follows: "It was not until 1161 that this political issue was decided. In that year Murchertach MacLochlainn was universally accepted etc." Rory O'Connor was the last high-king but had there been no Norman conquest how long would he have lasted? Five years like Murchertach MacLochlainn (1161-66), five years like Turloch O'Connor (1151-56)? The contemporary Irish historians had no such illusions. They called these kings "kings with opposition".

[a] Indeed, THOMAS O'RAHILLY (History, 116-7) has suggested that Dermot may well have had in mind the precedent of his legendary ancestor and 'founder of his race' who also left Leinster to seek help across the Irish Sea in recovering his kingdom.

[b] It may seem only natural that the Anglo-Normans should have looked to southern Ireland for fresh lands to conquer. It is hardly less obvious that they should look there for allies to assist them in their baronial wars and in their struggle with the centralizing English monarchy. For instance (CURTIS, Mediaeval Ireland, 49-50): when in 1100 the earl of Shrewsbury was expelled by King Henry I, his brother, the lord of Pembroke, fled to the Irish high-king "whose daughter he had espoused in order to bring Ireland into the feudal conspiracy" against the English crown. (See also: LLOYD, vol. ii, 409, 490).

lordship over the whole of Ireland – the first phase in a contest which was not to be concluded before the end of the sixteenth century.

It is, of course, not always possible clearly to separate the two struggles in which so many English kings were engaged. Nor is it possible to isolate them from the struggles which the English monarchy was to carry on within Great Britain. In fact, Irish history since the Anglo-Norman invasion is hardly more than a part of "the age-long strife between the stronger nation [England] and its weaker neighbours".[105]

THE LORDSHIP OF IRELAND (1171-1541)

Henry's 'political conquest' of Ireland (1171-2) was no mere whim on his part. The enterprise, which has been called "the culminating point of Henry's successful imperialism"[106], had been contemplated for a long time. The king had even sought, and ascertained, the approval of Rome to it. In 1155 Pope Adrian IV, by the bull *Laudabiliter*, granted him the lordship of Ireland. [a] In consequence, Henry got readily the sanction of the Irish hierarchy. In 1172 the English king was explicitly recognized as *Dominus Hiberniae* by all the bishops who assembled in synod at Cashel (except for the primate of Armagh who was said to be too old but who later confirmed the decisions). They also introduced further reforms which were based on 'English' models.[b] (That much stimulus for the reform movement in the Irish Church had already come from Canterbury, cannot have been without effect on the bishops.)

Such conception of 'national kingship' as existed in the Ireland of 1170 immediately collapsed. The resistance of the high-king was pathetically weak. If one did not realize how feeble an institution the high-kingship was, one would call the resistance contemptible. Indeed, the Gaelic kings found no difficulty in accepting Henry's overlordship. They saw in the English king a rather more powerful high-king: the implications of a feudal monarchy were unknown to them. When Henry wintered in Dublin (1171-2) almost all the kings came in to make submission, no doubt hoping that it would protect them from baronial attacks.

On the other hand, the newly established lordship was hardly more effective than the high-kingship. It is true, it was to last for almost four centuries and in unbroken succession. But, save for certain areas and mainstays which always remained loyal to the crown, its imposition was imperfect and only temporary. It is hard to see how it could

---

[a] Doubts have been cast – and are still cast by Nationalist authors – on the authenticity of the bull but the consensus of modern scholarship accepts it as genuine (cf. EGGERS, 78-9). It is, in any case, beyond doubt that in 1172 Pope Alexander III certified and confirmed the 'concession' in letters addressed to the bishops and nobles of Ireland (*Documents*, 19-22). Nor is there any doubt that the Irish, then and later, accepted it as genuine.

The principal passages of the grant may be rendered as follows: "We .. do hereby declare our will and pleasure that, with a view to enlarging the boundaries of the Church, .. correcting evil customs and planting virtue, and for the increase of the Christian religion, you shall enter that island, .. and also that the people of that land shall receive you with honour and revere you as their lord" (*Documents*, 17).

[b] It was resolved that "Divine offices shall be henceforth celebrated in every part of Ireland according to the forms and usages of the Church of England". As the contemporary historian of the conquest, the Welsh-Norman ecclesiastic Geraldus Cambrensus, commented: "For it is right and just that, as by Divine Providence Ireland has received her lord and king from England, she should also submit to a reformation from the same source" (*Documents*, 19).

have been otherwise. Apart from other factors, such as the irreconcilability of feudal and Gaelic law and the great difficulties of the terrain, no mediaeval English king had time, money, or men to enforce and to maintain any form of effective government throughout the island. [a] The same applies indeed to Scotland, even to Wales.[107]

The question presents itself whether Henry II, who has been pictured as "a man of great statecraft and demonic energy"[108], or his son and successor John, and a whole line of English kings, ever seriously contemplated the completion of the conquest. If they were not absorbed in domestic problems, they spent their energies and resources almost entirely on the continent. (According to G. W. S. BARROW[109], Henry II, of his thirty-five years as king, stayed some twenty south of the English Channel.[b]) Even as late as the fourteenth and fifteenth centuries, "England was not yet fully conscious of·her life apart" (from the continent), as GEORGE TREVELYAN puts it. If she had been, she would not have abandoned her task of "completing the British Empire by the assimilation of Ireland and Scotland".[110]

One of the few rulers who devoted greater attention to "England's insular affairs" was Edward I (1272-1307), the conqueror of Wales and the "Hammer of the Scots". He was the first English king, JAMES WILLIAMSON observes, who was possessed of the view that Great Britain was "a geographical unity, the natural home of a united kingdom".[c] However, Edward failed to give political reality to that idea, at least as far as Scotland was concerned.[d] For the next four hundred years England and Scotland developed not only along separate courses but actually in mutual antagonism.[111] The complete military failure of the English attempt to dominate Scotland, however, "in the long process of history has produced happier results to both countries than has the partial English success in Ireland".[112]

THE GAELICIZATION OF THE NORMAN BARONS

While the English kings did not establish any form of effective authority over the whole island, equally they did not properly control or – which also might have been possible – properly support the piecemeal conquest by the Norman barons.[113] As it was the barons took land where they could get it: if by royal grant all the better; if – in defiance of feudal law – from a Gaelic king, it sufficed. Thus they spread out over various parts of southern Ireland.

[a] Yet, while Henry II could not afford to keep up a powerful royal government in Ireland, he dared not let any of his feudal magnates obtain some kind of vice-regal authority (TREVELYAN, 204). It is true, Henry later transferred the lordship to his younger son John, which perhaps may be taken as showing that "he did not regard the political union between the two islands as indissoluble" (BECKETT, 19). Had his older son had an heir, John would not have succeeded to the throne (as he did in 1199) and, perhaps, he would have founded a kind of Norman sister kingdom in Ireland, left to work out its own salvation.

[b] It has also been calculated that from 1172 to the *Act of the Union, 1801*, reigning sovereigns spent exactly nine months in Ireland (NEWARK, 7).

[c] With him, WILLIAMSON (125) also notes, the idea of the 'natural frontier' took an early and clear cut form: "He was the greatest prince in an island, and therefore the whole island was his natural territory, to the elimination of frontiers altogether".

[d] It has been said that England's preoccupation with the Hundred Years' War secured Scottish freedom. FAWCETT (62) suggests that the length of the journey from the English lowland to Scotland, too, has helped the preservation of Scotland's independence, and still more the fostering and preservation of "its distinct national traditions and separate life".

It was this intrusion which revealed the toughness of Gaelic society. If the high-kingship had been replaced, as it were, almost without a blow by the overlordship of the English king, the barons never succeeded in conquering the whole country. It was the disparate units – the local kingdoms in whom real power had always resided from the nature of Gaelic society – that proved tougher nuts to crack. Gaelic society, being essentially organized in parts rather than as a whole, might be weak at the centre but it was sturdy in detail. Not till the end of the sixteenth century were the last Gaelic kings overthrown. Throughout the Middle Ages Gaelic society remained recognizably the society of pre-Norman times, indeed of pre-Viking times.

In fact, the barons could resign themselves to a sharing-out of the land with the Gaelic kings when the latter could not be ejected. After all, they were on both sides aristocrats. They intermarried freely: Norman barons married Irish wives, their daughters Irish kings. The fact that the Normans who penetrated into Ireland had already, by intermarriage, become half Welsh, probably helped their descendents to mingle easily with the Irish.[114] But they retained their original loyalty to the English crown, in a different way from the Irish chiefs who adopted it either by expediency or by compulsion.

In Irish school histories one story concerning the Anglo-Normans salves the national pride. They are said to have become, in the proverbial phrase, *Hibernis ipsis Hiberniores*, more Irish than the Irish. There is a good deal of truth in it. The statements of colonial parliaments denouncing this 'degeneracy' is evidence enough. Isolated in their palatine lordships, many Norman barons adopted Irish customs. They learned Gaelic – a language at that time at least as richly developed as English – and had Gaelic poets and wrote Gaelic poetry themselves.[115] (It should be taken into account that among the original invaders there had been few English speakers.[116])

But, if the barons tended to become gaelicized, the Irish princes[a] tended to adopt feudal institutions such as the right of the son to succeed the father. This "virtually changed the Gaelic chiefs, or 'the captains of nations', or 'lords of counties', as the English legal phrases called them, into Gaelic barons". One sees what O'FAOLAIN calls "the feudalization of their minds", too, in their introduction of standing armies and mercenaries.[117]

The patriotic legend also ignores the fact that there was an English colony in mediaeval Ireland, formed by civil servants, merchants, craftsmen, and farmers – the only real and permanent basis of English authority and culture in the island. Most of the 'first families' and their (Welsh and Flemish) dependents may have become, to a greater or less extent, gaelicized; not so the mass of the later immigrants, "the solid and industrious Anglo-Saxons", who only came with the planting of the towns and the organization of manors.[118] But by the end of the Middle Ages some of them, too, were threatened with 'absorption' by their Gaelic environment and the loss of their distinctive English characteristics.

---

[a] After their submission to Richard II, in 1395, the greater Irish chiefs dropped the title of 'king' (O'FAOLAIN, *Irish*, 63).

The English colony consisted of two parts. There was first Dublin with its immediate hinterland, a classic example of a coastal colony. [a] In Dublin there grew up a parliament which nominally had authority over the whole island but in reality only over the English colony and, at times, over (parts of) the 'normanized' areas.

The Dublin-based bridgehead expanded or contracted according as English power increased or decreased. At the beginning of the thirteenth century it extended over great parts of Leinster, parts of Munster, and a very small section of Ulster. To all these areas there was "a flow of inferior Englishry" (CURTIS). Various districts were, more or less effectively, manorialized. In a typical 'Anglo-Irish' manor the knightly or chartered tenants were almost all English, the renters and leaseholders mostly English, while nearly all the cottiers and labourers were Irish.[119]

The proportion of new-comers to natives of course varied. But it is clear that – as JEREMIAH HOGAN says in his study on *The English Language in Ireland* – "English established itself as the language of a great part of the country". The English spoken was a Southern English dialect of distinctive character. "Probably it was fairly uniform over the quarter of the island in which English race and speech were deepest rooted, that is, the country between Dublin and Wexford, inland of the Wicklow Hills".[120]

The "English life and culture", having grown up in the thirteenth century, declined in the fourteenth and fifteenth century when Gaelic recovered much of its original position.[121] At its smallest extent the English bridgehead still included parts of four counties on the east coast, namely Dublin, Kildare, Meath, and Louth: in fact, the most eastern section of the Central Irish Lowlands. This was what eventually became known as the 'Pale', a word which in Nationalist ears has acquired a sinister implication. [b] Part of the English yeomen and small freeholders in the outlying districts forsook the land and went to the Pale, if not back to England; others probably became gaelicized like the great Norman families.[122]

It has been said that in the course of the Middle Ages "the Pale grew narrower both in space and spirit". The English settlers and officials "came to regard almost everyone and everything outside the Pale ditch as belonging not to the 'English' but to the 'Irish' interest" – a distinction which set the tone of "a policy that for centuries was fruitful of mischief".[123] It was their 'garrison spirit' which framed the famous *Statute of Kilkenny* in 1366. This statute has often been represented as a kind of aggressive 'outlawing' of the Irish. In fact, it was essentially an expression of "a defensive 'colonial' policy" (BECKETT). The purpose was, according to CURTIS,

[a] HARVEY (99) has drawn a comparison between Dublin and New York, both trading depots with a large hinterland: "Viking Dublin was a ready-made bridgehead as convenient for the purposes of the Norman knights in 1170 as Dutch New Amsterdam was to the Duke of York's commanders in 1664". Its only possible rival was the kindred city of Waterford. Though very convenient as a port of entry from south Wales, it was not sufficiently central for the purposes of administration (CHART, 11-2).

[b] The term 'Pale' derives from Latin 'palus', meaning: a paling or fence. At the end of the fifteenth century the bridgehead was indeed defined – on the part "which mereth next unto Irishmen" – by a kind of dyke or stockade (CURTIS, *Mediaeval Ireland*, 402). Beyond the Pale (westward) lay forest and bog: "natural defences which the Irish strengthened by twining together branches and bushes in the woods, and by deepening the river-fords so as to render them impassable" (HOWARTH, 163-4).

"at the cost of abandoning a large part of the 'English land' to the Irish and the 'chieftains of English lineage' [the barons], to preserve the remainder for the English speech, race and law. Inside this 'land of peace' all Irish inhabitants were to be forced into English law and custom, which the Statute aimed at securing forever".[124]

At the time it certainly did not run in more than one-fifth of the island, and even in the 'land of the peace' it could not entirely be enforced. This "exclusive consolidation of the English elements in Ireland" reflected the change which was coming over the mother country: "England was ceasing to be an empire, ruling and tolerating many subject peoples and languages, and becoming a nation".[125] As HOGAN has shown, the reorganization of the English element in Ireland manifested itself in the language. In the first half of the fifteenth century French and Latin were being replaced by the new standard English as the official language: The speech of everyday life became transformed[a] into a mixture of new Midland forms and the old Southern English dialect, the whole influenced in varying degrees by Gaelic.[126]

The second part of the English colony is often overlooked: the numerous English towns and cities which were scattered over the greater part of the island (there were but a few in Ulster). The Anglo-Normans occupied all the Viking ports but also founded new coastal settlements and many towns inland. The biggest of the new walled urban settlements was probably Galway on the west coast.

Although Irishmen, by conforming to their laws, could – and did in large numbers – become citizens, these towns remained essentially English towns.[b] Their tradition was "unwaveringly English and plebeian": "enemies of feudalism – whether of Irish or Norman brand – they naturally allied with the Anglo-Irish state and the Lord of Ireland against 'English rebels and Irish enemies'" (CURTIS). They clung to their English speech (which resembled the dialect of the Pale) as "a safeguard of their privileges"; at the end of the mediaeval period, however, it was partly superseded by Irish. "Without these strongholds", CURTIS concludes, "Anglo-Ireland would have followed the Gaelicized Normans .. clean over to Irish speech and tradition; without them in the Tudor age the re-conquest would have been impossible".[127]

Chapter 11

IRISH, ENGLISH AND SCOTTISH ULSTER

THE GAELIC KINGDOMS OF ULSTER

The Anglo-Norman conquest made very little headway in Ulster. Down to the seventeenth century northern Ireland remained, as GERARD HAYES-McCoy observes, "to a

---

[a] In a few rural areas, *e.g.* in south Co. Wexford, the original dialect was preserved; it survived, unmixed except with Irish, until modern times (HOGAN, 5, 37).

[b] With the English towns we should count the chief ecclesiastical centres like Armagh, and the new monastic settlements. The aristocratic monastic orders, introduced in the twelfth century, were natural allies of the English feudal state. The democratic mendicant orders, introduced in the thirteenth century, however, tended to become the natural allies of Gaelic Ireland (FLOWER, 114).

great extent a *terra incognita* to the English authority in Dublin". He points out that the Gaelic part of Scotland, more specifically the western Highlands and Islands – which were "in active and constant communication" with northern Ireland – was also a kind of *terra incognita*. "The parallel", says HAYES-McCOY, "between Ulster as unknown and misunderstood by Dublin and the Isles and Highlands generally as similarly misunderstood by the Edinburgh Court is very striking". It is significant that the term "wild Irish" at one and the same time is applied by Dublin to the native Irish and by Edinburgh to the West Highlanders".[128]

Of the Gaelic princely families established in Ulster by the end of the twelfth century two had risen to great prominence, asserting their influence upon various 'tributary' kingdoms. They are usually known as the O'Neills and the O'Donnells, their kingdoms as 'Tyrone' and 'Tyrconnell'. (Both the O'Neills and O'Donnells were descendants of the 'northern' Uí Néill.)

Their power was based on typical 'highland bastions' or 'folk fortresses', the Sperrins and the Donegal mountains respectively.[129] Tyrone (from 'Tír Eoghain', literally: the land of Eoghain, English: Owen) included modern Cos Londonderry and Tyrone, and parts of Cos Armagh and Fermanagh. The kings of the Ulaid, who still held sway east of Lough Neagh and the river Bann (modern Cos Antrim and Down), were tributary to the kings of Tyrone. Tyrconnell (from 'Tír Conaill', literally: the land of Conall, English: Connell) covered modern Co. Donegal, and parts of Cos Fermanagh and Sligo.

The O'Neills and the O'Donnells – the 'princes of the north', as they were sometimes called – were the most unyielding opponents of King Henry II, feeling themselves sufficiently secure in their remote and inaccessible highland massifs to defy his authority. [a] In fact, the O'Donnells in detached Donegal did not acknowledge any central authority – whether English, Irish, or Scottish – until the sixteenth century. On the other hand, they kept up an age-long feud with the O'Neills. The two kingdoms rarely missed the chance of taking advantage of the other's misfortunes: every English attack on the one was paralleled by an attack of the other.

The O'Neills of Tyrone were definitely the most powerful. In later centuries they sometimes carried the main brunt of the Gaelic 'resistance' against the English. Thanks to their central position in Ulster they had most opportunity of expanding, but for the same reason they were also more vulnerable to attack. The O'Neills nursed the claim of the 'northern' Uí Néill to the high-kingship of Ireland, the claim that Brian Boramha had shattered at the end of the tenth century. But the O'Neills did not achieve the unity of Gaelic Ireland; indeed they never seriously attempted to accomplish such unity. Nearest their heart was their claim to the kingship of the old Ulster kingdom. From the thirteenth century onward the O'Neills styled themselves *kings of Ulster*. Whatever this title was meant to include[b], it was not recognized by the O'Donnells in west Ulster nor by the Anglo-Norman and Scottish settlers in east Ulster. In fact, the O'Neills did not achieve any effective unity of Gaelic Ulster until the end of the sixteenth century.

[a] A contemporary historian, Geraldus Cambrensus (cf. p. 125b), explained it by saying that in every country the northern people are the staunchest (*Handbook*, 8).

[b] Throughout the Middle Ages the term 'Ulster', in any of its forms (Irish, Latin, French, or English), was ambiguous. Sometimes it was used for east Ulster exclusively, sometimes it covered mid Ulster as well, and on some occasions also west Ulster (cf. ORPEN, vol. ii, 11n, 22; OTHWAY-RUTHVEN, 48).

In order to understand conditions in mediaeval Ulster it is not sufficient to look at the position of the Irish kingdoms. We should look at Scotland as well. One could say, perhaps, that mediaeval Ulster history reflects as much Scottish as Irish history.

This statement needs qualification. It is usual to think of mediaeval Scotland as a political entity which, to some extent, may be compared with the centralized English state. However, from the beginning of the twelfth till the end of the fifteenth century there were in fact two states in the north of Great Britain, not one united state: (1) the normanized and anglicized kingdom of Scotland centred on Edinburgh[a] (which enjoys almost all the attention of historians); and (2) the so-called lordship of the Isles, a Norse-Gaelic kingdom based mainly on the islands off the Scottish west coast (the Hebrides).[130] It was this lordship which had most intimate relations with Ulster, whether peacefully or otherwise. In the fifteenth century it was even to extend over part of Ulster!

As we have seen, the Norse (Vikings) established various colonies on the Scottish coast and in the Hebrides: territories which at the time were incorporated in 'Scottish' Dál Ríada (the cradle of the Scottish kingdom before it moved its centre eastward). These colonies did not preserve their cultural identity; they were soon absorbed by their Gaelic environment. Henceforth the Irish termed the island and coastal population of west Scotland 'Gall-Gáidil', literally: foreigner-Gael. They were in fact 'Norse-Gaels' – which in Norse was rendered as 'Víkinga-Skotar'.[131]

There is no doubt that their culture was Gaelic, though with Norse elements, but until the middle of the thirteenth century their political allegiance was primarily to the king of Norway. The attempts of the Scottish kings to recover their original possessions – by extending and consolidating their sovereignty over the lordships which had originated in the Viking colonies – were a constant factor in Scottish history down to the late Middle Ages. They had their first success in Galloway (from 'Gallaibh', literally: territory of the foreigners) – the region whence four hundred years later were to come the ancestors of many of the present Presbyterian population of Ulster. [b]

The main settlement of the Norse-Gaels was in the 'Insi-Gall', literally: islands of the foreigners, i.e. the Hebrides. These colonies were virtually independent of both Scotland and Norway up to the end of the eleventh century. After 1098 the kings (reguli) in the Hebrides were nominally subjects to the Norwegian crown. From about the middle of the twelfth century the most prominent 'royal house' (ruling family) was that of the MacDonalds, Irish: MacDonnells. The main strongholds of their power were in Argyll

[a] According to WALTER FITZGERALD Gaelic was recognized as the 'official' language of Scotland as late as the fourteenth century. Down to that time the speech of the Lowlanders (largely of Anglo-Saxon origin) was known as 'Inglis' (English). When the population of the Lowlands greatly increased, during the fifteenth and sixteenth centuries, its language was more widely spoken than the Gaelic of the High-lands. To continue to call it 'English' became "a slur on the nationality of the Lowlanders". Consequently, in the sixteenth century the Lowlands' speech came to be known officially as 'Scottish' (Europe, 18n).

[b] Galloway originally may have been a Pictish enclave. It seems to have been colonized, to some extent, either directly from 'Irish' Dál Ríada or from 'Scottish' Dál Ríada. It retained a separate existence as a Norse-Gaelic lordship till the end of the twelfth century, when it was brought into feudal subjection to the Scottish crown. Various attempts of the lords of Galloway to regain their independence were supported from Ulster and Man (MACNEILL, Phases, 207, 211). Meantime several Galloway magnates had been granted titles by Scottish kings, like the earl of Carrick and the earl of Atholl.

and the southern Hebrides. [a] The MacDonnell lordship is usually referred to as 'the Isles'. Though often weakened by internal dissension as any Gaelic kingdom, it remained a menace to the Scottish kings till the end of the fifteenth century. [b]

As AGNES MURE MACKENZIE says, the MacDonnells considered themselves "natives of Scotland, but rather allies than subjects of its Crown". They were frequently in alliance with its foes, *i.e.* England. In three treaties which King Edward III (1327-77) made with France the lord of the Isles signed as an allied sovereign between the duke of Gueldres and the doge of Genoa.[132] HAYES-MCCOY rightly observes that the significance of this lordship as "an entity apart from the Scotland which centred on Edinburgh" cannot be too strongly stressed.[133]

THE ANGLO-NORMAN COLONY IN EAST ULSTER (1177)

The Anglo-Norman conquest was brought to the north in 1177 when John de Courcy, acting as a true adventurer rather on his own account, overran the Ulaid kingdom in east Ulster and even penetrated into the north of Tyrone (mid Ulster). De Courcy styled himself *princeps Ulidiae*. This title probably referred only to the Ulaid kingdom (approximating to modern Cos Antrim and Down), but it could have included the whole north. CURTIS conjectures that there were Gaelic scholars to tell De Courcy that 'Ulster' had once stretched over the entire north of the island.[134] And, of course, the mythological tales, which refer to 'Ulster' in the original broad sense, were among the most popular tales of the period.

De Courcy consolidated his position by a marriage alliance to the most powerful of the Norse-Gaelic lords, the king of Man and the lord of the Isles. [c] But his career was soon cut short. He was one of the first great barons in Ireland to fall before the centralizing English monarchy. In 1205 he was overthrown by King John (1199-1212), whom CURTIS calls "the first effective foreign ruler over the greater part of Ireland".[135] However, De Courcy's undertaking had far-reaching effects.

De Courcy was in fact the founder of the Anglo-Norman colony in Ulster. This

---

[a] The 'ancestor' of this princely family is Somerled, who was son-in-law of the Norse-Gaelic king of Man. He owed allegiance to the king of Norway as well as to the king of Scotland, for his insular and mainland possessions respectively. In his rise against the Scottish crown in 1160 he had allies from Ireland (cf. MACDONALD, 77-9).

    Somerled's name is a reminiscence of the Viking raiders. It is the Norse 'Sumarliđi', which originally means "a man who sails during the summer". A similar name is 'Vetrliđi', originally: 'a man who sails in the winter'. Both names were originally nicknames but both became ordinary personal names during the Viking period and were fairly common during the Middle Ages in Norway and Iceland. They were still in use in some Norwegian districts in the seventeenth century, and at least 'Vetrliđi' still exists today in the form 'Vetle' (information from E. HALVORSEN, Oslo).

[b] There is, as MACNEILL (*Phases*, 215) remarked, a reluctance on the part of Scottish historians to recognize the kingdom of the Isles. They usually call it a 'lordship' but in Gaelic it is almost invariably referred to as a 'kingdom', like the Gaelic kingdoms in Ireland.

[c] De Courcy also got the king of the Ulaid on his side when the latter was attacked by the O'Neills of Tyrone in 1181 – though the O'Neills had at first assisted the Ulaid against the Norman invaders. Later De Courcy aided the Ulaid king in his attack on Armagh (CURTIS, *Mediaeval Ireland*, 89; ORPEN, vol. ii, 17-9, 117, 136). It is likely then that the king of the Ulaid had accepted De Courcy's overlordship. It is the last time we hear of him.

was, like the Pale north of Dublin, a typical bridgehead colony. It extended along the south–east coast of Co. Down, from Strangford Lough to Carlingford Lough where it linked up with the Pale. (By the end of the thirteenth century it was, like the Anglo–Norman settlement on Carlingford peninsula, actually considered as part of Co. Louth and falling within the Pale.[136])

The colony was based on a number of castles built on strategic points, usually at the water's edge so that they could be provisoned from the sea. The pivots of the Norman defence system were Strangford, Ardglass, Dundrum, Greencastle, and Newry–Narrow Water (built to defend the 'Newry gap'). They were to survive the Middle Ages as small trading centres.[137] (Some of these points, if not all, also had figured as footholds of the Vikings!) The main centre of the colony was Isle Lecale, the peninsula south of Strangford Lough, severed from the mainland by a broad line of marshes). Its religious and strategic capital was Downpatrick[138] (where St Patrick is said to have been buried).[a]

There were also a few settlements in Co. Antrim. The coastal castles of Carrickfergus (on the north coast of Belfast Lough) and Coleraine (at the mouth of the river Bann) gradually developed into small English walled towns. East of Coleraine were some Welsh colonists who, after they had become Gaelicized, were known as the MacQuillans.[139] De Courcy also introduced the first Scottish 'planters' into Ulster. When his Scottish cousin, the earl of Carrick, had come to his aid against the king of Tyrone, he was rewarded with a grant of land on the north coast.[140] (In the beginning of the fourteenth century the possessions and the title of the earl of Carrick passed to Robert Bruce, king of Scotland.)

THE EARLDOM OF ULSTER (1205–1449)

It was John de Courcy who laid the foundation of the Anglo–Norman earldom of Ulster. The first *earl of Ulster* was Hugh de Lacy, a baron at the time held in high favour by King John. In 1205 he was granted *totam terram Ultoniae*. It is again not clear whether 'Ultonia' was meant to cover the whole north.[141] *De facto* the earldom was confined to the territories which De Courcy had conquered. De Lacy continued De Courcy's policy. He also brought in Scottish colonists in order to secure his hold on the land. He enfeoffed Walter Bisset, a Scottish–Norman nobleman, with the island of Rathlin off the Antrim coast and with lands in the glens of north Co. Antrim.[142] These Bissets and their heirs were to play an important role in Ulster – a descendant, the *earl of Antrim*, is a prominent member of the present 'Ulster' establishment.

Hugh de Lacy, too, soon fell into disfavour (1210). King John, in his action against De Lacy, enlisted the support of three Scottish kinsmen of John de Courcy, the lord of Galloway and the earls of Atholl and Carrick, who were glad to avenge themselves on the instrument of their cousin's fall and equally eager for reward. Having crushed the De Lacy power they were granted big estates on the north coast and in south Co. Antrim (the earl of Carrick was already entrenched in north Ulster by grant of De Courcy).[143]

It should be noted that these grants were made by an English king to 'subjects' of

---

[a] Although the English hold on the peninsulas was often precarious, the names of the families installed by De Courcy still survive, like Hackett, Jordan, Logan, Russell, Savage, and White (CURTIS, *Earldom*, 76, · *Mediaeval Ireland*, 88, 274).

the Scottish king. At that particular time both kings were on rather friendly terms. The Scottish king did not interfere with John's war against his barons. On the other hand, John did not abandon the English claims on Scotland but, for reasons of expediency, he allowed them to lapse. John's grants of Ulster land may have been made in the hope of securing friends in Scotland (where the introduction of several Norman barons in the first half of the twelfth century had provided a Norman feudal basis). The grants were probably equally welcome to the Scottish king who may have been glad to see the energy of the recently rebellious Galloway house diverted to Ireland. The next king of Scotland, however, invaded England in support of the barons against John and there were no more grants by English kings to Scottish noblemen until the seventeenth century.

Meanwhile the MacDonnells, lords of the Isles, had also begun to take an interest in Ulster. The Anglo-Norman assaults on the O'Neills of Tyrone had provided the O'Donnells of Tyrconnell with an opportunity to attack them on the other side. In this venture they obtained the help of the MacDonnells, and of the earl of Atholl as well. The allies were duly rewarded with land. "Thus", says CURTIS, "was threatened a Scottish plantation of Ulster"[144] – a modest counterpart of the Welsh- and Anglo-Norman settlements in the rest of Ireland. But the O'Neills proved strong enough to call a halt to the Scottish invasion. They even got the help of – the De Lacys. The latter were temporarily restored to the earldom in 1227, but their restoration left the Scottish lords in most of their possessions, if not in all.

In 1264 the earldom of Ulster was granted to the De Burgos, a powerful baronial family already half gaelicized, who were established in Co. Galway. Richard de Burgo, earl of Ulster from 1280 till 1326, figured as "a provincial king after the Gaelic fashion" and that by direct sanction of the crown.[145] He was in a position to drive a wedge between the O'Neills and the O'Donnells by founding castles on Inishowen peninsula. The O'Neills even consented to hold their lands and regalities from him and to provide him with armed forces. De Burgo also pursued the policy of Scottish alliance: one of his daughters married the earl of Carrick, Robert Bruce[146] (to be crowned king of Scots in 1306).

De Burgo was the last earl of Ulster to exert real power. Soon after his death (which occurred in 1326) the earldom was invaded by an offshoot of the O'Neills, probably expelled from Tyrone by the O'Donnells who at the time expanded eastward at the expense of the O'Neills. In the next fifty years the O'Neills set up an entirely new kingdom, known as 'Clandeboye' (from 'Clann Aodha Buidhe', literally: the family of yellow-haired Hugh), which extended over south Co. Antrim and north Co. Down. Its 'capital' was at Castlereagh, today one of the suburbs of Belfast. The kingdom was based on the middle course of the river Lagan, a "great belt of woodland and bog", and it completely blocked land communications between Antrim and the south.[147] It survived down to the beginning of the seventeenth century.

Despite strong measures taken by later earls (some of whom acted as *lord lieutenants* in Dublin), the earldom never recovered its old position. However, on various occasions in the second half of the fourteenth and the first half of the fifteenth century the O'Neills and other Ulster chiefs – but rarely the O'Donnells of Tyrconnell – are reported to have done homage to the earls. In 1449 the earldom merged in the crown and thence shared in the general neglect of Irish affairs till the Tudor conquest in the sixteenth century.

If the Anglo-Norman influence in Ulster, small as it was, nearly melted away, the Scottish influence increased. Not only did it fill, to some extent, the vacuum left by the waning earldom, it also contributed greatly to the consolidation of the Gaelic kingdoms in the north.

When in 1258 Donald O'Donnell, who had been reared in the Isles and had married there, became king of Tyrconnell (on the death of his brother in a battle with the O'Neills of Tyrone), he brought with him a number of Norse-Gaelic soldiers. They probably were the first 'Gall-óglaigh', literally: foreign soldiers, anglicized: Gallowglasses, regularly to be employed by an Irish king.[148] During the fourteenth century there arrived considerable numbers of these traditional soldiers who had inherited the weapons and military skill of their Viking forefathers. They provided the Ulster kings, and later other Irish kings too, with "standing forces of well-trained soldiers"[149] who really were a match for the Anglo-Norman forces. [a]

It seems only natural that, when in 1306 Robert Bruce, the earl of Carrick, had become king of the Scots, Scottish affairs should impinge largely upon Ulster. The king not only had possessions in Co. Antrim but in 1302 he had married Elizabeth de Burgo, daughter of the earl of Ulster. As most of his kingdom was held by King Edward I of England, the king for some time after his coronation took refuge in Rathlin island (which was part of the Bisset dominion).[150]

After the Battle of Bannockburn (1314), which ended the English occupation of Scotland, the O'Neills, "pricked on no doubt by the example of Scotland", approached the king's brother, Edward Bruce, and offered to make him king of Ireland.[b] Edward, having helped his brother Robert to the Scottish crown, had no objection to winning the Irish crown for himself. And the new Scottish king did not refuse Edward his assistance as Edward's ambition was in keeping with his own interests. As AGNES MURE MACKENZIE says in her biography of Robert Bruce: "a free Ireland, under a king close kin to the royal house, should promise an invaluable ally, lying as she did on the flank of Ireland".[151]

In fact, the landing of Edward with a Scottish army in east Ulster in 1315 marks a new phase of the Scottish War of Independence (1297-1328), that of fighting England in Ireland.[152] (In the same year Robert Bruce invaded England.) After a short military campaign Edward Bruce was crowned *king of Ireland* near Dundalk (Co. Louth). But, says Miss MACKENZIE, he was master only of the north of Ireland, with a somewhat uncertain hold even of that (the O'Donnells of Tyrconnell stood aloof).[153] On the other hand, there had sprung up some sort of alliance between a number of Gaelic kings. This

---

[a] The Gallowglasses became an essential part of Gaelic society. Their chieftains acquired lands from Gaelic kings and founded various families who intermarried with the great Irish families. Their names still survive, like that of the MacSweeneys who served the O'Donnells of Tyrconnell to the end of the sixteenth century (cf. HAYES-MCCOY, 63-6). To the Gallowglasses, says CURTIS (*History*, 84) "we may attribute much of the resurgence of Gaelic Ireland in the next three centuries". However, they came to serve certain Norman magnates as well, and ultimately there are even instances of their employment by the English in Ireland (HAYES-MCCOY, 36-7; cf. MACNEILL, *Phases*, 325-6).

[b] In 1263 there had been a similar offer by the O'Neills to Haakon, the last sea-king of Norway, when he made a – fruitless – attempt to reassert his authority over his Scottish possessions (MACNEILL, *Phases*, 332-3; cf. MACDONALD, 106-11).

may be inferred from the *Remonstrance*, a lengthy document sent to the pope in 1317 by
"his devoted children Donald O'Neill, *rex Ultoniae*, and by hereditary right true heir
of the whole of Ireland, and also the under-kings and nobles and the whole Irish people".

The *Remonstrance* has many characteristics of a 'nationalist' declaration. It expresses
the claim of the Irish to the whole island of Ireland as theirs by immemorial right. It
questions the right of Pope Adrian to transfer the claim to the king of England. [a] The
papal grant is explained as a 'nationalist' act on the part of the pope, being an Englishman. [b]
The *Remonstrance* shows that, in any case, the terms of Adrian's bull had been broken. It
states that in vain the Irish had offered to hold their lands directly from the English king
according to the conditions of the bull, and that they had also sought a division of the
country between the Gaels and the English. (The second idea was latent in a previous claim
of the O'Neills to the *kingship of all the Irish of Ireland* – the first notion of Partition.)

The *Remonstrance* also stresses the difference in language and customs between the
Irish and the English. [c] Of the people of Scotland it says that they have retained to some
extent "our language and habits". It then states that the Irish now have called in Edward
Bruce, "who is sprung from our noblest ancestors", and have made him their king and
lord. The pope is asked to approve of their decision. [d] Finally the document emphasizes
the determination of the Irish to fight a just war.

The war, however, came soon to an end. In 1318 Edward Bruce was defeated, the
lords of the Isles and Argyll falling by his side. The victors were not an Anglo–Norman
feudal army but "a hastily-assembled force of colonists".[154] The earldom of Ulster was
soon restored but – as I have shown – not for long. In fact, nowhere in Ireland did the
conquest make any further progress and from this time on a stalemate reigned till the
Tudor conquest in the sixteenth century.

THE FIRST SCOTTISH COLONY IN EAST ULSTER

A new situation arose when in 1399 the heiress of the Bisset lordship, which at the time
extended over practically the whole of Co. Antrim[155], married a brother of the lord of

---

[a] The document must have owed much to Scottish example. In 1310 the Scottish clergy had issued a
protest against a renewed grant of Scotland to the English king by papal bull. It may also reflect the
rising influence of the democratic mendicant orders, especially the Franciscans, in thirteenth-century
Gaelic Ireland. They had introduced new ideas on the relations of king and pope and people.

[b] The document states that "at the false and wicked representation of King Henry of England .. Pope
Adrian, .. an Englishman not so much by birth as by feeling and character, did in fact, but unfairly, confer
upon that same Henry .. this lordship of ours by a certain form of words, the course of justice entirely
disregarded and the moral vision of that great pontiff blinded, alas! by his English proclinities". (For the
complete text of the *Remonstrance*, see: *Documents*, 38-46.)

[c] The document most fiercely denounces "the English of Ireland" who are said to differ so widely in their
principles of morality from those of England. They have striven "with all their might and with every
treacherous artifice .. to wipe our nation out", alienating "us from the king of England, hindering us
from holding our lands as voluntary tenants under the crown". In fact, the main grievance against
the English king is that he has not protected the Irish people from the oppressions of "the middle nation",
the English colony in Ireland, "who have compelled us to seek mountains, woods, barren tracts and even
caverns in the rocks to save our lives".

[d] The authors cannot have had great hopes of the pope's decision. Robert Bruce, "by the grace of God
most illustrious king of Scots", at the time was under sentence of excommunication. The *Remonstrance*
in fact led to the excommunication of mendicant friars and others who had preached rebellion.

the Isles. Their son, as well as being lord of Antrim, became lord of the Isles. Most of Antrim was thus included in the kingdom of the Isles. The extension of the lordship to the Irish mainland was not opposed by the English power in Ireland nor by the earls of Ulster. At the time the MacDonnells were allies of England and they did homage for their Ulster possessions to the earl of Ulster.

The lordship of Antrim and the Isles lasted throughout the fifteenth century, in spite of continuous pressure by the Scottish kings. By the end of the century, however, the Scottish part of the lordship was crushed by King James IV. The MacDonnells held only Islay and some minor islands. [a] The centre of the lordship then gravitated to Antrim where great numbers of Islanders took refuge. By 1550 James MacDonnell of Antrim, who still called himself *lord of the Isles*, commanded ten thousand 'Hebridean Scots' or 'Redshanks'.[156] They pushed the O'Neills of Clandeboye south and west. They were even strong enough to defeat one of the most formidable enemies of the Tudor state in Ireland, Seán O'Neill who styled himself *king of Ulster*.

Here then, in the middle of the sixteenth century, was a kingdom, half Scottish and half Irish, owing allegiance in name to two thrones – in Ireland to the Tudors and in Scotland to the Stuarts – but in practice in rebellion against both. However, this kingdom which acted as a kind of link between the two parts of the Gaelic world: Gaelic Ireland and Gaelic Scotland, is often overlooked. The Ulster part is usually seen as a mere Scottish Gaelic 'landing party', a kind of 'clan affair', which disappeared with the sixteenth century. Neither Northern nor Southern Irish authors give it much attention.[b] GALLAGHER in *The Indivisible Island* blankly refers to "the MacDonnells, a Scottish family who for two centuries had been established in Antrim".[157] They do not even rate a mention in his index. Thus is the kingdom of the Isles disposed of! "A Scottish family" – as who might say of the O'Neills: "an Irish family who had for some centuries been established in Tyrone".

Other anti-Partition apologists ignore the matter entirely. The reason is fairly obvious. To admit a Scottish colony in Ulster before the seventeenth century might tend to buttress the pro-Partition case – in terms of propaganda. On the other hand, the MacDonnells were to remain largely Roman Catholic (though not their head, the *earl of Antrim*) and today account for a rather strong Nationalist element in north Co. Antrim, thus giving little solace to Unionist propagandists.

The whole pre-Reformation history of this Scottish colony remains unwritten.

THE DEVELOPMENT OF THE ULSTER IRISH DIALECT

The divergence of political developments in the north and the south of mediaeval Ireland is clearly reflected by the development of the two main historical dialects in Irish, Northern and Southern Irish. According to THOMAS O'RAHILLY, in their latest phase the areas occupied by the two main dialects have a certain correspondence with the Northern and

---

[a] But, as KERMACK (58-9) notes, so strong a hold had the tradition of this Gaelic principality on the Western Highlands that armed attempts to restore the lordship were continued for more than half a century after its fall.

[b] This holds good also of Scottish historians, even of KERMACK who, in his history of the Scottish Highlands, dwells at rather great length on the lordship of the Isles.

the Southern Half. He is of the opinion that this correspondence, such as it was, is purely accidental.[158] One hesitates to criticize the views of such an outstanding scholar as O'RAHILLY but it would be difficult to believe that the conformity of the linguistic division with the other divisions between the north and the south – as separated by the Central Irish Lowlands – could be a mere coincidence.

Whereas Southern Irish "bears witness to the fact that the descendants of the Anglo-Norman invaders became absorbed in the historic Irish nation", as O'RAHILLY puts it, Northern Irish acquired its distinctive features as a result of "the partial assimilation of the pre-existing Northern Irish to the Gaelic spoken in Scotland some centuries ago", in consequence of the long-continued population movement from Scotland to the north of Ireland. "It had the advantage of rendering the Gaelic speakers on both sides of the North Channel easily intelligible to one another".[159] It is well to remember that

"To the Gaelic-speaking Scotsman of the past Ireland was the mother country, whose culture and whose traditions belonged no less to himself than to his kinsmen in Ireland. This feeling of racial unity among the sea-divided 'Gaoidhill' was so deeply rooted that, in despite of all obstacles, the same literary language as passed current in Ireland continued to be employed by Scottish writers down to comparatively recent times".[160]

The speech of the common people in Scotland, however, was deeply affected by "the numerous Norsemen who settled down in Scotland and became Gaelic speakers while retaining for a long time their own language as well". It was this Scottish Gaelic language which exerted a strong influence on the spoken language of Ulster, probably as early as the fourteenth century. (In the thirteenth century the Scots began to settle in increasing numbers in Ulster.) "Hence we find Northern Irish sub-divided into two lesser dialects, one of them situated in Connacht, the other mainly in Ulster". The latter dialect has conveniently been called 'Ulster Irish', "though from an historical standpoint some such term as Scoto-Irish would doubtless be more appropriate".[161]

Thus, while the literary classes in Scotland shared the same written language with Ireland, "the illerate people in Ulster and in the neighbouring parts of Scotland possessed in common something like an unwritten lingua franca for mutual spoken intercourse". This 'hybrid speech' proved itself a vigorous breed. When once it took root in Ulster – as it first did, probably, in Co. Antrim – it spread widely to the south and west.[162]

The influence of Scottish Gaelic continued strong until the end of the sixteenth century. Afterwards it declined, slowly at first, and then with increasing rapidity, owing to the political and social changes in Ulster and the spread of English in both countries. But "as long as Irish continued to be spoken in Co. Antrim the linguistic connection between the two countries was never entirely broken".[163]

CONCLUSION PART THREE

Both parts of the Irish Border, the land and the sea boundary, show conformity to age-old regional divisions over most of their length. As for the land boundary: it shows some conformity to the frontiers of one of the most important kingdoms of Gaelic Ireland, i.e. that of the O'Neills of Tyrone who for centuries claimed to be kings of Ulster and who remained virtually independent from Dublin till the end of the sixteenth century. The present land boundary also approximates to the southern frontier of the pre-Gaelic kingdom of Ulster, which was for some time strengthened by what is today known as the Black Pig's Dyke. The land boundary also reminds one of the division of Ireland into a Northern and a Southern Half. Originally this major north-south division was based on the Central Irish Lowlands but ever since the eastern coastal section of the Lowlands became a prominent seat of power the concept of 'the North' tended to coincide with 'Ulster'. (Since then 'the South' may be taken to include 'Munster', 'Leinster', and 'Connacht'.)

As for the sea boundary: the Irish Sea (including St George's Channel and the North Channel) has been recognized as a 'political frontier' since before the Anglo-Norman invasion, indeed before the Viking invasions. Throughout the period under consideration, however, Ireland was never effectively united, politically. If none of the Gaelic kings were ever able to establish complete control over all parts of Ireland, neither were any of the later English lords of Ireland. The Irish Sea, though of old it has been recognized as a (potential) 'political frontier', never was an effective ethnic, religious or linguistic barrier.

Cross-Channel contacts have been a constant feature of the history of the British Isles long since before the Anglo-Norman invasion of Ireland. All population movements into these islands, whether they arrived in Ireland or in Great Britain, spilled over into the neighbouring island. The exception is that of the Romans. The first historical people in the British Isles, the Pretani, probably spread from Great Britain into Ireland. The Gaels expanded from Ireland into Great Britain. The Vikings brought the two islands into closer contact. From their kingdoms in Ireland the ecclesiastical influence of Canterbury fostered the reformation of the Irish Church on English lines: the beginning of the forcible anglicization process – the main power welding the two islands together.

Of old, cross-Channel contacts tended to be: (1) between southern Ireland and Wales and England; and (2) between northern Ireland (Ulster) and Scotland. The latter-day Vikings, the Normans, who conquered great parts of southern Ireland, came from Wales. They paved the way for many English colonists who established English-speaking towns all round mediaeval Ireland outside of Ulster.

Cross-Channel contacts, because of the ease of travel across the North Channel, were most pronounced and continuous in the north. The first traces of man hitherto discovered in Ireland are found on the point nearest to Great Britain, *i.e.* in east Ulster. It seems inevitable that the pre-Gaelic rulers in Ulster should, under the pressure of the Gaelic invaders, seek refuge in Scotland. On the other hand, pressure on the Scottish Highlands and Islands in later mediaeval times led to a reverse colonization in east Ulster.

Expansion from the north of Ireland has permanently affected Great Britain in the Christianization and gaelicization of a large part of north Britain, which led to the formation of the Scottish (originally: Irish, or perhaps rather: northern Irish) state – a state which lasted as an independent entity till 1707. On the other hand, expansion from the south of Great Britain has permanently affected Ireland, firstly in the Christianization and eventually in the anglicization of large parts of southern Ireland. The modern Irish Republic ultimately goes back to the mediaeval English colony in (southern) Ireland.

Official Nationalist propagandists still labour under the delusion that it is necessary for 'prestige' purposes to establish that since the Anglo-Norman invasion of Ireland the Irish have fought for their 'national independence', as the Scots did. But no one can reconstruct a logical 'national' history of Ireland from 1170 till 1600 except by suppression and omission of facts. Mediaeval Irish history is not intelligible in terms of aggression and defence between two states. There is a problem of aggression and defence. But primarily the story is one of the confrontation of two very divergent civilizations, both of them very sophisticated, with two very different conceptions of statehood.

Even a casual acquaintance with the facts must show that throughout the Middle Ages there was very little warfare between the English and the Irish as compared with that between the English and the (Lowland) Scots. It is said that the Irish were fatally handicapped by the absence of a conception of national kingship. However, the decentralized nature of Gaelic society made it difficult to be destroyed (the political constellation of Gaelic Ireland fitted the fragmented physiographical pattern of the island). On the other hand, by its very nature Gaelic society was difficult to be assimilated into an Anglo-Norman lordship: the basis of law and custom was entirely different. The result was a stalemate which lasted till the sixteenth century – and was accepted on both sides.

The *Proclamation* of the Irish Republic (1916) passes cursorily over seven hundred years of Irish history in the vague phrase: "In every generation the Irish people have asserted their right to national freedom and sovereignty". The Irish successfully defended their own way of life over a great part of Ireland for four hundred years. But they did not assert a right to national freedom and sovereignty in the modern sense of the word. They recognized the English king as their overlord (on the pope's nomination). However, this meant very different things to the Irish and the English.

The Irish accepted the English king as a kind of high-king: they did not accept – they did not *understand* – the feudal implications. In contrast with the Irish, the (normanized) Scots did not recognize the English king as their overlord because to them it meant the same things as to the English: the Scots and the English shared the same concept of statehood. The English and Scottish concept was in fact a common European concept. (The Spaniards who came in contact with the sixteenth-century Irish found as great difficulty in understanding the Gaelic concept as did the English.)

Indeed, one of the most remarkable things about Ireland is the survival in this part of Europe (and in the Scottish Highlands!) of a peculiar archaic type of civilization down till its destruction by the Tudors in the sixteenth century. An outsider might expect that Irish Nationalists would be proud of having sprung from a civilization which so maintained itself to modern times. But, strange as it may seem, many Irish people are indignant when the distinctiveness of Gaelic civilization is pointed out – a tribute to the success of the anglicization process. (Modern Irish Nationalist theory owes its origins not to the Gaelic Irish but to the 'Anglo-Irish'.)

REFERENCES PART THREE

1 Cf. HOWARTH, 152; MACKINDER, 221, 299
2 EVANS, *Folk Ways*, 17
3 THOMAS O'RAHILLY, *History*, 168, 171-2
4 Cf. ibid., 204
5 Ibid., 166-7, 171. Cf. WALTER FITZGERALD, *Geography*, 35-6
6 THOMAS O'RAHILLY, *History*, 173. Cf. KENNEY, 392; MACNEILL, *Phases*, 234-6
7 Ó RÍORDÁIN, *Tara*, 9-10
8 Cf. THOMAS O'RAHILLY, *History*, 167
9 EVANS, *Folk Ways*, 16
10 THOMAS O'RAHILLY, *History*, 174

[11] Ibid., 191

[12] Ibid., 191

[13] Ibid., 173

[14] Cf. ibid., 173; MacNeill, *Phases*, 118

[15] MacNeill, *Phases*, 239; Thomas O'Rahilly, *History*, 222

[16] Cf. Brøndsted, 53

[17] *Society*, 54

[18] Thomas O'Rahilly, *History*, 176. Cf. Binchy, 14

[19] *Society*, 54

[20] Cf. Binchy, 11

[21] Thomas O'Rahilly, *History*, 347

[22] Ibid., 352, 205

[23] Ibid., 341-6. Cf. Dobbs, 66, 70

[24] Thomas O'Rahilly, *History*, 495

[25] Ibid., 222-3, 175-6; Binchy, 15. Cf. MacNeill, *Phases*, 117-8, 125-6

[26] Thomas O'Rahilly, *History*, 234, 229. Cf. Binchy, 14

[27] Thomas O'Rahilly, *History*, 223, 346. Cf. MacNeill, *Phases*, 129-30

[28] Cf. R. S. Rogers, *passim*

[29] Davies, *Archaeology*, 32; Macalister, *Archaeology*, 287-8; Raftery, 50

[30] *Handbook*, 2-3; Macalister, *Archaeology*, 288, *Tara*, 179; MacNeill, *Phases*, 131-2; Raftery, 50,215

[31] Ó Ríordáin, *Antiquities*, 15

[32] Davies, *Dyke*, 29-30

[33] Ó Ríordáin, *Antiquities*, 15. Cf. Curtis, *Mediaeval Ireland*, 402

[34] Davies, *Dyke*, 39

[35] E.g. Curtis, *History*, 5; Davies, *Archaeology*, 34, *Dyke*, 33

[36] Cf. Brøndsted, 161; Evans, *Folk Ways*, 106-7

[37] Thomas O'Rahilly, *Patricks*, 5

[38] Cf. Kenney, 319-29; *The Irish Times*, March 18, 1961

[39] E.g. Zimmer, 7-53

[40] Carney, 402-3

[41] Binchy, 16. Cf. Evans, *Portrait*, 52

[42] Binchy, 15. Cf. Zimmer, 17-24, 41

[43] Kenney, 159, 171. Cf. Zimmer, 42

[44] Thomas O'Rahilly, *Patricks*, 78

[45] Ibid., 41-4; Gougaud, 68-9; Jackson, *Language*, 122; Kenney, 171-82; Cecile O'Rahilly, 52-9; Zimmer, 66

[46] Binchy, 16

[47] Gougaud, 226-30

[48] Cf. Binchy, 13; Alice Green, 248; Kenney, 291-3, 747

[49] Bowen, 66

[50] Stamp, 21-5; Cf. Mackinder, 63, 314

[51] Stamp, 22-3

[52] Fox, *Personality*, 40

[53] Jackson, *Language*, 97, 116-7. Cf. Collingwood & Myres, 3

[54] Cf. Fox, *Personality*, 41

[55] Freeman, *Ireland*, 78; Stamp, 285-7

[56] Hawkes, 6

[57] Fox, *Personality*, 42, 44

[58] Cf. op. cit., 44

[59] Flatrès, 38

[60] Hawkes, 6; Zimmer, 16

[61] E.g. Cecile O'Rahilly, 36

[62] Jackson, *Language*, 154-5. Cf. Lloyd, vol. i, 97-8; Cecile O'Rahilly, 39-40

[63] Cecile O'Rahilly, 57

[64] *Historical Geography*, 284, 295

[65] Ibid., 135

[66] Lloyd, vol. ii, 398, 409; Cecile O'Rahilly, 74, 79

[67] MacNeill, *Phases*, 303-4

[68] Curtis, *Mediaeval Ireland*, 52

[69] Cecile O'Rahilly, 81-2

[70] Ibid., 83

[71] Cf. Kermack, 20

[72] Fawcett, 35

[73] Shearman, *Ulster*, 18-9

[74] Fox, *Personality*, 42

[75] *Belfast*, 76. Cf. *Ulster under H.R.*, 4

[76] Raftery, 158-9, 214

[77] R. de Valera, 36-48. Cf. Davies, *Archaeology*, 14-5

[78] *Belfast*, 79

[79] Thomas O'Rahilly, *History*, 223

[80] Kermack, 43; *Society*, 51

[81] Cecile O'Rahilly, 47

[82] Gougaud, 4; MacDonald, 12; Ritchie, xxviii

[83] MacNeill, *Phases* 194-5. Cf. MacDonald, 31

[84] Jackson, *Gaelic*, 77. Cf. Campbell, 40-2

[85] Jackson, *Language*, 27

[86] Jackson, *Gaelic*, 75-7. Cf. Campbell, 18-9

[87] Ritchie, xxviii

[88] Gougaud, 134-5; Kenney, 224, 422-6

[89] Kenney, 424

[90] Trevelyan, 74

[91] Ibid., 72; Gougaud, 392

[92] Goedheer, 109-10; Gougaud, 393

[93] Curtis, *History*, 28; Kenney, 353-4; MacNeill, *Phases*, 269-71

[94] Brøndsted, 101; Curtis, *History*, 29-30; Goedheer, 110, 117, 120; MacDonald, 61

[95] Cf. Curtis, *Mediaeval Ireland*, 9-10

[96] Gougaud, 398; Kenney, 757-63; Neill, 292

[97] Cf. Eggers, 30; Gougaud, 400-1; *History*, vol. ii, 37-8

[98] Curtis, *Mediaeval Ireland*, 6

[99] Ibid., 47; Beckett, 17; Aubrey Gwynn, 210-1

[100] BARROW, 171

[101] TREVELYAN, 163

[102] *Ulster under H.R.*, 15-6. Cf. MACNEILL,*Laws*, 135

[103] RITCHIE, xi

[104] COUPLAND, 21

[105] Ibid., xv

[106] BARROW, 170

[107] Cf. COUPLAND, 22-3

[108] BARROW, 170

[109] WILLIAMSON, *Evolution*, 121

[110] TREVELYAN, 122. Cf. WILLIAMSON, *Evolution*, 123-4

[111] ROWSE, 37

[112] TREVELYAN, 122; WILLIAMSON, *Evolution*, 124. Cf. O'FAOLAIN, *Story*, 17-20

[113] TREVELYAN, 163-4

[114] Cf. ibid., 162; COUPLAND, 22

[115] Cf. CURTIS, *History*, 114, 134-5

[116] Cf. HOGAN, 15

[117] O'FAOLAIN, *Irish*, 62

[118] CURTIS, *Mediaeval Ireland*, 52; HOGAN, 15

[119] CURTIS, *Mediaeval Ireland*, 182, 202

[120] HOGAN, 15

[121] Ibid., 22-3

[122] Ibid., 23

[123] TREVELYAN, 164-5. Cf. O'FAOLAIN, *Irish*, 58-9

[124] BECKETT, 31; CURTIS, *Mediaeval Ireland*, 285. Cf. *Documents*, 52-9

[125] CURTIS, *Mediaeval Ireland*, 320; HOGAN, 24

[126] HOGAN, 24-6, 30-1. Cf. GOAD, 200

[127] CURTIS, *Mediaeval Ireland*, 218-9; HOGAN, 29-30, 34-6

[128] HAYES-MCCOY, 4

[129] Cf. WALTER FITZGERALD, *Geography*, 13-4; MACNEILL, *Phases*, 311, 328

[130] HAYES-MCCOY, 8

[131] Ibid., 19, 17n

[132] MACKENZIE, *Scotland*, 291

[133] HAYES-MCCOY, 8-9

[134] CURTIS, *Mediaeval Ireland*, 89; ORPEN, vol. ii, 17-9, 117, 136

[135] CURTIS, *Mediaeval Ireland*, 111; ORPEN, vol. ii, 137-40

[136] BUCHANAN, *Barony*, 21; FARR, 14-5

[137] ARCHER, 9; CORR, 8; ORPEN, vol. ii, 19-20, 141; WARD, 11-5

[138] BUCHANAN, *Isle Lecale*, 14-6; ORPEN, vol. ii, 10, 20, 255

[139] CURTIS, *Earldom*, 76-80; MACNEILL, *Laws*, 9

[140] CURTIS, *Mediaeval Ireland*, 106; ORPEN, vol. ii, 134

[141] CURTIS, *Mediaeval Ireland*, 112

[142] Ibid., 230

[143] Ibid., 124-6, 130; ORPEN, vol. ii, 267, 290-3

[144] CURTIS, *Mediaeval Ireland*, 130, 142; HAYES-MCCOY, 20; ORPEN, vol. iii, 44-5

[145] CURTIS, *Earldom*, 67-9, *Mediaeval Ireland*, 168

[146] MACKENZIE, *Bruce*, 130-1

[147] CURTIS, *Mediaeval Ireland*, 273; E. R. R. GREEN, 18

[148] CURTIS, *Mediaeval Ireland*, 158; MACNEILL, *Phases*, 329

[149] HAYES-MCCOY, 16; *Handbook*, 9

[150] CURTIS, *Mediaeval Ireland*, 228; MACKENZIE, *Bruce*, 177-9

[151] MACKENZIE, *Bruce*, 289-90; Cf. CURTIS, *Mediaeval Ireland*, 228-9

[152] Cf. RAIT, 56-7

[153] MACDONALD, 124, 131; MACKENZIE, *Bruce*, 179, 293-4. Cf. CURTIS, *Mediaeval Ireland*, 234, 248

[154] CURTIS, *Mediaeval Ireland*, 244; MACNEILL, *Phases*, 219

[155] CURTIS, *Earldom*, 73-4; MACNEILL, *Phases*, 219

[156] CURTIS, *History*, 175-6

[157] GALLAGHER, 26. Cf. *Handbook*, 10

[158] THOMAS O'RAHILLY, *Dialects*, 263, 18

[159] Ibid., 260-1, 264

[160] Ibid., 123

[161] Ibid., 125, 248-9, 260

[162] Ibid., 261

[163] Ibid., 261

PART FOUR

REGIONAL CONTRASTS AND CONTACTS
OF POST-REFORMATION IRELAND

Chapter 12

THE TUDOR CONQUEST

THE STRATEGIC AND THE RELIGIOUS FACTOR

By the end of the fifteenth century, as CURTIS says, "both in England and Scotland the day of a new and powerful monarchy had come": in England by the accession of Henry VII Tudor (1485-1509), and in Scotland by the crushing of the Scottish part of the lordship of the Isles by James IV Stuart in 1499.[1] The sixteenth century was to see more and even more fundamental changes in the affairs of the two kingdoms – changes which have also largely affected the affairs of the sister island.

It was under the Tudors that "the conquest of Ireland, after being neglected for four hundred years, was at last undertaken in earnest".[2] It is, to some extent, more correct to speak of a re-conquest. The revival of the English interest in Ireland was chiefly dictated by strategic reasons. The Tudors could not for ever tolerate the existence of "a half-subdued dependency which, if not controlled by England, might soon be controlled by England's continental enemies".[3] "Mediaeval isolation was over", CURTIS observes, "and with the duel that now began of the new centralized monarchies of Europe this island might become a dangerous centre of intrigues against England".[4]

It took more than a lifetime, in fact the whole Tudor period, to complete the conquest. It was pursued primarily by diplomatic means but it was not consummated until after a long-drawn war. The conquest was both a success and a failure. It was successful in the sense that gradually all powers in Ireland, whether Irish, English or Scottish, were reduced to "order and obedience". It failed in the sense that it left "a foundation for continuing resistance to English power".[5] The main crux was religion.

It would be wrong to suppose that Tudor policy in Ireland was inspired by religion, *i.e.* by the idealism of the Reformation. According to O'FAOLAIN it was the Irish who identified their resistance with the idealism of the Counter-Reformation. Or it might be more accurate to say that the Irish were encouraged to do so by the emissaries of Spain and Rome who saw in Ireland the opportunity for a flank attack on Great Britain.[6] The religious motive, however, entered only gradually and ambiguously. It annotates the role of the religious factor that it was not until a Catholic queen came on the English throne that the 'psychological infiltration' of Ireland was accompanied by anything serious in the way of a conquest by force.[7] (Or as GALLAGHER puts it: "The change in religion merely intensified what was the permanent English aim".[8]) Religion became a major issue only after 1570 when Queen Elizabeth was excommunicated.

I agree with FALLS that it is at least a defensible proposition that Ireland might have become as closely united with England as Wales was, or as Scotland was to be, but for the failure of the Reformation in Ireland.[9] As WILLIAMSON says, "the underlying cause of all the blood-stained record of the past four centuries", as far as England and Ireland are concerned, is "the difference of religion rather than the difference of race".[10] Whereas the Reformation eased England's relations with Scotland, and ultimately smoothed the way for the political union of the two countries which has never been severed[a], it greatly contributed to the frustration of her relations with Ireland and ultimately it caused a breach which has never been repaired. Had the Reformation in Ireland succeeded, whether along English or Scottish (or Welsh) lines, there probably would not have been, today, an independent Irish Republic.

HENRY'S POLICY OF 'SURRENDER AND RE-GRANT'

There is a close parallel between the first phases of what became known as the Tudor conquest of Ireland, as undertaken by Henry VIII (1509-47) in the second quarter of the sixteenth century, and those of the Anglo-Norman conquest under Henry II in the final quarter of the twelfth century. The Tudor conquest, too, was initiated by the subjugation of feudal power (the Kildares in Leinster) and the imposition of royal authority on the entire island without a preliminary military conquest. In 1541 Henry VIII styled himself *king of Ireland*, while abandoning the title *lord of Ireland* bestowed on the English kings by the pope. The new royal title, publicly proclaimed in Dublin cathedral, was endorsed – like the previous title – by most Gaelic chiefs, if not by all (and, of course, by the 'Anglo-Irish' nobles). The Tudor conquest was also accompanied by a policy of reforming the Church on English lines. But here the parallel ends.

Henry VIII's new Irish departure aimed at the complete anglicization of the sister island: "Ireland was to be made if possible a second England through the complaisant bishops and nobility".[11] So far as the Church is concerned, Henry (who had broken with Rome in 1536) had little difficulty in forcing his programme through in Ireland. "The native Irish rulers had no reason for supporting papal authority, which had generally been exerted on the side of the English; the Anglo-Irish might naturally be expected to fall in line with a policy which had already been accepted in England".[12] And this is in fact what happened. Both Gaelic chiefs and Anglo-Irish lords took part in the scramble for the lands of the monasteries – which were never restored, not even under Queen Mary.[b]

The two main objects of Henry's civil policy were:

[a] It is well to remember that for more than 250 years after the Battle of Bannockburn (1314) Scotland remained England's enemy, invariably ready to take advantage of England's difficulties. Only what RAIT (61) calls "the accident of the Reformation" rendered it possible to disengage Scotland from her alliance with France, and to bring about a union with England. On the other hand, the postponement of the Anglo-Scottish Union till the seventeenth century enabled Scotland to work out her own ecclesiastical destiny "in the way best adapted to the nation's needs" (RAIT, 63).

[b] There was some opposition among the English clergy, led by the primate of Armagh. But when once the act of supremacy had been passed, the majority of the bishops seem to have conformed. The apathy of the native Irish in the whole question is clearly seen in the failure of the first Jesuit missionaries who arrived in Ulster in 1542 with letters from the pope and from Ignatius Loyola: "The northern chiefs gave them such a scant welcome that they were soon glad to make their escape to Scotland" (BECKETT, 50; cf. COONAN, 24; CURTIS, *History*, 165).

(1)   the fusion of the English colonists and the native Irish population, by "a complete abandonment of the policy of segregation" (the Pale!) and by the extension of English law and government to the whole island; and

(2)   the conciliation of the great lords, by confirming them and their heirs (according to English law) in their estates and granting them new titles (and by sharing with them the spoil of the religious houses)[13]; this conciliatory policy, which O'FAOLAIN calls "Henry's masterpiece of diplomatic strategy", is known as 'surrender and re-grant'.[14]

At first it seemed that the new Irish policy would succeed, but in the end it did not. The ecclesiastical changes which accompanied Henry's policy have sometimes been regarded as contributory to its failure. However, this is true, as BECKETT observes, only in so far as these changes prepared the way for the Protestantism of Henry's successor, his son Edward VI (1547-53).[15] One of the main reasons was the failure of the 'surrender and re-grant system'.

Conn O'Neill and other ambitious Gaelic chiefs were eager enough to be turned into English lords and thus to be brought into the circle of England's hereditary nobility. Thus Conn O'Neill was created *earl of Tyrone* (1542). The new system, however, was incompatible with Gaelic law. First of all, a Gaelic chief was not hereditary but elected for life. Secondly, he was not the owner of his whole 'country'. Of Gaelic law it would be almost true to say that 'it was the people who gave the land to the chief', while in the feudal system 'the chief gave the land to the people'.[16]

The new system – and, indeed, all other methods of anglicization employed in the Tudor age – made, relatively, most headway in Leinster, Munster and Connacht, *viz.* the 'south' in the modern sense of the word. It is well to remember that the mediaeval English influence had been almost confined to those provinces.[a] Throughout the sixteenth century Ulster remained the chief bulwark of the Gaelic tradition. It is significant that when Conn O'Neill, the first earl of Tyrone, died (1559), his subjects elected not his oldest but a younger son, Seán, as their chief, 'the O'Neill'. Thus the Gaelic principle of succession had triumphed over English law. (Seán O'Neill even revived the ancient claim of the O'Neills to the kingship of Ulster.)

MARY'S POLICY OF 'CONFISCATION AND PLANTATION'

Henry's policy of "Catholicism without the pope" had been accepted in Ireland as readily as in England. But with Edward VI's attempt to use the royal supremacy to bring about changes in doctrine and liturgy, "the differences between the two countries at once appeared". Except in the Pale, and in a few towns beyond it, the new ecclesiastical policy had little effect. As BECKETT points out, there had been in Ireland little of "that intellectual inquiry and criticism which had been growing in other parts of western Christendom". Not only was there no strong reform party in Ireland to counter the inevitable opposition, but most of the newly appointed bishops and clergy had very little zeal for reform measures. Moreover, the changes came at a time when the country was entering upon

---

[a]   Some of the greater families in the 'south', like the O'Briens in south Connacht who became – and remained – *earls of Thomond*, had already introduced a primogeniture principle by ensuring that the eldest son was elected as the 'chief of their name and nation'.

a new period of political unrest: the peace established by the policy of 'surrender and re-grant', superficial as it was, disappeared in a series of insurrections.[17]

The reversal of the ecclesiastical policy under Mary Tudor (1553-58) was almost universally welcomed in Ireland. [a] Mary, however, did not abandon her father's title – her proclamation as *queen of Ireland* was even confirmed by Pope Paul IV. In civil affairs she simply continued her half-brother's policy. As the new ecclesiastical policy had done nothing to reconcile the rebellious magnates, Mary's reign was almost wholly occupied in military operations against them. Mary also made an attempt to curb the increasing power of the Scottish lordship in Co. Antrim. But her measures came to nothing and the Scots continued to be "a great factor in the North" for forty years.[18]

It was Mary, too, who initiated the policy of 'confiscation and plantation', *i.e.* the expulsion of disloyal Gaelic chiefs and the distribution of 'their' forfeited lands among loyal English colonists. This policy served two purposes: it strengthened the basis of English power, and it provided an outlet for the growing population of the mother country. The various Irish projects of the sixteenth and seventeenth centuries are linked with the general movement towards overseas expansion. The plantation of Munster (1586) was even based in part upon Raleigh's proposals for Virginia, and Raleigh himself and others were engaged in plantation enterprises both in Ireland and in America.[19]

The first Irish plantation (1556) was that of the lands of the O'Moores, the O'Connors, and other families who, "from their secure retreat among the great bogs and woods" in the centre of the Lowlands, could easily attack the Pale.[20] The confiscated territory was converted into two counties which were named, in compliment to Queen Mary and her husband King Philip II of Spain, 'Queen's County' and 'King's County'. Their 'capitals' were called 'Maryborough' and 'Philipstown'.[b] (This plantation seems to have given the impulse to the cultivation, whether by settlers or natives, of large tracts of 'wilderness' in the midlands.[c])

None of the Marian and Elizabethan plantation schemes came up to expectations. This is due partly to incompetence and partly to the readiness with which 'undertakers' (planters), anxious for quick returns, accepted Irish tenants at high rents, in spite of their

[a] Even the Marian Restoration did nothing to further the cause of Protestantism as it did in England, because there were no martyrs. The reforming bishops were deprived but no proceedings were taken against them for heresy. "The fires of Smithfield and Oxford, which lit the way for a Protestant settlement in England", had no counterpart in Ireland (BECKETT, 52).

[b] In 1922 the two counties were renamed 'Leix' and 'Offaly', and the two towns 'Portlaoighise' and 'Daingean'.

[c] The sixteenth and seventeenth centuries saw a great reduction of the Irish woodlands. It is obvious that to the invading armies, and to the settlers who followed in their wake, the forests were a source of danger. "In these 'fastnesses' it was difficult for English horsemen to manoeuvre and dangerous for detached bodies of infantry to move: the 'passes' were only wide enough for horsemen to go in single file". But as well as being a danger the woods were a source of wealth. For that reason also they were destroyed, especially after the completion of the conquest, in the seventeenth century. "The planters wanted to make money as quickly as possible and one of the easiest ways was to utilize the timber on their estates. Apart from the use of wood for ordinary building and domestic purposes, there were four avenues of profit opened up to the new owners of woods: tanning of leather, shipbuilding, pipe and barrel-stave making, and iron smelting" (McCRACKEN, 287-9; cf. DAVIES, *Archaeology*, 2). By 1700 the woodlands had been reduced to a negligible area. (Reforestation began in the eighteenth century when landlords planted their lowland demesnes with exotic and native species of tree.)

agreement to bring in English".[21] (It may be noted that not all planters were Protestants.[22])
In the end the plantations were almost completely swept away by great insurrections.

THE POLITICAL CONSEQUENCES OF THE REFORMATION (1570)

It was during the long reign of Mary's half-sister Elizabeth (1558-1603) that the secular
and the spiritual issues were at last decided. For a right understanding of those stirring
times it is necessary to distinguish clearly between the four main cultural elements in
Ireland. They were, by seniority:

(1)   the *Gaelic Irish*, whose society had existed for over a thousand years; their strongest footholds were
       the O'Neill lordship of Tyrone (modern Cos Londonderry, Tyrone and Armagh) and the O'Donnell
       lordship of Tyrconnell (modern Cos Donegal, Fermanagh and Sligo);
(2)   the *Anglo-Irish*, henceforth called the *Old English*, the descendants of the pre-sixteenth-century
       colonists in the Pale and in the towns and some rural areas beyond the Pale – in so far as they had
       remained, culturally, recognizably English;
(3)   the *Norse-Gaelic Scots*, most strongly entrenched in Co. Antrim, the Irish part of the MacDonnell
       lordship of the Isles – greatly strengthened after the breakdown of the Scottish part of the lordship
       under James IV; and
(4)   the *New English*, the recently introduced officials of Church and state in Dublin and other main
       centres, and the planters established in the subdued parts of Leinster, Munster and Connacht – the
       nucleus of the future Ascendancy class.

I will deal first with the religious issue. When Elizabeth succeeded to the throne
Ireland was again subjected to a change-over in ecclesiastical policy. But, whereas under
Elizabeth England became substantially Protestant, Ireland remained substantially Roman
Catholic: the Gaels, the Old English, and the Scots alike. Every chance of winning the
people of Ireland over to Protestantism was neglected. The majority of the newly
appointed bishops and clergy showed no missionary zeal; many of them were absentees
and sinecurists. Moreover, as CURTIS says,

> "No attempt was made until it was too late to convert the people through the medium of their own
> language. It was not till the beginning of James I's reign that the prayer book and New Testament were
> published in Irish, nor was it till the reign of Charles I that the whole Bible was translated into Irish. So was
> set up in Ireland that Established Church on Anglican lines which the Irish called the 'Queen's religion'".[23]

The field of enterprise neglected by the Protestant clergy was soon seized upon by
a great number of travelling friars and priests from the continent [a] – a large proportion
of them being Jesuits – who were "far superior in learning, ability, and respectability of
life to the clergy displaced from their benefices".[24]

It was not till 1570, when Pope Pius V excommunicated Elizabeth and released her
subjects from obedience, that the political consequences of the Reformation began to
appear. "The papacy, for so long the ally of English power in Ireland, now became its

---

[a] Apart from the question as to whether it is possible to decide why any people became Protestant or
remained Roman Catholic, the reasons usually advanced as to why Ireland remained substantially Roman
Catholic (*viz.* the half-hearted attempts to 'convert' the Irish, and the Counter-Reformation with its
hostility to England) seem inadequate to explain why *no section whatever* of the pre-Reformation population
of Ireland – whether Gaelic, Anglo-Norman, English, or Scottish – showed a more than minimal interest
in Protestantism.

enemy" (BECKETT). [a] Whereas in England Protestantism and patriotism – and defiance of the Spanish enemy – gradually fell together, in Ireland (outside the Pale) "a slowly growing national sentiment came to be identified with the cause of the papacy" – and with that of Spain.[25]

Under these circumstances the position of the Old English by degrees became a very complicated one. The bulk of them were traditionally loyal to the crown but refused to accept the Reformation. Politically, then, they had common ground with the New English. Religiously, however, they found themselves at the side of the great majority of the Gaelic Irish. When the religious atmosphere heightened, it became more and more clear that the two loyalties were incompatible. It seems inevitable that, when the Old English remained faithful to the old religion, they were forced, willy-nilly, into the 'Irish camp'. It was most difficult for the Old English of the Pale and a number of cities beyond it, to whom the native Irish had always been the enemy. They managed to remain 'Queen's men' throughout Elizabeth's reign; they were only to throw in their lot with the majority under the first Stuarts.[26]

Thus "a common resentment against the new Establishment and the official policy on religion began to unite the two races, Gaelic and Old English, who were to become the Irish nation".[27] In the seventeenth century the greater part of the Antrim Scots, too, were merged in this new body politic.[b]

[a] Essentially, papal policy in regard to Ireland was only an appendage to papal policy in regard to Great Britain. The excommunication of Elizabeth and the release of her subjects from obedience was hardly more than a restatement of the bull of 1170. Henry VIII had repudiated that bull in declaring himself *king of Ireland*. The pope confirmed the new title to Henry's orthodox successor Mary Tudor, which means that he sanctioned the English sovereignty over Ireland. Elizabeth's Irish subjects were 'freed' of their allegiance. Had Elizabeth been succeeded – as was, at the time, not unlikely – by the orthodox Mary Stuart, the pope's decree might have been reversed and English rule in Ireland again recognized. Hugh O'Neill rebelling against a Protestant queen became a Counter-Reformation hero who was blessed by Rome. But Hugh O'Neill a rebel against a Catholic queen might well have been excommunicated as quickly as his ancestor Donald O'Neill – the man of the *Remonstrance*.

(There are anti-clerical elements in Irish revolutionary circles who maintain that papal policy has been consistently unfavourable to Irish 'national aspirations' – with the brief exception of the 1640-50 period. This exception was, as they see it, probably more due to the personalities of the papal nuncio in Ireland and the Irish envoy in Rome than to calculated policy. In 1690 the pope was a political ally of William of Orange; he even illuminated the Vatican to celebrate the Irish defeat at the Boyne – which to the pope was more importantly a defeat for Louis XIV.)

[b] How different was the outcome of the Tudor policy towards Wales (which had been 'incorporated' in England in 1536). The Welsh remained loyal to the English crown "throughout the dangerous storms of the Tudor period", even when "a great strain was put on their loyalty by the English Reformation", as TREVELYAN puts it. It is well to remember that the Tudors were of Welsh descent. This cut both ways: it was a 'source of pride' to the Welsh people (when Henry VII acceded to the English throne, his fellow-countrymen flocked to his court as the Scots a century later to the court of James VI and I), and it gave the Tudors an understanding of local conditions which, in the case of Ireland, they completely lacked (TREVELYAN, 262-3). On the other hand, the proximity of Wales and its accessibility via improved land routes served only to strengthen and to quicken the arm of the central government.

Protestantism came to Wales under the same guise as it came to Ireland: in a tongue little known, and by "an alien official clergy" without much missionary zeal. As in Ireland, it made little progress although there were few, if any, Roman Catholic clergy left and the Jesuit missions in Elizabeth's reign neglected Wales, "partly owing to a fierce domestic quarrel between the Welsh and English in the continental seminaries" (REES, 26-7; TREVELYAN, 263-4). Wales remained, more or less, Catholic (in a traditional way) until Wesley converted it to Methodism.

Whereas the religious issue in Ireland was largely decided in the first dozen years of Elizabeth's rule – the big landmark being 1570 – the political issue was decided only at the close of her reign. In fact, Elizabeth's most unyielding opponent, the lord of Tyrone, definitely submitted only some days after her death – being unaware of the fact that she had died.

Throughout her long government Ireland was "the danger point in Elizabeth's dominions".[28] It is true that Philip II, of whose aid the Irish Catholics held high hopes, proved "a very disappointing patron". During his long reign he never sent over more than a few hundreds of men directly to the Irish cause. The pope, while being more whole-hearted towards the Irish cause, had not the money or the armies to back Irish Catholic resistance.[29] But so long as Ireland was not entirely brought under control, an invasion by England's continental enemies was a factor constantly to be reckoned with.

By a combination of her father's more peaceful methods and Mary's policy of military conquest secured by plantation, Queen Elizabeth – "urged on by fear rather than ambition" – gradually extended her authority over Leinster, Munster, and Connacht. For more than thirty years Ulster, "cut off from the rest of the country by a natural barrier of mountains and lake", was left more or less alone. A factor to be taken into account is that "its remoteness discouraged European intervention".[30] On the other hand, the Ulster chiefs, the O'Neills and the O'Donnells, got far more – and far more effective – military aid from professional soldiers from the Islands and Western Highlands than the continental supporters of the Gaelic cause were ever able to supply. Until Ulster had been conquered it would be found impossible for the English government to prevent the enlistment of many thousands of these Scottish mercenaries – the successors of the older Gallowglasses.[31]

Elizabeth, by descent from the earls of Ulster, was *countess of Ulster*. This title was considered enough to entitle her to the whole north, regardless of 'native rights'. In particular John de Courcy's old lands in east Ulster were considered by law hers.[32] But for the time being this claim was allowed to lapse. Elizabeth, in dealing with the Ulster lordships, relied on diplomacy rather than on military action. Her policy was moderated of course by inadequate military and financial resources, and perhaps – in view of the links between Ulster and Scotland – by questions of Scottish policy. At any rate, so long as the O'Neills of Tyrone, the MacDonnells of Antrim, and the O'Donnells of Tyrconnell were rivals, there was no pressing need for embarking on a costly conquest.

In the early fifteen 'seventies there were undertaken several attempts at plantations in Ulster, *viz.* of parts of Cos Monaghan, Armagh, Down, and Antrim. They were foiled, however, by the O'Neills of Tyrone and by the O'Neills of Clandeboye and the MacDonnells of Antrim respectively.[33] In 1591 the English government scored a success by a 'surrender and re-grant' treaty with seven chief MacMahons and a MacKenna which included almost the whole of Co. Monaghan. As a result of this settlement, which recognized the rights of chiefs and native freeholders, Monaghan remained loyal and was not to be included in the final plantation of Ulster.[34]

Elizabeth's most formidable opponent in Ulster was Hugh O'Neill who, in 1593, was elected after the Gaelic fashion "the chief of his name and nation", 'the O'Neill'. He had already been created *earl of Tyrone* by Elizabeth. In fact, for a long time he had been the government's *protégé*: he had spent six years in the *entourage* of the queen in London and he had even served with English troops against Munster rebels. Like his predecessors as 'the O'Neill', Seán O'Neill[a] (1559-67) and Turloch O'Neill[b] (1567-93), Hugh O'Neill was quite prepared to be loyal so long as his loyalty did not clash with his personal ambition to secure recognition as 'the O'Neill' and, thereafter, to establish O'Neill supremacy in Ulster. But he was more far-sighted than his predecessors which may be apparent from the fact that he sought alliance with the O'Donnells of Tyrconnell, instead of trying to crush them.[35]

Although Hugh O'Neill did not seek war, knowing the weakness of his own position, at last the inevitable happened. The religious atmosphere had been heightening for some years and "in this uneasy position casual armed clashes led naturally to a national struggle" (1594).[36] As CURTIS remarks:

> "By geography Ulster was well fitted to make a desperate resistance, for on the south its border was one long chain of lakes, forests, and mountains, where the only passes were the Gap of the North beyond Dundalk on the one hand and the fords of the Erne at Enniskillen and Ballyshannon on the other. There was no English garrison on the northern coast, and this left open the communications with the Hebrides and with the citizens of Glasgow, who had no scruple in supplying Irish rebels with munitions of war".[37]

TYRONE'S WAR (1594-1603) AND THE FLIGHT OF THE EARLS (1607)

At the beginning of the war, which is generally known as Tyrone's War, Hugh O'Neill's demands were for religious toleration and security of possessions only in his own lands. As the war proceeded and spread to several parts of the island, it acquired a more 'national' character.[38] A number of Gaelic and Norman-Gaelic chiefs in the west and the south-west repudiated their obedience to the crown and rallied to O'Neill. Eventually some Anglo-Irish nobles, too, joined in the war. But all the towns, Roman Catholic though their burghers were, remained loyal to the crown.

For six or seven years O'Neill's Scottish and Irish forces were superior to the crown's forces. In 1598 they inflicted a crushing defeat on an English army[c] at the Battle of the

---

[a] Seán O'Neill was ready to acknowledge Queen Elizabeth as sovereign – he even saw Elizabeth herself in London – but he was resolute against the introduction of English law into Ulster. In his programme, CURTIS says, "religion or the union of Ireland counted less than the maintenance of the O'Neill kingship". He was encouraged to attack his Scottish rivals, the MacDonnells of Antrim (whom he defeated in 1565, killing James MacDonnell), but he was not allowed to become the absolute ruler of the north. When he was ready to attack the O'Donnells of Tyrconnell, the Dublin government hastened to their support by seizing Derry. The O'Donnells, however, proved more than a match for Seán. After being routed, he fled to Antrim where he was duly killed by the Scots (CURTIS, *History*, 181, 184-6).

[b] According to CURTIS, Turloch O'Neill "ruled Tyrone in general with satisfaction of the government". By marrying the widow of James MacDonnell of Antrim, who was a daughter of the earl of Argyll, Turloch got as a dowry some thousands of Scottish mercenaries. (James MacDonnell's daughter, who married Hugh O'Neill, did the same for her husband.) Turloch's Scottish wife was described by the English constable of Carrickfergus castle (on the northern shore of Belfast Lough) as "a great practiser for the bringing of that part of the realm [*i.e.* Ulster] to be Scottish" (CURTIS, *History*, 205; HAYES-MCCOY, 106, 132).

[c] The English army was commanded by Sir Henry Bagenal. At the time Hugh O'Neill was married to Bagenal's sister. He had eloped with her from Dublin and they were married by the Protestant bishop of Meath.

Yellow Ford (Co. Armagh) – a victory which still appeals to the imagination of many Irish people. But it became increasingly clear that, once the English summoned up all their strength, O'Neill's fate would soon be sealed. All his hopes were in Spanish aid which at last came: in 1601 four thousand troops landed at – of all places – Kinsale (Co. Cork) on the south coast. [a] When O'Neill's forces hastily rallied to them, they were decisively defeated at what came to be known as the Battle of Kinsale. (The Spaniards were glad to surrender on condition of being allowed to return home.)

Although his cause had now become a hopeless one, O'Neill, deprived of all his former allies, still held out for more than a year in his own Tyrone, only fighting now for satisfactory terms. His ultimate hopes were in the death of Queen Elizabeth and in her succession by King James VI of Scotland who had once expressed sympathy for his stand. Some years previously the Scottish king had received his envoys kindly, promising he would remember Tyrone "when it shall please God to call our sister the Queen of England to death".[39] James had even given O'Neill some underhand help by allowing recruitment of mercenaries and the purchase of munitions. The statement once common in Irish history books that James was O'Neill's secret ally[40], is however quite incorrect. It shows no appreciation of the harassed position of that monarch, let alone his religious opinions (he was a sincere Protestant but no lover of the Scottish divines). [b]

In 1603 Hugh O'Neill was finally forced to surrender, ringed round as he was by English forts and his country systematically laid waste. He is said to have wept with rage when he found he had submitted when Elizabeth was already dead and James VI of Scotland had become James I of England. However, James received him kindly in London and restored him to his earldom, though it was greatly limited (Rory, the son of Hugh O'Donnell, was similarly treated). But, to all intents and purposes, King James I of England had no more love of the overmighty subject than any Tudor. And inevitably he continued the Tudor policy where Elizabeth had left off.

The earl of Tyrone soon realized that his power was at an end and that the government was only waiting for a pretext to destroy him. Anticipating the decision he fled to the continent. In 1607 he sailed from Lough Swilly into voluntary exile, accompanied by the earl of Tyrconnell and nearly a hundred minor Gaelic chiefs of Ulster.

[a] It seems that O'Neill had plotted for a Spanish landing at Galway in the far west, hoping to win over this Roman Catholic, English, town. The fact that during Tyrone's War Galway remained loyal – as all the other walled towns – may have been one of the reasons why the Spanish fleet did not land there, which was near Tyrone and Tyrconnell, instead of the disastrous position of Kinsale in the extreme south.

[b] As a Scot, as a descendant of the Bruces – as one whose claim to the Scottish kingship went back to the same ancestors from whom the O'Neills had claimed the kingship of Ulster (and Ireland) – no doubt James had sympathy for Tyrone. If he did not succeed Elizabeth, Irish allies might be useful: the O'Neills had offered his grandfather the Irish kingdom. On the other hand, he would not antagonize Elizabeth. Moreover, if after all he did succeed to the English throne, he would have to deal with O'Neill: if O'Neill was a rebel, he was also a mighty subject.

Only after the Battle of Kinsale (1601), when Spanish help had failed and O'Neill was beaten back into his mid Ulster fortress, did James exert himself, with much publicity, against Tyrone. He even proposed the raising of a Highland muster against him. Here a last instance of pro-Irish feeling in Scotland may be mentioned. When James's proposed Highland levy came up for discussion at the Scottish parliament, there were (according to HAYES-MCCOY, 341) "many dissentient voices". The Irish, said some, "were closely related to the Highlanders and Islesmen by ties both of race-kinship and friendliness while the Saxons were nothing to them, and these latter had, furthermore, consistently oppressed the Irish".

The tragic "Flight of the Earls" was more than the disappearance of the last great opponents of English law and government. As Gaelic culture was completely bound up with the Gaelic aristocracy, the Flight meant practically the end of a distinctive culture. Gaelic society provided for the existence of a great literary class: families of poets, chroniclers and 'brehons' – all an essential part of the semi-tribal, semi-feudal, basis of that society. The weakness of Gaelic society was that it centred purely round a number of aristocratic families. (There were never Gaelic towns – the centres of Gaelic society were the dwellings of the tribal chiefs and these centres were of a semi-permanent nature.) When the aristocracy was destroyed, the literary class was destroyed too. [a] The classical poetry, which had maintained almost petrified though beautiful forms from the time of the Vikings, disappeared. Only the Gaelic language survived.

In conclusion: it is well to realize that, although the fight of the Ulster chiefs was an apparent failure, "nations are made in many ways, and among these is the heroic example of great men even when they seem to fail". [41]

Chapter 13

THE SCOTTISH COLONIZATION OF ULSTER

THE SECOND SCOTTISH COLONY IN EAST ULSTER (1606)

From the time of the Bruces to the close of Elizabeth's reign, the exclusion of Scots from the north of Ireland had been a constant feature of English policy – though not a very successful one in view of the entrenchment of the MacDonnells in Co. Antrim and the enlistment of thousands of Gallowglasses and mercenaries in the forces of the Ulster chiefs. It is hardly surprising that, after England and Scotland had become united under one king, the English policy underwent a radical change.

The English policy had been modified already since the consolidation of the Reformation in Scotland and the elimination of Mary Stuart had established a lasting peace on the Scottish Border. The shift in Elizabeth's policy, by which the Scottish colony in Antrim was in the early part of her reign savagely attacked and in the end of her reign encouraged and protected, can only be understood in the light of the changing scene in Scotland after Mary's flight. The succession of King James VI to the English throne only assured the position of the colony. Ronald MacSomhairle MacDonnell remained in

---

[a] One of the poets has expressed all that the Flight meant for those to whom the old Gaelic order was the only way of life they had known and who were now to see that order crumbling into ruins about them. From his long poem (cf. FLOWER, 166-8) I will cite a few of the last lines:

> "Sundered from hope, what friendly hand
> Can save the sea-surrounded land?
> Her chiefs are gone. There's none to bear
> Her cross or lift her from despair;
> The grieving lords take ship. With these
> Our very souls pass overseas".

undisturbed possession of the greater part of Co. Antrim and eventually was created *earl of Antrim.* [a]

The new English policy manifested itself immediately in Clandeboye, the lordship which embraced the southern fringe of Co. Antrim and the northern part of Co. Down. During Tyrone's War Clandeboye had "performed faithfully the duty of defending the eastern flank of Tyrone and containing the Carrickfergus garrison". After James's accession Conn O'Neill of Clandeboye was pardoned at the price of a great part of his lands. He was unable to retain the remainder of his estates which were sold off bit by bit.[42] In 1605 two Scottish favourites of the king received grants of land in south Clandeboye: James Hamilton on the southern shore of Belfast Lough and on the western shore of Strangford Lough, and Hugh Montgomery around Newtownards in the north of the Ards peninsula. [b]

The granting of lands in east Ulster to Scottish noblemen was in fact a revival of the policy of the Anglo-Norman earls of Ulster. The grants to the earls of Carrick and Galloway in the thirteenth century arose from identical geographical considerations as the grants to Hamilton and Montgomery who were lairds in Ayrshire. Historical reasons – the enmity between Scotland and England – had interrupted that policy. The union of the two countries under one crown naturally revived it.

Hamilton and Montgomery entered upon the development of their new estates with resolution. They called upon their whole kith and kin to aid them. In 1606 and the next few years at least ten thousand Scots of various ranks of life crossed the narrow North Channel.[c] Fortune smiled on the pioneers. Good grain harvests in the early years encouraged them to send home favourable reports and more thousands of settlers arrived. Within a few years small market towns were appearing.[43] The colonists soon formed congregations which called ministers from Scotland: thus were laid the foundations of Ulster Presbyterianism.

Many thousands of Scots also settled in Co. Antrim, most of whom were introduced by MacDonnell (which was an important reason for his creation as *earl of Antrim*[44]). The most numerous settlement was in the west of Antrim, in the valley of the river Bann. Another settlement was that of Glenarm, in the most southerly of the nine glens of Antrim. (According to EILA CAMPBELL and U. DONNELLY, the first generation of the Scottish Presbyterians who established themselves in Glenarm used to row back once a month to take Communion in their Ayrshire presbytery.[45])

There was a simultaneous immigration, on a smaller scale, from England into east Ulster, mostly in the valley of the river Lagan and on the northern shore of Belfast Lough (*i.e.* in north Clandeboye). These districts had been granted to Devon, Warwick and

---

[a] The earls of Antrim throughout the seventeenth century were to remain the most faithful adherents of the Stuarts in Ireland.

[b] The latter had arranged for Conn O'Neill's escape from his imprisonment in Carrickfergus castle on condition that he obtained part of his estates (HARRISON, 8-9).

[c] In a fair summer season, twice and sometimes three times a week, the pioneers were supplied from Scotland. Friends and relatives crossed regularly from Stranraer to attend Newtownards market with the produce and gossip of Galloway. It is said that sometimes on a long summer's day, "benefiting from a reaching wind for the passage out and home, a party would leave the Mull of Cantyre at dawn, hire horses on the Irish side to carry their wares to market, and be back in Scotland by night" (FALLS, 78; HARRISON, 60; LYTHE, 68).

Yorkshire gentlemen, and to the lord-deputy Chichester for his services in Tyrone's War. According to E. R. R. GREEN, the English colonists formed "a solid block" between the Scots of Antrim and Montgomery and Hamilton's settlers in Co. Down. Despite the heavy pressure from Scottish immigrants throughout the seventeenth century, the Lagan valley (with the eastern shore of Lough Neagh) retained its English character.

The same author has shown that these settlements caused an 'economic revolution' by bringing the centre of agricultural activity from the hillsides to the lowlands that man had so far lacked the desire, or equipment, to exploit. (The Anglo-Norman colonists in east Ulster had never ventured far into the inland regions.) After the clearance of the dense woods and the tillage of the swampy valley floor, the Lagan valley was to become "the great artery of intercourse between the Ulster interior and Britain".[46] The movement into the interior of Ulster is reflected in the gradual displacement of the ports of Carrickfergus and Carlingford by Belfast and Newry which were situated more inland at the head of estuaries.[47]

JAMES'S PLANTATION OF MID ULSTER

After the Flight of the Earls in 1607 all their estates were confiscated. In the same year the king gave his consent to a "scientific and strategic plantation" of these lands. Plans for the development of the forfeited territories were methodically framed, examined, and revised. But that was not all. They were, as THOMAS WILSON says, "executed with system and efficiency which were surprising in that age and would be impressive in any".[48] The development scheme recognized three ranks of grantees:

(1)   *undertakers*, who were allocated large estates, to hold of the crown in socage under such conditions as to settle their lands with Protestant English or 'inland Scottish' farmers, husbandmen, artificers and cottagers, and to build villages;

(2)   *servitors* of the crown, who had to comply with less favourable terms but who were allowed to take Irish tenants; and

(3)   *natives*, who might also take Irish tenants but who were to pay heavier rents than the servitors; on the other hand they were not required to take the *Oath of Supremacy* admitting the king to be head over the Church.[49]

There was a special plan for the development of Co. Londonderry and adjoining parts of Cos Donegal, Tyrone, and Antrim. This territory, which included the rich fisheries of the rivers Bann and Foyle, was transferred to the twelve *Companies of London*, such as the Drapers and the Mercers.

The Plantation scheme included the building of twenty-three towns which provided not only for defence but for the spiritual and material needs of the settlers.[50] (There were no towns in Ulster with the exception of a few coastal footholds, established by the Anglo-Normans, and Armagh.) According to GILBERT CAMBLIN, who has given a detailed account of the building of the new towns and the development of their rural setting, this scheme is one of the earliest examples of regional planning, if not the first such scheme in history. At any rate, the Ulster Plantation was the most important scheme for the building of towns to be carried out in the British Isles before the end of the Second World War.[51]

The Plantation of Ulster has been the subject of much misunderstanding. It is not always realized that it did not stretch over the whole administrative province of Ulster. It excluded Cos Antrim, Down, and Monaghan, whereas it embraced parts only of the other six Ulster counties, *i.e.* Londonderry, Donegal, Tyrone, Fermanagh, Cavan, and Armagh. Co. Donegal, for instance, was never planted except in the north-east. The plantation of Co. Cavan had hardly any success at all.[52]

It is often supposed that all 'Irish' inhabitants of the planted counties were driven to the hills and bogs. However, the extermination motif, which had been apparent in the Munster Plantation and other schemes, was absent in Ulster. According to RICHARD O'BRIEN, "contrasted with the treatment which their fellow-countrymen in the south had received under Elizabeth's 'plantation' policy, the Irish of the north were favoured".[53] Several hundreds of native freeholders received grants and were – like the 'servitors' – allowed to take Irish leaseholders. (Other native grantees already existed.) Moreover, the English 'undertakers', in particular the London Companies, ignoring the plantation terms, retained thousands of Irish as small tenants or cultivators on their lands.[54]

THE SUCCESS OF THE ULSTER PLANTATION

James's Plantation of Ulster made a permanent change in the face of Ireland in the sense that it moved a whole new population – can I say a whole new nation – into part of Ireland, where they remain to this day. Rich and poor, farmer and cottager, artisan and mill-hand, they have lived there and built a community with its own traditions and aspirations. The Marian and Elizabethan plantations, however, left little or no marks. The question presents itself why the Ulster Plantation differs so radically from the previous undertakings of that kind in other parts of the island.

The popular view in Ireland, held by both Nationalist and Unionist, is that Ulster as the last bulwark of Irish resistance was in a special position and therefore, when it was finally subdued, needed special treatment. This view attributes the success of the Ulster Plantation mainly to the forethought and thoroughness of the government. I do not quite agree. We must beware of seeing in the Jacobean state apparatus the vast bureaucracy of our times which can efficiently – and inhumanly – carry out great transfers of population. Elizabeth's plantation of Munster – with 'undertakers' and all the paraphernalia of the later Ulster Plantation – was merely a transfer of huge estates from Irish (and Old English) aristocrats to New English, with a feeble attempt to introduce 'settlers' at a lower level (farmers and labourers from Somerset). It came to nothing: there was no state apparatus at that time capable of carrying out such a scheme of rural re-settlement.[a]

That the Plantation of Ulster succeeded where other ambitious undertakings failed, is primarily due to the fact that it was mainly – and spontaneously – carried out by Scots. It was, by contrast to the previous – and later – undertakings of that kind, essentially a Scottish undertaking instead of an English.

First of all, it was presided over by a Scottish king. It will be objected that James

---

[a] The fact is often overlooked that outside Ulster, where the war had raged also, James acted just as his predecessors had done – and his successors were to do. The MacCarthys, the O'Sullivans, and other remnants of old Gaelic families – in Cos Leitrim, Longford, and Wexford, and elsewhere – lost their estates by confiscation to English loyal grantees (cf. SIMMS, 13), but there was no settlement of colonists as in Ulster.

planted Ulster as king of England (or Great Britain) rather than as king of Scotland. In fact, closer examination will show that almost the reverse is the truth. Had Elizabeth been able to conquer Ulster ten or twenty years previously, no doubt she, too, would have initiated a plantation. But she would not have dreamt of taking any measure in favour of Scottish lords and settlers as James did. The latter consented to the plantation of the lands of the O'Neills and the O'Donnells on condition that provision was made for his "loyal Scottish subjects" – a stipulation which no later king was ever to make in any of his dealings with Ireland.

In fact, the plan of the Ulster Plantation was, to a large extent, adjusted to – if not dictated by – the proximity of Scotland. Scotland was, compared with England, a rather poor country, at least in the west. There were a mass of small landowners and land-hungry farmers and a proletariat ready for crossing the Channel. They needed little encouragement. As HARRISON states in his essay on *The Scot in Ulster*:

> "The enthusiasm for colonisation was in exact reverse to the home comfort. The Scottish undertakers were poor men, many of them with estates deeply burdened with debt, and they belonged to a poor country... They had everything to gain by going to Ulster, and so had their relatives and humbler neighbours. Besides, Ireland was only across a narrow channel, and it was a country which they could see on any clear day... To London citizens, on the other hand, Ireland was a far-off savage country, for which they did not feel at all inclined to give up the comforts and the civilised activities of the metropolis".[55]

A fundamental difference between the Ulster Plantation and the other Irish plantation schemes is that it was not destined to create "an order of great landowners "– as Elizabeth had done in Munster – but to establish "a class of small proprietors".[56] The chief architect of the Ulster Plantation, Chichester, strongly – and successfully – opposed the desire of great English landowners, who were in search of lucrative investments, to obtain huge estates.[a] Nobody was allowed to hold more than three thousand acres each – and only two Englishmen and three Scots got as much. The average amount of acres held by each person was between one and two thousand.[57] The point is that what were petty grants to the rich English nobility were boons to poor Scottish noblemen. The sense of parcelling out the confiscated areas in small estates was that there were Scots at hand ready to accept these grants.[b]

Another point I want to stress is that the influx of Scots was part of a movement which had been going on – together with a movement in the opposite direction – as long as history records, in fact since man first settled on either side of the North Channel. A considerable part of the pre-Plantation population of Ulster was already 'Scottish'. The

---

[a] Chichester opposed and defeated Lord Audley – already a planter in Munster – who had set his mind on a grant of 100,000 acres. Chichester wrote with great sense of Audley's plan: "If the natives be not better provided for .. than I have heard of, they will kindle many a fire in Lord Audley's buildings before they be half-finished" (RICHARD O'BRIEN, 143-5).

[b] The success of the Ulster Plantation may also be due to the fact that James had already some experience of plantations on a similar basis in the Scottish Highlands where conditions were very much alike those in Ulster. Some years previously he had conceived the plan of ending the endemic unrest in the Scottish part of the former lordship of the Isles – and of increasing his revenue – by declaring the lands of various 'untrustworthy' clan chiefs forfeited and regranting them to 'adventurers' who would plant "colonies of answerable inland [Lowland] subjects" – and who would pay substantial rents. Although James continued to carry on his efforts in this direction after 1603, it may be said that the English succession prevented his giving effect to his scheme (KERMACK, 80-7; RAIT, 150-1, 155-6).

only real obstacle to Scottish expansion into Ulster prior to the seventeenth century had been the O'Neills; the English government had in the past proved helpless in preventing it. It was the O'Neill power which kept it in check and set a boundary to it. With the defeat of the O'Neills the only effective barrier to the westward expansion of the Scots was removed – and with a Scottish king on the English throne English dislike of Scottish expansion into Ireland was displaced by a paternal protection.[a]

The Plantation is, as everyone has recognized, one of the corner-stones of the modern 'Ulster problem'. But, had there been no Flight of the Earls and no Plantation, there would still be an 'Ulster problem', however great or small, today: there was already a strong body of Scottish Presbyterians in east Ulster before the Plantation was carried into effect. In fact, the Plantation was, to some degree, an extension of the recently established Scottish bridgehead in Cos Antrim and Down.[58] Many of the Scottish farmers, artisans and tradesmen who spread out in the Plantation counties came either from or via east Ulster.

A great proportion of the Scots, for instance, who settled in Co. Londonderry – often occupying vacated English lands – are known to have come from west Co. Antrim.[59] This east-west movement continued throughout the seventeenth century. (There was a similar movement of English settlers from the Lagan valley in south Co. Antrim and north-west Co. Down through north Co. Armagh and east Co. Tyrone into north Co. Fermanagh.[60]) According to HARRISON, the only county in which the Scots failed to take firm root was Fermanagh; there by 1618 a large number of the Scottish allocations had been sold to Englishmen.[61]

To summarize: the Plantation of Ulster served two purposes. Like the previous – and later – Irish plantation schemes, it originated in the desire of the English government to pacify rebellious Ireland. But it was also planned to provide for a surplus Scottish population a settled and prosperous community: a second Scotland. It is true that without the English conquest of Tyrone there could not have been a Scottish settlement in mid Ulster. And it is also true that the English government and James's English advisers saw in the Scots a most appropriate instrument for the pacification of these territories. But the Plantation of Ulster was more than a continuation of the Tudor conquest as hitherto carried on. In essence it was a continuation of a population movement from Scotland into Ulster which had been going on for much longer time.

The union of the crowns of England and Scotland under James I – and the triumph of the Reformation all over Great Britain, while Ireland remained substantially Roman Catholic – has served to obscure this population-movement aspect of the Plantation, and to identify the Plantation with the quite different English policy in the rest of Ireland. The difference is apparent from the fact that the Tudor plantations have left the population of Ireland as a whole untouched. This applies also to the later Cromwellian and Williamite 'land settlements' which dispossessed the remaining Roman Catholic landowners and substituted a new English landowning gentry who survived to the nineteenth century. However much these 'land settlements' may have contributed to the anglicization of Ireland, they have left no minority problem as has the 'scoticization' of Ulster.

---

[a] In 1614 an act was passed to repeal a law of Queen Mary's time (1556) that made it illegal to bring in, to retain, or to marry Scots (*History*, vol. ii, 561).

CONTACTS AND CONTRASTS BETWEEN THE SCOTTISH COLONISTS
AND THE 'NATIVES'

The fact that the large-scale immigration of Scots into Ulster in the seventeenth century may be seen as a successor to previous cross-Channel migrations is concealed by the religious change in Scotland. The conversion of the greater part of Scotland to Protestantism certainly created a barrier between the new and the older immigrants. In this Section I propose to deal with the relations between the Scottish immigrants – many of whom must have had distant Irish (*i.e.* Gaelic) ancestors – and the native population of the Ulster province – many of whom had also come fairly recently from Scotland. (The historical introduction to the *Handbook of the Ulster Question*, written under the guidance of that pioneer of Irish critical studies, Eoin MacNeill – who came from Ulster – says that the two population groups were identical in 'race'.[62])

According to various authors relations between settlers and natives were just as bad as those between the Irish and the English. S. G. E. LYTHE says that after the Reformation the mass of Scots agreed with King James that Ireland was a "proper dependance" and that anarchy there threatened the stability and security of England and Scotland alike.[63] E. STRAUSS and POLLARD go even further. STRAUSS states that the relations between the immigrants and the autochthons were on the same level as those between Palefaces and Redskins in North America. POLLARD remarks that the Calvinist Scots, like the Pilgrim Fathers, regarded themselves as "a people chosen to root out the Amalekite and Philistine natives".[64]

These theories seem to me very extremist ones. POLLARD is probably right about extremist divines: there is no evidence that the ordinary people looked at the autochthons of Ulster as Amalekites. The statements of extremists are often a poor guide, even if convenient for polemical purposes. And there is not the slightest evidence that the settling of the Scottish Presbyterians in Ulster led to savagery of any kind. On the contrary, as RICHARD O'BRIEN says, "for some time after their arrival, the Scots were chiefly supported by the Irish".[65] According to WOODBURN, they often intermarried.[66] The *Handbook*[67] observes that "English politicians were gravely perturbed at the readiness of the Scots to intermarry with the Irish".[a]

We should perhaps distinguish between two streams of immigrants. The first wave came mainly from Galloway and Strathclyde on the south-west coast. Within a generation, however, the prospects of Ulster were attracting Scotsmen from further afield. For instance, in two years in the early sixteen 'thirties about ten thousand persons went to Ulster from the country between Aberdeen and Inverness on the east coast; on some days, as many as three hundred sailed from Irvine on a single tide.[68] Though the southern (and south-eastern) parts of Scotland were the main source of immigrants after 1600, the pre-seventeenth-century drift of Highlanders and Islanders southward into north Co. Antrim did not entirely cease.[69] It seems not unlikely that the Scots from Galloway and other Norse-Gaelic districts on the eastern shore of the North Channel felt more easily

---

[a] In the session books of Presbyterian congregations, that go back to the middle of the seventeenth century, there are many members with such Irish names as O'Donnell and O'Neill. Many of these names have disappeared among the Ulster Scots, says WOODBURN (26), because when the Irish adopted the English language they also, in some cases, adopted English names.

at home in the midst of (Norse-)Gaelic Ulster than did the immigrants from the so-called 'inward parts' of Scotland.[70]

If there is any reason to distinguish between immigrants from nearby and farther-away places, it would also seem appropriate to distinguish between those natives who were still aware of their Scottish origin – in particular the 'Old Scots' of Antrim – and the others. It is not unlikely that part of the pre-Reformation Scottish immigrants had become Protestants like so many of their Scottish fellow-countrymen (John Knox is said to have sent a few of his followers to the Antrim Scots). [a] At any rate, today there exists a deep gulf between the Catholic and the Presbyterian Scots in Ulster: the former are staunch Nationalists and the latter staunch Unionists. And, as EILA CAMPBELL and DONNELLY have shown, in their study on the glens of Antrim, there are many other differences between these two groups.[b]

As far as the language is concerned, there was no clear-cut division between the immigrants and the 'natives'. It is fairly certain that many colonists of the first three decades of the seventeenth century who came from Galloway were Gaelic speakers. The same holds good for (later) immigrants from the Highlands whose descendants, in some cases, remained Gaelic-speaking[c] until the first half of the nineteenth century.[71] On the other hand, as G. B. ADAMS observes, some of the lesser Gaelic chiefs, especially in east Ulster, had accepted the Elizabethan Church settlement, either from conviction or policy, and had carried part of their followers with them so that there was "a nucleus of native population adhering to the Established Church before the English-speaking colonization began". They seem to have maintained their Gaelic language until the end of the seventeenth century at least. G. B. ADAMS concludes that

"From the late sixteenth to the early nineteenth century, there existed several population groups, apart from many individuals scattered here and there, partly of Irish and partly of Scottish origin, who were Gaelic in language and who belonged to one or other of the Protestant Churches; but being fairly widely scattered geographically as a linguistic minority among their co-religionists and a religious minority among the main body of Gaelic speakers they tended to become first bilingual and monoglot English-speaking at an earlier date than the latter".[72]

---

[a] On the other hand, in 1624 Franciscans from a convent in Ballycastle (Co. Antrim) were sent to the Islands and Western Highlands in order to revive Roman Catholicism there (KERMACK, 151).

[b] Of the nine glens (valleys) in the Antrim plateau, eight are predominantly Roman Catholic. Only the most southerly, Glenarm, is predominantly Presbyterian. EILA CAMPBELL and DONNELLY, who compared Glenarm with Glenariff, lying eight miles farther north, noted that Glenarm is characterized by large, freshly limed, houses with their air of prosperity, and Glenariff by small, grey-stoned, cottages. The latter, however, are rendered attractive by the profusion of flowers round the doors, whereas in Glenarm gardens are absent. "The thrifty and hard-working people of Glenarm" would not be given to spending much time or money on amusement. As the two authors comment: "flowers have no market value" (11. 14).

I wonder whether these and other differences between the Presbyterian and the Catholic glens are to be attributed purely to the denominational contrast. There is first the proximity of Glenarm to Belfast (marketing!). Secondly, the Scots of Glenarm came from Galloway (Ayrshire), whereas the Old Scots came from the Western Highlands and Islands (the lordship of the Isles).

[c] It is worth remembering that the 'second Scottish colony', that of Nova Scotia in Canada, begun in 1621, is still to some extent Gaelic-speaking. In the eighteenth century, when emigration from the Highlands was extensive, the Scottish Presbyterian Church sent many Gaelic-speaking ministers there.

A factor which probably has greatly influenced the relations between the Protestant Scottish immigrants and the autochthonous population is the progress of the Scottish Reformation, *i.e.* the trend to 'militant Calvinism'. Irish historians are often inclined to think of Scotland at the time of the Ulster Plantation as a solidly and stolidly Calvinist country – at least in the English– or Scottish-speaking Lowlands. This conventional picture is quite wrong: Protestant Scotland of that time may not be identified with post-Covenant Scotland. In the beginning of the seventeenth century there were in fact two Protestant parties in Scotland:

(1)   the *doctrinaire Calvinists*, whose ideal was a theocratic state; as AGNES MACKENZIE says, their power depended less on numbers than on "organization and geography": they had the advantage of being organized in "the main trading parts, with control of the capital";[73] and

(2)   the *moderate Calvinists*, who tended to Arminianism and who were more inclined to compromise with a secular state; they had their strongholds further from the centre of affairs. [a]

Now, the first wave of Scottish immigrants came mainly from districts where at the time 'moderate Calvinism' was still predominant and which verged into the area – from Glasgow east – where 'doctrinaire Calvinism' was predominant. This position, however, was soon to change. In the sixteen 'thirties the south-western parts of Scotland became the very stronghold of 'strict Calvinism' (and remain so to this day). This was largely due to the influence of David Dickson whose preaching stirred a wave of religious enthusiasm ('revivalism'). It is significant that this movement spread across to the colony in Ulster and took firm root there. Indeed, when the Covenant crisis arose – Dickson being a moving spirit – and when it was uncertain whether Calvinism or Arminianism would prevail, "certain fiercy spirits returned again from Ulster".[74]

It is likely, then, that the religious positions in Ulster only hardened in the 'thirties and 'forties. The contiguity of Ulster to the focus of Calvinist zeal in south-west Scotland was a significant factor in the continuing zeal of Ulster for strict Calvinism. (All the internal crises in the Church of Scotland in the eighteenth and nineteenth centuries were paralleled by similar ones in Ulster.) According to Miss MACKENZIE, "Dickson, through two of his lieutenants, John Livingstone and Robert Blair, is the spiritual father of modern Ulster".[75]

THE 'PEASANT REVOLT' OF ULSTER (1641)

It may be true that the Ulster Plantation was not planned to exterminate the Irish (*i.e.* the Catholics) and that the latter got the fairest deal they got in any plantation, both noble and peasant. But it is understandable that those who had been dispossessed brooded on revenge, whereas those who had been left undisturbed watched with envious eyes the growing prosperity of the immigrants – even when that prosperity was built on virgin territory. At any rate, the religious barrier between the immigrants and the autochthons seems soon to have become stable.

[a]   After his accession to the English throne King James was in a position to overawe the Kirk Assembly and the position of the bishops in Scotland was strengthened (1606, 1610). This continued to be the position till the attempt of his son, Charles I, to overthrow the compromise of 1610 and to enforce greater conformity with England (1637) caused "the Covenanters to spring from the earth in an incredible ardour of religious nationalism" (ASHLEY, 69–70, 226–7; RAIT, 154).

As early as 1628 far-sighted Englishmen prophesied that the dispossessed Irish Catholics would "rise upon a sudden and cutt the throts of the poore dispersed British". According to tradition this was exactly what happened in the so-called Ulster Rebellion of 1641, when thousands of Protestants in the planted counties are believed to have suffered the same fate as the American colonists who were surprised by the sudden raids of Red Indians upon outlying settlements.[76]

A few weeks before, the surviving Irish gentry in various parts of the island had risen in arms, taking advantage of the weakening of the Dublin government caused by the removal of the powerful lord-deputy Thomas Wentworth, earl of Strafford. This rebellion, however, was a strictly military affair carried out by Irish soldiers. Thereafter a popular element entered which THOMAS COONAN calls the 'peasant revolt' of Ulster: "The rising of the gentry afforded the Ulster peasantry the opportunity of solving after their own fashion the social problem created by the Plantation".[77] (These revolts were but the beginning of a ravaging civil war which lasted for no less than eleven years. [a])

Again according to tradition, as a body the Scots suffered relatively less from the rebellion than the English colonists. Presbyterian authors sometimes seek the explanation in the fact that under Wentworth many Presbyterians had fled to Scotland because of various actions of the State Church against Presbyterianism (see below). A recent history of the Irish Presbyterian Church, for instance, states that the few months of liberty which intervened between the execution of Wentworth and the beginning of the rebellion, were not sufficient to enable many to return: "the bishops, who had banished both pastors and people to Scotland, saved them from destruction".[78] I am not inclined to set much value on this argument.

A fact which is often overlooked is that, when the Irish gentry rose in rebellion, they expressly instructed their followers in Ulster not to attack the Scottish settlers under any pretext. It is not at all unlikely that the Irish leaders nursed greater hatred of the English than of the Scots. The decision to leave the latter unmolested may also have been prompted by King Charles's hope to see them united with their countrymen in Scotland in one common cause against his rebellious parliament.[79] It may surely also have been due to the fact that the Scots were too strongly entrenched in country where Scots of one kind or another had been settled for centuries. At that time the Scots in Ulster seem to have numbered about 150,000, whereas the English population probably was not much in excess of 20,000.[80] The Scots, at any rate those of east Ulster and other centres, were in a position to retaliate. After all, the Irish leaders were not romantics – or Red Indians.

But the efforts of the leaders of the rising to neutralize the Ulster Scots failed. The latter also suffered from attacks, however severe or futile. And if they had not suffered, would not they still have reacted to the danger to their colony? Links between the colony and the mother country were still so close that the Scottish parliament immediately stirred to help their countrymen. Thus for the first time in history the Scots sent an army

---

[a] In fact, the Irish warfare was closely connected with the many conflicts which raged over England and Scotland in those years. It is very unlikely that the Ulster Rebellion would have occurred at all but for the influence of the controversies which were soon to lead to civil war in England ("England's difficulty" was as usual "Ireland's opportunity"). The successful resistance in Scotland against royal authority in 1639-40, too, may have encouraged the Ulster malcontents (cf. BECKETT, 80; CURTIS, History, 243; FALLS, 339).

to fight against the Irish. They also may have taken into account that Ulster was very near to Scotland. [a]

The forces, which were sent to Ulster by the Scottish parliament in 1642, numbered about ten thousand men. They were quartered almost entirely on Cos Antrim and Down.[81] As an aggressive force they were an almost complete failure, mainly however because of circumstances outside their control. In 1646 they were defeated at the Battle of Benburb (Co. Tyrone) [b] and confined again to east Ulster. At the same time there can be no doubt that their presence preserved east Ulster from further invasion by the Irish.

The Scottish expeditionary force also promoted intercourse between Scotland and Ulster. The Scottish population of Ulster was augmented, and the army chaplains gave a definite impetus to the establishment of a separate Presbyterian Church in Ireland – the earliest daughter of the Church of Scotland. In 1642 the first Irish presbytery was formed in Carrickfergus.[82] Since then it can truly be said that the history of the Ulster Scots is to a large extent that of the Presbyterian Church. In fact, as HARRISON states, for many years the history of Ulster – so far as it had a separate history – was chiefly ecclesiastical.[83]

RELATIONS BETWEEN THE ULSTER SCOTS AND THE ENGLISH

A fact which present-day Ulstermen tend to minimize, whereas Nationalists tend to emphasize (if they are not entirely preoccupied with the griefs of the Irish, *i.e.* the Roman Catholics), is that throughout most of the seventeenth and eighteenth centuries the Scottish colonists suffered from various religious and civil disabilities. This applies, however, only to those who were – and remained – Presbyterian.

The English authorities in Dublin and, occasionally, those in London as well looked with great antipathy and mistrust at the powerful Scottish colony in Ulster, which legacy of James's Scottish prejudice was constantly to be reckoned with. The Ulster Presby-

---

[a] Some years previously, during the Bishops War, a plan had been mooted by Wentworth to send an army from Ireland to Scotland under MacDonnell, the earl of Antrim – who still had an equal interest in both Ulster and Scottish events as had the ancient kings of Dál Ríada and the mediaeval kings of the Hebrides. The champion of the Scottish Calvinists in their struggle with Charles I was Campbell, the lord of Argyll; the Campbells were the age-long rivals of the MacDonnells. Though Wentworth's invasion plan was abortive and contributed to his own destruction, when civil war broke out in Scotland MacDonnell indeed intervened in Scotland in aid of the earl of Montrose on the side of the Royalists against the Parliamentarians. MacDonnell, who had been created "His Majesty's General of the Isles and Highlands of Scotland", raised troops in Scotland as well as in Ireland – as his lords of the Isles ancestors might have done. MacDonnell's interest, however, was at least as great in destroying the attempted Campbell hegemony in the Highlands as in assisting the king (cf. BUCHAN, 312). But, of course, the earl of Antrim was as much Gaelic prince as royalist, and the Argylls (the Campbells) were nearer to Antrim than Stuart king or English parliament. In fact, as a result of this undertaking the MacDonnell sphere of influence in Scotland was preserved – though the Campbells remained most powerful.

[b] The Irish forces were commanded by Owen Roe O'Neill, a nephew of Hugh O'Neill, who had had a distinguished career in the Spanish army in the Low Countries. The Scottish forces were under the command of the Munro brothers who claimed descent from Irish chiefs in Co. Fermanagh who had emigrated to Scotland. It was one of the curious twists of history that a descendant of one Munro brother (deported from Scotland by Cromwell) became president of the United States (the father of the Munroe doctrine), while a descendant of the other was the general Munro who was executed in 1798 by the English after leading the *United Irishmen* of Ulster to the Battle of Ballynahinch (1798).

terians[a], in their turn, found it very hard, if not impossible, to comply with the pretensions of the Dublin establishment in civil and ecclesiastical affairs. They had hardly realized that, on crossing the North Channel, they entered another kingdom. They had looked at Ulster as an extension of Scotland rather than as an extension of Ireland. In the reign of James VI and I it made no difference but under his successors it did.

Throughout the seventeenth century they continued to feel first and foremost Scottish. This feeling weakened after the union of the Scottish and English parliaments in 1707, when their home country gradually lost interest in them.[b] One could say, perhaps, that anti-English sentiment, which had been very strong in Scotland in the past, remained very much alive among the Ulster Scots even when in Scotland it weakened (in both countries it has not yet entirely died). At any rate, anti-English feeling was fostered by the discriminatory legislative measures which successive Dublin governments thought fit to enact against all who defied the authority of the crown, whether in civil or in ecclesiastical affairs.

I will leave the question open whether the Ulster Scottish colony ever completely accepted the authority of Dublin in civil affairs – their descendants certainly do not today. On at least two occasions their offspring have even dared to defy the authority of London, *i.e.* at the end of the eighteenth century (in the Rising of 1798) and just before the First World War (when Home Rule for all Ireland was nearly carried into effect). There is one field in which the Presbyterians never gave in: that of religion. They offered most determined resistance to the anglicization, or rather 'anglicanization', of their Church life – a resistance which was no less effective than that of the Irish Catholics. The opinion of the seventeenth- and eighteenth-century State Church dignitaries is still re-echoed in the official history of the Church of Ireland which appeared in 1933. It states that the Scots who came over in Plantation times

"introduced into northern Ireland a source of weakness and dissension which impaired the ability of the Church of Ireland to combat the aggressions of the Roman Catholic missionaries and clergy. Undoubtedly it was a catastrophe of the first magnitude for the future of religion in Ireland that, at the one epoch when it seemed as if the Irish people were about to get, at long last, a good chance of having reformed doctrine taught them by that Church which they could feel was their own Church, .. there should have come into the country a number of men and ministers professing a type of religion which was alien in outlook and character from the Irish".[84]

[a] There were also some Presbyterians in Leinster and Munster but they were of English descent. Actually Presbyterianism came to Dublin as early as the sixteenth century. The first provost of Trinity College was an English Presbyterian minister. In the seventeenth century the number of English Presbyterians slightly increased. Apart from some Dublin congregations, the southern Presbyterians seem to have held aloof from the northern Presbyterians till 1854. In that year seven congregations were admitted to the General Assembly of the Presbyterian Church (cf. DAVEY, 23-4).

[b] CARGILL GRAHAM (an American of Scottish descent), in his study of Scottish emigration to North America in the eighteenth century (17-8), when contesting the view that the Ulster immigrants from Scotland continued to regard themselves as Scots, says: "They maintained their Protestantism, their hatred of Catholicism, and their contempt for the 'mere Irish'. But their environment and the divergence of their history from that of the parent country seem to have given them a sense of distinctness from all other peoples, even the Scots themselves." Although Ulster received constant reinforcements of population from Scotland down to the beginning of the eighteenth century, "her people had by then developed their own traditions and outlook, so that they formed virtually another nationality".

Initially the Presbyterians, though they had their own congregational life, were 'comprehended' within the State Church – albeit not without frictions. With the advent of the lord-deputy Wentworth (1633-40) a radical change took place. Wentworth's one aim was to destroy throughout the British Isles every force which stood against the absolute authority of the crown, in civil and ecclesiastical life. His militant action against the Ulster Presbyterians deprived many congregations of their ministers and caused some thousands of Presbyterians to fly to Scotland.[85] Great numbers of those who remained went to Scotland at Communion seasons. On one occasion five hundred persons crossed the Channel to receive the Sacrament at Stranraer. Wentworth's measures even led to an attempt at emigration to New England in 1636 – in the first ship known to have been built on Belfast Lough.[86]

I will pass by the vicissitudes of the Cromwellian, the Restoration and the Revolution periods. [a] Under the patronage of King William III (1691-1702) the Presbyterians were secure. It is no wonder, CURTIS says, that William of Orange is still "the hero of the North".[87] After William's death the Ulster Scots again suffered from discrimination. In 1704 the Dublin parliament enacted the *Test Act* which deprived them – like the Roman Catholics – of all effective participation in the political life of the kingdom. Throughout the greater part of the eighteenth century they could not vote at an election, or hold any office civil or military, without receiving the Sacrament in the State Church.[88]

Where one would expect the whole Protestant minority of Ireland to unite, as CURTIS observes, the Anglican Church was almost more hostile to the Presbyterians – "whose well-organized faith, uncompromising spirit, and widespread influence in the North especially made them so formidable "– than to the Roman Catholics. On the other hand, the Presbyterians, "whose frequent contacts with Scotland kept ever before them an example of Presbyterian triumph", made no effort to conceal their dislike of the Episcopalian establishment and its pretensions. One of the things which galled them most was the compulsory payment of tithes to the state clergy.[89]

In this light it is not surprising that there was, in the seventeenth and eighteenth centuries, little intermingling between the Presbyterian and the Episcopalian settlers in Ulster. After all, they represented two peoples with characteristic differences. In some rural districts this segregation still lingers on.[90] The segregation was cause and effect of the territorial *apartheid* which the earliest settlers observed. The corresponding minor regional differences are not yet entirely wiped out. Newtownards, for instance, is still as Scottish in its aspect as Armagh is English, while the English-settled Lagan valley still retains the neat parkland landscapes which distinguish it from both the Scottish and 'Irish' districts.[91] The former differences in agricultural method, however, have been overlaid by the economic and technological changes of the past hundred years. The differences in dialect, too, have practically gone: today it takes a highly practised ear to recognize a division of dialect to correspond with the difference of creed.[92]

---

[a] In 1672 Charles II began the payment – not very regularly maintained – of an annual grant to be distributed among the Presbyterian ministers. This so-called *regium donum*, however, was not so much a mark of favour as "a precautionary bribe": the Dublin government kept an anxious watch on the Ulster Presbyterians and their frequent contacts with Scotland (BECKETT, 93; CURTIS, *History*, 259).

In the reign of William of Orange the Presbyterian colony was considerably strengthened by immigration from Scotland.[93] The imposition of religious and other disabilities, however, called a halt to this movement. [a] It even led many groups of Presbyterians to emigrate to the American colonies. What first was a tiny trickle in 1718 became a flowing stream – ministers in some instances leading whole congregations across the sea. This stream continued till the American War of Independence (1775-83).[94] Thus, emigration *en masse* to America – which has been, until the present century, a constant feature of Irish life – began not with the Roman Catholic peasantry but with the more wealthy Ulster Presbyterians. Ulster farmers, just because they were comparatively prosperous, could afford to emigrate if they became dissatisfied with conditions at home.[95]

Religious intolerance was not the only factor leading to this emigration. A flow of emigrants was likely enough to arise in any case from among "a people of energetic character and pioneering instincts" as the Ulster Scots doubtlessly were.[96] There were also economic reasons.[97] The most important ones were: (1) the restrictions imposed upon the Irish trade by envious English parliaments (see below); and (2) the raising of rents when leases, formerly granted on easy terms, fell in.[b] By that time practically all Ulster landlords were Episcopalians. Therefore, even many of those who left Ulster primarily for economic reasons carried with them a grudge against anything English.

Estimates of the number of emigrants to the colonies of North America during the eighteenth century vary from 150,000 up to half a million.[98] By the time of the Revolution perhaps 200,000 had settled in America. As a result of the emigration the proportions of the three denominations, Presbyterians, Episcopalians and Roman Catholics, in several districts of Ulster underwent a great change. According to CURTIS, "considerable parts of the North" went back to "the Catholic and Irish-speaking peasantry". This applies particularly to the outlying districts of Ulster, *i.e.* what are today the Southern and Northern Border Counties. In some instances, however, the Presbyterians were replaced by Episcopalians.[99] (Ever since emigration to America began, the number of Presbyterians in Ulster has been declining.)

In America the Ulster Scots were often called 'Scotch-Irish'. It is interesting to note that they did not regard themselves as 'Irish'. In fact, nothing chagrined them more than to be dubbed 'Irish'. They were, they said, "people of the Scottish nation in Ulster".[100] Many American historians have paid tribute to the "stern Scotch-Irish". They are generally described as a hard-working, tough-minded people, "a sturdy, thrifty lot", who were usually set in their ways. [c]

---

[a] There was no further immigration from Scotland on any appreciable scale except that of industrial workers in the nineteenth century.

[b] It appears that wherever Protestant and Catholic tenants were mingled together the latter – "able to live more sparingly and more patiently under social wrongs" – often outbid the others in the bidding for farms (CURTIS, *History*, 292-3, 305-6; cf. STRAUSS, 24; WOODBURN, 221).

[c] Although they had no language barrier to separate them from their neighbours (as the Germans and Dutch had), they were not easy to assimilate. When Pennsylvanian authorities complained that the Scotch-Irish were settling on lands without legal title, they received the reply that it was "against the laws of God and Nature, that so much land should be idle when so many Christians wanted it to labour on" (BARCK and LEFLER, 288).

BARCK and LEFLER in their study on *Colonial America* say that the Ulster Scots exerted "a tremendous influence in shaping the history of the American nation". In Pennsylvania, South Carolina, and other colonies they became, as LOUIS WRIGHT says, "typical frontiersmen[a], hardy and determined, who led the vanguard of white conquerors of the great interior wilderness".[101] According to the same author the Scotch-Irish "early demonstrated a love of freedom combined with political acumen, a quality important in a nascent democracy". They were frequently agitators for political reform. As in their home country, they had as little as possible to do with the wealthy Anglican landed aristocracy.

The Ulster Presbyterians played a vigorous part in the War of Independence[b], especially in Pennsylvania where their prompt alignment with the American cause was perhaps of decisive importance. It seems that the first encounter between 'Americans' and 'British' was between Scotch-Irish of North Carolina and a British force. According to WERTENBAKER the Ulster Scots constituted "the very back-bone of Washington's army". TREVELYAN observes that they had more real wrongs to revenge on England than had most of those who followed the standard of Washington.[102]

Chapter 14

IRELAND AS AN ENGLISH COLONY

THE FUSION OF THE OLD IRISH AND THE OLD ENGLISH

It was in the seventeenth century that the two population groups who had been antagonistic for centuries, the Old Irish and the Old English, definitely merged into each other. The gradual integration of the two groupings has contributed a great deal to the anglicization of the Gaelic Irish. It is well to remember that the anglicization process really began with the mediaeval English colonists. Their alienation by religion from their fellow-subjects in England and the New English in Ireland – a process which had already

---

[a] It is often said that it was the Ulster Scots who led the way to the West. Their spread is evidenced by many place-names. In thirty-nine states there are towns with Ulster names. There are, for instance, eighteen towns named after Belfast and sixteen after Tyrone (MARSHALL, 25-30).

[b] CARGILL GRAHAM's conclusion that the 'Ulstermen', even as early as the eighteenth century, constituted "a new national group with its own, independent sense of community", and – in spite of similarities of religion and speech – played a separate role in history from the Scots, is borne out by the story of the American Revolution. During the revolutionary period – in spite of individual exceptions – the Scotch-Irish and the Scots who had emigrated directly from Scotland were at opposite political poles. The latter were overwhelmingly loyal to the British crown. (It is the confusion of the Scots with the Ulster Scottish immigrants that has resulted in the assumption that Presbyterian loyalists were practically unknown during the Revolution.)

The Scottish and the Ulster Scottish immigrants in America can also be distinguished in the peculiarities of their pattern of settlement: the former played only a minor role as frontiersmen. Another respect in which Scottish and Scotch-Irish immigration to America differed during the eighteenth century is that the numbers of the Ulstermen were far greater than those of the Scots proper. During the three years 1771-3 the figure of Ulster Scottish immigrants was 28,600 by exact statistics. Only about one-third as many Scots emigrated directly from Scotland to America in the same period, although this was the peak period of Scottish migration before the Revolution (CARGILL GRAHAM, 19-21, 148-9, 180-1).

begun under Elizabeth – did not mean that they abandoned their cultural heritage in order to become Gaels. On the contrary, it was the Old Irish who gave up their way of life and became anglicized: first the aristocracy, later the middle class, and finally the mass of the peasantry. The final result of the fusion was a completely new concept: the English-speaking Catholic Irish nation as we know it today.

The integration process was greatly accelerated during the warfare of the 1641-52 period. In this period even the mediaeval English towns joined in rebellion. In 1642 a kind of alliance was established between the Old Irish and the New Irish (*i.e.* the Old English who had remained Catholics), through the *Catholic Confederation of Kilkenny*. The Confederates set up a parliament of their own, accredited envoys to France, Spain and the Vatican, and received a papal nuncio. Their forces waged war on royal and parliamentarian armies (rather more half-heartedly with the first than the second, it is true). The ultimate objective of both parties was legislative independence for Ireland under the British crown, or what today is called Dominion status. They differed, however, as to method and interpretation of that objective.[103]

The Confederates, though bound together by religious persecution and the threat to landed property, were still very much aware of their different traditions.[104] This division continued for another generation but the religious division soon became the predominating one. The Counter-Reformation had now gathered much momentum. The well-trained priests and friars from the newly-founded seminaries on the continent came from both Old and New Irish families. For instance, the agent of the Confederates in Rome, Father Luke Wadding, was of old colonial burgher stock.[a]

It was Oliver Cromwell who helped to weld the Old and the New Irish closer together. After he had defeated the Scottish forces in Scotland (1648), he landed in Dublin with an army of twelve thousand men. Cromwell spared neither Irish or English: the latter suffered as well as the former. For instance, the three thousand people who were put to the sword in the Massacre of Drogheda were mainly English royalists. Cromwell spent nine months in Ireland (1649-50) and when he left the work of the re-conquest was still far from complete. But, as BECKETT says, "the vigour and cruelty of his campaign and the ruthlessness of the settlement that he subsequently directed have left a mark and a memory that succeeding centuries have not been able to wipe out".[105] It even figured in the conversations which Mr de Valera had with Lloyd George in the negotiations of 1921 which led to the formation of the Irish Free State.[106] There is still a saying: "the curse of Cromwell on you!"[b]

THE INTRODUCTION OF THE ENGLISH COLONIAL ASCENDANCY CLASS

When the re-conquest of Ireland was complete, a great number of Old and New Irish landowners and some royalist Protestant proprietors from various parts of Leinster and Munster, and even from certain districts of Ulster[c], were deprived from their estates.

---

[a] It was Father Wadding who had St Patrick, the Irish patron-saint, added to the Roman Calendar, so that ever since Patrick's feastday has been celebrated throughout the Roman Catholic Church.

[b] This saying was not confined to Ireland. It was (and perhaps still is) known in Scotland. Cf. Walter Scott's novel (published in 1818), *The Heart of Mid-Lothian* (Chapter viii).

[c] In 1653 there was put forward a proposal to remove a great number of Scots out of Ulster to the south

Those who had not left the country for Spain (1650–1)[107] were transplanted with their families (and their livestock) beyond the river Shannon into Connacht and Co. Clare. This policy became known as the policy of "to hell or to Connacht". As COONAN says, "this watchword was too provocative to be forgotten and has passed into the repertoire of Irish patriotism".[108] (The popular notion that the entire Irish population of various counties was ejected is, of course, groundless – only the landowners, great and small, were expelled.)

Of all the confiscations which in the course of a century and a half changed the ownership of the greater part of Ireland, the Cromwellian confiscation was certainly the most drastic.[a] It was also the first which was, as J. G. SIMMS observes, "frankly on a religious basis".[109] The expelled gentry were replaced by English 'adventurers', who had given loans for the Irish war[b], and by army officers whose pay was in considerable arrear. Thus Ireland had to pay for its own re-conquest. Ireland, in fact, was "the great capital out of which the Cromwellian government paid all debts, rewarded all services, and performed all acts of bounty".[110] The result of the so-called Cromwellian Settlement was the creation of a new landlord class which was considered "the best guarantee for the maintenance of English authority in Ireland".[111]

In addition many thousands of common soldiery were planted out as yeomen. Some of them sold their allocations and returned to England. Some of those who actually settled on the land were completely 'absorbed' by their Irish neighbours, for they were widely scattered and cut off by social barriers from the Protestant gentry. Not only did they marry Irish wives but many of them learnt the Irish language and their children often became Roman Catholics.[112] (A number of Irish speakers in the Gaeltacht who carry common English surnames are perhaps descendants of Cromwellian soldiers.) The rest formed the nucleus of the Protestant middle and working classes which were to develop in the towns of southern Ireland.

of Ireland, "where, by being mixed with the English, they would be less capable of mischief". The operation of the scheme was suspended and finally abandoned (GOOD, 14; WOODBURN, 124–6).

[a] It was this confiscation which made Ireland the first country in the modern world to be mapped from direct protractions. An initial difficulty of the confiscation and subsequent plantation was the lack of accurate knowledge of the territories concerned. The government then appointed William Petty (1623–87), who had studied in Leyden, to map the forfeited lands. Petty mapped all the Irish baronies, except of three Connacht counties, and all the townlands in almost half of the island. The fieldwork for this immense undertaking was done during the years 1655–7. Petty showed himself a remarkable pioneer in modern methods of surveying. Unfortunately the greater part of the manuscript maps were destroyed in two disastrous fires, that of the Dublin Customs House in 1711 and that of the Dublin Four Courts during the Civil War in 1922. Three collections of maps and copies survive; one of them, by another accident of fate, is in Paris. The 214 surviving barony maps contain some 250,000 place-names (cf. GOBLET, vol. ii, *passim*).

[b] One of the 'adventurers' who subscribed for Irish lands (1642) was a Dutchman, Gerard Boate, who had studied in Leyden and was 'royal physician' in London. In 1645 he wrote *Irelands Naturall History*, "Being a True and Ample Description of its Situation, Greatness, Shape and Nature; of its Hills, Woods, Heaths, Bogs; of its Fruitfull Parts and Profitable Grounds, with the severall way of Manufacturing and Improving the same; .. Conducting to the Advancement of Navigation, Husbandry, and other Profitable Arts and Professions". This book was published in 1652 "for the Common Good of Ireland, and more especially for the Benefit of Adventurers and Planters therein". This work is "a regional geography of quite exceptional merit" (TAYLOR, 132–3, 137) and looks quite modern (cf. EMERY, 264–6; GOBLET, vol. i, 147–8, 153).

The restoration of the Stuart monarchy in 1660 did not upset the Cromwellian Settlement to any considerable extent. A relatively small number of royalist English and Irish proprietors, including the earl of Antrim, had their former lands (or parts thereof) restored to them but the majority of the Cromwellian landlords remained firmly entrenched. It is hard to see how it could have been otherwise for it was the Cromwellian gentry who, obviously from self-interest, proclaimed Charles II (1660-85) *king of Ireland* – and not the royalist Irish.[113] On the other hand, according to an act passed in 1665, "the interests of His Majesty's Protestant subjects were his greatest care, and to be first provided for".[114]

An important consequence of the Restoration was the re-establishment of the Church of Ireland as the State Church and its acceptance by the Cromwellian Puritan landlords. Henceforth the English ruling class in Ireland was entirely Anglican – which served to accentuate the barrier between them and the Scottish Presbyterians of Ulster. (Their puritanism, however, gave the Church of Ireland as a whole its distinctively 'low church' character.) Thus was established the Episcopalian Ascendancy which was to be left in power and privilege until the nineteenth century.

It has been customary among Irish historians to depict the Cromwellian planters and their 'Anglo-Irish' descendants in the darkest colours. As the next pages will show, there is much reason for that. It is necessary to distinguish between the new landed gentry – who as a whole were and remained irresponsible landowners who had little care for the welfare of their tenants – and the many professional and business people, artisans, and peasants. The new English middle and lower classes have often been unjustly tarred with the Ascendancy brush.

It has been said that, though the Anglo-Irish (*i.e.* the descendants of the Cromwellian English colonists) resided in Ireland, Ireland was their *country* but it never became their *nation*. The colonists, however, grew to be a sort of nation of their own, "the Protestant Irish nation": Irish to the English and English to the Irish (like the mediaeval English colonists). But they were not altogether a separate enclave; they remained not entirely "an alien and detached strain". As O'FAOLAIN says, they brought to Ireland "a greater concentration of civil gifts than any previous, or later, colonizers". They created one of the richest of provincial English cultures which still forms the foundation of the culture of modern Ireland – however much it has changed in its adoption by the Roman Catholic democracy. In fact, in O'FAOLAIN's words, "culturally speaking, the Anglo-Irish were to create modern Ireland".[115]

The heyday of the Anglo-Irish was the eighteenth century. Their best-known monument is "Dublin's grace, roominess, magnificence and unique atmosphere". But all over the country the Ascendancy built gracious houses and pleasant seats, which are "the epitome of the classical spirit of that cultured and callous century". All the planned aspects of the prettier villages and towns in southern Ireland are also their handiwork.[116] The Anglo-Irish also founded the so-called Anglo-Irish literature and have produced all its great figures[a], such as Jonathan Swift (1667-1745), Oliver Goldsmith (1728-74), Richard

---

[a] Except for James Joyce (1882-1941), the first Roman Catholic Irishman whose works reached world-fame. Paradoxically he left Ireland, deliberately rejecting the English atmosphere of Dublin. Unlike other Irish writers he did not go to England but to the continent, where he always wrote of Ireland.

Brinsley Sheridan (1751-1816), Oscar Wilde (1856-1900), George Bernard Shaw (1856-1950), William Butler Yeats (1865-1939), and John Millington Synge (1871-1909).

The Anglo-Irish also provided Ireland with many of her greatest statesmen, from Henry Grattan (1746-1820) to Charles Stewart Parnell (1846-91). It was from the Anglo-Irish – and the Ulster Presbyterians – that the modern conception of Irish nationalism came, *i.e.* that of non-sectarian republicanism. The founder of Irish republicanism: Theobald Wolfe Tone (1763-98), its prototype martyr: Robert Emmet (executed in 1803), and its first intellectual: Thomas Osborne Davis (1814-45), were middle-class Anglo-Irishmen. Their doctrine was a tinder to the inflammable mass of Irish Catholic discontent. (How far the doctrine changed as the Roman Catholic majority adopted it, is another matter.) Even the founder of the modern Gaelic revival movement (1893) and the first *President of Éire* (1937-44), Douglas Hyde (1860-1949), was Anglo-Irish.[a]

THE JACOBITE WAR (1689-91) AND THE PENAL CODE (1695-1727)

The first chance for an attempt to upset the Cromwellian Settlement came with the Jacobite War (1689-91). It was in Ireland that King James II (1685-9), the first Roman Catholic on the English throne since Mary Tudor, after having lost two of his three kingdoms, could make his last stand. This was also what CURTIS calls "the last stand of Catholic Ireland". In 1689 James landed at Kinsale (Co. Cork) with French arms for ten thousand men, and immediately the Irish Catholics rallied to his cause. By now the identification of religious and political divisions was complete. As BECKETT[117] observes:

"Once the fighting began even Protestants who professed loyalty to James were disarmed and imprisoned. On the other hand, Anglicans and Presbyterians sank their differences in face of a common danger. The former distinctions between 'native Irish' and 'Old English' finally disappeared, and 'Irish' and 'Roman Catholic' became almost interchangeable terms. But the Gaelic aristocracy and its traditions had gone for ever; the Irish of the revolutionary wars were led mainly by men of English descent".[b]

James's only effective opponents were "the farming gentry and yeomen of the North". For the first time it was demonstrated "how much more effective the Ulster colony was as a 'garrison' than the Cromwellian Ascendancy thinly scattered over the island among a hostile peasantry". As TREVELYAN remarks, William of Orange was proclaimed king at Enniskillen and Londonderry with more heart-felt loyalty than in Whitehall and Edinburgh.[118]

[a] From the Ascendancy also came a good deal of the prevailing climate of morality in the Republic – odd though it may seem in a Roman Catholic country. The morality of the 'big house' was rather 'evangelical', as the foundation of the Ascendancy class by Cromwellian Puritans made almost inevitable and their isolation as a community ensured. O'FAOLAIN calls both the Anglican and the Roman Catholic Church in Ireland "notoriously 'low church' and puritanical" (*De Valera*, 169). The puritanism of the Irish Catholics finds expression in the recent condemnation by a bishop of the "trend to the continental Sunday" in Ireland. It has been suggested that this puritanism originates in Jansenist influences but this seems a rather thin hypothesis. I would be inclined to associate it with the climate of the Protestant Churches in Ireland.

[b] The final union of the two population groups is well typified in the Irish commander, Patrick Sarsfield (1650-93), earl of Lucan, who was Old English on one side and on the other Old Irish (CURTIS, *History*, 272). Sarsfield, who was a professional soldier of James's army in England, is the first Irish national hero who was English-speaking by birth. (He is also the first prominent Irish figure ever to bear the name of Ireland's patron saint.)

During the Siege of Londonderry a parliament was summoned in Dublin. This last gathering of the Old and New Irish gentry is known as the Patriot Parliament. The main objects of this English-speaking assembly[a] were: (1) legislative independence from England; (2) restoration of the Roman Catholic Church to a position of pre-eminence[b]; and (3) repeal of the Cromwellian and Restoration land settlements. James II, however, seems to have felt little sympathy for this program. He successfully resisted the drive for legislative independence: "he was still an English king and so bound to support the English interest in Ireland".[119] (To James – and to his ally, Louis XIV of France – a victory in Ireland was only a prelude to coming to grips with William of Orange in Great Britain.)

Anyhow, the new regime was not allowed to become consolidated. The Cromwellian plantation was not to be undone before the nineteenth century; the other aims of the Patriot Parliament were not fully to be achieved before the twentieth century. The hopes of James and of his Irish allies were dashed to the ground by the Battle of the Boyne (1690).[120] When French reinforcements failed to come, Sarsfield (the commander of the Irish forces) and Van Ginkel (the commander of the Williamite army) negotiated the famous Treaty of Limerick (1691). Only the military articles of the Treaty were fully observed. The civil articles, which required parliamentary confirmation, were only partly ratified.[c]

The great estates, left ownerless by those Catholic landlords who were so ill-advised as to submit immediately after the Battle of the Boyne, or who had been killed or had left for France, were confiscated. The earl of Antrim, one of the leaders of the Jacobite forces, was one of the Catholic aristocrates whose lands were saved. The outcome of the so-called Williamite Confiscation was, according to SIMMS[121], that the share of the profitable land owned by Roman Catholics declined from 22% in 1688 to 14% in 1703.

Between 1695 and 1727 the Dublin parliament, now entirely composed of Episcopalians, enacted a series of laws ostensibly intended for "the extirpation of popery". These Penal Laws have been compared with anti-Protestant legislation in France, Spain, Italy, and Poland. But the circumstances in which the Irish Penal Code was enacted and the ends which it served were very different. Firstly, the Irish laws were directed against the majority of the population and not against a tiny minority. Secondly, there was no effort to suppress Roman Catholic worship and to convert the body of the Irish Catholics to Protestantism. The Irish code arose not from missionary zeal, or "an authoritarian desire for uniformity", but from political fear.[122] It was essentially designed to preserve the

[a] The Ireland of 1641, even to a large extent in the English towns, was still Irish-speaking. By the end of the seventeenth century the surviving Old Irish aristocracy were already English-speaking. The next century saw the spread of the English language among the peasantry. By the end of the eighteenth century English was the common language of at least half of the Irish peasantry (cf. HOGAN, 54).

[b] A natural enough thing to demand in a country almost completely Roman Catholic, at least outside of Ulster. It was, however, a difference from 1641. In the Catholic Confederation there had been a certain ambivalence between the desire for toleration and the desire to restore Catholicism as the State Church. The Cromwellian Settlement, with its consequence of hatred towards the Ascendancy class, had naturally increased the anti-Protestant feeling.

[c] They guaranteed the Roman Catholics to enjoy such privileges in the exercise of their religion as they enjoyed under Charles II. They also provided that those who submitted would keep their former estates, privileges, and professions, on condition of taking a simple oath of allegiance to the king which excluded any abjuration of the papal spiritual power (cf. Documents, 171-5).

recently renewed land settlement by preventing Roman Catholics from obtaining land.[a]

The *Penal Laws* were – and indeed could not be – fully carried out. Many measures were mitigated by the London government, others were evaded by nominal conformity, and some became dead letters in a very few years after they were enacted. And not a single Roman Catholic was executed under these laws.[123] But they were effective in so far as they deprived the Roman Catholics of all power which might come from the possession of land. The Old and New Irish landed aristocracy was virtually destroyed in so far as they adhered to the Roman Catholic Church. According to PATRICK ROGERS, many of the Catholic gentry as a result of the Penal Laws conformed to the State Church (as, for instance, the earls of Antrim). Many of them even obtained seats in the Dublin parliament.[124] The great majority of the Catholics, however, were degraded to what KENNEY calls "a helpless and hopeless mass of ignorant agrarian helots".[125] From this time on O'Neill and O'Donnell, like FitzGerald and Costello, were peasant names.

SOCIO-ECONOMIC CONTRASTS BETWEEN SOUTH AND NORTH I

In 1726 it was stated: "The whole country, except the Scottish plantation in the North, is a scene of misery and desolation hardly to be matched on this side of Lapland".[126] The patent inferiority of the southern countryside to 'Scottish Ulster' was primarily due to its ruthless exploitation on behalf of the New English (Anglo-Irish) colonial oligarchy.[127] The worst feature of the Cromwellian Settlement, from the socio-economic point of view, was the spread of a bad system of land tenure over the greater part of Ireland. Its main characteristic was the subletting of very small holdings for absurdly short periods.

This custom of short leases was encouraged by an act of the Dublin parliament of 1702. This act – one of the most important and disastrous of the *Penal Laws* (CONRAD GILL) – forbade Roman Catholics to hold land for long terms of years or for life. The result was that by far the commonest lease in Ireland during the eighteenth century was for one year, with six months' grace.

"No tenant, even if he had paid rent regularly, and worked his land well, was secure in his holding; for in any year the land might be offered to a higher bidder, and the tenant would be driven away without compensation. If he would escape eviction he must pay, or at least promise, a higher rent than any competitor. Thus short leases meant rack-renting; and rack-renting meant that it was never worth while for a tenant to improve his land, because all the benefit would go to the landlord or the agent".[128]

Meanwhile the population was steadily increasing. According to K. H. CONNELL the Irish population increased from over $2\frac{1}{2}$ millions at the beginning of the eighteenth century, to over 3 millions in the middle and over $4\frac{3}{4}$ millions at the end of the century.[129] Ireland could have supported the increased population comfortably enough, even on a purely rural economy, if the land had been efficiently farmed. But social and economic conditions alike were against any improvement. "Behind this inefficiency lay the essential causes of Ireland's poverty" (BECKETT). Whether absentees or not, most Irish landlords

---

[a] By contrast with the laws against the Roman Catholics, which were primarily political, the Penal Laws against the Ulster Presbyterians were primarily religious (and therefore, perhaps, in one way more galling). There was, of course, the difference that the Presbyterians professed an uncompromisingly 'reformed' religion while the State Church – though being more evangelical in character in Ireland than in England – was anxious to retain various traditions and practices of the pre-Reformation Church.

were satisfied to draw what they could from their lands and give nothing in return.[130]

In a large part of Ulster another land system obtained. This was the *Ulster Custom* or *Ulster Tenant Right* which guaranteed the tenantry, Protestants and Catholics alike, (1) security of tenure so long as the rent was paid; (2) a fixed rent; and (3) the right to sell the tenant's interest in his holding. This land system is one of the important factors – if not the chief – which account for the greater prosperity of the Ulster countryside in the eighteenth and nineteenth centuries in comparison with the rest of rural Ireland[131], despite Ulster's less favourable conditions of soil (and, according to some, even of climate).

The *Ulster Custom* encouraged the proper cultivation of the land and drainage, fencing, building, and other improvements. It produced such a relatively high standard of cultivation as caused Co. Down to be styled "the Yorkshire of Ireland". And, as BRIAN KENNEDY and others have observed[132], it made the tenants industrious, rendered them law-abiding, and promoted in them "a spirit of self-reliance and independence".[a]

The *Ulster Tenant Right*, however, had no legal force. It was only legalized by Gladstone's *Irish Land Act, 1870*. But the custom was so strongly supported by public opinion in Ulster that few landowners dared to ignore it. It protected the tenants against eviction and against undue increase of rent. On the other hand, it was generally as profitable to the landlord as to his tenants: rents in Ulster were more regularly paid than elsewhere, the value of the tenant's saleable interest being a security against arrears.[133] Thanks to the land system, rural life in Ulster was not so often convulsed by disturbances and organized terrorism as was the rest of the island.

There is a general agreement among writers on this subject that the *Ulster Custom* arose in connexion with James's Plantation. It has been assumed that the right was a condition offered by 'undertakers' in the Plantation counties to attract colonists.[134] According to GILL, however, the custom was a claim that was gradually established rather than a principle admitted from the outset. GILL is inclined to think that the origin is not to be sought so much in the formal Plantation as in the gradual settlement of Cos Antrim and Down by Scottish colonists who would be used to 'kindly tenure'. As GILL points out, a tradition of fixed holdings and moderate rents would be more readily established during the piecemeal colonization of east Ulster than during the rapid reorganization of the other Ulster counties.

"But the tradition, once it was established in Antrim and Down, might spread over the whole province as a means, not of attracting, but of retaining tenants. The landlords depended very largely on settlers from

---

[a] In Chapter 6 I have given two widely accepted reasons for the various differences in way of life between northerners and southerners in Ireland. The differences of the kind alleged in the stereotypes – in punctuality, industry, thrift, etc. – are sometimes referred to the different land systems which have long prevailed in Ulster and in the rest of the island. The abominable Irish land system – as opposed to the Ulster Custom – in the eighteenth and nineteenth centuries far from rewarding industry and thrift actually penalized them. As LYNCH and VAIZEY (12) observe: the squalid conditions of his existence may have been among the factors that made the Irish peasant "thriftless and unproductive" (cf. GEORGE O'BRIEN, *History Union*, 446-7). ROBERT KANE – who was no fanatic or Nationalist – in his *Industrial Resources of Ireland* (1844), dealing with charges that used to be made against the character of the Irish people by some superior critics, wrote: "We were reckless, ignorant, improvident, drunken, and idle. We were idle, for we had nothing to do; we were reckless, for we had no hope; we were ignorant, for learning was denied us; we were improvident, for we had no future; we were drunken, for we sought to forget our misery" (cf. CARTY, *Ireland 1851-1921*, 6).

Great Britain for the improvement of their estates. ... In order to avoid a serious fall in land values the owners might very well be willing to offer generous terms, on the lines of the Ulster Custom, and eventually to extend them even to the descendants of those Irish peasants who had first been only tenants at will. The troubles of 1641 and later emigration may have helped this process".[135]

An argument which may strengthen GILL's thesis is that a large number of the tenants in the planted counties came from the densely-populated Cos Antrim and Down. It is likely that they would not have been willing to settle in mid Ulster if they had been offered terms which were less favourable than those obtaining in east Ulster.

SOCIO-ECONOMIC CONTRASTS BETWEEN SOUTH AND NORTH II

"As the policy of the Irish Parliament was to weaken and degrade the Catholics and the Presbyterians in order to render them helpless", as WOODBURN says, so it was the policy of the English parliament "to make Ireland so poor that it could never give any more trouble either by rebelling or by competing successfully with her in trade".[136] It was under Charles II that the English parliament passed the first of a series of commercial acts which in the course of some thirty years were to bring about the complete economic subjugation of Ireland to England.

The first measures were directed at the prohibition of direct trade between Ireland and the overseas colonies. "Thus Ireland could only get colonial goods through England or send her goods out through England, the building of a mercantile fleet for overseas trade was made impossible, and Ireland remained for over a century excluded from the trade of the Empire" (CURTIS). In 1666 the export of cattle to England was forbidden, because the landlord and farming interest in England resented the competition of cheap Irish cattle.[137] (These statutes were removed in 1759.)

Restrictions inflicted by successive English parliaments on the Irish trade culminated in the act of 1699 which prohibited the export of woollen manufactures to any country except England. (From England Irish woollen goods were already virtually excluded by heavy duties.) There is no doubt that the motive behind this act was partly commercial jealousy, for English manufacturers were alarmed at the competition of Irish goods in the continental market. The act was also prompted by "fear that an over-prosperous Ireland might yield the crown an independent revenue".[138]

Opinions differ as to the effects of this measure on the Irish economy. GEORGE O'BRIEN in his *Economic History of Ireland in the Eighteenth Century* says that, as the woollen manufacture was at that time the staple industry of Ireland, the 1699 act brought about "complete industrial ruin".[139] It is true that, after the import of cattle into England had been prohibited, sheep were substituted to a great extent all over Ireland. According to O'BRIEN this had caused a considerable growth of the woollen industry.[140] Modern economic historians, however, believe that "there was never a woollen industry in Ireland of the dimensions which popular historians have suggested".[141] The position has been well summed up by BECKETT:

"The practical effects of the restrictions were greatly exaggerated. In the most prosperous period of the industry woollen goods formed only a small proportion of total exports, and Irish manufacturers supplied only a fraction even of the home market. On the other hand, the industry was a growing one and had attracted both workmen and capital from England. Its restriction was a discouragement to further enterprise".[142]

The suppression of the woollen trade to some extent was compensated by the encouragement of the manufacture of linen – an industry which did not clash with any English interest. But, whereas the woollen industry had been spread over a great part of the island, the linen industry was mainly concentrated in Ulster. Hence, its benefits were localized.[143] The rapid growth of the linen industry served only to accentuate the socio-economic contrasts between the north and the south of Ireland.

There can be little doubt that the success of the linen industry in Ulster and its comparative failure elsewhere were due to the difference in land system more than to any other cause. [a] As GILL observes, the land system in the rest of Ireland was fatal to manufacture. Few tenants had enough capital to set themselves up as weavers. Even if they did begin weaving they would work under a continual threat of eviction. Above all, any income made from weaving would often have to go in increased rents, or in payment of arrears. In Ulster, however, the tenant had a fair chance of saving a little capital.

"He would also be more likely than the southern tenant to have a surplus of farm produce which he could sell at a market or fair on his own account. It is highly probable that many of the farmer-weavers in Ulster were in the habit of regular attendance as sellers at fairs and markets before the linen trade had grown to importance, and that the formation of special markets for linen and yarn was much easier in consequence".[144]

Other circumstances which certainly have favoured the development of the linen trade in Ulster are[145]:

(1) the capital, skill, and business habits of many of the Scottish immigrants who were "industrious townsmen, artisans, traders and small businessmen"[b]; and
(2) the arrival of Huguenots from the Netherlands at the invitation of William of Orange; many of them were experienced traders and highly skilled workers who had experience of bleaching gained at Haarlem and who installed a thousand Dutch looms.[c]

In the course of the eighteenth century the Dublin government often aimed at the development of the linen industry outside Ulster but the results were invariably disappointing. Even the best conceived plans of encouragement were defeated, not only owing to the defective land system but also to the "keen competition from the northern counties in both fine and coarse manufacture".[146] There are no figures to show the exact output of Ulster. The fast increase of the Ulster linen trade is reflected in the number of weavers: their number appears to have been about 35,000 in 1770 and 40,000 in 1784.

In the last quarter of the eighteenth century there grew up a second textile industry in the heart of the linen-producing district: the cotton industry. The cotton industry was

[a] The foundations of the Ulster linen trade are commonly said to have been laid by two king's deputies, Wentworth (in the 1630s) and Ormonde (in the 1660s), who introduced flax-seed, spinning-wheels, and even some workers from the Netherlands. GILL (8-9, 13, 61) has shown that they had no more than a trifling influence on the trade; Dutch merchants did much more than either Wentworth or Ormonde to lay the foundations of the Irish export trade.
[b] That there was hardly any linen industry in Co. Fermanagh may have something to do with the fact that there were practically no Scottish colonists.
[c] The great promotor of the Ulster linen industry was Louis Crommelin who decided to settle in east Ulster after a careful survey of the whole island. In Ulster he found already the nucleus of an export trade, and a congenial spiritual atmosphere. The Huguenots found in the Ulster Presbyterians "a people akin to their nature, with whom they could work and share their knowledge" (GILL, 17, 27-8; KNOX, 28-9).

"the great herald of the Industrial Revolution" both in Great Britain and Ulster. The new industry was a contrast to linen in many ways, notably in the fact that the raw material was imported and that the yarn was produced by machinery. It had far-reaching effects on both the linen industry and Belfast. It set an example of advanced methods, such as steam spinning, and it made Belfast the centre of the Irish textile industry. [a] The use of steam power for cotton spinning led to the organization of a coal supply to Belfast, and as coal could be had more cheaply at the quayside than further inland, the spinning mills were naturally built near the port. It first brought masses of industrial workers into the town.[147]

As the spiritual foundations of modern Ulster had been laid by the Presbyterian Church, the economic foundations were in fact laid by the linen industry. As the Presbyterian Church provided Ulster with its first regional assembly: the Synod of Ulster[b], it was the linen industry which gave it its capital city: Belfast. Throughout the eighteenth century a considerable part of the Ulster linen trade to England [c] still went through Dublin, mainly because of its banking facilities. But in the second half of the century the direct trade from the northern ports, especially from Belfast, with England and other countries increased notably. At the beginning of the nineteenth century the hegemony of Dublin as the chief market for linen export was transferred to Belfast.[148]

THE EFFECT OF THE AMERICAN REVOLUTION (1775)

In the course of the eighteenth century the religious fanaticism of the Ascendancy cooled in the spread of scepticism from Great Britain. The natural result of the passing away of religious intolerance among the dominant Protestant caste was the great increase of ecclesiastical activity among the Roman Catholics. As PATRICK ROGERS says, the first ten years of the reign of George III (1760-1820) saw in reality the Roman Catholic Church in Ireland rising from the Catacombs.[149]

At the same time there awoke among the Ascendancy a spirit of independence of England, a kind of 'colonial patriotism' (some authors even speak of 'nationalism').

---

[a] Belfast was "marked out by nature" to become "the commercial, industrial, and cultural capital of the North before it became its political capital following Partition". The advantages of its situation were threefold:

(1)   the streams from the Antrim plateau with their steep gradients helped to make Belfast a notable centre of industry in the days of waterpower (they still determine the location of its main industrial quarters);

(2)   its location at the head of the Lagan valley gave it ease of access to the Central Ulster Lowlands (which were, in EVANS's phrase, "fatefully separated from southern Ireland by the difficult hills of south Armagh") by road, by canal (1754-63), and by railway (1835-9); and

(3)   its proximity to the peoples and the coalfields of south-west Scotland and north-west England: from the sheltered waters of Belfast Lough the passage by sea to the Clyde and the Mersey was quite short (EVANS, *Site*, 171, 175-6; GILL, 182).

[b] Like the general synod of the American Presbyterian Church, prior to the election of the first Congress, it was "the only assembly that covered the whole country, or was in any sense representative of it" (cf. MARSHALL, 33; *Ulster since 1800*, vol. ii, 22).

[c] Not only were English people themselves by far the largest customers, but even the cloth that was sent abroad went for the most part by way of English ports (GILL, 177). This tradition has remained for quite a number of exports from the north of Ireland.

The driving force of this movement was largely economic grievances. Its main object was the removal of the economic disabilities which successive English parliaments had jealously imposed on the Irish trade. Claims to legislative independence – later generations might have spoken of 'Home Rule' – naturally followed. The decline of 'sectarian animosity' and dissatisfaction with English legislation led to some form of contact, if only slight, with the Roman Catholics, especially with the Catholic merchant and professional class which had emerged in the towns.[a] There grew even a demand for relaxation of the civil part of the *Penal Code*.[b]

There was, as BECKETT observes, a fatal weakness in this movement. The Episcopalian aristocrats – "in origin and purpose a colonial garrison" – could never ally themselves wholeheartedly with the mass of the people, for the religious barrier was too strong. On the other hand they could not push their quarrel with London beyond a certain point, for their own supremacy depended upon military force which, in the last resort, they might have to call upon England to supply.[150] And it should not be forgotten that, whatever patriotism there was among this oligarchy, their spiritual home was England – and, as they were notorious absentees, as often as not their real home.

Anyhow, this first reform party which emerged in Ireland managed to secure various important concessions from the London government. It is not unreasonable to regard these concessions – as STRAUSS does – as "a mere by-product of the American Revolution".[151] The American War (1775-83) certainly made for greater indulgence on the part of the English government. When, after the withdrawal of the British troops from Ireland, with France, Spain and the Netherlands joining in against England, an invasion of Ireland became conceivable, a volunteer force was formed (1778). The *Irish Volunteers*, representing "the armed property of the Protestant nation", became a powerful instrument in the hands of Grattan and the other leaders of the reform movement.[c] In 1779 Ireland practically obtained free trade, and in 1782 she was granted legislative independence.

However, once the American War was over, the British parliament hardened and the extent of the concessions to Ireland was reduced (1785). Great Britain retained the monopoly of the imperial trade and protection against Irish trade with England (the admission to which was to be one of the baits offered at the Union of the two kingdoms in 1800).[152] The constitutional experiment of 1782 was continued but it was to last for

---

[a] The economic provisions of the *Penal Laws* had affected directly only the acquisition and disposal of real property; personal property did not, for the most part, fall under the law. "So the more energetic Catholics turned to trade as the only sphere in which they could make any progress". According to PATRICK ROGERS, the new Catholic commercial class – "wealthy and, on the whole, educated, in spite of the Penal Code" – formed "in character and ideas as great a contrast to the broken and dispirited nobility which still remained loyal to the Faith, as to the ignorant and torpid mass of the peasantry" (8-9). The richest of them were very rich indeed, richer than most of the landlords. It was natural that they should wish to match their rising mercantile influence with a proportionate political influence which the *Penal Laws*, by excluding Roman Catholics from parliament, prevented.

[b] Acts for "the relief of His Majesty's subjects professing the popish religion" were passed in 1771, 1774, 1778, 1782 and 1793 (cf. *Documents*, 194-202).

[c] The rapid decline of the Volunteer movement shows on what a weak foundation the 'colonial nationalism' was based. But its symbols lingered. Many present-day popular Nationalist symbols, such as the green flag and the harp, derive from the *Irish Volunteers*. They were used again by the *United Irishmen* in 1798 and by later Nationalist movements. (The national emblem of the Republic, the harp, actually goes back to King Henry VIII who adopted it as the seal of Ireland.)

eighteen years only. It might have succeeded but for the French Revolution which encouraged all the elements of unrest in Ireland and made it more and more difficult to maintain the authority of government.[153]

Before turning to the 'fatal effects' of the French Revolution I should point to the great impression which the American Revolution – and the distinguished part of the Scotch-Irish in it – made in Ulster. The links between the Ulster emigrants and their friends at home (among whom a liberal spirit, in politics as well as in theology, was at this time very strong) fostered the exchange of ideas. "Both laboured under a sense of oppression, and in both there grew up a desire to assert their independent rights".[154] The Ulster Scots "made no secret of their desire for a British defeat and they openly rejoiced when it came".[155] The American Revolution obviously prepared the ground for the influence of the French Revolution in Ulster.

THE EFFECT OF THE FRENCH REVOLUTION (1789)

In Ireland, as in England, the outbreak of the French Revolution produced a wave of enthusiasm among the supporters of reform, particularly among the Presbyterians. In Belfast – being a new, quickly expanding, industrial city and more acutely aware of the strangling hand of landlordism than the older cities – the Fall of the Bastille was celebrated along with the commemoration of the Battle of the Boyne, both being regarded as "victories for liberty".[156] Though the Presbyterians had been relieved of the *Test Act* which had excluded them from every influential office, "the weight of prejudice against their admission to such posts had as yet scarcely lifted".[157]

The principles of civil, political and religious liberty found most response in the *Society of United Irishmen*, founded in Belfast in 1791 by Theobald Wolfe Tone, a young Dublin barrister of English descent. The aim of the new organization was to promote "a brotherhood of affection, an identity of interest, a communion of rights, and a union of power amongst Irishmen of every religious persuasion". At first the United Irishmen concentrated upon obtaining parliamentary reform. When the government attempted to suppress them, and their circle narrowed, they naturally grew more revolutionary in their aims and more violent in their methods.[158]

However sincerely the United Irishmen embraced the cause of Catholic Emancipation, they did not win over the leading Roman Catholics, the hierarchy, the few remaining gentry, and the new middle-class. These were by no means inclined to revolution – the course of the French Revolution did not make for any sympathy with France, the welcome ally of 1690. Even among "that very respectable body, the men of no property" – the down-trodden Catholic peasantry on whom Tone pinned high hopes – the revolutionary philosophy made little appeal (apart from certain districts which had a well-organized United Irish movement).

As far as "the radical North" was concerned: the main strength of the movement lay in the middle class of Belfast and in the farming population of parts of Cos Antrim and Down. Wherever Protestant and Roman Catholic elements in the population were more evenly balanced, sectarian rivalry was more potent than the notion of universal brotherhood.[a] The founding of the *Orange Institution* (in 1795 in Co. Armagh), at the time composed almost exclusively of Episcopalians, "both indicated and helped to perpetuate a division of opinion hopeless at variance with the ideals of Tone and his friends".[159]

Tension mounted till 1798. Then a rising broke out. There was no general insurrection.[b] The main action took place in Co. Wexford. This was primarily a revolt of the peasantry goaded by oppression.[c] Hardly had the Wexford rebels been crushed (by 13,000 troops), when a small French force landed in the west. They were joined by a large number of the Connacht peasantry. After some initial success they were defeated at Ballinamuck. Though these actions came to nothing, they showed that the hatred which the Catholic peasants bore their Protestant landlords was capable of serious explosion. All through the eighteenth century the peasants had laid dormant, leaderless.[d] Now a new element had entered the Irish political scene – the peasantry in arms, under their own leaders: farmers and priests (and an odd Anglo-Irishman who was very liberally inclined).

There was also a short-lived revolt in the Presbyterian stronghold of east Ulster. Despite all intimidation some hundreds of *United Irishmen* turned out, including a few Roman Catholics. This was the first – and last – time that Ulster Presbyterians joined with Roman Catholic Irishmen to assault English power. There are Nationalists who never tire of recalling that "there was a period, not long distant, when the aspirations of Ulster coincided with those of the rest of Ireland".[160] We should beware of idealizing this alliance. The numbers of Catholics and Presbyterians who took an active part in the Rebellion were relatively small. Did "the aspirations of Ulster", *i.e.* of Presbyterian Ulster, really coincide with those of the rest of Ireland, *i.e.* the Roman Catholic Irish? They did in so far as both groups wanted to be free from the English (Episcopalian) yoke, the Ulster Presbyterians no less than the Irish Catholics – and no less than their co-religionists in America.

If they had seen any real prospect of establishing a democratic Irish republic on the

---

[a] There was in this steadily increasing animosity between Protestants and Catholics a strong economic factor. FITZHENRY (45) notes that emigration and the Belfast industries had drawn many Protestant smallholders from the farms. "Gradually Catholics filtered into the vacant holdings and their coming was bitterly resented by their Protestant neighbours. Local feuds broke out, and the magistrates, all members of the Established Church, did little to check the attacks on Catholics".

[b] A quick move of the government had deprived the movement of most of its leaders. Wolfe Tone at the time was in France planning an invasion by French troops. He was taken when a small French naval squadron was intercepted and forced to surrender. (There had been another unsuccessful French expedition in 1796.)

[c] CURTIS notes that "the most determined, indeed the only formidable, rising took place in the quarter where no one would have expected it". In the early days of the Anglo-Norman conquest Co. Wexford had been planted with Normans, Flemings, and Saxons. Though the northern parts were Irish, the southern baronies were still occupied by an "Old English population speaking an old-fashioned Saxon dialect" (CURTIS, *History*, 341-2). The action of these sturdy Catholic peasants indicates that the fusion of the Old English and Old Irish population elements had become complete.

[d] The elimination of the Catholic landed gentry had obviated the chance of a nation-wide insurrection, officered by aristocrats. Even the 1715 and 1745 risings in the Scottish Highlands had no effect on Ireland – though causing alarm in Dublin and the latter one leading to some alleviation of the *Penal Code*. The only agitations were agrarian, intended to curb the greed of the Anglo-Irish oligarchy. But they never amounted to more than 'terrorist outrages'. (The hierarchy attempted to suppress these disturbances.)

principles adopted by the United States, or as developed by Tone – supposing that the English could be defeated – the majority of Ulster Presbyterians probably would have joined in the Rebellion. They apprehended, however, rightly or wrongly, that in an independent Irish state, in which the Roman Catholic Church was bound to dominate, these principles would count for little. Anyhow, they had never felt any particular attachment to Ireland at large: their interests did not reach farther than the boundary of Ulster. On the other hand, many of those who actually felt inclined to rise seem to have become disillusioned by what CURTIS calls "the Catholic nature of the peasant revolt in Wexford". According to BARRINGTON the Wexford Rebellion had many of the characteristics of a Holy War and "the massacre of Protestants at Scullabogue had a profound effect on Protestant opinion in the north".[161]

The significance of the Rebellion lies rather in the fact that it established "a tradition of revolutionary violence which, from that time onwards, has exercised an influence, varying in strength but never negligible, on Irish politics". This tradition still contains "all those incongruous elements that were at work in 1798 – national feeling, radical discontent, religious fanaticism and humanitarian philosophy".[162] It was Wolfe Tone who forged the key-phrase of Irish republicanism: "to break the connection with England, the never-failing source of all our evils", and "to replace the name of Catholic, Protestant [Episcopalian] and Dissenter with the common name of Irishman".

The immediate effects of '1798' were also fateful. The Rebellion dealt the death-blow to the constitutional experiment of 1782 and prepared the way for the Union of Great Britain and Ireland (1801). The 'aristocratic nationalism' of the Irish Volunteers shrank to "a sentimental regret for the glories of the Irish parliament"; the 'revolutionary nationalism' of the United Irishmen left only "a brief postscript" in Robert Emmet's abortive insurrection of 1803.[163] Thus the Rebellion marks the end of an era in the history of Anglo-Irish relations and the beginning of a new one: to present-day Irish Nationalists "a period of oppression and degradation", to the Irish Unionists "a great experiment which went wrong", whereas to the historian its main characteristic is – as BECKETT sees it – that it made possible the Irish nation of today.[164] And, as I might add, the 'Ulster nation'.

Chapter 15

IRELAND IN THE UNITED KINGDOM

THE UNION OF GREAT BRITAIN AND IRELAND (1801)

On the first of January, 1801, a new flag was hoisted in London, Edinburgh, and Dublin: the *Union Jack*, formed by the crosses of St George, St Andrew, and St Patrick. The kingdom of Ireland, proclaimed in 1541, and the Dublin parliament, only recently endowed with greater powers, had ceased to exist. Ireland was merged completely – or almost completely[a] – into the United Kingdom, henceforth to be known as 'the United

---

[a] Ireland retained a separative executive and many laws were to be passed which applied exclusively to Ireland. The Union of North and South Britain in 1707 likewise had not involved the complete legislative absorption of Scotland.

Kingdom of Great Britain and Ireland'. The new kingdom was to last exactly one hundred and twenty years – from the Napoleonic Wars to the end of the First World War: "It coincided with the period of England's industrial and political supremacy, and its end marks, though it did not cause, the end of England's expansionist imperialism".[165]

From the English point of view the Union of Great Britain and Ireland was little short of a military necessity. For Great Britain, once more alone in the struggle with France, a restless Ireland was a source of intolerable danger. Ireland conciliated and closely bound to Great Britain would be a source of strength, especially to the armed forces[166], for at this time the island held approximately one quarter of the total population of the British Isles. It was not only strategic reasons which settled the matter. Another factor were "the apprehensions of British manufacturers and farmers that a privileged enclave with special tariffs would grow on their doorstep".[167]

However, according to its chief architect, William Pitt, the Union was not designed solely for the English interest. Ireland would also benefit by it. In the House of Commons in 1799 Pitt listed the following advantages which Ireland would derive from the Union:

"the protection which she will secure to herself in the hour of danger, the most effectual means of increasing her commerce and improve her agriculture, the command of English capital, the infusion of English manners and English industry, necessarily tending to ameliorate her condition, to accelerate the progress of internal civilization ..".[168]

Opinions in Ireland on the Union were divided. Although too much generalization on the matter is dangerous, it seems reasonably to say that it was unpopular with the majority of the Protestants, Episcopalians and Presbyterians alike, whereas the majority of the Roman Catholics regarded it with indifference – if not with approval.[169] Of the two most influential bodies in Ireland, the Ascendancy class and the Roman Catholic hierarchy, the former was generally opposed to the idea of the Union whereas the latter supported it. The Ascendancy were naturally loath to lose their privileged position – they had to be 'bribed' to accept the Union. The hierarchy supported it because of their dread of revolution and because they were led to believe that the Union would entail Catholic Emancipation.[a]

The attitudes of the two religious groups towards the Union were soon reversed. Later it was the majority of Protestants who were most anxious for its continuance and the majority of the Catholics who were most anxious for its repeal.[170] (Repeal of the Union in nineteenth-century Ireland did not mean the setting-up of a sovereign Irish republic: it implied only such self-government as Ireland had enjoyed prior to 1801.) From an overall British Isles point of view, the most fateful political developments in post-Union Ireland were the 'alienation' of the Irish Catholics which ultimately led to the creation of the Irish Free State, and the 'appeasement' of the Ulster Presbyterians which ultimately produced Northern Ireland which remained within the United Kingdom.

In the course of the nineteenth century contacts between the various parts of the British Isles increased considerably. The Union greatly facilitated the intermingling of the peoples of the British Isles – a process which had been going on from the earliest times and which has not abated since 1921 (at least as far as Great Britain is concerned).

---

[a] The Catholic peasantry did not protest. But they were hardly in a position to protest – even if they had felt that way inclined. The parochial clergy for the most part also remained silent.

Economically, the whole of Ireland became indissolubly tied to Great Britain, though for north and south the ties differed. These economic links still remain. Of the regional contrasts which existed between Ulster and the rest of Ireland and between the two parts of Ireland and Great Britain at the time of the Union, some were blunted or disappeared altogether. Other contrasts, however, remained and received new emphasis as in the case of religious allegiance.

The nineteenth century saw the near completion of the process by which a single culture was extended over the whole British Isles: both the south and north of Ireland became thoroughly anglicized, though each part in its own way. Indeed, the Union led, in Pitt's words, to the increase of commerce and the improvement of agriculture, and to the infusion of English manners. Whether or not it accelerated "the progress of internal civilization" is a matter of dispute.

The present-day pattern of regional differentiation in Ireland is well known but how this pattern evolved since the beginning of the nineteenth century? This Chapter is restricted to an outline of the main processes which have determined this pattern. I will concentrate upon the factors which have set these processes in motion.

This Chapter deals only with the impact of the Union on Ireland. It is not amiss to point out that Great Britain, too, was greatly affected by the Union. One of the few authors who have dealt in a systematic way with Ireland's influence on Great Britain from the time of the Union is STRAUSS. In his work on *Irish Nationalism and British Democracy* he has shown how Irish problems and the Irish members of parliament became one of the most powerful factors in British political life. The analysis of this influence provides an important clue to the understanding of the growth of British democracy. STRAUSS says:

"Even on the most superficial view, the extent of the Irish influence on British politics between Waterloo and Versailles is astounding. The fall of British ministries on Irish questions or through the use of the Irish vote was for many years more the rule than the exception.[a] .. Ireland's influence on the modernisation of the relations between Great Britain and the Dominions, though less obvious, has also been considerable".[171]

One of the subjects worth more detailed consideration than it has so far received is the contribution of Irish migrants, both from the south and the north, to British industry and commerce, to the arts, and to Church life in Great Britain. Before the onset of the Industrial Revolution the movement of population between the two islands flowed almost exclusively westward into Ireland. During the later part of the eighteenth century this movement showed the first signs of a reversal. In the nineteenth century there was both emigration westward and eastward. In the twentieth century only the eastward movement continued.[172] This has not changed since the Separation of the Free State.

THE ALIENATION OF THE IRISH CATHOLICS I

The view is widely held today, both in the Republic and in Great Britain, that the Union of 1801 – "conceived in iniquity and born in sin" (GEORGE O'BRIEN) – was doomed to inevitable failure. I agree with MOODY, O'BRIEN and others that, if the British parliament

---

[a] This influence was strengthened by the fact that Ireland became increasingly over-represented in the British parliament.

had operated the Union of 1801 "with the right state of mind and the right state of heart", and had immediately set itself to remedy Ireland's ailments, it might have proved not only tolerable but satisfactory to Ireland[173], like the Union of 1707 and the Union of 1536 have proved tolerable and satisfactory to Scotland and Wales respectively. The Union of 1801, however, was not a complete failure. It failed in so far as it failed to satisfy the demands of the largest population group in Ireland, the Roman Catholics, when roused to political self-consciousness. The second largest population group, the Ulster Presbyterians, soon acquiesced and in the end became its strongest upholders, as far as Ulster was concerned at any rate.

The history of Anglo-Irish relations in the nineteenth century may well be summed up in O'BRIEN's words: "Agitation succeeds where reason and justice fail; the inevitable surrender is made too late; and relief, when it comes, comes with a bad grace".[174] The failure of the Union is often attributed to socio-economic factors, the most important of which was the continuation of the degrading land system in the south of Ireland. According to many authors the cardinal struggle in nineteenth-century Ireland was the agitation against landlordism, the so-called Land War. Others regard as the cardinal struggle the agitation for Catholic Emancipation, *i.e.* the removal of the remaining political restrictions on Roman Catholics, and especially those excluding them from membership of parliament and other public posts. I also believe that the failure of the Union as a political arrangement is due to the delay of Catholic Emancipation [a] rather than to the delay of Land Reform.

O'BRIEN is right, I think, when he says that if Catholic Emancipation had been granted without delay, the whole course of politics in nineteenth-century Ireland would probably have run on different lines. As it was, the energies of the Catholic Irish were concentrated for nearly thirty years on securing "an act of elementary justice". This created a feeling of dissatisfaction with the Union which nobody strove to allay until it was too late. The result was that "the first great Irish popular agitation was given a religious tinge, which tended to colour later agitations concerned with quite different matters".[175]

That Catholic Emancipation was at last secured (1829) – followed by other much-needed reforms, such as tithe reform (1838), the *Poor Law* (1838), and municipal reform (1840) – was mainly due to one figure: Daniel O'Connell (1775-1847), "the Liberator".[b] O'Connell was a pioneer in bringing the force of public opinion to bear on government in a constitutional and yet aggressive way. "By the colossal force of his personality, untiring energy, wily adaptability, legal ingenuity, floods of oratory, and an inexhaustible

---

[a] Pitt had hoped to carry this through immediately after the Union, but the opposition was stronger than he had expected, the measure had to be dropped, and he resigned in protest (BECKETT, 148). Whatever hopes the Irish Catholics may have entertained were swiftly and rudely disappointed: "Anti-Catholic prejudice and intolerance seemed to increase rather than diminish. The king dismissed Grenville from office for proposing to introduce a measure allowing Catholic soldiers the free exercise of their religion – this in the midst of a great war, when one-third of the British army was composed of Irish Catholics" (CARTY, *Ireland 1783-1850*, xxvii).

[b] O'Connell, who was a successful Dublin barrister and who became the first Roman Catholic lord mayor of Dublin since the Reformation, came from a family of small landowners, a remnant of the Gaelic aristocracy. One of his modern admirers calls him "a southern Irish Catholic landlord, or rather chieftain" (cf. *O'Connell*, 52).

patience in organization" (O'FAOLAIN), O'Connell used the cause of Emancipation to
inspire the hitherto silent and inert Catholic masses with a sense of united purpose such
as they had never known before.[a] "He gradually lifted them out of their torpor, gave
them hope and self-respect, discipline and self-reliance".[176]

The question whether Irish nationalism begins with O'Connell or not has elicited a
good deal of controversy. According to ROCHE, the period of his public career marks
"the early stage of that transition from the eighteenth-century rationalist 'patriotism' to
the state of mind known to us as 'national self-consciousness', which knows no satisfaction
save in complete autonomy".[177] Another of O'Connell's admirers says that it was he who
set going "the movement which through a century's changes and chances vindicated for
the Irish people their ancient right to a separate national identity".[178]

It is well to distinguish between two main traditions of Irish nationalism, the moderate
and the extremist one, both of which date from the first half-century after the Union.
They are definable not only in terms of aims but in terms of methods as well:

(1)   the *constitutional* tradition or moral-force school steadfastly backed by the Roman Catholic Church,
      accepting the essential unity of the British Isles as symbolized by the British crown, and seeking what
      Professor Galbraith was later to christen 'Home Rule' for Ireland to be won by consent with England;
      and

(2)   the *revolutionary* tradition or physical-force school steadfastly opposed by the Church, rejecting
      any idea of the unity of the British Isles, and seeking the establishment of a sovereign Irish republic
      to be achieved by force.[179]

O'Connell was no Republican or Separatist. He certainly did not take Wolfe Tone
and the United Irishmen as his inspiration; he was rather in the tradition of Henry
Grattan and the Irish Volunteers.[180] O'Connell was opposed to physical force and nothing
could be further from his temperament, as TIERNEY says, than "the 'blood-sacrifice'
mystique which was to inspire the Rebellion of 1916".[181] All his life he remained perfectly
loyal to the British crown. His action for Repeal of the Union was essentially a demand
for Home Rule. In 1832 he said to an English audience: "We only want a parliament to
do our private business, leaving the national business to a national assembly".[182] O'Connell,
then, may be regarded as the creator of the Home Rule idea.

If the delay of Catholic Emancipation was the principal cause of the failure of the
Union as far as Catholic Ireland is concerned, it had, as O'BRIEN puts it, "the further evil
result of associating Irish nationalism with Catholicism in the mind of the British public"[183]
– and in the mind of the Protestant Irish. O'Connell's political creed was, in McDOWELL's
words,

"basically a mixture of Catholicism and nationalism, so closely blended, that though his genial good
nature and realistic appreciation of the requirements of the situation made him strive to obtain Protestant
co-operation, he frequently seems to have identified the Irish nation with Irish Catholicism".[184]

---

[a] According to ROCHE (in: *O'Connell*, 52), "O'Connell seemed to call to the deeps of the Irish Catholic
nature and to stir it as none but one of their flesh and blood, and a leader of genius at that, could do"
(cf. CURTIS, *History*, 359). It has also been observed that "he left his mark indelibly on the national mind
so that to understand fully the mentality of a modern Irishman it is necessary to study him" (O'FAOLAIN,
Story, 37). O'Connell is the only modern Irish leader who grew up in a Gaelic tradition: he spoke Irish
from birth and to the end of his life he prayed in Irish. But he was not interested in Irish and thought
English more 'useful'.

As BECKETT says, O'Connell linked the cause of Irish nationalism and the cause of the Roman Catholic Church so firmly together that succeeding generations have hardly been able to prise them apart. (Such a linking-up was perhaps the only means of providing the feeling of solidarity without which an Irish popular movement could hardly have emerged; there was no general sentiment against the Union.) O'BRIEN, too, is of the opinion that no Nationalist movement since O'Connell, whether moderate or extremist, has succeeded in being regarded as religiously neutral.[185]

There were Protestants who joined the Repeal Movement, and some played an important part in it, but they were not representative of any considerable body of Protestant opinion.[186] This applies also to later Nationalist movements and it holds good both for the Episcopalians and the Presbyterians.

THE ALIENATION OF THE IRISH CATHOLICS II

According to Giuseppe Mazzini (1805-72), one of the foremost exponents of nationalism in mid-nineteenth-century Europe, O'Connell's Repeal Movement was lacking in "the essential marks of nationality" as it did not plead for "any distinct principle of life or system of legislation, derived from native peculiarities, and contrasting radically with English wants and wishes".[187] Irish nationalism in this romantic and doctrinaire sense of the word begins with Thomas Davis (a young Anglo-Irishman) and his friends who founded a new journal, *The Nation* (Dublin, 1842). By naming their movement *Young Ireland*, in imitation of Mazzini's *Young Italy*, they showed their kinship with the contemporary movements on the continent.[188] They were the first to define 'Irish nationality' (1844 in *The Nation*):

"It is the summary name for many things. It seeks a literature made by Irishmen, and coloured by our scenery, manners and character. It desires to see art applied to express Irish thoughts and belief. It would make our music sound in every parish at twilight, our pictures sprinkle the walls of every house, and our poetry and history sit at every hearth. It would thus create a race of men full of a more intensely Irish character and knowledge, and to that race it would give Ireland".

The Young Irelanders, says O'FAOLAIN, were idealists who created a brilliantly refracted picture of the past greatness of their country.

"They created or gave wide currency to all those symbolic images which have ever since become the metaphorical language of Irish politics; Davis in particular went back eagerly to the Gaelic tradition which O'Connell rejected.[a] .. Much of what they wrote was superficial .. but it was always heroic and generous and uncompromising, and this was precisely the element that O'Connellism, with its coarser and more opportunist technique, inevitably lacked".[189]

The Young Irelanders derived much of their inspiration from Tone.[b] Not only did they take up Tone's conception of non-sectarian republicanism but they also revived his idea of physical force: "They looked for an Ireland in which men of all faiths would

---

[a] It was an ironic situation: O'Connell, the Catholic and Irish-speaking 'Gael', who could "witness without a sigh the gradual disuse of Irish", was faced by the Protestant and English-speaking 'Anglo-Saxon' Thomas Davis, who wished for a revival of interest in the Irish language though he had a very imperfect knowledge of anything to do with that language.

[b] In fact, the modern veneration for Tone begins in 1844 with the erection of the monument over his grave, for which Davis wrote the inscription.

mingle freely and they were willing, it seemed at times almost anxious, that it should be won by a people in arms".[190] They may have been rather futile and pathetic revolutionaries [a] but the influence of their short-lived movement on later Irish and British politics has been formidable. This applies especially to *The Nation* and to the polemic writings of John Mitchel (1815-75) which provided the gospel for all later revolutionaries.[b] "The intransigence, the unwillingness to compromise or bargain, and the cult of physical force which has been so marked a feature of our politics during the past half-century", says TIERNEY, "all undoubtedly derive from the influence of *The Nation*".[191]

It was Young Irelanders who founded and inspired the I.R.B., the *Irish Republican Brotherhood* (Dublin, 1858), the core of the so-called *Fenian Movement*.[c] This secret society was also dedicated to the task of winning an independent Irish Republic by force. In two respects, however, Fenianism differs from Young Ireland. Firstly, its leaders were all Roman Catholics (though some of the most prominent were non-practising). Secondly, it was not confined to Ireland: it found its most determined adherents among the Irish exiles in America and Great Britain. At the end of the eighteenth century it had been the Presbyterian emigrants who exerted influence upon home opinion. Now it was the Roman Catholic emigrants who affected Irish political affairs. Their influence, however, was more forcible and lasted much longer. In fact, it still exists in the modern extremist I.R.A. and its associate groups in the United States.

Fenianism, however great its membership may have been, was never in any sense a popular movement like O'Connell's Repeal Movement and the later Home Rule and parliamentary Nationalist parties. (It was constantly opposed by the hierarchy.) But it greatly impinged on Anglo-Irish relations. It was the Fenian Rising of 1867, though "no more than a gesture of armed defiance" (BECKETT), which convinced Gladstone of "the intensity of Irish national feeling" and made him declare (when entering upon his first ministry in 1868): "My mission is to pacify Ireland".[192] His first step in that direction was the disestablishment and the partial disendowment of the Episcopalian Church of Ireland.[d]

---

[a] In 1848 they attempted an insurrection. This rebellion fizzled out in an attack on a police-barrack in Co. Tipperary. Its leader forbade the cutting of trees to make a barricade without first securing the permission of the landowner on whose land they stood. When the rebellion began, one of the most fiery of their supporters, a priest, had his ardour cooled by a direction from his bishop and excused himself from participating.

[b] John Mitchel was an Ulster Presbyterian. Two of his daughters, however, became Catholics. Of his eldest daughter he says (*Jail Journal*, 408) that "she was greatly influenced by her very strong Irish feeling, and had a kind of sentiment that one cannot be thoroughly Irish without being Catholic". Mitchel was a true disciple of Wolfe Tone. This may be apparent from the way in which he stood up for the "Anglo-Irish and Scottish Ulstermen" (*Aedh O'Neill*, vii-viii): "Whatever god or demon may have led the first of them to these shores, they have now far too old a title to be questioned: they were a hardy race, and fought stoutly for the pleasant valleys they dwell in. .. And have not those men and their fathers lived, and loved, and worshipped God, and died there? .. A deep enough root those planters have struck into the soil of Ulster, and it would now be ill striving to unplant them".

[b] The name 'Fenian' is derived from the mythical 'Fianna', ancient Irish warrior-bands (of the *Ossianic legends*). The Fenians were the first Irish movement to give themselves a name from the Gaelic past. This was due to the influence of one of the founders, John O'Mahony, who was a Gaelic scholar (he died in New York in 1877).

[c] The *Act of Union* had provided "that the churches of England and Ireland, as now by law established, be

It was a revived Irish Republican Brotherhood which, seeing in the First World War "Ireland's great opportunity to play for her own freedom" (O'HEGARTY), organized the Rising of Easter Week, 1916. This Rising, too, was no more than "a gesture of armed defiance". According to one of the members of the supreme council of the I.R.B. who planned the Rising, it was "a forlorn hope and deliberate blood sacrifice". The men who planned it and led it knew that they could not win. They also realized that at the time their action would be very unpopular but "they counted upon being executed afterwards".[193]

The immediate reaction of Nationalist opinion as a whole was to condemn the Rising as "criminal folly". At the time the demand for a completely independent Irish Republic had little popular support.[a] It was, as BECKETT notes, the government's treatment of the affair, however natural in the circumstances, that produced "an immediate revulsion of feeling". Indeed, the sentiments aroused by the subsequent executions – the Sacrifice of the Fifteen Men (1916) – together with the threat of conscription (1917) deprived the great Home Rule party of most of its supporters. They rallied to Sinn Féin (literally: We Ourselves), a more extremist party (founded in 1905), which provided "the machinery to take advantage of the rising tide of republicanism"[194] and which eventually obtained Dominion status for twenty-six counties in 1921.[b]

Thus it was the I.R.B. which dealt the death-blow to the Union. As GEORGE O'BRIEN comments: "an organisation which was not founded until 1858, and would probably never have been founded if the Union had been differently operated".[195]

THE IMPACT OF THE INDUSTRIAL REVOLUTION

The Union of 1801 is often condemned because of its alleged adverse influence on the Irish economy. There was, however, not one Irish economy but two. At the beginning of the nineteenth century Ireland, from the economic point of view, could roughly be divided into:

united into one protestant episcopalian church, to be called 'The United Church of England and Ireland'". By the provisions of the *Irish Church Act, 1869*, the union between the two Churches was dissolved. According to NEILL in his study on *Anglicanism* (294), Gladstone regarded the disestablishment of the Church of Ireland as "the discharge of a debt of civil justice, the disappearance of a national, almost a world-wide reproach, a condition indispensable to the success of every effort to secure the peace and contentment of that country; finally, relief to a devoted clergy from a false position, cramped and beset by hopeless prejudice, and the opening of a freer career to their sacred ministry". (In 1861 the Church of Ireland embraced 12% of the total population of Ireland.)

[a] The 1916 leaders rallied less than three thousand men. There were over a hundred thousand volunteers from the South fighting in the British army in France and Belgium, and some thirty thousand more rallied in Ireland to oppose the 1916 Insurrection.

[b] After 1921 Sinn Féin soon fell into the background. The story of its break-up on the Treaty issue and of Mr de Valera's expulsion is too well known to need repetition here. Today Sinn Féin is but a shadow of its former self. In 1961 it lost its last four seats in the Dublin parliament (it polled only about 3% of total votes cast). The party had already lost its seats in the London and Belfast parliaments (Sinn Féin representatives never took part in parliamentary proceedings). As there is no other extremist party the decline of Sinn Féin may be taken to prove that intransigent republicanism has almost become extinct in Ireland. (Even such election-cries as "the expulsion of the British occupying forces from the Six Counties" and "the repudiation of all treaties, pacts and laws that in any way curtail the nation's independence" have had their day.)

(1)   'Scottish Ulster' with Dublin and the other coastal towns of the south – which PATRICK LYNCH and
      JOHN VAIZEY call 'maritime Ireland' – with an advanced cash economy based on commerce and
      closely linked with that of the greater part of Great Britain by ties of credit and trade; in fact, this
      economy was not an autonomous unit but formed in almost every essential an integral part of the
      rapidly expanding capitalist economy of the British Isles; and
(2)   the rest of the island peopled largely by moneyless peasants who held a tenuous and temporary
      interest in small patches of land and who lived mainly on potatoes; this part was characterized by a
      largely static subsistence economy and formed a large-scale counterpart of the remote parts of Scotland
      and Wales which had not yet been assimilated into the 'maritime economy' of the rest of Great
      Britain.[196]

The Union did not immediately affect the subsistence economy. The 'maritime
economy', however, underwent great changes. In the first decades of the nineteenth
century various industries declined. This is generally attributed to the reduction, and
later on the abolition (1824), of the customs barrier between Ireland and Great Britain.
Thus were "Ireland's struggling industries" deprived of protection and encouragement
and exposed to "the unfettered competition by English manufacturers".[197] It is doubtful,
however, whether all Irish industries would have been able to maintain themselves if
there had been no Union.

LYNCH and VAIZEY rightly point out that the collapse of certain industries in maritime
Ireland is almost contemporary with their decline elsewhere and that it is in part "a
replacement of hand-methods of production by cheaper manufactured imports". This
process began in the textile industries and continued in other craft or hand-trades throughout the century:

"The logic of the situation was that the industries of any region flourished until technical change,
aided by falling transport costs, led to the eventual triumph of manufacturing industry. Since manufacturing
industry was based largely upon coal and iron, .. it was to be expected that most of its growth was in
the north of England and the midlands, rather than in Ireland or elsewhere in the United Kingdom".

The elimination of small trades was accelerated by the reduction in cross-Channel
transport costs after 1830 brought about by the introduction of steamships in 1824.[198]
On the other hand, certain trades continued to grow. These industries, however, were
almost entirely confined to Ulster. As STRAUSS says, it was only in Ulster that the forecasts
of the optimistic supporters of the Union came to life:

"It enabled the Ulster business interests to participate in the triumphal progress of British industry
as a sturdy, if modest auxiliary. At first mainly in the textile industries, later on as an integral part of the
shipbuilding and manufacturing empire of north-west England and south-west Scotland, the Belfast area
became one of the major industrial centres of the United Kingdom".[199]

The industrialization of Ulster, or rather of east Ulster, in the first half of the nineteenth century is often looked upon in Ireland as a novel development which clearly
stands on its own. It is true that it is not paralleled by any comparable industrial development in the rest of Ireland. It definitely does not fit into the sad picture of post-Union
Ireland painted by so many Irish authors. But the industrialization of Ulster is by no
means remarkable when it is seen in its proper perspective, in the context of the 'northern
half' of the British Isles. Indeed, industrial Ulster is "a province of the industrial empire
of north-west England and south-west Scotland".[200] There was a constant flow of capital

and machinery from across the Channel.[a] The industrial development of Ulster merely epitomizes the historical intertwinement of the north of Ireland with the north of Great Britain.

It is a general misconception that the industrialization of Ulster was a by-product of the Union. The extensive textile industry was firmly rooted in the linen trade which had been established long before the Union was proposed. The shipbuilding industry, too, may be traced back to pre-Union times.[b] A novel aspect of post-Union history is the rise of Belfast to dominance over the north of Ireland. The growth of Belfast virtually began in the seventeen 'eighties when the town became the chief centre of the cotton industry. In 1800 Belfast already counted about 20,000 inhabitants. By the middle of the century "the Irish Liverpool" (as it was called by contemporaries) reached the 100,000 figure. By the end of the century that figure had been trebled.[c]

The growing importance of Belfast is shown by the re-orientation of routes in the north. Hitherto Dublin had been the great radiating centre for all main roads in Ireland. The Industrial Revolution made Belfast a second focus. Main roads in Ulster now tended to be those running in an east-west direction, linking the province with Belfast, rather than those running in the old north-south direction towards Dublin. The Lagan valley became the most important artery of the north, connecting Belfast with the Central Ulster Lowlands, and via Clones and Enniskillen with north Connacht. This great land route was extended by sea to Glasgow and Liverpool.[201]

As a matter of fact, communications with the Mersey and the Clyde became far more important to Belfast than those with Dublin. Accordingly Belfast was more concerned in developing its harbour facilities than in improving the land connexion with Dublin. Indeed, modern Ulster owes much to the far-sightedness and the tenacity of Belfast's *Harbour Commissioners* who saw to it that their port facilities made the transportation of coal and iron to Belfast easier than to many places on the British mainland.[202]

---

[a] For instance, the beginning of the cotton industry in Belfast may be dated from the establishment of a cotton spinning venture with the help of a Lancashireman (1784). The first large-scale undertaking in linen thread making was a migrant branch of a Scottish industry (Lisburn, 1784). The first steam-engine ever to be seen in Ireland (Lisburn, 1790) was introduced by a Yorkshireman (E. R. R. GREEN, 81-2, 85, 95, 99). At the same time two other innovations – both significantly Scottish in origin and name as EVANS says – began to penetrate Ireland by way of east Ulster: the 'Scots cart' and the 'Scots plough', which were to become "important agents in transforming the cultural landscape of Ulster by speeding up the agrarian and industrial revolution" (*Ulster since 1800*, vol. ii, 62).

[b] The pioneer of modern shipbuilding in Belfast was a Scot, William Ritchie (1791). The rapid rise of Belfast's shipbuilding dates from the eighteen 'fifties and is very largely due to Edward Harland (who, too, came from Scotland). Harland was the first to break away from the traditional form of the sailing ship, and take full advantage of the possibilities of iron and, later, steel for shipbuilding. It was he who originated the long narrow-beamed steamship with iron deck, the shape of hull which is familiar today (*Modern Ireland*, 175-6; *Ulster since 1800*, vol. i, 52-4). Harland's shipyard later, as Harland & Wolff's, became the largest single unit of its kind in the world. On twenty-four occasions it had the largest annual tonnage output of shipbuilding firms throughout the world (SHEARMAN, *Ireland*, 75-6; *Ulster Year Book 1956*, 109-10; cf. BLAKE, 546-9).

[c] An idea of the growing importance of Belfast as a port may be obtained from the following figures. In 1727 Belfast's share in the total tonnage of ships arriving in Irish harbours was 5.3%; in 1856 it had risen to 24.9%. Dublin's share amounted to 52.2% and 28.6% respectively (STEWIG, 105). By the early eighteen 'nineties customs revenue showed Belfast to be the third port in the British Isles, coming after only London and Liverpool (SHEARMAN, *Ireland*, 75).

Belfast's independence of Dublin is clearly shown in the activities of the *Ulster Railway Company*. In the eighteen 'thirties there were set up two railway systems [a], one Belfast-based and the other Dublin-based. It is of economic as well as of political significance that the link between Dublin and Belfast was not completed until 1855.[203]

THE IMPACT OF THE GREAT FAMINE (1845-48)

For Ulster, and especially for east Ulster, the decades following the Union were on the whole an age of great economic advance. For the rest of Ireland, however, this was "a period of depression, disappointment, and disaster". This applies not only to the maritime fringe of southern Ireland where industry was declining (except, for instance, brewing), but even more so to the inland parts with their subsistence economy.[b] In some ways the history of these parts in the first half of the nineteenth century resembles what FREEMAN in his *Pre-Famine Ireland* calls "a tragedy rising to its devastating climax". The greater part of rural Ireland was heading for a human disaster which came with greater force and horror than anybody could possibly anticipate.[204]

Under the then existing economic and social conditions rural Ireland was undeniably overpopulated.[205] Nevertheless its population was still increasing rapidly. This growth can be attributed to three factors:

(1)   the habit of early marriages, and the high birth-rate;
(2)   the increase in numbers of small tillage farms, accelerated by the repeal of the laws which prevented Roman Catholics from holding land (1785), and the encouragement by the landlords of the subdivision of holdings; and
(3)   the ubiquity of the potato as the main diet of the peasantry.[206]

These three factors were related as both causes and effects. Early marriage was not discouraged by a fear of being unable to acquire a smallholding and to feed a family. The role of the potato was not confined to the mere supply of plenty of food with a minimum of effort. It also greatly reduced the area from which a family could gain its living:

"It provided abundantly from a fraction of the land required to get its nutritional equivalent from grain or pastoral products; it thrived on mountain and bog that was useless in other branches of arable farming; increasingly, in the years before the Famine, the planting of a more prolific potato meant that a family could gain its food from an even more confined area".[207]

In the autumn of 1845 in rather less than half of Ireland the potato harvest failed. In the summer of 1846 there was a second and universal potato blight.[c] In 1847 the blight struck again, though not as heavy as in the previous year. In 1848 the failure was total and

[a]   One of the vary rare occasions during the last century when Ireland did not slavishly follow British practices was the adoption of a broad gauge, broader than the *standard gauge* (the gauge of the English mailcoaches which was employed for most railways in Western Europe). The Irish gauge measures 5ft 3in (1600 mm) (MURRAY, 7; ROLT and WHITEHOUSE, 136-7).
[b]   According to WILLIAM ADAMS (335, 365, 410-26), between 1815 and 1845 about a million Irishmen emigrated to the New World (they laid "the solid foundation of Roman Catholicism in the United States"). To this number of emigrants we have to add the very considerable number who went no further than England and Scotland. In 1841 there were 419,000 people of Irish birth resident in England (CONNELL, 28-9).
[c]   The failure of the potato was due largely to the overcrowding of the soil with the crop, so that to check the spread of the disease was almost impossible once it had begun (LYNCH and VAIZEY, 163).

complete. In 1849 the crop failed partially and in 1850 slightly. The potato blight struck many parts of Europe (including Great Britain) but nowhere else did it produce such disaster as in Ireland, for nowhere else did so many people maintain an exiguous existence based almost entirely on the potato.[208] The Great Famine is the ominous name which embraces all the horrible suffering caused by the visitation of the potato blight in five seasons running. [a] In fact, the Great Famine was no mere natural catastrophe. It was also a social catastrophe in so far as "the combination of the archaic semi-feudal Irish land system and the market economy and *laissez faire* principles of Great Britain" helped to produce all the effects of a great famine.[209]

The Great Famine was very much of a watershed in Ireland's social and political history.[210] Its significance arises primarily from the fact that "it cut the Gordian knot of the question of disproportion between resources and population by drastically reducing the latter".[211] From 1845 to 1851 well over a million people emigrated.[b] The stream of emigrants was swelled by the victims of the clearance movement, *i.e.* the eviction of small tenants, many of whom were in arrears. The evictions opened the way for the consolidation of holdings which henceforth were let as grazing farms.[b] All told, in five years the population of Ireland as a whole was reduced by a quarter, from eight to six million, and the population of the non-maritime, rural, economy by about a third, from six to four million.[d]

For those who remained life was materially better than before. The Famine marks the

---

[a] Above half a million, but less than a million, people died directly from the Great Famine from 1845 to 1851. Probably about a third of the deaths were from typhus, a rather smaller portion from dysentery and diarrhoea, and the remainder from starvation and other causes (*Famine*, 312). It is not amiss to point out that it was not the lack of food as such, but the destruction of the subsistence of the poor, who had no money to buy other food, which brought many thousands to starvation (STRAUSS, 84).

[b] This emigration affected Anglo-American relations by establishing in the United States "a huge Irish population whose sense of national solidarity was based mainly on hatred of Britain" (BECKETT, 158). "Most of the hostility, and much of the lack of understanding", which has from time to time dogged Anglo-American relations, can be traced to the feeling of bitterness – "almost religious in its uncritical fervour" – which developed in the minds and hearts of the ragged, starved, Irish immigrants of the middle of the last century, and which feeling has been passed, like an heirloom, to their descendants, "now influential and prosperous lawyers, politicians and party managers, who play so potent a part in moulding American public opinion" (SALAMAN, 316, 321).

[c] The chief cause of the evictions was the abolition of the *Corn Laws* which was occasioned by the Famine. The repeal of these laws permitted the free entry of cheap corn from abroad. As soon as protection was withdrawn, corn growing in Ireland for export ceased to be profitable. In the years 1847-53 84,000 peasant families, or close on half a million people, were evicted from their smallholdings. Whatever its economic justification, the grievance of eviction rankled bitterly in the hearts of the peasantry, since they had no alternative occupation to which they could turn. The result of the clearance movement was that the number of holdings of 5 acres and less, which amounted to 310,000 in 1841 (45% of all holdings), fell to 88,000 in 1851 (15%), whereas in these years the number of holdings of 30 acres and upwards increased from 48,500 (7%) to 150,000 (26%) (BARKER, 11, 45; SALAMAN, 317-8; cf. *Vanishing Irish*, 24-5).

[d] The Famine was most severe, and consequently depopulation most heavy, in Connacht and Munster. Ulster suffered least (cf. WEIR, *passim*) – "not because of its Protestantism or its loyalty, as is sometimes argued even to-day, but because it possessed in the *Ulster Custom* a measure of tenant-right which prevented the northern agriculturist from sinking into the bog in which the hapless cottier of the south and west was submerged" (*Handbook*, 23). In Ulster there was the widest range of supplements to the potato in the dietary of the people (CONNELL, 237).

end of the old subsistence economy and the assimilation of the last parts of Ireland into the maritime economy of the rest of the British Isles.[212] This assimilation led to rural Ireland's as a whole specializing in livestock husbandry. Henceforth what GOTTMANN calls the rural landscape of Ireland was organized not so much for the purpose of supplying local needs as to complement the economy of Great Britain.[213] Since then the pattern of regional specialization within the British Isles has not profoundly altered as far as Ireland is concerned. Even the secession of the Free State from the United Kingdom has meant no fundamental change.[a] For even the industrialization policy of successive Dublin governments has to a great extent been based on free access to the United Kingdom market. (The decentralization policy of Dublin has been matched by similar policies in the United Kingdom.)

THE RETREAT OF THE IRISH LANGUAGE

The population losses caused by the Great Famine and subsequent mass emigration were greatest in the poorest parts of Ireland which were also the most Gaelic parts. Consequently the number of Gaelic speakers was greatly reduced, both absolutely and relatively. At the beginning of the century probably about the half of the population were still Irish-speaking.[214] In 1851 the number of Gaelic speakers had fallen to about a quarter of the population. At the time of Partition (1921) their number had been further reduced to less than one-seventh (cf. Table 11).

The decline in the number of Gaelic speakers cannot be ascribed to emigration only. Other explanations usually offered include: (1) the hostility towards the language shown by officialdom; (2) the spread of education (always through the medium of English); and (3) the widespread recognition of the usefulness of a knowledge of English. While I do not wish to detract anything from the factors named I would lay stress on two other factors which are too often neglected: the attitude of the Church, and the attitude of almost all Nationalist leaders in nineteenth-century Ireland towards the Irish language.

That great importance should be attached to the attitude of the Church is clearly demonstrated by the history of the Welsh and Scottish Gaelic languages.[b] The stand of the Protestant Churches in Ireland against Gaelic is largely irrelevant: the great majority

---

[a] A report on the economic potentialities of the Republic (1952) calls it somewhat of an enigma that the overall pattern of the cattle industry in the South is still organized in "a fashion that serves the convenience of the economy of the United Kingdom rather than its own economy": its product is still to a very great extent disposed of through export shipments of *live* cattle (*Appraisal*, 73).

[b] That Welsh, alone among the Celtic languages today, has "the vigorous growth and development of a living cultivated language" – it is still spoken by something more than a quarter of the Welsh population (that is by well over 700,000 people) – is probably due largely to the spread of Bible-reading in Welsh and to the usage of the language in Protestant divine services (cf. GRIFFITH 20-1; Ó CUÍV, 31; CECILE O'RAHILLY, vii). That Scottish Gaelic is still spoken by nearly 100,000 Highlanders and Islanders has a similar explanation. For a long time practically all the literature available to Gaelic speakers in Scotland were translations of seventeenth-century Calvinist divines. The 'strongholds' of the language are the Protestant Churches in the Highlands and Islands with their Gaelic Bible, catechism, metrical psalms (1694), and sermon (CAMPBELL, 25-6, 45-6, 61).

Table 11. The number of persons in Ireland, able to speak the Irish language[a], by county or province (numbers and percentages of total population), at the censuses of 1851 and 1911.

	Numbers		Percentages	
	1851	1911	1851	1911
Co. Antrim	3,050	2,724	1.2	1.4
Belfast C. B.	295	7,595	0.3	2.0
Co. Down	1,153	2,432	0.4	1.2
East Ulster	*4,498*	*12,751*	*0.7*	*1.6*
Londonderry C.B. & Co.	5,406	4,039	2.8	2.9
Co. Tyrone	12,892	7,584	5.0	5.3
Co. Fermanagh	2,704	1,563	2.3	2.5
Co. Armagh	13,736	2,792	7.0	2.3
Northern Border Cos	*34,738*	*15,978*	*4.6*	*3.4*
Co. Donegal	73,258	59,313	28.7	35.2
Co. Cavan	13,027	2,968	7.5	3.3
Co. Monaghan	10,955	5,430	7.7	7.6
Southern Border Cos	*97,240*	*67,711*	*17.0*	*20.4*
Dublin C.B. & Co.	4,707	17,743	1.2	3.7
Rest of Leinster	54,469	22,482	4.3	3.3
Munster	815,785	228,694	43.9	22.1
Connacht	512,849	217,087	50.8	35.5
Rest of Ireland	*1,387,810*	*486,006*	*30.6*	*17.3*
Total Ireland	1,524,286	582,446	23.3	13.3

of Protestants never spoke the language.[b] The fate of Irish was largely sealed when English became in effect the official language of the Roman Catholic Church. As THOMAS O'RAHILLY says: "In the short space of a century and a half at most, the Church, when it might have been the bulwark of the national language (as the Nonconformist churches were in Wales), had, on the linguistic side, definitely turned its back on the Irish tradition".[215] This attitude may have been one of mere indifference.[216] According to MÜLLER-Ross the Church regarded the Irish language as an impediment to its efforts to gain influence in England by way of Ireland.[217] (It must be admitted that today Gaelic – as "a

[a] The totals of Irish speakers include monoglots. In 1851 the number of people in Ireland who spoke Irish only amounted to 319,602 (20.9% of all Irish speakers). In 1911 they numbered only 16,873 (2.9% of all Irish speakers in the island). The corresponding figures for Co. Donegal are 34,882 (47.6%) and 4,733 (8.0%); for the province of Connacht 137,283 (26.7%) and 9,367 (4.3%); for the province of Munster 146,336 (17.9%) and 2,766 (1.2%); and for all other parts of Ireland taken together 1,101 (0.9%) and 7 (0.01%).

[b] Curiously enough, the only regular divine services in Gaelic in present-day Ireland are in the Church of Ireland: every month in Dublin and occasionally in other parts of the Republic. In Dublin cathedral there is an annual service in Irish in memory of the 1916 Rising: at the time, however, the Rising was described by the Protestant archbishop of Dublin as "an awful crime" (*The Ulster Protestant*, July 1959).

guardian of the Faith" – finds many zealous supporters among the clergy and in monastic establishments; here one thinks first of all of the *Christian Brothers* who run hundreds of schools.)

The decay in the Gaelic language was also aided by the use of English by the Nationalist leaders. To an outsider it seems rather paradoxical that throughout the nineteenth century patriotic ideals and Nationalist doctrines were expressed almost invariably in the English language. In other countries, "political nationalism and the native culture were related as theory and practice". In Ireland, "not only were the two not mutually complementary, but the growth of the former was accompanied by a catastrophic decline in the latter".[218] According to CURTIS, "Political agitation had to be in English, for the eyes of Ireland were turned towards Westminster".[219] Perhaps the greatest harm was done by Daniel O'Connell who addressed his 'monster meetings' all over the island in English. In 1835 he declared:

"Although the Irish language is connected with many recollections that twine round the hearts of Irishmen, yet the superior utility of the English tongue, as the medium of all modern communication, is so great that I can witness without a sigh the gradual disuse of the Irish".[220]

In O'Connell's time the language was practically nothing but a vernacular. As DANIEL CORKERY says:

"It was alive in a peasant mind, and nowhere else. And it was these very peasants who most worshipped O'Connell. He was one to be listened to. They must have translated his phrase into: keep Irish from the children. Only too well they did so in the years to come".[221]

The first Nationalist leader to pay lip-service to the cause of the language was Thomas Davis who declared:

"A people without a languge of its own is only half a nation. A nation should guard a language more than its territories – 'tis a surer barrier and more important frontier than fortress and river. .. Nothing can make us believe that it is natural or honourable for the Irish to speak the speech of the alien, the invader, the sassenach [English] tyrant, and to abandon the language of our kings and heroes".[222]

These words are often quoted in the Republic. Davis's ideal, however, was a bilingual nation. Davis who, unlike O'Connell, did not speak Irish himself, is best remembered as the father of Irish patriotic verse in the English language, which replaced the Gaelic songs of the seventeenth and eighteenth centuries. So he, too, fostered the anglicization process.

It was only towards the end of the century that a Gaelic Revival movement began to take shape. Its core was the *Gaelic League*, founded in 1893 with the double object of arresting the decline of the language and of encouraging its use in literature and daily life. Its president was Douglas Hyde, a Protestant scholar and, like Davis, of English descent. He never tired of advocating the necessity for "de-anglicizing Ireland". In 1892 he declared:

"It has always been very curious to me how Irish sentiment .. continues to apparently hate the English, and at the same time continues to imitate them; how it continues to clamour for recognition as a distinct nationality, and at the same time throws away with both hands what would make it so".[223]

The League from the beginning was "essentially a townsmen's organization, centralized in Dublin", and never took real root in the Irish-speaking districts.[224] Unlike the

Gaelic Athletic Association (1884), which became Ireland's biggest sporting organization[a], the Gaelic League never had anything of a popular appeal.[b] The League, however, though not avowedly political at all, became "a hotbed of republicanism". In the League the language movement took on "a character of inspiration and self-sacrificing devotion that was almost religious".[225] The "Irish-Ireland atmosphere" of the League was one of the main sources of inspiration for the leaders of Sinn Féin and the 1916 Rising. According to Padraic Pearse, who was to be president of the Irish Republic of Easter Week, "the Irish Revolution really began in 1893, when the Gaelic League was founded".[226]

THE TERMINATION OF THE CROMWELLIAN SETTLEMENT

There remain for consideration two further processes which have greatly contributed to the shaping of present-day Ireland: the termination of the Cromwellian Settlement, and the consolidation of the Ulster region or nation. Both developments are usually dated in the second half of the century, to be accurate, in its final quarter. I would prefer to say that they culminated in the last decades of the century. Both processes began virtually with the passing of the *Act of Union*. I will deal first with the disposal of the Cromwellian Settlement, that is the deposition of the Ascendancy from their political, social, and economic power.

The Union, instead of completing and stereotyping "the triumph of the Ascendancy"[227], dealt the first great blow to their position. By surrendering their own parliament, the Ascendancy lost their power to defend their privileges in the future.[228] Ever since the advent of O'Connell the ground trembled under their feet. The second blow to the status of the Ascendancy was Catholic Emancipation (1829): at last Irish Catholics were legally, at any rate, on an equal footing with Protestants. But neither Catholic Emancipation nor the other reform acts secured by O'Connell's great agitation struck at the roots of Ascendancy power, *i.e.* their landed property.[c]

It was the biggest social upheaval in modern Ireland, the Great Famine, that seriously reduced the influence of the Protestant landlords as a class by ruining about one-third of them and impoverishing many others. The *Encumbered Estates Court*, created in 1849 for the purpose of selling out insolvent landlords, disposed within eight years of more

---

[a] The G.A.A., founded at a time when "the people were turning almost willingly into little Britons", in order "to turn the steps of the nation back to its own paths" (*The Sunday Press*, Oct. 6, 1957), failed in the urban centres but spread like wildfire into every country parish. Indeed, according to DAVID GREENE, "it was the G.A.A. which may be said to have created the county also as an object of local patriotism, for the shiring of the country had been an act of the English administration and the county boundaries had little more than legal significance until the inter-county matches began to be played" (*Modern Ireland*, 80-1).

[b] It undoubtedly awakened an interest in the language. This was reflected by the introduction of facilities for bi-lingual education in Gaelic-speaking districts. In 1901 Irish was made one of the optional subjects in the school certificate examinations (SHEARMAN, *Ireland*, 130). At the time of the 1911 census the number of pupils in Irish schools receiving instruction in Irish was 166,800 – of whom 165,800 were Roman Catholics.

[c] The 'land question' was never made the object of a crusade by O'Connell. His defenders generously explain this by saying that the land question which really appealed to his imagination and "stirred the depths of his soul", was the ancient expulsion of the Catholic owners of the soil, and their replacement by Protestants, rather than the wrongs of the actual uncongenial land system (cf. POMFRET, 24).

than three thousand estates. To the surprise of the authorities over 90 per cent of the eight thousand purchasers were Irishmen.[229] The land system as such, however, was left unimpaired; the clearance movement had even the effect of consolidating it.

The discontent of the peasantry manifested itself in the *Irish Tenant Right League* (1850), and in various secret societies which assaulted landlords and their agents. These 'agrarian crimes' often took on a religious tinge. But the 'land war' as a whole was not directed specifically against the remaining Protestant landowners but against landlordism in general. As POMFRET points out, the peasants had little reason to rejoice at the disappearance of so many of their old masters as the new landowners managed their estates upon "strictly business principles" and were less indulgent to their tenants than their encumbered predecessors.[230]

It was Gladstone (who had disestablished the Church of the Ascendancy in 1869) who introduced the first of an impressive series of remedial measures by which the greatest excesses of the Irish land system were removed and a completely new system was eventually established. Gladstone was the first British statesman to recognize fully the fundamental differences between the land systems of England, Ulster, and the rest of Ireland. His first "Act to amend the law relating to the occupation and ownership of land in Ireland" (1870) legalized the *Ulster Custom* and practically stopped eviction by the indirect method of making it costly for the landlord. It failed, however, to protect the tenants from increases in rent. His second *Irish Land Act, 1881*, gave the tenant security of tenure at a fair rent.

Both the acts of 1870 and 1881, like the *Irish Church Act, 1869*, contained provisions which enabled tenants to purchase their holdings with government aid. The *Purchase Act, 1885*, for the first time permitted the tenant to borrow the whole of the purchase money for his holding from the state. Acts passed in 1888, 1891 and 1896 further extended the facilities for land purchase. Under the various acts passed from 1870 to 1896 73,800 holdings were transferred. The act of 1903, amended in 1909, greatly induced land purchase transactions by offering the landowner a bonus on the purchase money. By the time of the proclamation of the Free State well over 300,000 peasants had become owners of their holdings. Thus Ireland was made essentially a land of peasant proprietors.[231]

THE APPEASEMENT OF THE ULSTER PRESBYTERIANS

"The six northern counties of Ireland are so very differently circumstanced from the rest, that they very well deserve a separate consideration, if there be really any intentions of restoring the tranquillity of the country". This statement could easily have been taken from an account of the state of affairs in Ireland shortly after the Rising of 1916 and on the eve of the Separation of the Irish Free State from the United Kingdom. It is borrowed, however, from an account of the state of affairs in Ireland shortly after the Rising of 1798 and on the eve of the Union of Great Britain and Ireland. The quotation is from *An Enquiry into the Causes of Popular Discontents in Ireland* by "an Irish Country Gentleman".[a]

What makes "the six northern counties" so different from the rest of Ireland, according to the author of the *Enquiry*, is that they are almost entirely composed of

---

[a] According to the University Library, Edinburgh, the author was W. PARNELL. He was the first to consider the six counties of present-day Northern Ireland as a group.

Presbyterians. He notes that it is not generally understood in England "how formidable the body of Presbyterians is in Ireland", and how active a part they took in the recent rebellion.[a] He dwells at length on their grievances against the government. The fact that they still have to contribute to the payment of the Episcopalian clergy, he says, is "quite sufficient to keep alive the zeal and animosity of a party, and to give it a very pernicious direction in opposition to Government". The author recommends that the government "should not lightly disclaim all compromise with a sect, which is the most enlightened, proud, and in moral force, the most important body of men in Ireland".[232]

The only gesture which the British government thought fit to make towards the Ulster Presbyterians in the wake of the Union (1803) was to augment the *regium donum* (a compensatory annual payment to their ministers), with the obvious intention of 'buying their loyalty'.[233] Meantime the government kept close watch on them, and continued to do so for many years. Gradually, however, it became clear that it was unnecessary as the Presbyterians turned strong supporters of the Union. Whatever their initial opinions might have been, the Ulster Scots soon came to realize that the Union was essential to "the Protestant and the trade interest". The Ulster Presbyterians' attitude reminds us of that of the Scottish Presbyterians towards the Union of 1707, as sketched by WALLACE NOTESTEIN:

"By every rule of logic those who hoped to keep Scotland within the Presbyterian fold had to support the Union. Scotland had 'to drink the potion [of the Union] to prevent greater evils'. .. Both nations needed the Union, England to guard herself against Jacobite plots, Scotland to save herself from even more economic discrimination than she had endured, and to preserve herself as well from the possibility of Catholic rule".[234]

There is little doubt that the Ulster Presbyterians, on the whole, felt the justice of the claim for Catholic Emancipation, however much they seem to have disliked O'Connell's policy of "close alliance with and dependence upon the Roman Catholic clergy".[235] They had nothing to fear from Catholic Emancipation as the Protestant population of the United Kingdom greatly outnumbered the Catholics. But they opposed the idea of Repeal of the Union. The prospect of their being placed again under a Dublin parliament by no means appealed to them – they had never felt great love for a Dublin parliament – the more so as, after Catholic Emancipation, that parliament would be predominantly Roman Catholic. Thus what later was to be termed 'Ulster Unionism' really dates from O'Connell's time.[236]

The rising influence and self-confidence of the Irish Catholics, stirred up by the demand for self-government, not only stiffened the Presbyterians in their 'loyalism' but also made for conciliation with the mass of the northern Episcopalians. (The growing strength of Roman Catholicism was also brought home to Presbyterians and Episcopalians

---

[a] "In England", W. PARNELL states, "all the disturbances in Ireland are referred to the Catholics only, but with very little truth; for had the Presbyterians been allowed to take the lead, it would not only have been called a Presbyterian instead of a Catholic rebellion, but I am afraid would have proved a Presbyterian revolution". According to the same source, the Roman Catholics got the start of the Presbyterians, and hence the failure of the rebellion. "The moment the Catholics acquired force, the Presbyterians took the alarm; the old jealousy and hatred of the Puritans to the Catholics revived in all its force in the breasts of their descendants" (22-3).

alike by the great influx of Catholics into Belfast.[a] Another factor which greatly contributed to the healing of the friction between the descendants of the Scottish and English
colonists was the spread of the 'evangelical movement' from Scotland to Ulster. (In
Scotland 'moderatism' had already been on the decline since the last years of the eighteenth
century.[b]) Evangelicanism produced in both the Presbyterian congregations and Episcopalian parishes what McDowell calls "a more vigorous and earnest Church life and a
stiffening of doctrinal standards".[237]

The gradual disappearance of ill-feeling between the Presbyterians and the Episcopalians in the north was also aided by the deprival of the Episcopalian Church of its
privileged position by the *Tithe Act, 1838* (which eased the burden of the upkeep of the
established clergy), the *Municipal Corporations Act, 1840* (which reformed local government
in a more democratic way), and other measures, culminating in the disestablishment of the
Episcopalian Church by the *Irish Church Act, 1869*. Land Reform, too, contributed to the
appeasement of the Ulster Presbyterians: the great Episcopalian landlords were sacrificed
with as little regret in Ulster as elsewhere.

The more stable and coherent the Protestant Ulster society became, the more it
tended to draw away from the opinions and purposes which dominated the rest of
Ireland.[238] As George O'Brien says, by the time of the introduction of the first Home
Rule Bill in the 'eighties the Ulster Protestants were more united in their desire to maintain
the Union, and more united in voicing that desire, than they had been at any earlier
period.[239]

THE GROWTH OF ULSTER UNIONISM

Earnán de Blaghd (who was a prominent member of the Free State government,
1922-32) in his study on Partition attaches great importance to the fact that during the
nineteenth century the general body of Irish Catholics, while struggling to throw off the
political authority of England, did their utmost to become indistinguishable from
Englishmen in everything except religion. In the circumstances the Protestants were
bound to feel subconsciously – in cases in which they were not consciously convinced –
that Repeal of the Union was being sought solely in the interest of Catholicism.[240] That

---

[a] The enormous expansion of Belfast drew its people from a far wider area than Cos Antrim and Down
where Protestants were in the majority. Newcomers came from all over Ulster and even beyond, from
areas that were predominantly Catholic. In 1800 the Roman Catholics were estimated to number 6%
of the Belfast population; in 1861 they were 34% of a much greater total (*Essays*, 218-20; *Ulster since 1800*,
vol. i, 90, and vol. ii, 96). "The sense of competition and separation", produced by the policy of some
eighteenth-century Episcopalian landlords of introducing Roman Catholic tenants to undercut and
replace Protestant tenants, continued among the nineteenth-century industrial workers on account of
undercutting of wages by Roman Catholic workers (Shearman, *Ireland*, 21, and *Ulster*, 131).

[b] It is well to remember that many of the Ulster Presbyterian ministers, and lawyers, physicians, etc., were
trained in Glasgow and Edinburgh (they were debarred by doctrinal tests from Trinity College, Dublin).
"This close connection with Scotland had considerable influence in the formation of Ulster opinion",
Beckett says; "an influence most readily observable in Protestant theology, but to be seen in other fields
also, as, for example, in literature and education" (*Ulster since 1800*, vol. ii, 20). The influence of the
Scottish universities was even noticeable in the Scottish accent of the professional middle class (cf. G. B.
Adams, 70-1).

Home Rule would mean 'Rome Rule' became for almost all Ulster Protestants an unanswerable indictment.[241]

The ideological gulf between 'Protestant Ulster' and the rest of Ireland was further widened by the spread of the Industrial Revolution from Great Britain into the north-east of Ireland.

"Industrial Ulster was linked to Great Britain by vital material interests which made any idea of repealing the Union, with the chance of customs barriers between the two countries always in the background, anathema to the Ulstermen, while in the South the need for protection from superior British competition assumed in the course of time the dignity of an indisputable axiom".[242]

The interests of the new industrial middle class in Ulster completely fused with those of the British business classes of which it formed an integral part. The working-class movement, too, reflected the integration of industrial Ulster and Great Britain: more than half of the Ulster trade-unionists joined cross-Channel unions. This organic union was not confined to common interests and ideals. As STRAUSS rightly emphasizes, it was, to a large extent, a matter of 'physical identity':

"To all intents and purposes, Belfast forms one corner of an industrial triangle based on Lancashire in England and Lanarkshire in Scotland[a], and an unceasing ebb and flow of workers moving to and from Belfast, the Mersey and the Clyde, was the necessary result of this set-up. The economic interests of the shipyard engineers and linen workers of Belfast were naturally identified with the system of which they formed a part".[243]

The Protestant farmers adhered to Unionism almost without question. They had always been in a privileged position compared with the mass of the southern peasants. This difference, and particularly "their violent hostility to the neighbouring Catholic peasants in south Ulster"[244], made them no less reliable supporters of the Unionist cause than the industrial population.

It seems strange that none of the Irish Nationalist leaders in the nineteenth and early twentieth century appreciated the religious aspect of Ulster Unionism – nor its firm social basis. As its own internal frictions were removed, 'Protestant Ulster' manifested at each Home Rule crisis, in 1886, in 1893, and in 1912, "a spontaneous solidarity, a capacity for self-organisation, and a hard unshakeable resolution" (THOMAS WILSON), which proved that "here was a State in the making". If the Union could be saved for Ireland as a whole, it would be content, but, if not, it would at least save the Union for itself.[245]

In the 'eighties the raising of an army of hundred thousand volunteers had already been planned. But the first Home Rule crisis passed so quickly that there was not enough time to set these plans in motion.[246] Twenty-five years later, however, when Asquith's government announced the third Home Rule Bill, the old plans were executed with great determination and efficiency: on Easter Tuesday, 1912, a hundred thousand *Ulster Volunteers* paraded in Belfast. In September of the same year over 470,000 Ulster people

[a] The school-text view that Belfast is "the industrial capital of Ireland", which is reflected in MÜLLER-Ross's study on the Partition problem (cf. Chapter 2), is a fallacy. Belfast is really "an outpost of industrial Britain" – the sister city of Glasgow and Liverpool rather than of Dublin (E. R. R. GREEN, 37; SHEARMAN, *Ireland*, 76; STRAUSS, 232).

signed the *Ulster Covenant* (a declaration based on the Scottish Covenant of 1643) pledging themselves "to stand by one another in defending for ourselves and our children our cherished position of equal citizenship in the United Kingdom". The next year the formation of a *Provisional Government of Ulster* was publicly announced, its chairman declaring that if Ulster were coerced into submission to a Dublin parliament, it would have to be ruled as a conquered country.

ST. JOHN ERVINE in his biography of Lord Craigavon (Northern Ireland's first prime minister) rightly observes that

"Ulster's opposition to Home Rule was not manufactured, as was often alleged, by men at the top, but sprang spontaneously from the people. .. No one could have originated Ulster's resistance to Home Rule if it had not been broad-based upon the people's will. Whatever critics may say against it, they cannot deny that it was a democratic movement".[247]

As EARNÁN DE BLAGHD puts it in his *Briseadh na Teorann*: "The Unionist movement in the North was as democratic and as earnest as the Nationalist movement in the South". The Ulster Protestants, Presbyterians and Episcopalians alike, rallied almost unanimously to Unionism – but "less than a practically unanimous rally could not have been decisive".[248] Hence, once Separation became a fact, Partition (of one kind or another) was inevitable.

PARTITION

The idea of Partition was first put forward as a suggestion, as "a minor point of argument" (GALLAGHER), by Lord Macaulay in 1833 when replying to Daniel O'Connell's plea for Repeal of the Union. "I defy the honourable and learned member", Lord Macaulay said, "to find a reason for having a parliament at Dublin which will not be just as good for having another parliament in Londonderry". The subject was not seriously referred to again until 1843 when the question of a separate parliament at Belfast was raised anonymously in a Belfast newspaper. The proposal to partition Ireland did not again rise until the 'eighties when Gladstone set out a plan for Home Rule for Ireland. In 1886 Joseph Chamberlain said that he would be glad "if there could be conceded to Ulster a separate assembly". According to GALLAGHER Chamberlain's and contemporaneous Partition proposals were advanced "not as a practical solution but to make any solution impracticable".[249]

When after 1910 self-government for Ireland became again a live issue the suggestion of providing some sort of separate treatment for Ulster, too, was put forward again as a possible compromise to meet the bitter opposition of the Ulster Unionists. In April 1912 Mr Churchill proposed to afford "the characteristically Protestant and Orange counties" the option of a moratorium of several years before acceding to the Irish parliament. He thought of three counties, *viz.* Antrim, Down, and Londonderry. A few months later two young liberals, Agar-Robartes and Neil Primrose, suggested that Co. Armagh, too, should be excluded from the operations of the Home Rule Bill. A later proposal referred to three counties and part of three others. The Ulster Unionists, however, demanded the exclusion of all nine counties of the province of Ulster, which were to continue under the jurisdiction of the Imperial Parliament.[250]

The actual decision to exclude some part of Ulster from the new Irish legislature was taken, very reluctantly, by Asquith's government in March 1914, "as the maximum concession which it was possible to make to the Opposition". The electors of any county in Ulster would be permitted to vote for the exclusion of their own county from the jurisdiction of the new Dublin parliament. But, those counties which might decide in favour of exclusion would remain out for six years only; then the Home Rule Act would come into operation for the whole island.[251]

The Ulster Unionists, and their Conservative allies in England, however, were by no means satisfied with this compromise. They continued sedulously to prepare for armed resistance; in April 1914 they landed a large consignment of rifles and ammunition (the so-called Larne Gunrunning). On the other hand, when the commander-in-chief in Ireland was instructed to strengthen the crown's forces in Ulster (March 1914), there was a mass-refusal by his officers to obey his orders (the so-called Curragh Mutiny). While leading British statesmen and politicians, urged on by threats of civil war, were trying feverishly to achieve a settlement of the Ulster question on the lines of exclusion of some sort, the danger of the outbreak of hostilities in Europe became suddenly immanent after the assassination of the Archduke Franz Ferdinand at Serajewo (June, 28).

On the eve of the First World War King George V, invoked as an arbiter, invited "representatives of parties, British and Irish" to a conference (July, 18). This so-called Buckingham Palace Conference ended abortively (July, 24) when parties concerned were "unable to agree either in principle or detail" upon the area to be excluded from the operations of the new Act. The main stumbling-block was Co. Tyrone which was claimed by both the Irish Nationalists and the Ulster Unionists. If the attempt to reach a settlement by consent had failed completely for the time being, the Buckingham Palace Conference, according to DENIS GWYNN, produced "one extremely important result, by introducing for the first time as a practical suggestion the proposal that only six counties instead of nine should be excluded"[252], *i.e.* the six counties of Northern Ireland.

The outbreak of the European War put an abrupt end to the negotiations. The Home Rule question was shelved until the British government decided to re-open negotiations with the Nationalist and Unionist leaders in 1916, apparently with a view to conciliating (Irish-)American opinion which had been greatly influenced by the execution of the leaders of the Rising of Easter Week. Lloyd George's proposal that the Home Rule Act should be brought into immediate operation subject to the condition that six counties of Ulster would have to be excluded, was accepted by both parties. The negotiations broke down, however, on the question whether the exclusion of the six counties was to be considered merely "a temporary emergency war measure" or a permanent settlement.[253]

Demands for a settlement of the Irish question from America (and the Dominions) continued to haunt the British government. Meantime the influence of John Redmond's Irish Party was declining rapidly, *Sinn Féin* gaining ground from month to month by winning all by-elections. [a] A "Convention of Irishmen of all parties", summoned by Lloyd George (now prime minister) "for the purpose of producing a scheme for Irish

[a] The sudden trend towards extremism in the south of Ireland is well typified by the fact that when Willy Redmond (brother of the leader of the Nationalist Party), who was a volunteer in the British army, was killed in action in Flanders, his seat for East Clare was won by Mr de Valera who had recently been released from prison. The latter had been interned after having taken part in the 1916 Rising (he had escaped execution as he was born in America).

self-government" (May 1917), lost itself in protracted discussions which had "an air of unreality" (GWYNN) as *Sinn Féin* refused to take any part in the proceedings.[254]

In December 1919 Lloyd George offered a new compromise which again was based on a division of Ireland into twenty-six and six counties. In contrast with previous proposals this settlement provided for the establishment of *two* parliaments and governments in Ireland, each having identical, very limited, powers: one in Belfast for 'Northern Ireland' and the other in Dublin for 'Southern Ireland'. Designed to placate the objections of both the Nationalists and Unionists, the new proposal satisfied neither side. It was carried solely by British votes (December 1920)!

In so far as 'Southern Ireland' was concerned, the *Government of Ireland Act, 1920*, was "so ludicrously inadequate" (GWYNN) that it was never even considered seriously[255]: partly because, as NEWARK observes, "Irish nationalism had advanced far beyond the limited degree of Home Rule which might have been acceptable in 1914", and partly because Irish nationalism insisted on "the essential unity of all the island of Ireland". In so far as 'Northern Ireland' was concerned, the act was received with mixed feelings. Though it gave security from the fear of domination by a Dublin parliament, it involved the creation of a Belfast parliament which had never been asked for: the Unionists had always demanded that 'Ulster' should continue to be governed as it had been since the Union of 1801, by the Imperial Government. Added to this, 'Northern Ireland' was not to be the whole province of Ulster (nine counties) but only the six counties where there was the greatest concentration of Unionists.[256] (A separate parliament for the whole province would of course have had a very precarious existence.)

The *Government of Ireland Act, 1920*, is usually referred to by Irish Nationalists as the *Partition Act*. It is true that this act established Partition. It is often overlooked, however, that it contemplated and afforded every facility for union between the two parts of Ireland. It empowered the two Irish parliaments by mutual agreement and joint action to abolish the land boundary and to set up one parliament and government for the whole island.

The political division of Ireland, then, was envisaged and carried through as a temporary expedient. But, however many provisions of the *Government of Ireland Act, 1920*, have been altered, impaired or superseded since its enactment – especially in regard to what soon became known as the Irish Free State – Partition remained. Apart from the study by the *Boundary Commission* (1924-5), there has not even been question of any revision of the land boundary as it was defined in 1920. The Irish land boundary is not the only state frontier in Europe which was designed as a temporary compromise but was destined to have a longer life – merely because the parties concerned were unable to agree on its revision. And, as I see it, the Partition of Ireland in its present form is likely to continue for many years to come.

CONCLUSION PART FOUR

From what has been said above it is apparent that the question why Ireland does not form a political entity cannot be separated from the question why the British Isles no longer form a political entity. In my opinion the main problem is not why the majority of the people of the 'Six Counties' refused to cut through their constitutional links with

Great Britain and throw in their lot with the people of the 'Twenty-Six Counties', but rather why the majority of the people of the 'Thirty-Two Counties' desired to withdraw from the United Kingdom of Great Britain and Ireland. However that may be, the two questions come to virtually the same thing: both Separation and its immediate aftermath Partition ultimately derive from religious cleavages.

Separation and Partition alike bear witness to the vital importance of the religious factor in the shaping and maintenance of the major socio-cultural regional contrasts in the British Isles. In Ireland undoubtedly it is religion which provides the most distinguishing element. The popular idea that Separation and Partition both derive from ethnic contrasts, *i.e.* between the 'Irish' and the 'British' (or rather English and Scottish) peoples, is a fallacy. On the eve of the Reformation there were three 'peoples' in Ireland:

(1)   the 'mere Irish' (Gaels), later sometimes referred to as 'Old Irish';
(2)   the long-settled English colonists in southern Ireland and south-east Ulster, eventually known as 'Old English' as distinct from later English immigrants; and
(3)   the Scottish settlers in north-east Ulster, eventually known as 'Old Scots' as distinct from later Scottish immigrants.

At the Reformation the Old Irish, almost to a man, adhered to the Roman Catholic Church. Practically all the Old English and Old Scots, too, remained Roman Catholics – in contrast with the majority of the English and Scots in Great Britain who became Protestants. It was the religious factor which brought the Old Irish and the Old English – and later also the Old Scots – together into a common resistance against the English (British) crown and against new waves of immigrants from England and Scotland: immigrants who were practically all Protestants. In the pre-Reformation period 'Irish' had meant 'Gaelic'. After the Reformation 'Irish' gradually became identified with 'Roman Catholic' when the Gaels (the 'Old Irish') and the Old English and Scots (or 'New Irish') were welded together as 'Papists' by discrimination and suppression on a politico-religious basis. Thus was formed the modern 'Irish nation.'

The Union of Ireland with Great Britain (1801), if the grievances of the Irish had immediately been removed, might have made the Irish forget the wrongs of the past – as the Scots have forgotten. As it was, the delay of Catholic Emancipation, more than anything else, encouraged the development of Irish Nationalist demands. Thus, Irish nationalism as we know it today is based in the enduring devotion of the pre-Reformation inhabitants of Ireland to the Roman Catholic Church. The break with the pre-Reformation Gaelic past is perhaps most apparent from the fact that Irish nationalism has nearly always expressed itself in the English language. Only for sixty or seventy years have a minority of Irish Nationalists – albeit an influential minority – been alive to the idea of reviving the Gaelic language.

Ulster regionalism or nationalism, too, can be traced back to the seventeenth century. It is rooted in the self-assurance of the seventeenth-century Scottish Presbyterian 'planters' in the former Gaelic kingdom of Ulster and the Anglo-Norman earldom of that name. This colonization was a mass immigration which provided a new middle class and 'proletariat' – in fact, a whole new society – in northern Ireland. A subsidiary result was the introduction of Scottish land tenures contrasting sharply with the 'English colonial' tenures of the rest of Ireland. The spread of the Industrial Revolution since the end of the eighteenth century accentuated the different socio-economic basis of this settlement.

Beginning as an extension of Scotland, political developments in Great Britain, especially the disappearance of Scottish independence, led to the isolation of this compact colony which could no longer call on Scottish sympathy or even military aid (as in 1641). The Ulster Presbyterians had neither the ambition nor the strength to attempt to spread outside of Ulster – ever since the end of the seventeenth century their position has been weakening, numerically (as a result of emigration but also because of the influx of English Episcopalians and Irish Catholics into northern Ireland). No Ulster Scot was ever to occupy any position of authority in the Dublin administration. Indeed, the English government in Dublin was as anxious to check the influence of the Ulster Scots as was the mediaeval English government in Dublin to curb Scottish immigration into Ulster.

But while the pre-Reformation Scottish immigrants were intruders from a foreign state (Scotland) into an English lordship (Ireland), the post-Reformation immigrants were co-citizens of Great Britain. They were, however, of a different religion: they were Presbyterians whereas those in power in Dublin were exclusively Episcopalians (Anglicans). It was primarily on a religious basis that the Ulster Scots were, throughout the greater part of the seventeenth and eighteenth centuries, subjected to various disabilities (except in the reigns of their fellow-Scot, James VI and I, and their 'fellow-Presbyterian', William of Orange). This discrimination by successive Protestant, *i.e.* Episcopalian, governments has greatly contributed to the persistence and the invigoration of Ulster regionalism.

In the course of the nineteenth century, when the Ulster Presbyterians came to enjoy the same civil rights as the other Protestant citizens of the United Kingdom, Ulster regionalism did not die. On the contrary, it was considerably strengthened as a result of the development of Irish Nationalist political demands. The prospect of self-government for Ireland and the fear of Roman Catholic domination even led to a *rapprochement* between the Scottish Presbyterian and English Episcopalian population groups in northern Ireland – a *rapprochement* which the Home Rule crises in the late nineteenth and early twentieth century only served to consolidate. Thus the modern Ulster nation embraces not only the descendants of the post-Reformation Scottish immigrants (with an admixture of some Old Irish and Old Scots who had become Protestants), but also many descendants of the post-Reformation English immigrants.

Apologists of Separation often fall back on pre-Reformation regional divisions of the British Isles, *i.e.* on age-old socio-cultural contrasts between Ireland and Great Britain. Apologists of Partition in their turn sometimes fall back, though less convincingly, on ancient divisions between the north and south of Ireland. Those regional divisions, however, are at best locational, not functional, predecessors of the present state frontier. Both Separation and Partition originate in the desire to preserve, or to accentuate, regional contrasts which are, fundamentally, religious contrasts – and, therefore, are not older than the Reformation (and Counter-Reformation) period. Viewed in this light, both sections of the Irish Border, the sea and the land boundary, are in the last resort religious frontiers.

REFERENCES PART FOUR

1 CURTIS, *History*, 155
2 TREVELYAN, 206
3 BECKETT, 44, 54
4 CURTIS, *History*, 159
5 BECKETT, 68
6 O'FAOLAIN, *Story*, 22
7 Ibid., 22
8 GALLAGHER, 19
9 FALLS, 18
10 WILLIAMSON, 162
11 CURTIS, *History*, 170. Cf. BONN, vol. i, 185-6
12 BECKETT, 50; FALLS, 18
13 BECKETT, 48; CURTIS, *History*, 167-8. Cf. *Documents*, 107-9
14 O'FAOLAIN, *Story*, 22. Cf. BONN, vol. i, 212-7
15 BECKETT, 48-9
16 CURTIS, *History*, 178-9
17 Ibid., 173-4; BECKETT, 49-51
18 BECKETT, 52; CURTIS, *History*, 174-6
19 BECKETT, 59; CURTIS, *History*, 174-7; FREEMAN, *Ireland*, 94-6; TREVELYAN, 265
20 CURTIS, *History*, 176-7
21 BECKETT, 60
22 Cf. CURTIS, *History*, 200
23 Ibid., 182-3
24 BECKETT, 53; FALLS, 19-20
25 BECKETT, 53; CURTIS, *History*, 194. Cf. *Constitution*, 259
26 BECKETT, 53-4; CURTIS, *History*, 203; KENNEY, 28
27 CURTIS, *History*, 184
28 TREVELYAN, 265
29 CURTIS, *History*, 197-8
30 BECKETT, 56, 60-1
31 CURTIS, *History*, 205; HAYES-MCCOY, 121
32 CURTIS, *History*, 206
33 Ibid., 206; BONN, vol. i, 273-4; WOODBURN, 44-5
34 CURTIS, *History*, 209
35 Ibid., 206-7; BECKETT, 63
36 BECKETT, 64
37 CURTIS, *History*, 209
38 Cf. *Documents*, 119-20
39 CURTIS, *History*, 213
40 E.g. *Handbook*, 11
41 CURTIS, *History*, 220
42 E. R. R. GREEN, 20-3; WOODBURN, 54-6
43 HARRISON, 19-21; LYTHE, 67-8; WOODBURN, 76
44 HARRISON, 26-7
45 CAMPBELL & DONNELLY, 11
46 E. R. R. GREEN, 26. Cf. GILL, 164

47 Cf. WARD, 101-2
48 *Ulster under H.R.*, xiii
49 *Documents*, 128-33
50 Cf. *Ulster under H.R.*, xv-xvi
51 CAMBLIN, vii
52 Cf. WOODBURN, 72
53 RICHARD O'BRIEN, 147
54 BECKETT, 71-2; CURTIS, *History*, 231-2; STRAUSS, 19-20
55 HARRISON, 45-6. Cf. RICHARD O'BRIEN, 161-2; STRAUSS, 20; TREVELYAN, 290
56 RICHARD O'BRIEN, 138
57 Ibid., 148
58 Cf. *Handbook*, 11
59 Cf. RICHARD O'BRIEN, 165; WOODBURN, 70
60 WOODBURN, 70-3
61 HARRISON, 52. Cf. WOODBURN, 71
62 *Handbook*, 11
63 LYTHE, 67
64 *Constitution*, 260-1; STRAUSS, 20-1
65 RICHARD O'BRIEN, 162
66 WOODBURN, 26-7
67 *Handbook*, 13
68 LYTHE, 67-8; WOODBURN, 24-5
69 G. B. ADAMS, 69
70 Cf. LYTHE, 67
71 G. B. ADAMS, 69; *Handbook*, 11. Cf. BLAGHD, 100
72 G. B. ADAMS, 68-9
73 MACKENZIE, *Scotland*, 232
74 Cf. ibid., 363
75 Ibid., 333n. Cf. WOODBURN, 76-89
76 Cf. STRAUSS, 21
77 COONAN, 111
78 BARKLEY, 9
79 COONAN, 102; WOODBURN, 104
80 Cf. COONAN, 114; GOOD, 9
81 *Essays*, 124
82 Ibid., 129-31; WOODBURN, 111-3, 128-30
83 HARRISON, 54
84 *History*, vol. ii, 559-60, vol. iii, 14
85 BARKLEY, 6-9; BECKETT, 77-80; WOODBURN, 95-9
86 BARKLEY, 8-9; HARRISON, 60; WOODBURN, 93-4
87 CURTIS, *History*, 288
88 Cf. ibid., 287; DAVEY, 22; WOODBURN, 181-4
89 BECKETT, 107; CURTIS, *History*, 281-2, 287-8
90 Cf. HARRIS, 192
91 *Belfast*, 22; *Ulster under H.R.*, xv. Cf. E. R. R. GREEN, 31
92 Cf. E. R. R. GREEN, 27-8; HUME, *Elements*, 116-8; *Surnames*, passim

[93] GOOD, 20–1; WOODBURN, 172

[94] Cf. MARSHALL, 12–25; WOODBURN, 212–22

[95] CURTIS, *History*, 292; *Ulster since 1800*, vol. i, 12

[96] *Ulster under H.R.*, xvi

[97] Cf. MARSHALL, 10–1; WOODBURN, 179, 213, 216–7

[98] Cf. BARCK & LEFLER, 285; CARGILL GRAHAM, 19; MARSHALL, 24; WERTENBAKER, 22; WOODBURN, 213, 227; WRIGHT, *Cultural Life*, 46, 66–7

[99] CURTIS, *History*, 293; WOODBURN, 228. Cf. WILLIAM ADAMS, 396–7; MARSHALL, 23,56–7

[100] CARGILL GRAHAM, 18–9; MARSHALL, 14–5. Cf. WERTENBAKER, 20; WRIGHT, *Cultural Life*, 65

[101] BARCK & LEFLER, 288; WERTENBAKER, 23; WRIGHT, *Atlantic Frontier*, 218, 274, 304

[102] Cf. CARGILL GRAHAM, 20; MARSHALL, 28–9; TREVELYAN, 361–2; WERTENBAKER, 23–4; WOODBURN, 222–7; WRIGHT, *Cultural Life*, 19, 67–71

[103] COONAN, 152–3. Cf. *Documents*, 148–58

[104] Cf. CARTY, *Ireland 1607–1782*, 59–61

[105] BECKETT, 86

[106] ASHLEY, 92–3

[107] PRENDERGAST, 96

[108] COONAN, 321

[109] SIMMS, 13–4. Cf. PRENDERGAST, xvi, 100

[110] CURTIS, *History*, 252–4; PRENDERGAST, 72

[111] BECKETT, 86–7

[112] TREVELYAN, 266, 305–6; WOODBURN, 126–7. Cf. ASHLEY, 191; *Documents*, 313

[113] BECKETT, 88–91; CURTIS, *History*, 254–8; PRENDERGAST, xvi. Cf. *Documents*, 158–69

[114] PRENDERGAST, vii

[115] BRIAN FITZGERALD, 12–3; HOGAN, 53–4; INGLIS, 11, 20; O'FAOLAIN, *Irish*, 87–8

[116] O'FAOLAIN, *Irish*, 87–8

[117] BECKETT, 98

[118] TREVELYAN, 359–60

[119] BECKETT, 100

[120] Cf. ARMOUR, 36–7; WOODBURN, 171

[121] SIMMS, 160–2

[122] BECKETT, 105; CURTIS, *History*, 277–8

[123] WOODBURN, 177–8

[124] PATRICK ROGERS, 41

[125] KENNEY, 48–9

[126] GEORGE O'BRIEN, *History 18th Century*, 91

[127] Cf. ibid., 24–7, 386–7; PATRICK ROGERS, 20–1; STRAUSS, 21–2

[128] GILL, 24

[129] CONNELL, 25

[130] BECKETT, 114; POMFRET, 19

[131] Cf. RICHARD O'BRIEN, 173–6; POMFRET, 55–6

[132] *Ulster since 1800*, vol. i, 41; *Ulster under H.R.*, xvi

[133] BECKETT, 116–7

[134] E.g. STRAUSS, 22; WOODBURN, 356–7

[135] GILL, 29–30. Cf. BONN, vol. i, 346–7; RICHARD O'BRIEN, 158–67

[136] WOODBURN, 178

[137] CURTIS, *History*, 260–1. Cf. BECKETT, 117

[138] BECKETT, 112; GEORGE O'BRIEN, *History 18th Century*, 182, 387

[139] GEORGE O'BRIEN, *History 18th Century*, 5

[140] Ibid., 181

[141] E.g. O'DONOVAN, 44

[142] BECKETT, 113

[143] Ibid., 113; STRAUSS, 22

[144] GILL, 25–7

[145] Ibid., 16–20; E. R. R. GREEN, 57; STRAUSS, 21

[146] GILL, 102, 135–7

[147] Ibid., 227, 234–6, 318; E. R. R. GREEN, 97, 111; *Ulster since 1800*, vol. i, 30–2

[148] GILL, 175, 181, 183; E. R. R. GREEN, 70–1

[149] PATRICK ROGERS, 2–6

[150] BECKETT, 103–4; CURTIS, *History*, 300–3

[151] STRAUSS, 56

[152] CURTIS, *History*, 326–7

[153] BECKETT, 134

[154] *Ulster since 1800*, vol. i, 12

[155] O'CONNELL, 64

[156] BECKETT, 134; *Ulster since 1800*, vol. i, 15

[157] FITZHENRY, 43

[158] *Ulster since 1800*, vol. i, 16

[159] Cf. ibid., 16–7; CURTIS, *History*, 329, 336–7; SHEARMAN, *Ireland*, 57–9; STRAUSS, 24–5

[160] Cf. MANSERGH, *Government*, 82

[161] BARRINGTON, 383; CURTIS, *History*, 343–5; *Ulster since 1800*, vol. ii, 23–4; WOODBURN, 289–90, 309

[162] BECKETT, 137

[163] Ibid., 147

[164] Ibid., 181

[165] STRAUSS, 67

[166] BECKETT, 138–9

[167] LYNCH & VAIZEY, 20

[168] *Documents*, 229

[169] GEORGE O'BRIEN, *Fields*, 74; O'CONNELL, 120; WOODBURN, 313

[170] GEORGE O'BRIEN, *Fields*, 73–4

[171] STRAUSS, 70–1

[172] Ibid., 118–22

[173] GEORGE O'BRIEN, *Fields*, 14; *Ulster since 1800*, vol. i, 29

[174] GEORGE O'BRIEN, *Fields*, 12

[175] Ibid., 11, 72–3

[176] BECKETT, 150; O'FAOLAIN, *Story*, 36; STRAUSS,72

[177] O'CONNELL, 53

[178] Ibid., i

[179] Cf. CURTIS, *History*, 366; *Essays*, 306

[180] Cf. *The United Irishman*, March 1958

[181] O'CONNELL, 155

[182] Ibid., 152
[183] GEORGE O'BRIEN, *Fields*, 69-70. Cf. BARRINGTON, 382-3
[184] *Famine*, 73
[185] BECKETT, 148, 154; GEORGE O'BRIEN, *Fields*, 77-8
[186] BECKETT, 154
[187] *Féilscríbhinn*, 121. Cf. MANSERGH, *Age*, 56-9
[188] BECKETT, 154-5
[189] O'FAOLAIN, *Story*, 38
[190] BECKETT, 155; *Féilscríbhinn*, 121, 125; PAUL-DUBOIS, 59
[191] O'Connell, 152
[192] BECKETT, 162; CURTIS, *History*, 373; *Essays*, 307
[193] O'HEGARTY, 1, 4
[194] BECKETT, 172, 175
[195] GEORGE O'BRIEN, *Fields*, 14
[196] Cf. LYNCH & VAIZEY, 4, 9-10, 31
[197] E.g. STRAUSS, 64-5, 76
[198] LYNCH & VAIZEY, 31-2
[199] STRAUSS, 231
[200] Cf. GILL, 186; E. R. R. GREEN, 96, 98, 105, 107; PRIESTER, 7
[201] E. R. R. GREEN, 29; SHEARMAN, *Ireland*, 73-4; *Ulster since 1800*, vol. i, 35-7
[202] *Ulster since 1800*, vol. i, 53, 126
[203] E. R. R. GREEN, 54. Cf. CONROY, 5, 358; HOWARTH, 208-13; MURRAY, 54; PRIESTER, 44
[204] FREEMAN, *Pre-Famine Ireland*, 3, 10; *Ulster since 1800*, vol. i, 27
[205] Cf. FREEMAN, *Pre-Famine Ireland*, 11
[206] Cf. CONNELL, 81-2, 133-4, 166-74; LYNCH & VAIZEY, 11; SALAMAN, 189-221
[207] CONNELL, 242
[208] *Famine*, *passim*; SALAMAN, 274, 278
[209] STRAUSS, 87
[210] *Famine*, vii
[211] GEORGE O'BRIEN, *History Union*, 222-3
[212] LYNCH & VAIZEY, 7, 168-9
[213] GOTTMANN, *Europe*, 186
[214] Cf. Ó CUÍV, 20-2
[215] THOMAS O'RAHILLY, *Dialects*, 10-2
[216] Cf. CURTIS, *History*, 371
[217] MÜLLER-ROSS, 49

[218] BREATNACH, 130
[219] CURTIS, *History*, 371-2
[220] O'Connell, 4
[221] CORKERY, 112-3
[222] *The United Irishman*, July 1958
[223] *Documents*, 310-1. Cf. HYDE, vii
[224] *Modern Ireland*, 80
[225] KENNEY, 80. Cf. PAUL-DUBOIS, 383-95
[226] Cf. CORKERY, 127-8; KENNEY, 79; *Modern Ireland*, 80; O'SULLIVAN, 33
[227] *Handbook*, 20
[228] BECKETT, 181
[229] POMFRET, 43-4
[230] Ibid., 45, 25
[231] Cf. *Documents*, 262-9; POMFRET, *passim*
[232] PARNELL, 22, 24
[233] Cf. BLAGHD, 104; CURTIS, *History*, 356; *Famine*, 65
[234] NOTESTEIN, 185
[235] BECKETT, 154; CURTIS, *History*, 360
[236] Cf. *Ulster since 1800*, vol. i, 25; *Ulster under H.R.*, xx, 57
[237] *Ulster since 1800*, vol. i, 23-4, vol. ii, 27
[238] *Ulster under H.R.*, xx
[239] GEORGE O'BRIEN, *Fields*, 70
[240] BLAGHD, 109-14, 126; *The Leader*, Jan. 12, Aug. 3, 1957
[241] *Ulster since 1800*, vol. i, 131
[242] STRAUSS, 231. Cf. SHEARMAN, *Ireland*, 121, *Ulster*, 130-1
[243] STRAUSS, 234
[244] Ibid., 233
[245] *Ulster under H.R.*, xx
[246] D. C. SAVAGE, 203
[247] ERVINE, 187
[248] BLAGHD, 74; *The Leader*, Aug. 3, 1957
[249] GALLAGHER, 57-9
[250] DENIS GWYNN, 41-4, 48-9
[251] Ibid., 39-41; GALLAGHER, 95-6
[252] DENIS GWYNN, 115-34
[253] Cf. ibid., 144-57; GALLAGHER, 110-26
[254] DENIS GWYNN, 159, 164. Cf. GALLAGHER, 128-37
[255] DENIS GWYNN, 185-8
[256] *Ulster under H.R.*, 23

POSTSCRIPT

THE IRISH REPUBLIC DURING THE SECOND WORLD WAR

In 1939 the South of Ireland, alone among the Dominions, exercised the right of neutrality in a War whose call to sacrifice was plain to all the others. Of all reflections cast by British observers on this decision it is certainly one of the mildest that it was anomalous for a people "to enjoy the advantages without having taken up the duties of British citizenship".[1]

The Republic's neutrality is often taken to prove how much the (Southern) Irish and the British have become estranged from one another. An analysis of present-day Anglo-Irish relations does not, I believe, bear out this conclusion. The War years, too, demonstrate how many are the ties by which the South of Ireland is linked to the rest of the British Isles, or at least to Great Britain. Here I do not even think of the fact that all through the War the Republic recognized King George VI as "the external Head of the Irish State" [a] – a link which involved the Republic and the United Kingdom alike in all sorts of paradoxes and absurdities.[b] As I see it, a brief analysis of the position of the Republic during the War brings out very clearly some of the main theses which this study maintains.

According to M. J. MacManus (a Nationalist author) in his biography of Mr de Valera, when the War broke out there was never any doubt as to the attitude (Southern) Ireland would adopt: "The whole of its history, ancient and modern, weighed the scales down crushingly on the side of neutrality." De Valera had paved the way that made neutrality possible; now he had merely "to interpret the people's will".[2]

There are different versions of Mr de Valera's motives. Mr Gray (the American ambassador in Dublin during the War) holds that Mr de Valera believed that the Axis would win the War and that, in payment for keeping the Allies out of the Southern Irish ports, he would obtain Northern Ireland on his own terms. "This would have enabled him to invoke his formula of 'exchange of populations', expel 800,000 Ulstermen, and invite in an equal number of 'exiles'". When it became clear that he had backed the loser he advanced the proposition that he could not in conscience help the Allies while "the crime of Partition" lasted, that is "while Britain prevented the North from joining Eire".[3]

Mr de Valera himself stated (Detroit 1948): "You cannot ask a small nation to fight for you for justice when you are inflicting an injustice on that small nation". As his

---

[a] The so-called 'external association' of the Republic with the British crown was by no means a vestige of British colonial rule. Mr de Valera had abolished all these vestiges but had, of set policy, retained this arrangement as "the final solution" for Anglo-Irish political relations. He had thought it out long since, before 1921, and held unwaveringly to it. It was his opponents who abolished it in 1948.

[b] The German minister in Dublin, who remained on his post till the bitter end (like the Japanese consul), was accredited to King George. When, at the height of the War, the post of minister to Germany became vacant Mr de Valera appointed a new representative. The German government, however, would not accept the new minister without the usual letters of credence. As the latter still had to be signed by the British king, and George VI hardly could be expected to accredit a minister to a power with which he was at war, the Irish legation in Berlin was left in charge of a *chargé d'affaires* (a Protestant). The legation premises were demolished by an R.A.F. bomb in 1943 (Smyllie, 319).

biographer put it: Partition was "the rock on which, to the great majority of Irishmen, Britain's claim to be fighting the battle of democracy breaks".[4] R. M. SMYLLIE (a Southern Protestant and editor of *The Irish Times*) was perhaps nearest the truth when he wrote that Mr de Valera wanted to be able

"to prove the world at large that, after more than seven hundred years of subjection to England, the twenty-six counties of Southern Ireland at last were really free. What better proof of national independence could there be than the fact that, while Great Britain was fighting for her very life, Mr de Valera and his three million Irish citizens could remain at peace on England's doorstep?"[5]

Whatever his reasons may have been, all through the War Mr de Valera stuck to his declaration of neutrality. When the first American troops landed in Belfast (January 1942) he sent formal protests against "the occupation of Irish soil by United States troops" to the American minister in Dublin – as did the head of the Irish hierarchy.[6] Even at the end he was careful to observe the very niceties of protocol in formally presenting the condolences of his government to the government of the Third Reich on the death of the Head of State, Herr Hitler.[7]

The neutrality of the Republic was respected by both sides. It seems that the Germans toyed rather seriously with plans for an invasion of Ireland.[8] The real danger to the Republic's neutrality came not from the Germans but from the British – and eventually the Americans.[9] As in the First World War the Allied cause turned upon the security of the Atlantic sealanes. But the Admiralty rights at Cork, Berehaven and Lough Swilly, retained under the Treaty provisions, had been transferred to the Republic by Mr Chamberlain's government in 1938. The elimination of these ports presented the Allies with great difficulties. As BRINTON says, "the price in lives of Allied seamen we have paid for the neutrality of Eire can never be calculated".[10]

In these circumstances the Northern Irish ports and air bases came to be vital – not only in defensive operations covering the 'north-western approaches' to Great Britain but also in all manner of offensive preparations.[a] As General Eisenhower has testified (Belfast 1945), without Northern Ireland he did not see how the American forces could have been concentrated to begin the invasion of the continent.[11] Mr Churchill has left no doubt that, without "the loyalty of Northern Ireland", the British should have been forced to come to close quarters with the Dublin government.[12] Thus it may be argued that Partition saved the Republic's neutrality.[13]

There are many people in the South who maintain that the Republic's neutrality was a facade. There is no doubt that, as SMYLLIE says, "with the insignificant exception of a small minority of irreconcilables" the people of Southern Ireland were wholeheartedly on the side of the Allies. The same held good for most members of the government, including – however strange it may seem to outsiders – Mr de Valera. Even among those "who for historical or political reasons always had made at least a show of anti-

---

[a] The chief functions of the Southern ports came to be combined in Londonderry C.B. This Border town rose to be the largest escort base in the United Kingdom. Larne (Co. Antrim) grew into an important trawler base for mine-sweeping and anti-submarine operations. Outside Belfast Lough great convoys assembled and dispersed. Vast aerodromes were constructed throughout the North, and an immense seaplane base for transatlantic air traffic was built near Enniskillen (Co. Fermanagh) on Lough Erne (BLAKE, 45-6).

British feeling", there was a fairly strong dislike of the nazis. The only Irishmen who, because of their inveterate hatred of England, were inclined to be actively and ostentatiously pro-German, were the extreme Republicans.[14] (Long before the War there was a link between the *Abwehr* and the I.R.A.[a])

SMYLLIE characterizes Mr de Valera's policy as "a brave and at times even an aggressive show of neutrality".[15] It certainly was no farce in so far as the Allies – and the Germans – were prevented from using the territory of the Republic for military bases. On the other hand, Mr de Valera did not follow the example of other neutral countries by passing a Foreign Enlistment Act, making it an offense, punishable by loss of all civil rights, to join the fighting services of any of the belligerent powers.

All through the War citizens of the Republic were completely free to join the British forces. The volunteers from the South have been reckoned at 180,000 – a number which, as SMYLLIE notes, "provides almost a complete answer to those who have been holding Eire up as a hate-ridden nation, eager for Britain's humiliation and defeat".[16] After the War it was stated in the Dublin parliament that about four thousand members of the Irish army, or almost exactly 10 per cent of the total force, had deserted during the War to join the British army.[b]

It was not only by her contribution to the British forces that the Republic helped the Allied War effort. According to official figures 183,200 people from the Republic took jobs in Great Britain and Northern Ireland between 1940 and 1945. And every available ounce of foodstuffs, particularly in the shape of livestock, was sent across the Irish Sea.[17] The Southern weather stations continued to supply the British with all their informotion. British and American aircraft which landed in the South were returned, as were also the pilots[18] (German pilots were interned). On the other hand, the forces of the Republic were armed by the British.[19] Recently it has come to light that there was a secret liaison between the high commands of North and South.[20] The police forces of North and South always co-operated closely to keep the I.R.A. under control.[c]

In conclusion it may be said that – contrary to popular belief in the English-speaking

---

[a] Ever since the First World War it had been an axiom of the German Secret Service that "the key to all sabotage and espionage operations in England is to be found in Ireland". There undoubtedly was a certain amount of espionage on behalf of the Germans, particularly in the early years of the War, but it seems never to have got very far. According to an *Abwehr* chief, "every undertaking we attempted proved abortive". All the I.R.A. people were interested in was "guns to fight the English" – on their own account and for their own interest only. It has been suggested that the 'Teutonic' and 'Celtic' characters were too unlike to ever permit any real understanding (ABSHAGEN, 275-8; SMYLLIE, 325; WIGHTON & PEIS, 38, 67).

[b] These deserters, having received a fairly thorough training (on British principles) in the Republic, were particularly welcome in the British forces, many of them becoming commissioned officers in a very short time. When one of them was arrested and tried on a charge of desertion on his return to Dublin after V-E Day it was argued by his lawyer in open court that the man could not be guilty of desertion in the military sense of the word, because desertion meant running away from danger to a place of safety, whereas in his case precisely the opposite procedure had been adopted. The 'deserters' were excluded from government jobs and relief schemes – if they chose to return to the South (SMYLLIE, 321).

[c] All through the War, and especially up to March 1943, there was "a limited measure of scattered and partially co-ordinated I.R.A. activity" in Northern Ireland, consisting of bomb attacks and of occasional raids on banks for money and on police barracks and military units for arms and ammunition. In 1939 the I.R.A. was rather active in England (BLAKE, 82; CARSON, 23; *War*, 235-6). They are also held responsible for the sabotage in New York harbour of the great French liner *Normandie* when the ship was about to be converted into a troop transport (WIGHTON and PEIS, 54).

world – the neutrality of the Republic was operated in favour of the United Kingdom, or in CYRIL FALLS's words: "Eire behaved generally as a benevolent and friendly neutral".[21] The Republic was not the only neutral to operate her neutrality in favour of one belligerent or other. But she certainly made more dramatic noises than other neutrals to display her neutrality. Even so long after, the condolences for Hitler seem rather extravagant. In fact, this incident does not run counter to, but is essentially in line with, Dublin policy since 1922. This policy can perhaps best be characterized as: the principle of formal independence emphasized, with a shrewd eye to the realities of the social and economic unity of the British Isles.

REFERENCES POSTSCRIPT

[1] WILLIAMSON, History, vol. ii, 348

[2] MACMANUS, 330

[3] CARSON, v

[4] MACMANUS, 374, 353

[5] SMYLLIE, 317. Cf. Foreign Relations, 755; War, 237-8, 253-4

[6] BLAKE, 271; CARSON, 49. Cf. Foreign Relations, 755-63

[7] MACMANUS, 357-8; War, 252

[8] BLAKE, 154-5; War, 243-4

[9] BRINTON, 117

[10] Ibid., 117

[11] CARSON, viii

[12] CHURCHILL, 667

[13] SHEARMAN, Developments, 158

[14] SMYLLIE, 319-20; 322-3. Cf. War, 242

[15] SMYLLIE, 322

[16] Ibid., 319-20. Cf. War, 248n

[17] SMYLLIE, 321-2; War, 248n

[18] Foreign Relations, 755, 767-76

[19] Cf. ibid., 756, 760

[20] Ibid., 760, 762-3

[21] Ulster under H.R., 82

BIBLIOGRAPHY

ABSHAGEN, KARL HEINZ, *Canaris: Patriot und Weltbürger*. Union Deutsche Verlagsgesellschaft, Stuttgart 1949

ADAMS, G. B., *The Emergence of Ulster as a Distinct Dialect Area*. In: *Ulster Folklife* (Belfast) IV (1958), 61-73

ADAMS, WILLIAM FORBES, *Ireland and Irish Emigration to the New World from 1815 to the Famine*. Yale University Press 1932

ANDREWS, J. H., *The 'Morning Post' Line*. In: *Irish Geography* (Dublin) IV (1960), 99-106

Appraisal of Ireland's Industrial Potentials, An. I.B.E.C. Technical Services Corporation, New York 1952

ARCHER, ELSIE M. D., *The Port of Newry*. Diss. B. A. (Hon.), The Queen's University of Belfast 1955

ARMOUR, W. S., *Ulster, Ireland, Britain: A Forgotten Trust*. Duckworth, London 1938

ASHLEY, MAURICE, *England in the Seventeenth Century*. Pelican Books A 268, 1958 (3d ed.)

Aspects of International Relations, Geographic. Ed. by CHARLES C. COLBY. University of Chicago Press 1938

BARCK, OSCAR THEODORE, and HUGH TALMAGE LEFLER, *Colonial America*. MacMillan, New York 1958

BARKER, ERNEST, *Ireland in the Last Fifty Years: 1866-1916*. Clarendon Press, Oxford 1917

BARKLEY, JOHN M., *A Short History of the Presbyterian Church in Ireland*. Church House, Belfast 1959

BARRINGTON, DONAL, *Uniting Ireland*. In: *Studies* (Dublin) XLVI (1957), 379-402

BARROW, G. W. S., *Feudal Britain: The Completion of the Medieval Kingdoms, 1066-1314*. Arnold, London 1956

BECKETT, J. C., *A Short History of Ireland*. Hutchinson, London 1958 (2nd ed.)

Belfast in its Regional Setting: A Scientific Survey. Ed. by E. ESTYN EVANS, R. A. R. GRESSON, R. H. SEMPLE and EMRYS JONES. Publ. for the British Association for the Advancement of Science by the Local Executive Committee, Belfast 1952

BINCHY, D. A., *The Background of Early Irish Literature*. In: *Studia Hibernica* (Dublin) I (1961), 7-18

BLAGHD, EARNÁN DE, *Briseadh na Teorann*. Sairséal & Dill, Dublin 1955

BLAKE, JOHN W., *Northern Ireland in the Second World War*. H.M.S.O., Belfast 1956

BLANCHARD, JEAN, *Le Droit Ecclésiastique contemporain d'Irlande*. Thèse Université de Paris. Pichon & Durand-Auzias, Paris 1958

BLANSHARD, PAUL, *The Irish and Catholic Power: An American Interpretation*. Verschoyle, London 1954

BLOOMFIELD, W. A., *The Kingdom of Mourne*. Thesis Mod., Trinity College, Dublin 1953

BOGGS, S. WHITTEMORE, *International Boundaries: A Study of Boundary Functions and Problems*. Columbia University Press 1940

BONN, MORITZ JULIUS, *Die englische Kolonisation in Irland* (2 vols). Cotta, Stuttgart-Berlin 1906

Border must be, Why the. Northern Ireland Government, Belfast 1956

Boundary, The Ulster. In: *Foreign Affairs* II (1923), 328-329

BOWEN, E. G., *The Settlements of the Celtic Saints in Wales*. University of Wales Press 1954

BOWMAN, ISAIAH, *The New World: Problems in Political Geography*. Harrap, London 1926 (rev. ed.)

BREATNACH, R. A., *Revival or Survival? An Examination of the Irish Language Policy of the State*. In: *Studies* (Dublin) XLV (1956), 129-145

BRINTON, CRANE, *The United States and Britain*. Harvard University Press 1945

BROGAN, D. W., *The English People: Impressions and Observations*. Hamilton, London 1946 (2nd ed.)

BRØNDSTED, JOHANNES, *The Vikings: An Illustrated History of the Vikings, Their Voyages, Battles, Customs, and Decorative Arts*. Pelican Books A 459, 1960

BROOKFIELD, H. C., *Ireland and the Atlantic Ferry: A Study in Changing Geographical Values*. In: *Irish Geography* (Dublin) III (1955), 69-78

BUCHAN, JOHN, *Montrose*. Nelson, London 1950 (8th ed.)

BUCHANAN, RONALD HULL, *Isle Lecale: Some Aspects of its Personality*. Diss. B. A. (Hon.), The Queen's University of Belfast 1953

—, *Stapple Thatch*. In: *Ulster Folklife* (Belfast) III (1957), 19-28

—, *The Barony of Lecale (Co. Down): A Study of Regional Personality*. Thesis D. Ph., The Queen's University of Belfast 1958

CAMBLIN, GILBERT, *The Town in Ulster*. Mullan, Belfast 1951

CAMPBELL, EILA M. J., and U. DONNELLY, *Peasant Life in the Glens of Antrim*. In: *Economic Geography* (Clark University) XXIII (1947), 10-14

CAMPBELL, JOHN LORNE, *Gaelic in Scottish Education and Life: Past, Present and Future.* Johnston, Edinburgh 1950

CARNEY, JAMES, *Studies in Irish Literature and History.* Dublin Institute for Advanced Studies 1955

CARSON, WILLIAM A., *Ulster and the Irish Republic.* Cleland, Belfast 1957

CARTY, JAMES, *Ireland from the Flight of the Earls to Grattan's Parliament, 1607-1782.* Fallon, Dublin 1949

—, *Ireland from Grattan's Parliament to the Great Famine, 1783-1850.* Fallon, Dublin 1949

—, *Ireland from the Great Famine to the Treaty, 1851-1921.* Fallon, Dublin 1951

CHADWICK, H. M., *Early Scotland: The Picts, the Scots, and the Welsh of Southern Scotland.* Cambridge University Press 1949

CHARLESWORTH, J. K., *The Geology of Ireland: An Introduction.* Oliver & Boyd, Edinburgh 1953

CHART, D. A., *The Story of Dublin,* Dent, London 1932

CHATTERTON-HILL, G., *Irland und seine Bedeutung für Europa.* Curtius, Berlin 1916

CHURCHILL, WINSTON S., *The Second World War, VI: Triumph and Tragedy.* Cassell, London 1954

CLARKSON, J. DUNSMORE, *Labour and Nationalism in Ireland.* Columbia University Press 1925

COLE, GRENVILLE A. J., *Ireland the Outpost.* Oxford University Press 1919

COLLINGWOOD, R. G., and J. N. L. MYRES, *Roman Britain and the English Settlements.* Clarendon Press, Oxford 1956 (2nd ed.)

COLUM, PADRAIC, *Arthur Griffith.* Browne & Nolan, Dublin 1959

CONNELL, K. H., *The Population of Ireland, 1750-1845.* Clarendon Press, Oxford 1950

CONROY, J. C., *A History of Railways in Ireland.* Longmans, London 1928

Constitution, The New Irish: An Exposition and Some Arguments. Ed. by J. H. MORGAN. Hodder & Stoughton, London 1912

COONAN, THOMAS L., *The Irish Catholic Confederacy and the Puritan Revolution.* Columbia University Press 1954

CORKERY, DANIEL, *The Fortunes of the Irish Language.* Irish Life and Culture IX. Cultural Relations Committee, Dublin 1954

CORR, T. J., *An Historical and Geographical Account of Newry.* Diss. B.A. (Hon.), The Queen's University of Belfast 1945

COUPLAND, REGINALD, *Welsh and Scottish Nationalism.* Collins, London 1954

CRONE, JOHN S., *A Concise Dictionary of Irish Biography.* Talbot Press, Dublin 1928

CURRAN, FRANK, *Ireland's Fascist City.* Derry Journal, Londonderry 1946

CURTIS, EDMUND, *The Mediaeval Earldom of Ulster, 1333-1603.* In: *Proceedings and Reports of the Belfast Natural History and Philosophical Society* 1930-31, 67-80

—, *A History of Mediaeval Ireland from 1110 to 1513.* Talbot Press, Dublin 1938 (2nd ed.)

—, *A History of Ireland.* Methuen, London 1945 (5th ed.)

DAVEY, J. ERNEST, *The Story of a Hundred Years, 1840-1940: An Account of the Irish Presbyterian Church from the Formation of the General Assembly to the Present Time.* Baird, Belfast 1940

DAVIES, O., *The Archaeology of Ulster.* Repr. from: The Ulster Journal of Archaeology. Graham & Heslip, Belfast 1949

—, *The Black Pig's Dyke.* In: *The Ulster Journal of Archaeology* (Belfast) XVIII (1955), 29-36

DEMANGEON, ALBERT, *The British Isles.* Heinemann, London 1949 (2nd ed.)

DEWAR, M. W., *Why Orangeism?* Grand Orange Lodge of Ireland, Belfast 1958

—, *Protestant Portraits: A 'Brave Thirteen'.* Broadacre, Bradford 1960

DICKINSON, ROBERT E., *The German Lebensraum.* Penguin Books 1943

DOBBS, MARGARET E., *The Dál Fiatach.* In: *The Ulster Journal of Archaeology* (Belfast) VIII (1945), 66-79

Documents, Irish Historical. Ed. by EDMUND CURTIS and R. B. McDOWELL. Methuen, London 1943

DÖRRIES, HANS, *Die Britischen Inseln.* In: *Handbuch der Geographischen Wissenschaft;* West- und Nordeuropa in Natur, Kultur und Wirtschaft. Athenaion, Potsdam 1934

DOYLE, LYNN. *The Spirit of Ireland.* Batsford, London 1939 (3d ed.)

DUIJKER, H. C. J., and N. H. FRIJDA, *National Character and National Stereotypes.* North-Holland, Amsterdam 1960

EGGERS, ANNA, *Die Urkunde Papst Hadrians IV. für König Heinrich II. von England über die Besetzung Irlands.* Ebering, Berlin 1922

EMERY, F. V., *Irish Geography in the Seventeenth Century*. In: *Irish Geography* (Dublin) III (1958), 263-276
ERVINE, ST. JOHN, *Craigavon: Ulsterman*. Allen & Unwin, London 1949
Essays in British and Irish History in Honour of James Eadie Todd. Ed. by H. A. CRONNE, T. W. MOODY and D. B. QUINN. Muller, London 1949
EVANS, E. ESTYN, *The Site of Belfast*. In: *Geography* (London) XXII (1937), 169-177
—, *Portrait of Northern Ireland*. Collins, London 1951
—, *Irish Folk Ways*. Routledge & Kegan Paul, London 1957
—, *Irish Heritage: The Landscape, the People and Their Work*. Dundalgan Press, Dundalk 1958 (7th ed.)

FALLS, CYRIL, *Elizabeth's Irish Wars*. Methuen, London 1950
Famine, The Great: Studies in Irish History, 1845-52. Ed. by R. DUDLEY EDWARDS and T. DESMOND WILLIAMS. Browne & Nolan, Dublin 1956
FARR, SIDNEY, *A Regional Survey of the Carlingford Peninsula*. Diss. B.A. (Hon.), The Queen's University of Belfast 1950
FAWCETT, C. B., *Frontiers: A Study in Political Geography*. Clarendon Press, Oxford 1918
Féilscríblinn Torna. Tráchtaisí léanta in onóir don Ollamh Tadhg Ua Donnchadha. Ed. by SÉAMUS PENDER. University Press, Cork 1947
FELS, EDWIN, *Irland, die grüne Insel: Länderkundliche Skizze*. In: *Zeitschrift für Erdkunde* (Frankfurt a. M.) IV (1936), 481-497
FENNELL, DESMOND, *The Northern Catholic: An Inquiry*. Mount Sales Press, Blackrock (Co. Dublin) 1958
FINLAY, IAN, *Scotland*. Chatto & Windus, London 1957
FITZGERALD, BRIAN, *The Anglo-Irish: Three Representative Types, 1602-1745*. Staples Press, London 1952
FITZGERALD, WALTER, *The Historical Geography of Ireland*. The Geographical Teacher, Suppl. 1. Philip, London 1925
—, *The New Europe: An Introduction to its Political Geography*. Methuen, London 1946 (2nd ed.)
FITZHENRY, EDNA C., *Henry Joy McCracken*. Talbot Press, Dublin 1936
FLATRÈS, PIERRE, *Géographie rurale de quatre contrées Celtiques: Irlande, Galles, Cornwall et Man*. Plihon, Rennes 1957
FLOWER, ROBIN, *The Irish Tradition*. Clarendon Press, Oxford 1947
Foreign Relations of the United States. Diplomatic Papers 1942, vol. i. United States Government Printing Office, Washington 1960
FOX, CYRIL, *The Boundary Line of Cymru*. In: *Proceedings of the British Academy* XXVI, 1-28
—, *The Personality of Britain: Its Influence on Inhabitant and Invader in Prehistoric and Early Historic Times*. National Museum of Wales, Cardiff 1959 (4th ed.)
FREEMAN, T. W., *Pre-Famine Ireland: A Study in Historical Geography*. Manchester University Press 1957
—, *Ireland: A General and Regional Geography*. Methuen, London 1960 (2nd ed.)
Frontiers of the Future. Lectures delivered under the Auspices of the Committee on International Relations. University of California Press 1941

GALLAGHER, FRANK, *The Indivisible Island· The History of the Partition of Ireland*. Gollancz, London 1957
GIDEL, GILBERT, *La mer territoriale et le zone contiguë*. In: *Recueil des Cours, Académie de Droit International* (Paris) XLVIII (1934), 133-278
GILFILLAN, S. COLUMB, *European Political Boundaries*. In: *Political Science Quarterly* (Columbia University) XXXIX (1924), 458-484
GILL, CONRAD, *The Rise of the Irish Linen Industry*. Clarendon Press, Oxford 1925
Glasgow Region, The: A General Survey. Ed. By RONALD MILLER and JOY TIVY. Publ. for the British Association by the Local Executive Committee, Glasgow 1958
GOAD, HAROLD, *Language in History*. Pelican Books A 416, 1958
GOBLET, Y. M., *La transformation de la géographie politique de l'Irlande au xviie siècle dans les cartes et essais anthropogéographiques de Sir William Petty* (2 vols). Berger-Levrault, Paris 1930
GOEDHEER, ALBERTUS JOHANNES, *Irish and Norse Traditions about the Battle of Clontarf*. Diss. Utrecht. Tjeenk Willink, Haarlem 1938
GOOD, JAMES WINDER, *Ulster and Ireland*. Maunsel, Dublin 1919
GOTTMANN, JEAN, *Geography and International Relations*. In: *World Politics* (Princeton University) III (1951), 153-173

—, *La politique des états et leur géographie*. Colin, Paris 1952

—, *A Geography of Europe*. Holt, New York 1961

GOUGAUD, LOUIS, *Christianity in Celtic Lands: A History of the Churches of the Celts, their Origin, their Development, Influence, and Mutual Relations*. Sheed & Ward, London 1932

GRAHAM, IAN CHARLES CARGILL, *Colonists from Scotland: Emigration to North America, 1707-1783*. Cornell University Press, Ithaca N.Y. 1956

GRAHAM, JOHN M., *A Study of Drumlins, and their Influence on Settlement and Farming in Northern Ireland*. Diss. B.A. (Hon.), The Queen's University of Belfast 1951

GREEN, ALICE STOPFORD, *History of the Irish State to 1014*. Macmilland, London 1925

GREEN, E. R. R., *The Lagan Valley, 1800-50: A Local History of the Industrial Revolution*. Studies in Irish History III. Faber & Faber, London 1949

GRIFFITH, WYN, *The Welsh*. Pelican Books A 215, 1950

GRUBBE, PETER, *Jenseits der Grenze*. In: *Merian* (Hamburg) XII (1959), 15-18

GWYNN, AUBREY, *Ireland and the Continent in the Eleventh Century*. In: *Irish Historical Studies* (Dublin) VIII (1953), 193-216

GWYNN, DENIS, *The History of Partition, 1912-1925*. Browne & Nolan, Dublin 1950

Handbook of the Ulster Question. Issued by the North Eastern Boundary Bureau. Stationery Office, Dublin 1923

HARRIS, ROSEMARY LOIS, *Social Relations and Attitudes in a Northern Irish Rural Area*. Diss. M.A., University of London 1954

HARRISON, JOHN, *The Scot in Ulster: Sketch of the History of the Scottish Population in Ulster*. Blackwood, Edinburgh 1888

HARVEY, JOHN, *Dublin: A Study in Environment*. Batsford, London 1949

HAWKES, JACQUETTA and CHRISTOPHER, *Prehistoric Britain*. Chatto & Windus, London 1947

HAYES-McCOY, GERARD A., *Scots Mercenary Forces in Ireland, 1565-1603*. Oates & Washbourne, Dublin 1937

HENDERSON, GEORGE, *The Norse Influence on Celtic Scotland*. Maclehose, Glasgow 1910

Historical Geography of England before A.D. 1800, An. Ed. by H. C. DARBY. Cambridge University Press 1951 (4th ed.)

History of the Church of Ireland from the Earliest Times to the Present Day (3 vols.). Ed. by WALTER EDISON PHILLIPS. Oxford University Press 1933-34

HOGAN, JEREMIAH J., *The English Language in Ireland*. The Educational Company of Ireland, Dublin 1927

HOWARTH, O. J. R., *A Geography of Ireland*. Clarendon Press, Oxford 1911

HUME, A., *Surnames in the County of Antrim*. In: *The Ulster Journal of Archaeology* (Belfast) V (1857), 323-335

—, *The Elements of Population in Down and An'rim*. In: *The Ulster Journal of Archaeology* (Belfast) VII (1859), 116-130

HYDE, DOUGLAS, *A Literary History of Ireland from Earliest Times to the Present Day*. Fisher Unwin, London 1899

INGLIS, BRIAN, *The Story of Ireland*. Faber & Faber, London 1956

Ireland: An Introduction to her History, Institutions, Resources and Culture. Department of External Affairs, Dublin 1950

IRWIN, GEORGE S., *Enniskillen: A Study of the Development of an Ulster Market Town*. Diss. B.A. (Hon.), The Queen's University of Belfast 1953

JACKSON, KENNETH, *Common Gaelic: The Evolution of the Goedelic Languages*. In: *Proceedings of the British Academy* XXXVIII, 71-97

—, *Language and History in Early Britain: A Chronological Survey of the Brittonic Languages, First to Twelfth Century A.D*. University Press, Edinburgh 1953

JONES, EMRYS, *Problems of Partition and Segregation in Northern Ireland*. In: *The Journal of Conflict Resolution* (Chicago) IV (1960), 96-105

—, *A Social Geography of Belfast*. Oxford University Press 1960

JONES, J. MERVYN, *British Nationality Law*. Clarendon Press, Oxford 1956 (rev. ed.)

KEDOURIE, ELIE, *Nationalism*. Hutchinson, London 1960

KENNEY, JAMES F., *The Sources for the Early History of Ireland: An Introduction and Guide, I: Ecclesiastical*. Columbia University Press 1929

KERMACK, W. R., *The Scottish Highlands: A Short History, c. 300-1746*. Johnston & Bacon, Edinburgh 1957.

KNOX, S. J., *Ireland's Debt to the Huguenots*. A.P.C.K., Dublin 1959

KRISTOF, LADIS K. D., *The Nature of Frontiers and Boundaries*. In: *Annals of the Association of American Geographers* IL (1959), 269-282

LEMASS, SEÁN, *One Nation*. Fianna Fáil, Dublin 1959

LINTON, ANNE E., *Ballyconnell and Derrylin: The Effect of the Border on their Functional Areas*. Diss. B.Sc. (Hon.), The Queen's University of Belfast 1957

LLOYD, JOHN EDWARD, *A History of Wales from the Earliest Times to the Edwardian Conquest* (2 vols). Longmans, London 1948 (3d ed.)

LOGAN, J., *Ulster in the X-Rays*. Stockwell, London [c. 1925] (2nd ed.)

LYNCH, PATRICK, and JOHN VAIZEY, *Guiness's Brewery in the Irish Economy, 1759-1876*. Cambridge University Press 1960

LYTHE, S. G. E., *The Economy of Scotland in its European Setting, 1550-1625*. Oliver & Boyd, Edinburgh 1960

MACALISTER, R. A. S., *Tara: A Pagan Sanctuary of Ancient Ireland*. Scribner, New York 1931

—, *The Archaeology of Ireland*. Methuen, London 1949 (2nd ed.)

MACBRIDE, SEÁN, *Our People, Our Money*. Browne & Nolan, Dublin 1949

McCARTHY, MICHAEL F., *Five Years in Ireland, 1895-1900*. Hodges & Figgis, Dublin 1901

McCRACKEN, EILEEN, *The Woodlands of Ireland circa 1600*. In: *Irish Historical Studies* (Dublin) XVI (1959), 271-296

McDERMOTT, R. P., and D. A. WEBB, *Irish Protestantism To-day and To-morrow: A Demographic Study*. A.P.C.K., Dublin [1945]

MacDONALD, COLIN M., *The History of Argyll up to the Beginning of the Sixteenth century*. Holmes, Glasgow [1951]

MACKENZIE, AGNES MURE, *The Scotland of Queen Mary and the Religious Wars, 1513-1638*. Maclehose, London 1936

—, *Robert Bruce, King of Scots*. Oliver & Boyd, Edinburgh 1956

MACKINDER, H. J., *Britain and the British Seas*. Heinemann, London 1902

McKNIGHT, W. A., *Ireland and the Ulster Legend: The Truth about Ulster*. King, London 1921

McLAREN, MORAY, *Understanding the Scots*. Muller, London 1956

MacMANUS, M. J., *Eamon de Valera: A Biography*. Talbot Press, Dublin 1957 (6th ed.)

MacNEILL, EOIN, *Celtic Ireland*. Dublin 1921

—, *Early Irish Laws and Institutions*. Oates & Washbourne, Dublin [1934]

—, *Phases of Irish History*. Gill, London 1937

MANSERGH, NICHOLAS, *The Government of Northern Ireland: A Study in Devolution*. Allen & Unwin, London 1936

—, *Ireland in the Age of Reform and Revolution: A Commentary on Anglo-Irish Relations and on Political Forces in Ireland, 1840-1921*. Allen & Unwin, London 1940

MARSHALL, W. F., *Ulster sails West*. The Belfast News-Letter, Belfast 1950 (3d ed.)

MEGHEN, P. J., *How they order it in France*. In: *Administration* (Dublin) III (1955), 95-105

MILLIGAN, CECIL DAVIS, *The Relief of Derry*. The Londonderry Sentinel, Londonderry 1946 (2nd ed.)

MILROY, SEAN, *The Case of Ulster: An Analysis of Four Partition Arguments*. Talbot Press, Dublin 1922

MITCHEL, JOHN, *The Life and Times of Aedh O'Neill, Prince of Ulster*. Duffy, Dublin 1845

—, *Jail Journal*. Gill, Dublin (repr.)

MITCHEL, N. C., *Ireland*. In: *Focus* (American Geographical Society) VI (1955), 1-6

Modern Ireland, The Shaping of. Ed. by CONOR CRUISE O'BRIEN. Routledge & Kegan Paul, London 1960

MOGEY, JOHN M., *Rural Life in Northern Ireland: Five Regional Studies*. Oxford University Press 1947

—, *The Community in Northern Ireland*. In: *Man* (London) LVIII (1958), 85-87

MÜLLER-ROSS, FRIEDRICH, *Die irische Grenzfrage: Ulster, Irland und Grosz-Britannien*. Diss. Friedrich-Wilhelms-Universität Berlin. Ohlau i. Schl. 1931

MUMFORD, LEWIS, *The Culture of Cities*. Secker & Warburg, London 1946

MURRAY, KEVIN, *The Great Northern Railway (Ireland): Past, Present and Future*. G.N.R., Dublin 1944

NEILL, STEPHEN, *Anglicanism*. Pelican Books A 421, 1958

NEWARK, F. H., *Notes on Irish Legal History*. Boyd, Belfast 1960

NOTESTEIN, WALLACE, *The Scot in History: A Study of the Interplay of Character and History*. Cape, London 1946

O'BRIEN, GEORGE, *The Four Green Fields*. Talbot Press, Dublin 1936
O'BRIEN, GEORGE [AUGUSTINE THOMAS], *The Economic History of Ireland in the Eighteenth Century*. Maunsel, London 1946
—, *The Economic History of Ireland from the Union to the Famine*. Longmans, London 1921
O'BRIEN, RICHARD BARRY, *The Irish Land Question, 1829-1869*. Sampson Low, London 1880
O'Connell, Daniel: *Nine Centenary Essays*. Ed. by MICHAEL TIERNEY. Browne & Nolan, Dublin 1949
Ó CUÍV, BRIAN, *Irish Dialects and Irish-Speaking Districts*. Dublin Institute for Advanced Studies 1951
O'DONOVAN, JOHN, *The Economic History of Live Stock in Ireland*. Longmans, London 1940
O'FAOLAIN, SEAN, *De Valera*. Penguin Books 1939
—, *An Irish Journey*. Longmans, London 1940
—, *The Story of Ireland*. Collins, London 1943
—, *The Irish*. Pelican Books A 184, 1947
O'HEGARTY, P. S., *The Victory of Sinn Féin*. Talbot Press, Dublin 1924
O'RAHILLY, CECILE, *Ireland and Wales: Their Historical and Literary Relations*. Longmans, London 1924
O'RAHILLY, THOMAS F., *Irish Dialects Past and Present*. Browne & Nolan, Dublin 1932
—, *Early Irish History and Mythology*. Dublin Institute for Advanced Studies 1946
—, *The Two Patricks: A Lecture on the History of Christianity in Fifth-Century Ireland*. Dublin Institute for Advanced Studies 1957
Ó RÍORDÁIN, SEÁN P., *Antiquities of the Irish Countryside*. Methuen, London 1953 (3d ed.)
—, *Tara: The Monuments on the Hill*. Dundalgan Press, Dundalk 1960
ORPEN, GODDARD HENRY, *Ireland under the Normans, 1169-1333* (4 vols). Clarendon Press, Oxford 1911-1920
O'SULLIVAN, DONAL, *The Irish Free State and its Senate: A Study in Contemporary Politics*. Faber & Faber, London 1940
OTWAY-RUTHVEN, JOCELYN, *Place-Names in Ireland*. In: *Irish Geography* (Dublin) II (1950), 45-51

PANHUYS, H. F., VAN, *The Rôle of Nationality in International Law: An Outline*. Diss. Leiden. Sijthoff, Leiden 1959
[PARNELL, W.,] *An Enquiry into the Causes of Popular Discontents in Ireland*, by an Irish Country Gentleman. Wallis, London 1805 (2nd ed.)
PARTRIDGE, ERIC, *Origins: A Short Etymological Dictionary of Modern English*. Routledge & Kegan Paul, London 1958
PAUL-DUBOIS, L., *L'Irlande contemporaine et la question irlandaise*. Perrin, Paris 1907
POMFRET, JOHN E., *The Struggle for Land in Ireland, 1800-1923*. Princeton University Press 1930
PRENDERGAST, JOHN P., *The Cromwellian Settlement of Ireland*. Mellifont, Dublin 1922 (3d ed.)
PRIESTER, HERMANN, *Die Oberflächengestalt und Lage Irlands und ihre verkehrsgeographische Ausnutzung durch den Menschen*. Diss. Rostock. Strecker & Schröder, Stuttgart 1908

RAFTERY, JOSEPH, *Prehistoric Ireland*. Batsford, London 1951
RAIT, ROBERT S., *An Outline of the Relations between England and Scotland, 500-1707*. Blackie, London 1901
REES, J. F., *Studies in Welsh History*. University of Wales Press 1947
Regionalism in America. Ed. by MERRILL JENSEN. University of Wisconsin Press 1952
REILLY, W. C., *The Distribution of Settlement round Lower Lough Erne*. Diss. B.A., The Queen's University of Belfast 1949
RENAN, ERNEST, *Discours et conférences*. Lévy, Paris 1887
Reports Commission on Emigration and other Population Problems, 1948-1954. Stationery Office, Dublin 1955
Republic of Ireland. A Financial Times Survey, London 1960
RITCHIE, R. L. GRAEME, *The Normans in Scotland*. University Press, Edinburgh 1954
RODGERS, W. R., *The Ulstermen and their Country*. Longmans, London
ROGERS, PATRICK, *The Irish Volunteers and Catholic Emancipation, 1778-1793: A Neglected Phase of Ireland's History*. Oates & Washbourne, Dublin 1934
ROGERS, R. S., *The Folklore of the Black Pig's Dyke*. In: *Ulster Folklife* (Belfast) III (1957), 29-36
ROLT, L. T. C., and P. B. WHITEHOUSE, *Lines of Character*. Constable, London 1952

[Rose, A. J.,] *Ireland*. In: *Current Affairs Bulletin* (University of Sydney) XVIII (1956), 179-191
Rowse, A. L., *The Spirit of English History*. Cape, London 1943
Rumpf, Erhard, *Nationalismus und Sozialismus in Irland: Historisch-soziologischer Versuch über die irische Revolution seit 1918*. Diss. Heidelberg. Hain, Meisenheim am Glan 1959

Salaman, Redcliffe N., *The History and Social Influence of the Potato*. Cambridge University Press 1949
Savage, D. C., *The Origins of the Ulster Unionist Party, 1885-6*. In: *Irish Historical Studies* (Dublin) XII (1961), 185-208
Savage, Roland Burke, *Ireland To-morrow*. In: *Studies* (Dublin) XLIV (1955), 1-4
Saville, John, *Rural Depopulation in England and Wales, 1851-1951*. Routledge & Kegan Paul, London 1957
Scarlett, W. D., *The Economic and Social Effects of Partition on Clones (Co. Monaghan)*. Diss. B.A. (Hon.), The Queen's University of Belfast 1957
Shearman, Hugh, *Anglo-Irish Relations*. Faber & Faber, London 1948
—, *Ulster*. Hale, London 1949
—, *Recent Developments in Anglo-Irish Relations*. In: *World Affairs* (London) III (1949), 152-163
—, *Modern Ireland*. Harrap, London 1952
Sheehy, Michael, *Divided we stand: A Study in Partition*. Faber & Faber, London 1955
Sheridan, John D., *Irish Writing to-day*. In: *Studies* (Dublin) XLIV (1955), 81-85
Simms, J. G., *The Williamite Confiscation in Ireland, 1690-1703*. Studies in Irish History VII. Faber & Faber, London 1956
Smyllie, R. M., *Unneutral Neutral Eire*. In: *Foreign Affairs* XXIV (1946), 317-326
Social Life in Ireland, 1800-45. Ed. by R. B. McDowell. Irish Life and Culture XII. Cultural Relations Committee, Dublin 1957
Society, Early Irish. Ed. by Myles Dillon. Irish Life and Culture VIII. Cultural Relations Committee, Dublin 1954
Sölch, Johann, *Die Landschaften der Britischen Inseln* (2 vols). Springer, Vienna 1952
Speeches and Documents on the British Dominions, 1918-1931: From Self-Government to National Sovereignty. Ed. by Arthur Berriedale Keith. Oxford University Press 1933
Stamp, L. Dudley, *Britain's Structure and Scenery*. Collins, London 1960 (5th ed.)
Stamp, L. Dudley, and Stanley H. Beaver. *The British Isles: A Geographic and Economic Survey*. Longmans, London 1959 (5th ed.)
Stanford, W. B., *Faith and Fiction in Ireland now*. A.P.C.K., Dublin 1945
Stewig, Reinhard, *Dublin: Funktionen und Entwicklung*. In: *Schriften des Geographischen Instituts der Universität Kiel* XVIII, 2 (1959)
Strauss, E., *Irish Nationalism and British Democracy*. Methuen, London 1951
Survey of Merseyside, A Scientific. Ed. by Wilfred Smith. Publ. for the British Association by the University Press, Liverpool 1953.

Taylor, E. G. R., *Late Tudor and Early Stuart Geography, 1583-1650*. Methuen, London 1934
Trevelyan, George Macaulay, *A Shortened History of England*. Pelican Books A 443, 1959

Ulster since 1800: A Political and Economic Survey (2 vols). Ed. by A. E. Moody and J. C. Beckett. British Broadcasting Corporation, London 1955, 1957
Ulster under Home Rule: A Study of the Political and Economic Problems of Northern Ireland. Ed. by Thomas Wilson. Oxford University Press 1950
Unification of Ireland. Hearing before the Committee on Foreign Affairs, House of Representatives, April 28, 1950. United States Government Printing Office, Washington 1950
Ussher, Arland, *The Face and Mind of Ireland*. Gollancz, London 1950

Valera, Eamon de, *Recent Speeches and Broadcasts*. Talbot Press, Dublin 1933
Valera, R. de, *The Court Cairns of Ireland*. In: *Proceedings of the Royal Irish Academy* (Dublin) LX, C2 (1960), 9-140
Vanishing Irish, The: The Enigma of the Modern World. Ed. by John A. O'Brien. Allen, London 1954
View of Ireland, A: Twelve Essays on Different Aspects of Irish Life and the Irish Countryside. Ed. by James Meenan and David A. Webb. Publ. for the British Association by the Local Executive Committee, Dublin 1957

VISSCHER, CHARLES DE, *Théories et réalités en droit international public*. Pedone, Paris 1955 (2nd ed.)

War and the Neutrals, The. Ed. by ARNOLD TOYNBEE and VERONICA M. TOYNBEE. Survey of International
    Affairs, 1939-1946. Oxford University Press 1956

WARD, SYBIL, *Geographical Factors in the Growth and Decline of the Ports of North-East Ireland*. Thesis M.A.,
    The Queen's University of Belfast 1940

WEIR, ROSEMARY H., *The Historical Geography of the Potato in Ulster from 1841 to 1871*. Diss. B.A. (Hon.),
    The Queen's University of Belfast 1961

WERTENBAKER, T. J., *Early Scotch Contributions to the United States*. Glasgow University Publications LXIV.
    Jackson, Glasgow 1945

WHEARE, K. C., *The Constitutional Structure of the Commonwealth*. Clarendon Press, Oxford 1960

WHITE, J., *Partition*. In: *The Month* (London) XVII (1957), 151-158

WIGHTON, CHARLES, and GÜNTER PEIS, *They Spied on England*. Odhams Press, London 1958

WILLIAMSON, JAMES A., *The Evolution of England*: *A Commentary on the Facts*. Clarendon Press, Oxford
    1944 (2nd ed.)

—, *A Short History of British Expansion* (2 vols). Macmillan, London 1947 (3d ed.)

WINANT, JOHN GILBERT, *A Letter from Grosvenor Square*. Hodder & Stoughton, London 1947

WOODBURN, JAMES BARKLEY, *The Ulster Scot: His History and Religion*. Allenson, London 1914

WRIGHT, LOUIS B., *The Atlantic Frontier: Colonial American Civilization, 1607-1763*. Knopf, New York 1947

—, *The Cultural Life of the American Colonies, 1607-1763*. Harper, New York, 1957

ZIMMER, HEINRICH, *The Celtic Church in Britain and Ireland*. Nutt, London 1902

INDEX